Excursions in Identity

Excursions in Identity

Travel and the Intersection of Place, Gender, and Status in Edo Japan

Laura Nenzi

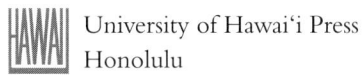 University of Hawai'i Press
Honolulu

© 2008 University of Hawai'i Press
All rights reserved
Printed in the United States of America
13 12 11 10 09 08   6 5 4 3 2 1

LIBRARY OF CONGRESS CATALOGING-IN-PUBLICATION DATA
Nenzi, Laura Nenz Detto.
Excursions in identity : travel and the intersection of place, gender, and status in Edo Japan / Laura Nenzi.
   p. cm.
Includes bibliographical references and index.
ISBN 978-0-8248-3117-2 (hardcover : alk. paper)
1. Japan—Description and travel. 2. Japan—Social conditions—1600–1868.
3. Travelers' writings, Japanese—History and criticism. I. Title.
DS808.N46 2008
306.4'819095209034—dc22
                              2007048453

University of Hawai'i Press books are printed on acid-free paper and meet the guidelines for permanence and durability of the Council on Library Resources.

Designed by Paul Herr, University of Hawai'i Press production staff
Printed by Edwards Brothers, Inc.

To nonna Elena

Contents

Acknowledgments / ix

Introduction: Everything Flows / 1

PART I: RE-CREATING SPACES

1. Maps, Movements, and the Malleable Spaces of Edo Japan / 13
2. At the Intersection of Travel and Gender / 45

PART II: RE-CREATING IDENTITIES

3. Women on the Road: Identities in Motion / 71
4. Palimpsests: The Open Road and the Blank Page / 92

PART III: PURCHASING RE-CREATION

5. Print Matters: Popularizing Past and Present / 121
6. Icons of Escapism / 141
7. Bodies, Brothels, and Baths: Travel and Physical Re-creation / 165

Conclusion: Dreaming of Walking near Fuji / 186

Notes / 191
Bibliography / 231
Index / 249

Acknowledgments

COMPLETING A BOOK is like completing a long journey. Not unlike the travelers whose adventures I examine in this study, I too have needed guidance, advice, and support in order to reach the end of this road. And not unlike some of them—Kita and Yaji of *Shank's Mare* fame come to mind—I too have been a clumsy traveler at times, losing track of my destination on more than a few occasions. At times I have stopped to enjoy the view, aware that my journey would be delayed but that the overall process would be far more rewarding.

Here I wish to acknowledge a number of people who have accompanied me along the way, giving directions and much needed advice. When in doubt about how to proceed, Edo period travelers could consult one of the many guides and manuals available in the bookstores. In my case, guidance came first and foremost from Luke Roberts, my graduate adviser at the University of California, Santa Barbara. His command of Edo period documents and his generosity as a scholar have made this a rewarding and enriching adventure from beginning to end. I also wish to thank Joan Judge for her invaluable editorial help and for her suggestions on issues of gender. Allan Grapard guided me as I stepped onto sacred territory and followed my travelers along the winding paths of numinous mountains. When I found myself unable to make sense of the distant voices and cryptic comments of some wayfarers, I turned to Haruko Iwasaki; my dialogue with Edo period travelers and authors would not have been as fruitful without her. Many heartfelt thanks also go out to Anne Walthall for her continuous support and for her insightful suggestions on ways to improve the original version of the manuscript. Patricia Crosby at University of Hawai'i Press believed in this project from day one and chose two conscientious readers whose help and suggestions were instrumental in the making of this book. Invaluable advice at different stages of my research has also come from Peter Kornicki, Atsuko Sakaki, Jilly Traganou, Itasaka

Noriko, Joshua Fogel, Valerio Alberizzi, Erik Esselstrom, Robert O. Collins, Aurora Morcillo, Karen Garner, Asuncion Gómez, and Lynne Barrett. All shortcomings, it goes without saying, are solely my fault.

Edo period travelers often used confraternities to sponsor their journeys. For me, financial support has come from a variety of sources, beginning with the Graduate Division and the History Department at the University of California, Santa Barbara. I owe a great debt of gratitude to the Japan Foundation, whose generosity in funding a research trip to Japan in 2001 I wish to recognize. At Florida International University, the College of Arts and Sciences granted me a Faculty Development Program Award in 2005 and a semester of teaching relief in 2007 that allowed me to focus solely on the manuscript. Travel grants to complete my research also came from the Asian/Pacific Studies Institute at Duke University (with special thanks to Kristina Troost) and from the Harvard-Yenching library.

At the Historiographical Institute of Tokyo University (Shiryō Hensanjo) I am indebted to Hōya (Kumazawa) Tōru for being my adviser and to Gonoi Takashi for his warmth and generosity. My gratitude also goes out to Robert Campbell, who helped me access a collection of women's diaries made temporarily unavailable by renovation works in the library of the Komaba campus, and to Shinno Toshikazu of Tsukuba University for providing me with a list of useful documents.

Earlier versions of parts of Chapters 4 and 6 were originally published as "Cultured Travelers and Consumer Tourists in Edo-Period Sagami" in *Monumenta Nipponica* 59:3 (Autumn 2004): 285–319. I wish to thank the editor, Kate Wildman Nakai, for kindly granting me permission to use this material. Earlier versions of other portions of Chapter 4 appeared as "Women's Travel Narratives in Early Modern Japan: Genre Imperatives, Gender Consciousness and Status Questioning" in *Journeys, The International Journal of Travel and Travel Writing* 5:1 (May 2004): 47–72, and are reproduced with permission of Mark Stanton, managing editor of Berghahn Books.

My exploration of Edo roads began long ago at the University of Venice (Università degli Studi di Venezia), when I informed my then adviser Adriana Boscaro that I had chosen the Tōkaidō as the topic of my research. From her enthusiastic reaction I knew I had a long but fascinating road ahead of me, and I have not been disappointed. She has been an inspirational teacher first and a great friend later, and deserves my utmost gratitude.

Many others have walked stretches of this road with me. My colleagues at Florida International University have provided constructive criticism, encouragement, and technical support. I am particularly indebted to Steven Heine and to the preternaturally efficient staff of the Institute for Asian

Studies for their assistance, and to Stacey West and Asuka Haraguchi for their help with maps and copyright letters. Sincere thanks also go out to William Scott Wilson, Christopher (Chip) Dewell, Ethan Segal, Kimura Ken, Kimura Kiyoko, and Kimura Kazu in Funabashi, to Ōhashi Akiko at the Shiryō Hensanjō, and to the Koyama family in Tokyo.

Over the years, family and friends in Italy, Japan, and the United States have followed with interest and curiosity my journeys in academia. Though at times puzzled by my choices and amused by my exuberant enthusiasm, my parents, Giorgio and Carla, and my sister Francesca have especially understood and supported my commitment to this adventure of a lifetime.

Last but certainly not least, Peter deserves a special recognition for his patience, his humor, and his ability to show me on a daily basis that life also exists outside the Edo bubble wherein I generally reside.

Miami, July 2007

Introduction
Everything Flows

> Living only for the moment, turning our full attention to the pleasures of the moon, the snow, the cherry blossoms and the maple leaves; singing songs, drinking wine, diverting ourselves in just floating, floating; caring not a whit for the pauperism staring us in the face, refusing to be disheartened, like a gourd floating along with the river current: this is what we call the *floating world*.
> —Asai Ryōi, *Tales of the Floating World* (*Ukiyo monogatari*, 1665)

THE EDO PERIOD (1600–1868) was the age of movement par excellence. Motion characterized and imbued its every aspect, from the gourd of the floating world slowly descending along the river to the fluid creations of linked-verse poets, from the dynamism of an expanding society to the innovative spatial logic of its made-for-strolling gardens.[1] It was only normal, and inevitable, that in a place and time where movement reigned supreme travel would become an activity through which life itself could be defined: "Days and months are travellers of eternity. So are the years that pass by," sang poet and traveler Matsuo Bashō (1644–1694) at the onset of *The Narrow Road to the Deep North* (*Oku no hosomichi*, 1689).[2] The general goal of the pages that follow is to examine some of the ways in which early modern travel intersected with life in and around the floating world, and to assess its impact, pervasiveness, and functions against the background of Edo culture and society.

Travel was by no means an invention of the Edo period. In the centuries that preceded the rise to power of the Tokugawa, soldiers and merchants, poets and entertainers, pilgrims and wanderers had trodden the roads in search of inspiration or profit, enlightenment or escapism. With a few notable exceptions, however, journeys through the seventeenth century were prominently utilitarian or generally undertaken out of necessity.[3] Wayfarers were mostly concerned with the destination rather than the road, for movements through space were essentially contingent to the accomplishment of other goals.

Uncomfortable and dangerous, travel was the unavoidable price one had to pay to "get things done" elsewhere. The expeditions of the frontier guards sung in the *Anthology of Ten Thousand Leaves* (*Man'yōshū*, eighth century), the imperial pilgrimages to Kumano between the eleventh and thirteenth centuries,[4] and the journeys of merchants in the medieval period provide fitting examples of travel as a military, political, or commercial obligation. In the early modern period a new type of journey became prominent: travel as a conscious sociocultural act, undertaken not out of practical necessity but from the simple desire to break with the ordinary and engage with an out-of-the-ordinary space and time—a goal only the lifelong peregrinations of wandering monks, nuns, and mountain ascetics (*yamabushi*) had approximated in the past. With the shift in focus the road took on a new function. No longer the inert, flat line between two points of interests, it became an active stage on which meanings could be "discovered, created, and communicated."[5] For many a traveler reaching the final destination became subordinate to the greater goal of being in motion and, as novelist Jippensha Ikku (1765–1831) aptly put it, "enjoying all the delights of the road."[6]

In the Edo period, physical mobility (travel along horizontal lines) was tightly regulated and social mobility (travel along vertical lines), though not impossible, was not always a viable option. Parameters based on status and gender permeated every facet of one person's life, and to a certain extent travel was no exception. I contend, however, that recreational travel, as a space and time apart, provided a convenient platform to question and alter some of these parameters. Shaped by multiple interpretations, the spaces of travel constituted malleable terrains that stood in sharp contrast to the predominantly static spaces of the ordinary. When travelers began their journeys and were no longer "tied by convention as when they live[d] in the same row of houses,"[7] they eagerly exploited the flexibility and the "anything-goes" atmosphere of the open road to redraw both horizontal and vertical lines, reshaping personal hierarchies and, on more than one occasion, temporarily crafting new identities. Along the road, recreation (as in "leisure") became synonymous with re-creation (as in "regeneration," or "creation of a new self").[8] The modalities of such re-creation were not static, and diversified over time in parallel with the evolution of the Edo period into an age of pervasive commercialism and widespread literacy.

This cartography of self-assertion on the part of the individual emerges more prominently at the junctures of travel with space, gender, status, literacy, the economy, and the body. These are the main intersections to which this study is dedicated. Although I remain aware that crossing such vast categories of inquiry forced me to make inevitable selections, and that by choosing certain avenues of investigation I had to walk away from many others, I nevertheless believe that the complexity of early modern travel culture as a site of creations, re-creations, and challenges is best understood through a combination of all of the above. When projected onto the plane of travel, issues of spatial control, gender, status, literary prowess, economic necessity, and physicality manifest themselves as mutually interdependent and often indivisible. Their inseparability affected the structure of this work: although each of the chapters deals with one major theme, common issues and problems constantly resurface.

In its first part ("Re-creating Spaces") this study introduces the notion that the spaces of travel were malleable and could be continually reconceptualized across interpretive frames.[9] Divergent views on the degree to which gender and status should affect mobility, the weight of religious and cultural precedent, and ever-powerful economic considerations all played a decisive role in the formation of a plurality of spatial hierarchies and of highly polysemic terrains. Consequently, the modalities of a traveler's interaction with the landscape were never cast in stone. By the simple act of looking at a space through a different lens travelers discovered that they could successfully question the geography of power envisioned—if ever attained—by officialdom. In a silent yet fierce tug-of-war, landscapes were continuously appropriated, shaped, defined, and contested. Far from being static backgrounds, the complex spaces of travel proliferated in a myriad of loci where one person's center was another's periphery.[10] The multifaceted character of landscapes buttressed a sense of autonomy and agency on the part of the traveler vis-à-vis the institutions and the social pressures that regulated life in the space of the ordinary.

Once physical detachment from one's preassigned niche took place, individual travelers began to interact with the landscapes through the set of conventions they found more congenial. In the course of the seventeenth and eighteenth centuries educated travelers, mostly of high social standing, engaged with landscapes in a conscious effort to establish a connection with the sites' lyrical heritage, hence confirming their own position within pre-existing cultural hierarchies (Part II: "Re-creating Identities"). They used travel to, or through, revered lyrical sites as a way of asserting and enhancing their roles and identities. By the mid-eighteenth century the dynamics and goals of self re-creation through cultural engagements began to diversify as the popularization of culture and the rise of commercial printing ushered in a new wave of informed travelers—commoners who had discovered the layered meanings of sites in the pages of popular literature and in woodblock prints. The forging of a link with a hallowed past and the self-identification with its icons empowered this new brand of wayfarers to put identity up for debate, not so much (or not exclusively) for the purpose of asserting their worth within cultural circles as to escape, if only for the length of the journey, some of the handicaps that limited their agency in the space of the ordinary.

Men and women alike engaged in the recovery of literary precedent and in the intellectual acquisition of the spaces of travel. Gender, however, affected their respective approaches. While educated travelers of both sexes turned their movements into sociocultural acts by investing them with rich literary meanings, women seemed particularly devoted to the search for validation in preferred sites of lyrical authority and gendered power. I have chosen to devote special attention to the case of female travelers, not only because they have thus far been relatively neglected in the pages of Western language historiography on the topic, but also because looking at gender most forcefully highlights the disjunction between modes of control on one side and practices on the other.

I approached the gendered history of travel in early modern Japan informed by the notion that, historically, women have always been the silenced, immobile, and confined ones. In a study of travel practices across cultures, for instance, Eric J. Leed affirms, "In a vast portion of human history, men have been the travelers; and travel literature is—with a few significant, and often modern, exceptions—a male literature reflecting a masculine point of view. [...] There is no free and mobile male without the unfree and sessile female."[11] The Tokugawa period in particular, as Martha Tocco has observed (and refuted), tends to be "widely understood to represent the nadir in the status of Japanese women."[12] The intersection of travel and gender in early modern Japan simply proves that the picture was far more nuanced, and that women were remarkably capable of achieving mobility by exploiting the discrepancies between overlapping spatial discourses.

As travel became pervasively commodified in the nineteenth century, so did the dynamics of the interaction between wayfarers and landscapes. When educated divertissements met commercial pressure, the recovery of literary or historical precedent became but one of the many ways in which visitors bonded with the spaces of travel. In its final part this study looks at the intersection between recreational travel and the rising commercial economy, which allowed visitors to appropriate landscapes through new means: monetary transactions, acquisition of tangible icons, or physical intercourse (Part III: "Purchasing Re-creation"). The process that had begun in the seventeenth century had by the nineteenth reached its zenith. In the final century of Tokugawa rule the culture of recreational travel combined with consumerism to generate a proliferation of simulacra: miniature pilgrimage circuits as alternatives to full-scale circumambulations across provinces; souvenirs that distilled the identity of a site into purchasable units; and an array of services and icons that offered a convenient alternative—or complement—to the intellectual interaction with the landscape. The cultural discovery of a site and an educated engagement with its history ceased to be the sole coordinates along which visitors mapped and seized space. The many spaces of travel became increasingly complex, now invested with a multiplicity of meanings, values, and symbols to better respond to the rapidly rising demands of the market. Material icons such as souvenirs, gastronomic specialties, or local courtesans worked just as effectively as quotations from the classics in the travelers' process of integration with the extraordinary landscapes of travel, and in the reelaboration of their own identities: "I buy, therefore I am" was the new mantra of nineteenth-century recreational travelers.

The Many Cultures of Movement

As a cultural practice, travel has received extensive attention in scholarship, both across disciplines (anthropology, the social sciences, literature, history) and across diverse geographical regions. The works of John Urry, Judith Adler, Dean MacCannell, or James Buzard, just to name a few, have placed the phenomenon under the microscope, highlighting practices and agendas, short-lived fads and long-lasting trends, challenges and individual responses to novelty.[13] Though I use them sparingly, these studies, conceptualized to explain Western (and often modern) manifestations of the cultures of movement, have helped me bring the recreational travels of early modern Japan into better focus. Mostly I resorted to Western theories when studies on the specific case of Edo period Japan were not available; the field has only recently been gathering momentum and there is still much work to be done. In other cases I used them to provide food for thought, though never with the intention to engage in a comparative study of travel practices in the "East" versus travel practices in the "West." Theories formulated for the understanding of Western historical phenomena can still serve as valid tools to interpret, in this case, a Japanese tradition either by way of comparison or by way of contrast, as long as they do not force or distort interpretations.

In the more confined field of early modern Japanese history, the works of Constantine N. Vaporis in English and the extensive publications of Kodama Kōta, Maruyama Yasunari, Igarashi Tomio, and many others in Japanese have offered a tremendous contribution to the knowledge of Edo period travel. In the majority of cases, it ought to be noted, scholars have focused primarily on the institutional side of the story, mostly honing in on the detailed travel legislation put forth by the Tokugawa. Titles such as *A Basic Study of Early Modern Post Stations, A Basic Study of Early Modern Checkpoints,* or *Study of the Post Station System in the Early Modern Period* reveal a tendency to define travel almost exclusively in terms of official edicts, government-mandated post towns and checkpoints, and legally sanctioned stages for the transportation of official goods and correspondence.[14] In this view from above, rarely if ever does leisurely travel appear as a category in itself. If mentioned, it is frequently within the convenient frame of the clash between legality and disobedience.

Government-centered institutional histories also tend to define recreational travel—when they define it at all—for what it is not (i.e., nonofficial) rather than for what it is, and to peruse it from the viewpoint of the authority. The result is often a plot that bases its social characterization on a convenient dichotomy between samurai and commoners—the epitome of officialdom being the former, the embodiment of defiance the latter. Alternatively, recreational travel is quickly introduced as a superficial, frivolous activity akin to modern tourism and is associated almost exclusively with the lower echelons of society (the masses of "mass tourism").

More nuanced, in this respect, is Constantine N. Vaporis' *Breaking Barriers,* a monograph that, while focusing largely on the institutional organization and control of movements (as the subtitle *Travel and the State in Early Modern Japan* indicates), also brings the voices of actual travelers into the picture. In his concluding chapter Vaporis offers one of the most substantial contributions to the history of early modern recreational travel to date, outlining the rise of popular leisurely journeys despite and against the will of the Tokugawa, who, all evidence to the contrary notwithstanding, still "did not recognize the concept of tourism."[15] This volume departs from the point where Vaporis leaves off by focusing as much as possible on the view from within. Starting from a reexamination of the ways in which many travelers "broke the barriers" erected by the government and moved somewhat freely along the roads, this study seeks to evaluate the deeper meaning and the short- and long-term repercussions of such movements and of the narratives and commercial transactions they generated. It goes without saying that writing a comprehensive social and cultural history of travel is well beyond the scope of this work. As Hiruma Hisashi suggests, there were "many cultures of movement," and while they all deserve equal attention, this study presents a selection of themes in the hope of generating debate and stimulating further inquiries.[16]

Travel and Pilgrimage

Even outside of strictly institutional frames of interpretation recreational travel in Japan has hardly been granted a historiographical identity of its own, for in most cases it has been presented as an offspring of pilgrimage, simultaneously assuming that the religious experience per se was inherently devoid of any mundane aspects and that it automatically excluded the possibility of amusement. Several schools of thought have attempted to explain the intricacies of the relationship between faith and fun, prayer and play, sacred and profane, both within and without the sphere of travel.[17] Some, perhaps believing that statistics are the key to uncontestable truths and that numeric coordinates can measure the human experience, have even set out to quantify the ratio to which faith and leisure mixed on the road. Konno Nobuo establishes that by the late Edo period the proportion was 80:20 in favor of recreation, while Shinjō Tsunezō settles for a 70:30 ratio.[18] The works of scholars who avoid mathematical formulations to explain the "emergence" of recreational travel still tend to present an *evolutionary* process that culminates with the metamorphosis of an essentially religious act into a mixed concoction of pleasure and devotion.[19]

Other studies, however, have challenged this view. In line with the argument that "a tourist is half a pilgrim, if a pilgrim is half a tourist,"[20] they have asserted that the two elements of recreation and devotion were in fact thoroughly combined, promoting the notion that "prayer and play were complementary and indeed inseparable."[21] As evidence bolstering their claim, the supporters of the *complementarity* theory point to such examples as the boisterous dance the gods staged before the cave where the Sun Goddess Amaterasu had gone into hiding (an episode narrated in *Record of Ancient Matters, Kojiki,* 712), to religious phenomena that feature a remarkably entertaining character (such as exhibits of sacred icons during festivals and *kagura* dances), and to recreational events that bear the signs of an intrinsically religious origin (sumo wrestling and rural festivals, to name a few).[22] Further proof of the interconnectedness of the two spheres, they argue, is the ambivalence of terms that overlap the two semantic fields of pleasure and religion. Words such as *tayū* (by which both Shinto priests and high-ranking courtesans in pleasure quarters were identified) and *gozen* (literally meaning "those who serve the deities," but also a synonym for "prostitute") are the most eloquent examples of such complementarity.[23] The proponents of the "inextricable conjoining of faith and pleasure" reject the distinction between sacred and profane by asserting that, throughout the early modern period, "religion was one form of enjoyment, [. . .] one of the great pleasures of life."[24]

Following in the footsteps of these scholars, I do not intend to draw at any point a precise line of separation between travel as "religion" and travel as "leisure," for I regard them as inseparably linked at all stages of Edo history.[25] The memoir written by an eighteenth-century woman to commemorate her journey, for example, confirms that certain travelers tended to invest space with ever-changing meanings, depending on location, time of the year, and personal inclinations. They also did not think it inappropriate to shift freely from times and spaces of the sacred to times and spaces of the mundane, for they saw no boundaries between the two. In 1777 Arakida Reijo (1732–1806), the wife of an Ise priest, traveled through a series of famous locations in western Japan. On 1777/3/20 she left Yoshino to reach the Hall of Five Hundred Arhats in Sumiyoshi. After spending time in this sacred space, she headed to Noda to enjoy a seasonal spectacle, the sight of blooming wisterias. While in Noda, she once again put secular amusements aside and paid homage to a shrine dedicated to Kasuga no Kami.[26] Should we define Reijo's tour as "just" a pilgrimage or as "primarily" a pilgrimage? Was it an excursion through places celebrated in literature intertwined with occasional stops at sites of cult, or was it "tourism" pure and simple? As in many other cases, Reijo's journey defies a clear-cut definition in these terms and shows that the character of Edo period recreational travel was multilayered and adaptable.

Maps and Texts: The Original Stones

In the pages that follow I will use maps to look at the manifold ways in which spaces were interpreted, assigned specific meanings, re-presented, and, ultimately, exploited. I am using the word "map" as a general term of convenience to describe *all* types of visual representations of a given space—from cartography to art, from textbook illustrations to board games, from mandalas to woodblock prints. The recent works of Marcia Yonemoto and Jilly Traganou have effectively demonstrated that mapmaking and spatial illustrations were in fact dense, complex languages, and that as such they provided a fertile terrain, not only to outline political agendas, but also to bend and invert the established order with satirical twists and irreverent parodies.[27]

An analysis of the contrasting creations and definitions of space, however, cannot stop at the visual level. Equally significant was the verbal production of landscapes effected through edicts, annotations, explanations, jottings, mantras, evocations, and narratives that, more often than not, complemented visual images. Language (in the strict verbal sense) appropriated spaces and affirmed authority just as pervasively, effectively, and decisively as images. Official edicts, village records, and documents issued by religious institutions are discussed in conjunction with educational textbooks, travel guides, and popular fiction to cast a light on the different discourses and meanings overlapping in the spaces of travel. The occasional use of fiction (and comical fiction, no less) as a source of historical investigation is in part a reflection of my love for the works of Jippensha Ikku, and in part a deliberate decision dictated by my belief that every documentary source is ultimately distorted in its own way. I am fully aware that the interest of commercial authors like Ikku never lay with a realistic rendition of Edo life but rather with creating farfetched situations that would amuse the readers and sell the books. At the same time, however, the very fact that many popular works of fiction courted the theme of travel speaks volumes about the role of movement as a pillar of Edo culture and about travel as a marketable commodity.

Above all, the view from within that this study wishes to present is achieved by using personal diaries as windows into the experiences of individual travelers.[28] It is only recently that historians have turned to travel diaries as fully legitimate sources of investigation. Both Herbert Plutschow and Marcia Yonemoto, for example, have pointed at the degree of empirical curiosity and even scientific observation that defines some Edo period travelogues.[29] In this study prominence is given to the ways in which travel narratives enabled their authors to affirm personal orders as they crossed extraordinary terrains, and to the ways in which such authors reimagined their roles and forged relations with space through the written word or through material items. By complementing the view from above of existing histories with a view from below and within, it becomes clear that the open road offered travelers *across the social spectrum* a platform to re-create themselves through a variety of means, some elaborate and some quick and easy. Warriors and literati, townspeople and farmers, men and women all looked at the road as a stage, and used it to fulfill personal goals and aspirations far more profound than a mere diversion.

All in all, "maps," narratives, and tangible objects associated with movement reverberate with a chorus of fresh voices that compel us to adjust, or at the very least complement, some long-standing arguments about early modern travel. They show us that authority could be mediated and challenged without direct confrontation, that identities could be quietly re-created, that even government officials constructed personal hierarchies that stood in sharp contrast to the existing geopolitical order, and that ordinary travelers—including women—easily identified and successfully exploited specific areas (the open road, the blank page, the body) where conventions could be invisibly yet effectively questioned without fear of repercussion or punishment.

No one document, of course, is more reliable or tells a greater truth than another. Every source, while opening a new window, necessarily forces the historian to look in certain directions only. A combination of access points, however, can approximate—without ever reaching it—an ideal 360-degree view: "Whatever one does, one always rebuilds the monument in his own way. But it is already something gained to have used the original stones."[30]

PART I

Re-creating Spaces

CHAPTER 1

Maps, Movements, and the Malleable Spaces of Edo Japan

I did not want to establish any particular direction for my stroll:
I strove for maximum latitude of possibility so as not to fatigue my
expectant mind with the obligatory foresight of a particular path.
—Jorge Luis Borges

The map's role of authenticating travel can be seen as a perennial
possibility.
—Stephen Bann, "The Map as Index of the Real"

RECREATIONAL TRAVEL in the Edo period opened the door to an extra-ordinary space where the dogmas and obstacles of everyday life could be questioned and bypassed. This was made possible first and foremost by the very character of the landscapes across which travel occurred. The Tokugawa's conceptual organization of the territory never completely succeeded in permeating—much less in stifling—travel practices, largely because the logic of officialdom was never able to overcome the variety of individual spatial constructions that coexisted with it and that generated multiple, malleable spaces of travel.[1] An array of different parameters, including considerations based on sacredness, historical prestige, and cultural excellence, helped craft such individual hierarchies. Government cartographers *(ezukata)* and artists, wandering monks and poets converged at the crowded intersection of travel and space, measuring and charting landscapes in an effort to control them. Each one of them mapped specific areas of interest, each read and rewrote space, each outlined boundaries, and each prioritized different elements of the travelscape. Each, in short, added different nuances and layers of meaning, making Edo space into a disputable entity.

Distinctive frames of interpretation—political, religious, and lyrical are the ones examined hereafter—inevitably tended to prioritize segments of space that reflected individual standards and agendas. Through the cartographers, for instance, political discourse mapped space with symbols that facilitated the

Tokugawa's penchant for control and their constant quest for stability.² The landscape as interpreted by governmental mapmakers and Road Magistrates (*dōchū bugyō*) was dominated from above and organized in order to reinforce notions of centrality based on military and political prominence, to convey a sense of pervasive authority, and to buttress a social hierarchy founded prominently on status and gender. For the rulers, land equaled power in countless ways, offering at the same time possibilities for reward (territorial concessions to local lords) and punishment (exile and forced transfers, as in the case of the untrustworthy outer lords, or *tozama daimyō*), for financial gain (taxation)[3] and economic growth (the "assisting village" network, also known as the *sukegō* system),[4] for surveillance (alternate attendance), and for the practical display of status (the closer to the "center," the higher the prominence).[5]

Historically, the political domination of space had always had to come to terms with a formidable contender, the religious establishment. Religious discourse had traditionally mapped space—*the same* space—with a different brush, privileging exclusive areas of karmic superiority, spaces of cleanliness, and peaks endowed with sacred meanings. Not exclusively an Edo period phenomenon (as the example of *Mandala of a Pilgrimage to Mount Fuji,* discussed later, demonstrates), the religious alternative to official mapmaking continued to increase and diversify itself in the early modern period.

The plurality of representations became ever more evident as educated travelers put their own spin on spaces, developing yet new geographies of interest. Early works of art and literature on the topic of travel tended to celebrate locations selected by virtue of their prominence within a respected cultural heritage, thus bypassing the protocols imposed upon the landscape by political and religious bodies. As diverging interpretations and variations on the theme of landscape piled up, the multiplicity of discordant voices allowed individual travelers to choose the one more in tune with their ears.

The Spaces of Travel in Political Discourse

> Item: It is forbidden to travel arbitrarily off the road.
> —Ordinance posted on roadside board under Tokugawa Hidetada, 1611/3/19[6]

Under the rule of Tokugawa Ienari (r. 1786/9–1837/4) the government sent out orders for a comprehensive survey of all main roads in the country. Officials were dispatched across the provinces (Figure 1) in preparation for the imminent issuance of what would become the massive road map collection

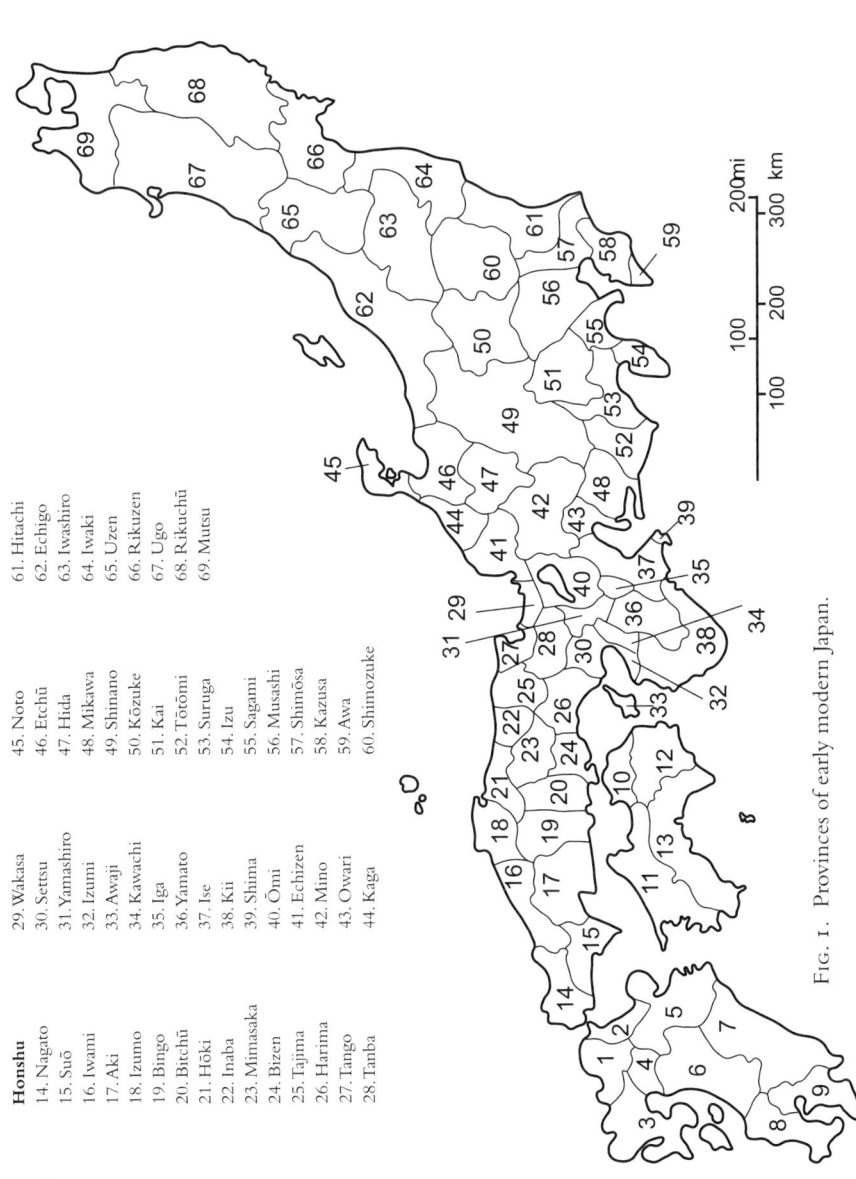

Fig. 1. Provinces of early modern Japan.

Kyushu
1. Chikuzen
2. Buzen
3. Hizen
4. Chikugo
5. Bungo
6. Higo
7. Hyūga
8. Satsuma
9. Ōsumi

Shikoku
10. Sanuki
11. Iyo
12. Awa
13. Tosa

Honshu
14. Nagato
15. Suō
16. Iwami
17. Aki
18. Izumo
19. Bingo
20. Bitchū
21. Hōki
22. Inaba
23. Mimasaka
24. Bizen
25. Tajima
26. Harima
27. Tango
28. Tanba
29. Wakasa
30. Settsu
31. Yamashiro
32. Izumi
33. Awaji
34. Kawachi
35. Iga
36. Yamato
37. Ise
38. Kii
39. Shima
40. Ōmi
41. Echizen
42. Mino
43. Owari
44. Kaga
45. Noto
46. Etchū
47. Hida
48. Mikawa
49. Shinano
50. Kōzuke
51. Kai
52. Tōtōmi
53. Suruga
54. Izu
55. Sagami
56. Musashi
57. Shimōsa
58. Kazusa
59. Awa
60. Shimozuke
61. Hitachi
62. Echigo
63. Iwashiro
64. Iwaki
65. Uzen
66. Rikuzen
67. Ugo
68. Rikuchū
69. Mutsu

known as *Illustrated Map and Survey of the Five Main Roads (Gokaidō bunken nobe ezu).*[7] *Illustrated Map and Survey of the Five Main Roads* was the last in a series of maps compiled by order of the Tokugawa since the early seventeenth century, and that included not only itinerary (road) maps, but also country maps, provincial maps, and maps of cities and castles.[8]

While all five major highways of Japan (Tōkaidō, Nakasendō, Kōshūdō-chū, Ōshūdōchū, and Nikkōdōchū, collectively known as Gokaidō, Figure 2) would be included in the collection, the Tokugawa's latest cartographic effort remained profoundly informed by specific notions of reciprocal prominence and hierarchical value. Strategic considerations played an important role in establishing rank among these officially sanctioned main roads. Connecting the headquarters of the Tokugawa in Edo to the imperial capital of Kyoto in the Kansai region, the Tōkaidō stood out as the main artery in the country. The ability to provide official travelers with adequate services and to facilitate their movements to and from Edo also affected a road's placement in the list. In 1799, for example, the Road Magistrate evaluated the availability of horses and porters along Nakasendō and Kōshūdōchū by comparing it to the standards set by the Tōkaidō.[9] In the 1770s the domain lords en route from the west and from the islands of Kyushu and Shikoku received official warnings about the state of neglect, poverty, and discomfort of most secondary roads *(wakimichi),* and were encouraged to journey only along the main highways *(hongaidō).*[10]

Such major highways were thus the primary concern of the official cartographers, whose maps mirrored the government's political and strategic priorities. Like many of the road charts produced by the Road Magistrate office since Hōjō Ujinaga and Ochikochi Dōin first surveyed the territory in 1651,[11] the 1830s' *Illustrated Map and Survey of the Tōkaidō (Tōkaidō bunken nobe ezu,* part of the larger Gokaidō survey, Figure 3) provides a bird's-eye view of the landscape—the view from above of the political center. As suggested by the horizontal layout of the map, political discourse interpreted the space of travel as a linear sequence of relay stations. Unless they appeared to be strategically relevant, the smaller settlements falling in between did not benefit from inclusion in the selected group of official post stations. In the cartography of officialdom these communities barely stand out—often represented by a few, scattered constructions, at other times simply acknowledged by the scribbling of their name. The edicts of officialdom supported this hierarchy, ordering defiant travelers to ignore the services offered in these "midway villages" *(aida no muramura)* and to do business only in the officially recognized post towns.[12]

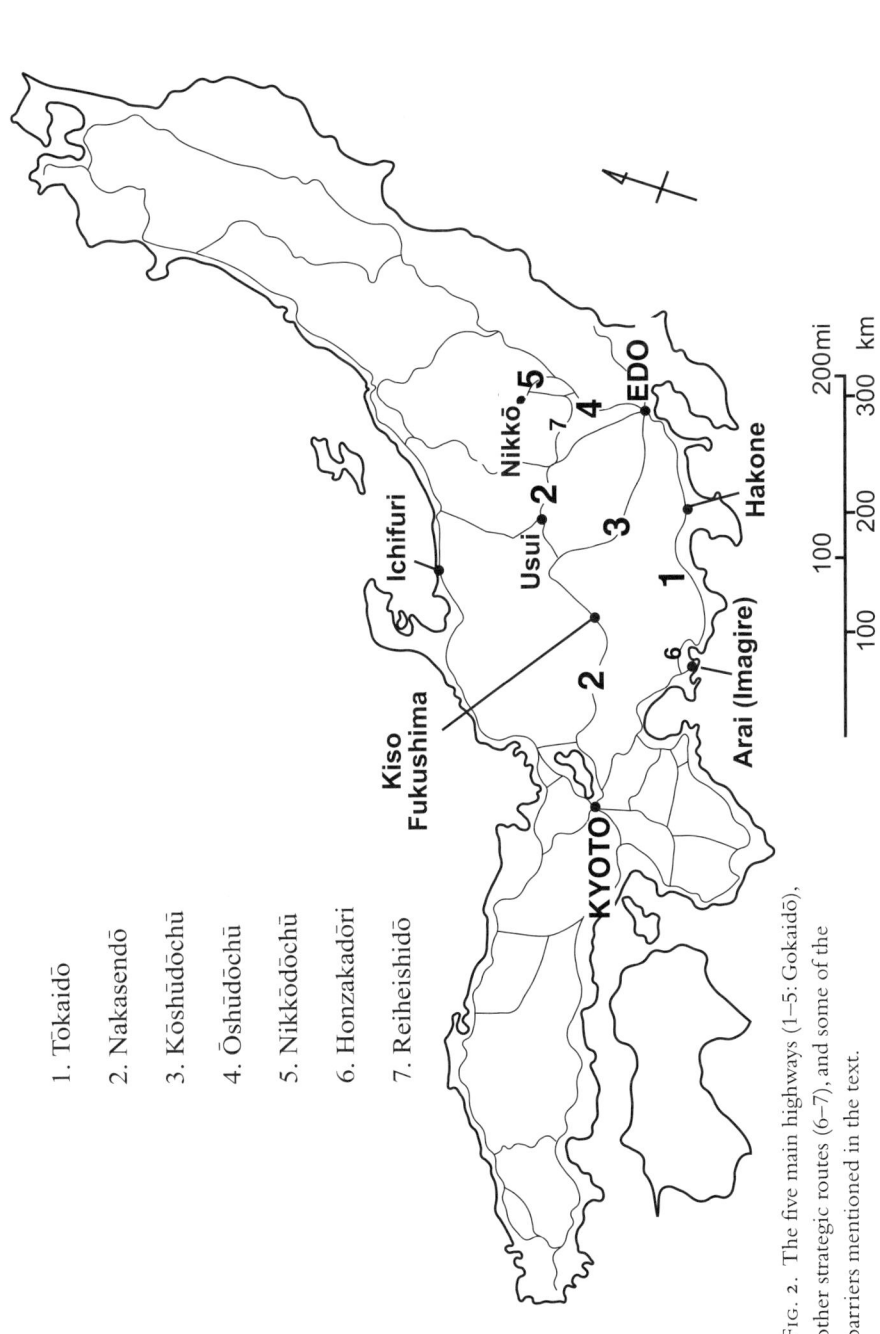

FIG. 2. The five main highways (1–5: Gokaidō), other strategic routes (6–7), and some of the barriers mentioned in the text.

1. Tōkaidō
2. Nakasendō
3. Kōshūdōchū
4. Ōshūdōchū
5. Nikkōdōchū
6. Honzakadōri
7. Reiheishidō

Fig. 3. Mount Fuji in an official map. *Illustrated Map and Survey of the Tōkaidō (Tōkaidō bunken nobe ezu)*. Image from TNM Image Archives (http://TnmArchives.jp/). Courtesy Tokyo National Museum.

Illustrated Map and Survey of the Tōkaidō accurately details the position and layout of such post stations and the intersections of the main highway with smaller secondary roads. It records the names of each district and outlines the borders between provinces. It also includes details on each station's revenue, the width and depth of the major rivers that crossed the route, and the distances between post towns. Even such seemingly objective details in fact concealed the social and political agendas of the government. As Herman Ooms indicates, from the early Edo period the cartographies of officialdom made it a point not to include, in the computation of distances between two points, the stretches of the road that passed through outcast villages, effectively depriving such communities of any voice and of any relevance.[13] Most significant, the illustrations depict all the material icons of governmental authority and ubiquity: billboards onto which ordinances would be posted, fences designating areas of competence, and bridges that on one hand symbolized the power of the Tokugawa to reach across natural obstacles and into the farthest corners of the country, and on the other revealed their ability to compromise strategy with practical necessity.[14] Such icons of authority received preferential treatment over all other elements of the landscape. In *Illustrated Map and Survey of the Tōkaidō,* as Jilly Traganou has pointed out, the road is not drawn to scale; it is purposely enlarged to emphasize its importance in the context of the Tokugawa geopolitical order.[15]

Finally, *Illustrated Map and Survey of the Tōkaidō* illustrates an array of natural and man-made features of the landscape: rivers and forests, hills and lakes, houses and temples, shrines and bright-red gates. The map is so rich in detail that at a first glance the observer would be tempted to declare that it includes everything down to each single tree along the Tōkaidō highway.[16] A closer look, however, reveals one significant and telling omission. Unlike on other road maps, there are no people journeying across this space. Despite being produced during the 1830s, at the peak of what many scholars recognize as the era of a veritable "travel boom,"[17] this map of officialdom represents a silent, immobile landscape undisturbed by any human activity or presence.[18] Like the government that had demanded its creation, this map is ubiquitous yet aloof.

Some of the stylized fences reproduced in *Illustrated Map and Survey of the Tōkaidō* mark the access to the compounds of checkpoints *(sekisho).* Not only their presence throughout the country, but also the fact that they referred prospective travelers to an array of local branches of government to obtain transit permits characterized *sekisho* as pervasive symbols of the Tokugawa's long-reaching arm.[19] Checkpoints, and the array of ordinances and laws that came with them, established and maintained a hierarchy of space that, from early on, set the spaces "this side of the barriers" *(seki yori uchi)* apart from those "which are far beyond" *(engoku no bun).*[20] As a result, these strongholds of Tokugawa authority became the instruments by means of which the government simultaneously achieved, enforced, and reiterated its comprehensive organization and management of the territory.

By allowing transit only between certain hours, checkpoints provided the government with the illusion of controlling not only space but also time. As a general rule, barrier gates were open only between six in the morning and six in the evening. In line with the hierarchical principles that informed Tokugawa policies, exceptions were made to accommodate official travelers, known as the bearers of the "packhorse red seal" *(tenma shuin).* In 1651 the barriers of Hakone, Imagire (Arai), and Kiga were reminded that, apart from high-ranking envoys and official couriers, no other traveler could transit at night.[21] On 1710/7 the senior council *(rōjū)* felt compelled to indicate to the stations of the Tōkaidō highway and of the Mino Road when exactly the night hours began, since "there have been cases in which it was not understood."²²

Domain lords were particularly affected by the Tokugawa's strict policies on movement. Since the enforcement of the alternate attendance system *(sankinkōtai)* in 1635, not only their journeys but also the cycle of their yearly obligations had become painstakingly regulated.²³ According to the principles of *sankinkōtai,* domain lords were to spend every other year in Edo, removed from their power bases at home and under the careful watch of the Tokugawa. An edict of 1635/6/21 included in the *Laws for the Military Households (Buke shohatto)* clearly specified that the lords were to begin their journeys "every year during the summer, in the middle of the fourth month."²⁴ The sixth shogun, Ienobu (r. 1709/1/11–1712/10/14), revised the *Laws for the Military Households* and included a reminder that "the alternate attendance [journeys] shall not occur outside the established period."²⁵ In his *Miscellany of Literary Encounters (Bunkai zakki,* 1749), Confucian scholar Yuasa Gentei (1708–1781) also remarked on the accuracy with which the dictates of the alternate attendance system regulated the movements of domain lords:

> When the months for the alternate attendance of the various lords were established, a general investigation was held. It was decided that the lords of Owari, Kii, and Mito would travel to Edo on the third month, and all the outer lords on the fourth. [...] It was [also] decided that the hereditary vassals *(fudai)* would alternate on the sixth month. [...] In the eighth and ninth months, when the winds pick up on the Western sea, the lords from Tsukushi [Kyushu] do not go to serve in Edo.²⁶

Mapmaking, checkpoints, and the regulations pertaining to the alternate attendance system were some among many of the strategies the rulers employed to regulate spaces and movements. The attention to detail manifested in textual documents also reflects the government's obsession with pervasive and accurate management of the territory. In 1674, for example, the offices of the Finance Magistrate *(kanjō bugyō)* sent out an ordinance to all the stations of the Gokaidō network. In their zeal to secure complete authority over strategic points, the authors of the ordinance considered the settlements around river crossings *(kawagoshi)* and the offices out of which operated the providers of ferry services *(funawatari)* as virtual post stations. The total number of Tōkaidō stages thus rose to sixty-six (rather than the usual fifty-three), if only in this specific document.²⁷ Whenever certain stretches of the road became strategically relevant, the Tokugawa acted swiftly to claim authority over them. In 1764 the government secured control of the Honzakadōri and of the Reiheishidō by placing them under the management of the Road Magistrate.²⁸ While the former connected Hamamatsu to Yoshida and Goyu along the northern shore of Hamana Lake, sparing travelers a much feared ferry ride, the latter branched off the stretch of Nakasendō known as Kiso Road to join the Nikkō Road, the ever important stage of the official parades to Ieyasu's mausoleum (Figure 2). Reminders that certain spaces fell first and foremost under the jurisdiction of official magistrates were issued incessantly. On 1811/6/17, for example, the Finance Magistrate responded to an inquiry by clarifying which stations constituted the initial and final stages of each major highway. The Tōkaidō began at Shinagawa and ended at Ōtsu, while Naitō Shinjuku was the initial stage of the Kōshūdōchū.²⁹ By so doing, the Magistrate reclaimed the government's monopoly over the spaces of official mobility.

Language was a critical factor in the Tokugawa's endless quest for spatial control. Fearing that an imprecise designation of road names might generate confusion, in 1716 the authorities had issued an edict clarifying the exact denomination and spelling of all Gokaidō highways. This was meant to avoid, or at least reduce, the risk of misunderstandings and the creation of loopholes generated by the coexistence of multiple names (a segment of the Nakasendō, for instance, was also commonly known as Kiso Road) and of alternate spellings. The name Nakasendō was written using at least two interchangeable characters for *sen,* an ambiguity the 1716 edict meant to straighten out once and for all.³⁰

The Tokugawa's attention to detail extended to all the tools through which they asserted their authority—road maps, edicts, checkpoints. The general goal was not only to maintain control over the order they had established, but also to claim a central role therein. Politically, early modern Japan consisted of what Mark Ravina has described as "an intricate patchwork of distinct governments," a combination of territories under the direct control of the Tokugawa, domains entrusted to vassals, lands managed by temples and shrines, and imperial landholdings. This generated "broad areas of ambiguous and overlapping authority"³¹ and prompted the Tokugawa to renew their efforts toward pervasive supervision while seeking a pivotal position in the geopolitical map they were drawing.

Centers of Political Discourse

As part of a larger political plan, the early Tokugawa rulers made a conscious claim to identify Edo as the core of all roads by the simple stratagem of planting mile markers *(ichirizuka)* that displayed the distance between each post station and Nihonbashi.[32] Built in 1603, the center of the road network was aptly named the "bridge of Japan." While it would be anachronistic to speculate that there existed an embryonic sense of "nationwide" cohesion on the part of the government, it is safe to argue that, in naming the site, the Tokugawa may have been inspired by a strong centripetal vision. According to a chronicler of the time, Miura Jōshin (1565–1644), notions of centrality had in fact affected the choice. The province of Musashi, Jōshin tells us, was chosen as the departure point "because it coincides with the center of the country's east-west [axis]."[33] By establishing a symbolic point of origin for all movements, the Tokugawa made of mile markers what they would later make of checkpoints: powerful reminders of the government's geopolitical ubiquity and efficacious tools in its appropriation of space. Little did it matter that the original segment of the Tōkaidō highway, which had existed since the eighth century, actually departed from Kyoto.[34] By disregarding historical accuracy and shifting the Tōkaidō's point of origin to the east, the Edo-based government deliberately rearranged geography in order to make a bold political statement. In this respect, Edocentrism was officially born in 1604, when the edict ordering the placement of mile markers along every road was first issued.[35]

At the time, Edo was only beginning to develop its identity as a "capital." Aware of Edo's growing political clout, Miura Jōshin looked at historical records to explain and justify the simultaneous presence of two political centers (Edo and the imperial capital, Kyoto). He pointed at the existence of an eastern capital in China under the Zhou dynasty (1027?–256 BC) as evidence that such coexistence was not only possible but also vouched for by respectable historical precedent.[36] In Japan, he found an antecedent in the Kamakura period (1185–1333), when the seat of the samurai government in Kamakura had been bestowed with the denomination "the other capital." Finally, he cited a more metaphysical case in point, the parallel existence of a heavenly capital and of the mythological palace of the dragon under the seas. Jōshin rebutted the objection that "heaven does not have two suns, the earth does not have two kings," and that "there is only one king in the realm and one capital" by claiming that "all places of peace and prosperity ought to be called capitals."[37] Despite Jōshin's endorsement, the centralization of Edo required a great deal of work on the part of the Tokugawa. Again, language played a prominent role in their efforts.

The existence of multiple centers subtly conditioned the terminology with which movement was defined. The prominence of a site over all others had been historically ratified by the use of terms such as *noboru* or *kudaru*—to move up to, or down from, the imperial capital, perceived as a higher landmark. Visitors would "ascend" toward Kyoto and "descend" away from it. Overall, the legislation issued by the Tokugawa—whose claim as legitimate rulers depended on an alleged deferral of power on the part of the Kyoto court—was careful to respect, at the level of linguistic choices, the superior position of the imperial capital. The 1601 ordinances requiring each Tōkaidō post station to maintain a fixed minimum number of packhorses use the term "ascend" in reference to the western region, and "descend" for horses and porters traveling east, toward Edo.[38] When the first shogun, Ieyasu, traveled to Kyoto in 1605 to hand over his position to his successor Hidetada, he issued a set of guidelines to regulate what he called his "ascent to the capital" (*jōraku*).[39] For a long time the language of official documents continued to use *noboru* as synonymous with "leaving Edo" (to go west). The 1667 ordinance regarding the inspection methods at the Imagire barrier, for instance, specified that "All firearms going down toward Edo *(kudari)* must pass with the authorization of the senior council, which is not required for those leaving Edo *(nobori)*."[40] Again in 1748, in preparation for Princess Isonomiya's journey from Kyoto to Edo, the Tokugawa government sent an edict to all the lords whose domains were located along the Nakasendō. The ordinance informed them that the princess would be traveling east to marry the future tenth shogun, Ieharu, and ordered them to have all roads and bridges repaired and cleaned. The edict uses the expression "to head downwards" *(gekō)* in reference to the princess's journey, still recognizing the prominence of Kyoto in relation to the east.[41]

In an effort to show respect for the pivotal role of the imperial capital while cementing their own authority, the Tokugawa in fact operated under conflicting logics that were never really resolved and ended up coexisting. While official edicts paid verbal homage to the superiority of Kyoto, mile markers buttressed the Tokugawa's attempts to counterclaim Edo as a center. So did the network of checkpoints established throughout the provinces. Not only did their guidelines spell out minutely what and who could move in which direction, but their function as the controllers of "*incoming* guns and *outgoing* women" *(iriteppō deonna)* speaks clearly about the Edocentric ambitions of Tokugawa political discourse.[42]

As the longevity and apparent solidity of the Tokugawa rule became manifest, occasional appropriations of the status of higher landmark for Edo were bound to take place also in official edicts. One such slip of the brush occurred on 1720/12/21 under the rule of the eighth shogun, Yoshimune. On that day, the official in charge of directing naval traffic issued an ordinance addressing the vessels "traveling up" *(noboru)* east, from Shimoda (in the Izu peninsula) to Edo.[43] This was not an isolated case. The same use of *noboru* in reference to ships traveling east to Edo reappears in the guidelines for the Uraga checkpoint issued the following year.[44] The endowment of Edo with the badge of higher landmark was neither final nor absolute. Rather, it represented a shift toward the notion that the relative supremacy of the two centers allowed both to claim the label of capital.

As they weaved their intricate tapestry of power, the Tokugawa remained acutely aware of the complex web of vertical lordship relations.[45] As careful as they were to maintain a facade of subordination vis-à-vis the imperial court, they quickly switched to a different terminology when the balance of power shifted their way. If in the higher spheres of political protocol Edo remained theoretically subordinate to Kyoto, at the lower levels of bureaucracy the hub of the Tokugawa explicitly claimed a higher stand. Such was the case for the journeys to Edo of domain lords and foreign ambassadors. Alternate attendance ordinances never required a provincial lord to "descend" to Edo. Generally, the term of choice would be *sankin,* where the component meaning "to attend" *(tsutomeru,* here read *kin)* spelled out in itself the lords' subordination to the Tokugawa.[46] The 1710 version of *Laws for the Military Households* refers to the alternate attendance lords as "summoned *(mesu)* to Edo," another verbal choice that, far from being casual, explicitly suggests compliance on the part of the daimyo with an order from above, thus situating Edo as a virtual center in the maps of the Tokugawa's retainers.[47]

In the course of the Edo period some of the same lords who were asked to report to Edo for duty were also, on occasion, the recipients of several missives concerning the preparations for the visits of Korean ambassadors. Relations with the Korean government were conducted on the basis of parity, yet the pomp and circumstance with which the Tokugawa organized, controlled, and commemorated the event betray an effort to centralize the position of Edo not only on a national but also on an international scale.[48] Local lords were told that the Korean envoys would be "coming to Japan" *(raichō),* "proceeding" *(sankō)* to Edo, and "returning home to their country" *(kikoku).*[49] The envoys never descended (nor, to be fair, did they ascend) toward Edo: they "advanced" *(keika),* "came and went" *(ōrai),* "transited" *(tōru),* or "traveled" *(ryokō).* Most significantly, they "came invited" *(raihei).*[50] As the edicts addressed to post stations and local lords in preparation for the transit of the foreign envoys did not reach the ears of the Koreans, the use of politically charged terms posed no risk of tarnishing or compromising existing diplomatic relations. Still, prudence was of the essence in the choice of terminology. While the respectability of the Tokugawa as a legitimate center of power was at stake on the one hand, the possibility of committing a faux pas and of altering the precarious balance of post-Hideyoshi normalization lurked on the other.

On the surface, retainers acknowledged the Tokugawa's centripetal efforts and, ever the loyal subordinates, bestowed upon Edo the dignity of a higher landmark, making it a (but hardly ever "the") center. In his *Collection of Things Seen and Heard in the Keichō Era (Keichō kenmonshū),* Miura Jōshin reveals how, as early as the first decade of the seventeenth century, the people of Kyoto summoned to Edo on official duty responded to the invitation by saying, "I obey the order, and I must go up" *(makarinoborubeki sōrō),* or "I am going up to serve." Once in Edo, he continues, "they would say 'I came up yesterday,' or 'I came up today.' They started [the trend], and now people from every province 'come up' to Edo. Isn't Edo then the capital?"[51]

Jōshin's rhetorical question implies that many retainers acknowledged Edo's leading role within a few years of its establishment as the headquarters of the Tokugawa. What happened outside the realm of officialdom, however, was a different story. In the private diaries of government officials, centers shifted freely according to individual preferences and personal agendas. One would expect to see the centripetal pull of Edo increase exponentially through the seventeenth, eighteenth, and into the nineteenth centuries, as the city grew in size and developed its own identity. While (as we shall see later) many nineteenth-century travelers did recognize the prominence of Edo in their writings, others—even government officials—used personal memoirs to challenge Edo's absolute placement on the geopolitical pedestal.

Morioka Sadakata offers a poignant case in point. An officer in Tosa domain, in 1843 Sadakata was sent to Edo as part of an embassy *(oreimairi)* whose purpose was to thank the twelfth shogun, Tokugawa Ieyoshi, for accepting Lord Yamauchi Toyosuke's resignation and for permitting Lord Yamauchi Toyohiro to replace him. Referring to his journey from Tosa to Edo, Sadakata chooses terms that emphasize the official character of the mission and the subordinate position of the province vis-à-vis the hub of the Tokugawa. In his writings Edo is identified as Kōfu, the "administrative headquarters of officialdom," and the travel itself is "an attendance" *(go-sankin).*[52] However, in relation to the travel to Edo of two court nobles (Lord Hino and Lord Tokudaiji, both related to the Fujiwara clan) from the Kamigata region, Sadakata carefully rearranges the hierarchy and chooses to employ verbs that unquestionably place Edo in a subordinate position: "Having heard that the lords Hino and Tokudaiji are going down to Edo *(Edo go-kudari)* to deliver a message, and will transit through Kusatsu, we delayed today's departure and stayed."[53] It is possible that such verbal choices could in fact have been conceived not by Sadakata but by his grandson Sadayoshi, who edited the original diary and, in the introduction, admits to having polished his grandfather's jottings. Authorship, however, has only relative importance in this case. Whether chosen by Sadakata or by Sadayoshi, these verbs unquestionably demonstrate the relativity of centers and peripheries. Mid-nineteenth-century southwestern retainers in particular may have been especially inclined to present the Tokugawa's hub as ever-so-subordinated to the imperial capital.

Equally prone to geopolitical relativity—at least in their personal diaries—were the provincial representatives of the government's bureaucracy. In 1865 the elder retainer *(toshiyori)* Nishikiori Gobei Yoshikura traveled from his village of Moto Katada, in Ōmi, to Edo to discuss with his lord the impact of corvée labor on the community. The private memoir of his journey constantly identifies his homeland, the Kamigata region (and Kyoto in particular), as the center. He refers to the departure for Edo as "leaving to go to the government headquarters" *(shuppu)* and calls the journey itself "a descent" *(go-gekō)*. The first scroll of Gobei's diary, recounting the journey to Edo, is titled "Downward bound" *(kudari),* while the second scroll, in which he records the return trip along the Tōkaidō, is named "Upward bound" *(nobori)*. Traveling to Kyoto is "an ascent to the capital" *(jōkyō)*. Another curious, yet not innocent, annotation betrays Gobei's personal inclination to see the imperial capital as the center of his world. On the way home Gobei comes to Yakushi Nitta, a place that, he claims, is "right midway between Kyoto and Edo."[54] At the time Gobei was traveling from the east to the west along a road, the Tōkaidō, which in the proclamations of officialdom, familiar to an officer such as himself, unquestionably originated from Edo Nihonbashi. It would have been more appropriate for him to identify Yakushi Nitta as the halfway point between Edo and Kyoto, and not the other way around. But in his personal jottings Gobei was free to use the language that most fit his priorities, and his choice of seeing the road as stretching from the west to the east was not a slip of the brush, it was a conscious assertion of a personal spatial hierarchy.

The Spaces of Travel in Religious Discourse

Like the political sphere, religion too was inextricably linked to notions of spatiality and movement. Pilgrimages, coming-of-age ascents to sacred peaks, the incessant peregrinations of mountain ascetics, dynamic practices such as ritual dances (the dancing *nenbutsu*), and the allusive character of terms such as "leaving home" *(shukke)* as synonymous with "entering priesthood" are but a few examples of the historical interconnectedness between faith and movement.⁵⁵ Circuit pilgrimages and the climbing of sacred peaks, in particular, are examples of how religious discourse saw certain landscapes as earthly projections of heavenly realms and associated travel through geographical settings with progress across various levels of spiritual knowledge.⁵⁶

Mandalized maps in the vein of Kanō Motonobu's (1476–1559) *Mandala of a Pilgrimage to Mount Fuji* (*Fuji sankei mandara,* Figure 4) provide an example of a spatial order engendered by religious priorities.⁵⁷ Manifestation mandalas *(suijaku mandara)* of this kind first developed in the sixteenth century; originally produced in temple and shrine ateliers, they had reached popular audiences by the seventeenth.⁵⁸ While some variations in style occurred over time, these works for the most part "became fixed and frozen icons, accepted as canonical and transmitted through centuries largely unchanged."⁵⁹ In this respect, Motonobu's work anticipates many Edo period attitudes toward sacred spaces.

Motonobu reproduces the same landscape later captured by the Road Magistrate's cartographer (Figure 3); yet he sees it in a completely different light. In the map of the official cartographer the road, artificially enlarged, stands out as the focal point, while Mount Fuji, its towering majesty notwithstanding, remains a distant fixture of the landscape. In the religious representation, on the other hand, the road, though included, does not count. The vertical layout suggests that the focus is on the mountain and on its role as the space of a spiritual ascent. Distances, measurements, cardinal directions, and any other symbols of a rational and calculating approach to space are completely absent. The authors of mandalas, artists who created commissioned works in harmony with the canons of the sacred, made no attempt to give their illustrations the faintest semblance of a rationally laid-out chart. A hierarchy of the sacred replaces the fences and clear district boundaries of geopolitical discourse. Like other mandalized maps of the land, *Mandala of a Pilgrimage to Mount Fuji* includes natural elements endowed with sacred meanings.⁶⁰ The moon and the sun, simultaneously rising at the time of the equinox, challenge conventional dichotomies and call for a cosmogony of nonduality. Bridges and boats suggest passages into another world or dimension—departure, death, and rebirth. Waterfalls, pools, and rivers evoke purification, while gates *(torii)* indicate thresholds into the sacred.⁶¹

Unlike the all-inclusive maps of officialdom, in mandalized maps "solemnity is more important than accuracy."⁶² Because the gaze of the political authorities aimed at pervasiveness, *Illustrated Map and Survey of the Five Main Roads* presented a clear and undisrupted view of the road, with its every nook and corner immediately revealed to the eye.⁶³ On the other hand, the interest in the mandala is neither straightforward clarity nor the instantaneous

FIG. 4. Mount Fuji as a sacred peak. Kanō Motonobu (1476–1559), *Mandala of a Pilgrimage to Mount Fuji (Fuji sankei mandara)*. Courtesy Fujisan Hongū Sengen Jinja.

comprehension of the landscape, but a gradual appropriation of the principles embedded therein. The lower slopes of the mountain are partially concealed by lingering veils of mist and low clouds that gradually guide the observer's gaze to the upper portion of the picture, the summit. Here, three avatars reward with their presence those who complete the climb.[64] To make their message resonate more clearly, mandalas did not refrain from manipulating geography for their convenience. Elizabeth ten Grotenhuis discusses cases of mandalas whose creators moved entire mountains from their actual locations in order to give them a more prominent position and mandalas that unrealistically combined east/west and north/south perspectives—illogical yet perfectly functional in the larger theological goals of the patron temples.[65]

The same numinous hierarchy envisioned in Motonobu's work carried over into the early modern period, when the popularity of sacred peaks as travel destinations spread at a fast pace. By the mid-Edo period, with the gradual development of Fuji confraternities, more and more mandalas of the mountain were produced using woodblock-print technology. Smaller in size than their earlier counterparts, and therefore easier to carry and to distribute as promotional items, they took on the function of virtual Fuji amulets.[66] But even in the age of commercialism and commodification peaks and passes maintained their function as entry points into the supernatural.

Historically, mountains indicated the convergence of sacred and worldly and the ideal projections of paradise onto earth.[67] To the practitioners of mountain asceticism *(shugendō)* in particular, "entering the mountain" *(nyūbu)* was a standard expression that indicated the act of engaging in a spiritual journey across the most sacred of spaces. While traveling through the most renowned holy peaks in the country between 1812 and 1818, the ascetic Noda Senkōin (1756–1835) came to Jigenji, a Zen mountain temple in Kyushu. He walked along a river to an area he identified with the Buddhist paradise. Further into the depths of the mountain he reached Hōfukuji, a sacred area *(reichi)* inaccessible to women, "hence supremely clean."[68] Secular travelers were just as aware of the divine aura that peaks exuded. In 1855 Confucian scholar Kiyokawa Hachirō (1830–1863) commented that the summit of Mount Maya, in Settsu Province, was "a thoroughly numinous place, and one feels it." During the same journey one of his travel companions even drew a parallel between Kiyomizu Temple in Kyoto and Fudaraku, the paradise of Kannon.[69]

Difficult to conquer, dense with mystery, and projecting upwards toward the heavens, mountains resonated with religious metaphors and provided a great many religious institutions with the perfect terrain to project their spiritual constructions.[70] Economically and strategically relevant, the plains operated, if not exclusively at least largely, under the careful scrutiny of secular political authority. Isolated and mostly uninhabited, mountains were by definition the spaces of the sacred.[71] Their ruggedness made them particularly inaccessible during the snowy winter months. Permitting access to their mountain compounds only during the "open mountain" season helped temples and shrines to establish a self-regulating religious calendar that also included annual festivals, exhibits of sacred images, and seasonal celebrations.[72] As such, sacred mountains and sacred places sustained the efforts of the religious establishment to map a geography (and establish a calendar) independent from that of the government.

As the foci around which religious discourse mapped a significant part of its space, mountains claimed a spatial hierarchy of their own. The geography of power in the religious arena was based not on association with and proximity to the inner circles of government but rather on the dynamic opposition between cleanliness and pollution. Social activities, mobility, and uncleanliness were confined at the bottom of the peak; the hustle and bustle of ordinary life gradually decreased along the slopes; and the very top embodied timeless calm, purity, and untamed wilderness.[73]

Yet for all its otherworldly atmosphere the space of the sacred was not aseptic. Hallowed grounds were intended as areas where pilgrims could interact with holiness and begin their ascent toward a higher state—in both the physical and the spiritual sense. Consequently, religious interpretations of space like *Mandala of a Pilgrimage to Mount Fuji* display none of the detached immobility of maps in the league of *Illustrated Map and Survey of the Five Main Roads*. The eye of the authorities produced a freeze-frame of a politically idealized land, a somewhat surreal travelscape where buildings, bridges, and billboards were at the service of no one, except perhaps the few administrators who had access to these maps. In the mandala, on the other hand, countless individuals move around the mountain. The illustration is a dynamic portrayal of the quest for the sacred, which begins in the lower segment of the picture with everyday activities (a man carrying goods in baskets, fishermen at work on their boats) and ascends progressively across higher levels of holiness (the gate, the ablution pool, the waterfall, the zigzagging line of white-clad pilgrims climbing the slope) until it reaches the benevolent deities at the top.

Aside from mountains, religious circuits *(junrei)* also mapped the space of the sacred around the notion of spiritual progress. Pilgrimage circuits (Figure 5) such as the eighty-eight-stage Shikoku tour (Shikoku *henro*), the thirty-three-stage Western Provinces circuit (Saikoku *henro*), the thirty-three-stage

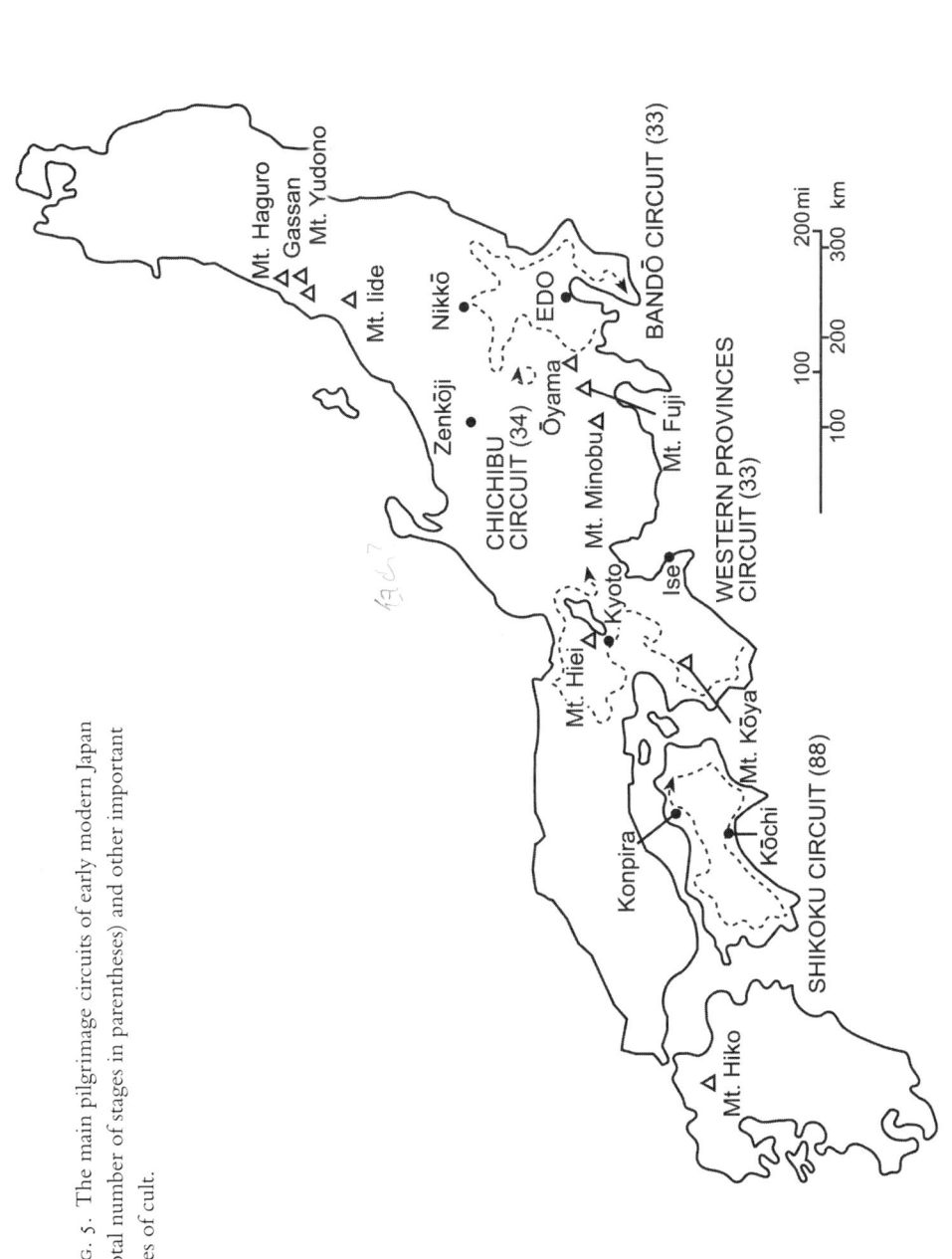

FIG. 5. The main pilgrimage circuits of early modern Japan (total number of stages in parentheses) and other important sites of cult.

Bandō circuit, and the thirty-four-stage Chichibu circuit (these last three combined formed the megacircuit of the one hundred Kannons of Japan) enjoyed a vast popularity among travelers throughout the Edo period.[74] Whereas the directionality of political discourse was conceived around the notion of linear movement between established centers (Edo Nihonbashi and the imperial capital), in the case of circuits movement occurred in a circular route (circumambulation, or *mawari*) along a number of stages, or *fudasho*.[75] As Figure 5 shows, Shikoku pilgrims progressed along a clearly circular route. Other circuits were more open-ended, but by no means were they organized along straight lines. The Western Provinces circuit, for instance, began at Nachi Falls in Kumano, progressed through the Kii peninsula, then stretched toward Kyoto and farther west as far as the shores of the Inland Sea. From there it turned north, then east, and reached its final stage in what corresponds to modern Gifu Prefecture (early modern Mino Province), completing, if not a perfect circle, a route defined by continuous directional changes.[76]

Some sacred mountains also required circular progressions around their complexes. The practitioners of the branch of mountain asceticism known as Murayama *shugendō* who climbed Mount Fuji, for instance, circled the crater on the summit in a practice called *ohachi meguri*.[77] During his extensive travels, the mountain ascetic Noda Senkōin reached the top of Mount Fuji on 1817/6/16 and marched in circles around the mouth of the volcano.[78] On the slopes of Mount Fuji linearity was outlawed and circularity was enforced by the prohibition against "splitting the mountain" *(yama o saku* or *yama o kiru),* which forbade pilgrims who entered the complex through a particular access point to exit the area from the same location, or from the one directly in line with it. For instance, travelers who reached Mount Fuji via its northern access at Yoshida could neither turn back and exit through Yoshida nor use the southern gates of Ōmiya and Murayama.[79] Suzuki Shōzō, a traveler from Shimōsa who climbed Mount Fuji in 1828, entered the sacred complex at Yoshida and exited from the eastern gate of Subashiri, conveniently en route to his next destination, Ōyama and the celebrated sites of Sagami Province.[80]

Circumambulations in the name of faith occurred also on a larger scale, outside or across the routes of circuits. Iwahana Michiaki has observed that many of the pilgrims who visited the cluster of three sacred peaks in Dewa (Gassan, Haguro, and Yudono, Figure 5) also included stops at some—if not all—stations of the Chichibu or Bandō circuits and returned home after completing a full circle. Iwahana explains their circular motions by arguing that the space crossed by pilgrims, once trodden, appropriated, and recorded in diaries, lost its aura of inaccessibility (synonymous with sacredness), hence prompting the necessity to move in circles, off to new and untapped holy places.[81]

It is also undeniable that a hefty dose of utilitarianism on the part of pilgrims contributed to the circular shape of religious travel. Confraternity-sponsored pilgrimages by proxy *(daisan)* moved along preestablished routes that had been designed to reap as many worldly benefits as possible by including a high number of religious centers and sacred locations. Individual travelers, many of whom justified their journeys in religious terms, also sought to take full advantage of what was often a once-in-a-lifetime experience by visiting as many locations as possible. In this respect, circular routes allowed them to achieve their goal more effectively than linear ones. Many such travelers combined a visit to Ise with one to the other great center of faith, Zenkōji in Shinano Province. By using alternatively the Tōkaidō and the Nakasendō, they traveled in full circle across some of the most renowned sites in the country.[82] The commoner Kuwahara Hisako (1791–1853), for instance, departed from Ebitsu in her native Chikuzen Province (Kyushu) in 1841 and completed a full and tortuous circumambulation of the central part of Honshu. She reached Osaka and turned south toward the Kii peninsula, passing by Nara and Yoshino before coming to Ise. From there she traveled to Nagoya, entered the Nakasendō, and walked all the way to Zenkōji. She then moved east and visited Nikkō. At that point she began her return journey, coming down to Edo first, then traveling west along the Tōkaidō until she came to Fujisawa. There, she turned her back to the coast and moved inland again, headed to Suwa (Shinano). The circle was completed when she descended to Nagoya, reached Kyoto, and then came back to Osaka before returning to Kyushu.[83] Equally circular, albeit on a much smaller scale, was the ascending movement visitors experienced upon visiting one of Edo's most famous attractions, the Turbo Hall (Sazaedō) at the Temple of the Five Hundred Arhats (Gohyaku Rakandō). Its spiral stairs generated the illusion of perpetual motion—so much so that the hall was also known by the alternate name of Entsūkaku, or Turret of Rotating Motion.[84]

Sacred mountains, the mandalized representations of space, and religious circuits all provided an alternative to the logic of official discourse, for they transcended the hierarchy and bipolarism (from/to, up/down) implied in the linear motion of governmental maps and edicts. Linearity spells simplification, while circularity entails complexity. It requires the attention of a constant quest, startles with sudden changes of direction, provides the illusion of infinity, and nurtures the rejection of commonly accepted notions of directionality. The verses that Saikoku pilgrims inscribed on their sedge hats reflect an acute awareness of such complexity, not to mention a thorough disregard for the geopolitical rationale of officialdom:

> Awakening from illusion, the three worlds are a palace.
> Originally, *there is neither East nor West*.
> Enlightenment is empty, the ten directions are empty.
> *Where is North and [where is] South?*[85]

Centers of Religious Discourse

As with political discourse, decentralization occurred at various levels in the sphere of the sacred. With the rise of the Tokugawa shogunate, the old order that gravitated around the cultural (and imperial) capital of Kyoto and the holiest of the holy in Ise became complemented, according to Herman Ooms, by a new order whose foci were the Tokugawa government in Edo and its heavenly satellite in Nikkō. When the emperor granted Tōshō Shrine the denomination of *gū* (prominent shrine) in 1645, Nikkō emerged as the eastern equivalent of Ise in the hierarchy of the sacred. Ieyasu, deified as the Great Avatar of the East, shone over this new center much like Amaterasu did in the west.[86] Further evidence of the Tokugawa's attempt to create a parallel between the Great Shrine and Ieyasu's mausoleum was Iemitsu's order to dismantle and rebuild the Tōshōgū every twenty years, following a tradition practiced in Ise.[87] Although the plan did not survive Iemitsu's death in 1651, its termination does not detract from its significance as a political act. The efforts of the early Tokugawa rulers to recenter the political landscape by replicating the relation between power and the sacred existing in the west were not limited to Nikkō: while the imperial court in Kyoto benefited from the protection of Mount Hiei—which safeguarded the capital from the inauspicious northeastern corner—the Tokugawa headquarters throve under the auspices of the "Mount Hiei of the East" (Tōeisan Kan'eiji), built in 1625 by order of Hidetada.[88]

Aside from Mount Hiei, many other holy mountains, once identified as the unique nuclei of a cosmological order, multiplied in the course of the early modern period. Fuji cult practitioners of the early Edo period such as Kakugyō (1541–1646) and Jikigyō Miroku (1671–1733) had considered Mount Fuji the pillar of the universe, the source from which sprang life, the sun, the moon, and the entire geopolitical order.[89] By the mid-Edo period, however, the mountain's surge in popularity not only attracted visitors from all social standings, but also spurred a trend for iconization and imitation sustained by the rising commercial economy.[90] Imitation in particular occurred on two fronts. The first was that of popular culture and the publishing industry. Initially represented in refined mandalas and in elegant works of art only accessible to few wealthy patrons, by the second half of the Edo period images of Fuji (and of many other numinous sites) multiplied, making their appearance in countless woodblock series, in the pages of popular literature, and in an array of travel guides. The second front involved more concrete attempts at reproduction. Small-scale copies of sacred sites popped up throughout the country. Replicas of sacred peaks such as Mount Fuji and Mount Kōya abounded in Edo. Followers of Kōbō Daishi (774–835) living in the East no longer needed to journey to Shikoku to pay homage to the master, for by the mid-eighteenth century replicas of the circuit he had allegedly founded had appeared in a number of Edo wards. Another copy of the circuit existed at the foot of Mount Tenmoku, in Kai Province.[91] The appearance of surrogate mountains, miniature pilgrimages, and affiliate establishments not only remapped the world of faith, but also added density and meaning—even ubiquity—to the geography of the sacred.

The existence, by the late Edo period, of multiple centers of faith (Ise and Nikkō, or Mount Hiei and Kan'eiji at the intersection of religion and politics; the various stages of circuits at a more popular level), and of surrogates and icons, was in part the result of a political strategy effected by the Tokugawa, in part the outcome of the religious establishment's attempts at expansion, and in part the inevitable consequence of economic and cultural changes that had opened the door to commodified, commercialized travel. As the number of religious centers multiplied, so did the range of options available to prospective, nonofficial travelers. At the same time, the maps of lyrical discourse were also promoting their own spatial hierarchies and their own centers.

The Spaces of Travel in Lyrical Discourse

> A human life cannot be graphed, whatever people may say, by two virtual perpendiculars, representing what a man believed himself to be and what he wished to be, plus a flat horizontal for what he actually was; rather, the diagram has to be composed of three curving lines, extended to infinity, ever meeting and ever diverging.
>
> —Marguerite Yourcenar[92]

Adding to the chorus of voices that narrated the same space in a multitude of distinct idioms were artists, poets, and lyrical travelers. Poetic discourse categorized the spaces of travel according to yet another hierarchy, one that, oblivious to notions of karmic prominence or geopolitical clout, valued first and foremost literary recognition. While it came of age by percolating through all levels of society in the Edo period, poetic travel was by no means a new trend of the times. The late medieval poet Shōtetsu (1380–1459) had already captured the essence of literary space when he wrote, in his *Shōtetsu's Tale* (*Shōtetsu monogatari,* 1448): "If someone were to ask me what province Mount Yoshino is in, I would answer that when it comes to cherry blossoms I think of Mount Yoshino, when it comes to bright autumn leaves, I think of Mount Tatsuta. I would write my poems accordingly, *not caring whether these places are in Iga or Hyūga Provinces.* It is of no practical value to remember which provinces these places are in."[93]

In their diaries, Edo period poetic travelers confirm Shōtetsu's view that literary assonances stand to the fore as the necessary prerequisites to make space worthy of recognition. The lyrical traveler by definition, Matsuo Bashō was so "absorbed in the wonders of the surrounding countryside and the recollections of ancient poets" at the barrier of Shirakawa that he found himself momentarily at loss for words.[94] In the writings of the itinerant nun and poetess Kikusha-ni (1753–1826) the northern region of Rikuoku became transmogrified into a series of lyrical sites, her journey a passage from one poetically celebrated location to the next—Okinoishi, Sue no Matsuyama, the Abukuma River, the barrier of Shirakawa.[95]

Literary precedent had inspired educated travelers to take to the road in the first place. Hōshō Hakuō, who wrote under the nom-de-plume Senbai, opened the diary of his 1759 journey with a two-tiered homage to the authors of the past: "The travel diary of a man of old [says that] the writings of Ki [no Tsurayuki], of [Kamo no] Chōmei, and of the nun Abutsu are infused with emotions, and for this reason everyone imitated them without improving on what they have left behind."[96] Not only does Senbai directly mention three writers of the ancient and medieval period (Tsurayuki, Chōmei, and Abutsu), he also does so by borrowing the words of a fourth literary icon: the "man of old" Senbai refers to is none other than Bashō, and the diary in question is *The Records of a Travel-Worn Satchel* (*Oi no kobumi,* 1687). The words and emotions of authors from the ninth to the seventeenth centuries informed Senbai's relation with the travelscape.

The relationship between precedent and sites was one of reciprocal support, for the landscapes of lyrical travel served as perennial reminders of the classics just as much as the classics gave meaning and value to the landscapes.

Only when she began a journey from Edo to Izumi Province (1806) did the magistrate's wife Tsuchiya Ayako "truly come to see and understand the real meaning [lit. *kokoro*, spirit] of the poems of old."[97]

Indifferent to schemes of linearity or circularity, a journey through poetic space occurred along a series of lyrically induced emotional pinnacles. Post towns and amulet offices, barriers and torii did not constitute the landmarks of poetic travel; in this case, evocative place-names *(utamakura)* served the purpose. Originating from sites with religious assonances where travelers experienced a sense of communion with the sacred, *utamakura* had indicated areas of high lyrical intensity since the Heian period (794–1185).[98] With time, these catalysts of emotional involvement became incorporated into the literary and poetic heritage and assumed new layers of significance. Mount Yoshino, in Yamato Province, became the standard epitome of impermanence by virtue of its splendid though short-lived cherry blossoms, while the villages of Suma (Settsu Province) and Akashi (Harima Province), on the Inner Sea, owed to Genji's exile (narrated in the eleventh-century novel *The Tale of Genji*) their consecration as the embodiments of sadness, detachment, loneliness, and the ephemeral.[99] Because of their evocative power, *utamakura* charted the routes of poets by providing a unit of measurement based on emotional valence and lyrical resonance. The lack of proper sanctification in the classics affected literary space as much as the absence of strategic value or karmic relevance diminished the worth of sites in the maps of officialdom and of religious discourse. The true literary traveler would consciously disregard any sight not validated by literary antecedent—so much so that the sites located between one *utamakura* and the next floated in the same vacuum as the "midway villages" between official post towns and as the cloud concealed areas in the mandala.

Just as malleable and independent as space was the time of lyrical travel. Journeys into the space of poetic nostalgia were generally immune from the dictates of religious or official calendars. Unlike mountains and temporary displays of sacred icons, *utamakura* and moss-covered monuments were almost always accessible, their evocative charge undiminished—in fact enhanced—by the dramatic effect of seasonal change and by the passing of time. In the words of Matsuo Bashō: "In this ever-changing world where mountains crumble, rivers change their courses, roads are deserted, rocks are buried, and old trees yield to young shoots, it was nothing short of a miracle that this monument alone had survived the battering of a thousand years to be the living memory of the ancients. I felt as if I were in the presence of the ancient themselves, and, forgetting all the troubles I had suffered on the road, rejoiced in the utter happiness of this joyful moment, not without tears in my eyes."[100]

Fig. 6. Mount Fuji as a poetryscape. Tawaraya Sōtatsu (active 1600–1640), *The Descent to the East from Tales of Ise.* Courtesy The Gotoh Museum, Setagaya-ku, Tokyo.

The same Mount Fuji that quietly rose behind the main road in the cartographies of political power, and that could be transmogrified into the embodiment of spiritual progress in the maps of religious discourse, took on yet another role in the representations of the poetically inspired. Those who invoked the sanctification of the classics to assign meanings to landscapes were more inclined to see in Mount Fuji one of the stages of Ariwara no Narihira's (825–880) "descent to the East" *(Azuma kudari)* as narrated in

Tales of Ise (tenth century). So did, for example, numerous professional artists who painted on commission, creating unique pieces for wealthy patrons. Ōgata Kōrin (1661–1716), various members of the Kanō and Tosa schools, and Tawaraya Sōtatsu (active 1600–1640) all produced elegant works centered on the link between Narihira and Mount Fuji.[101]

Sōtatsu's contribution to the sanctification of lyrical space is titled *The Descent to the East from Tales of Ise* (*Ise monogatari Azuma kudari*, Figure 6). Produced in the first half of the seventeenth century, it encapsulates many of the tenets that would define lyrical mapmaking throughout the Edo period: a symbiotic relation between the site and the work of literature associated with it, an understanding of space based on lyrical parameters, and the creation of an imaginary bridge between past and present. If in *Illustrated Map and Survey of the Tōkaidō* the road was enlarged to underscore its prominence, and in *Mandala of a Pilgrimage to Mount Fuji* the mountain rose as the nexus between this world and the next, in Sōtatsu's illustration Narihira and the peak stand out as equals. Such balance is not so much a matter of perspective as it is the application of a fundamental concept of lyrical maps: the literary icon and the geographical site are indispensable to one another, for it is by means of their reciprocal encounter that lyricism is created and meaning assigned.

More than one image of Narihira's descent to the East is attributed to Sōtatsu. While the one reproduced here is purely visual, other similar versions include poetry as well.[102] Whenever verses are included with the image—as in the early seventeenth-century scroll of the Tosa school (Figure 7)—they always cite the lines Narihira wrote in admiration of the snow-capped mountain:

Toki shiranu	Fuji is a mountain
yama wa Fuji no ne	That knows no season.
itsu tote ka	What time does it take this for,
ka no ko madara ni	That it should be dappled
yuki no fururan	With fallen snow?[103]

Informative notes also appeared in the maps of government cartographers, but with a profoundly different function. There, they quantified landscapes by means of rice bushels *(koku)*, yards *(ken)*, and miles *(ri)*. In the maps of lyricism, on the other hand, they measure the worth of space in syllables—the 5-7-5-7-7 sequence of traditional Japanese poetry.

These renditions of Mount Fuji do not project heavenly realms onto the slopes of the mountain, nor do they turn the peak into the accessory of a greater political project. In the conception of lyrical discourse, Mount Fuji

Fig. 7. Another version of Mount Fuji as poetryscape. School of Tosa (early seventeenth century), *Tales of Ise, Episode 9, Fuji*. Hanging scroll, ink, color, and gold on paper; 16.2 x 15.3 cm (left-card pictorial), 16.1 x 15.3 cm (right-card inscription). Photograph © Museum of Fine Arts, Boston, gift of Mr. and Mrs. Alan J. Strassman. Courtesy Museum of Fine Arts, Boston.

becomes the pretext for an emotional engagement with the landscape both on the part of Narihira—who is inspired to conceive one of his celebrated verses—and of the external observer—who is able to create an instant bond with literary tradition. Whereas the cartographies of the Tokugawa spoke of a political present and the mandalas revealed timeless paradises, the maps of lyricism brought the observer on a journey back in time. Gazing at Fuji from the same spot from which Narihira had admired the peak, the viewer identifies with the literary icon and partakes of his emotional connection with the landscape.[104] The sudden revelation that time can be transcended by means of a cultural act provides literary travelers with an alternative to both the flat and monotonous linearity of the road map and the gradual, step-by-step revelation of the mandala. In other words, the seizure of the literary past offers instant gratification.

The diverging iconographic representations produced by the Road Magistrate's officers, by the mandala artists, and by the transmitters of literary values not only ascribed different meanings to the same landscapes, they also created geographical hierarchies whose centers and peripheries intersected but seldom overlapped.

Centers of Lyrical Discourse

Since becoming the seat of imperial power in the late eighth century Kyoto had embodied the focus not only of political but also of literary attention. The hierarchy of poetic space placed the Kansai region at its top, the imperial capital at its core, and the remote regions away from Kyoto at its margins. The center of this universe was a space of comfortable stability, wealth, and cultural excellence best exemplified by the Heian notion of *miyabi,* the refinement and elegance of the imperial court. By contrast, the peripheries spelled discomfort, backwardness, and unknown dangers. It did not matter that misery, ugliness, and violence might in fact lurk around the wards of the capital, as they often did, nor did it matter that corruption and machinations had forced the political center to shift more than once in the past. In the gaze of the poets and writers of all times, the dichotomy between the safe haven of the center and the wild perils of the peripheries was the yardstick with which travel was measured, as hardships grew in direct proportion to the distance from the capital: "as we traveled from province to province, farther and farther away from the capital, the trees growing on the mountains and the shapes of the rocks appeared increasingly rough to us," Minamoto (Koga) Michichika (1149–1202) had written in 1180.[105] On the maps of lyrical discourse, distances had always been measured in cultural achievements rather than exact mileage, as Lady Nijō (1258–ca. 1328) revealed when, upon reaching Enoshima (Sagami Province) after a long journey from Kyoto, she wrote, "I realized I had truly come from two-thousand miles away."[106] Her exaggeration speaks volumes about the perceived cultural gap between her center and the remote province.

The poetic prominence of the imperial capital maintained its influence over educated travelers well into the early modern period. At the onset of her trip from Ise to Kyoto in 1777, Arakida Reijo, the wife of a shrine priest, expressed her excitement as she prepared to visit "each and every *utamakura*" along the way.¹⁰⁷ While visiting the Silver Pavilion, a famous Kyoto landmark, she composed verses that celebrated its exceptional value as the nexus between past and present:

Toshi o hete	As the years go by
kumonaranu ike no	the glimpses of the past
kagami ni wa	remain clear
mukashi no kage zo	in the mirror
sayaka nari keru	of the unclouded pond.¹⁰⁸

The relatively new city of Edo, born out of a swampland in the late 1500s, could hardly provide such a window into the past, and for this reason many a cultured traveler chose to ignore it altogether. Steven D. Carter cites the case of two court poets from the eighteenth century, Reizei Tamemura (1712–1774) and Karasumaru Mitsuhide (1689–1748), who during their 1746 journey to the East composed a number of poems at lyrically relevant sites along the Tōkaido, but wrote nothing at all of their stay in the hub of the Tokugawa. Their diaries note the travelers' approach to the city and then abruptly end, only to resume with the return segment of the trip.¹⁰⁹

Despite Edo's shortcomings in the higher spheres of lyricism, in the course of the seventeenth century individual authors were already at work to give the city a semblance of literary dignity, one that was, if not thoroughly independent, at least somewhat detached from Kyoto's model. Some of the modes of engagement with the space of lyrical travel that had been established in the classic courtly tradition eventually came to inform erudite travelers in the eastern regions, who, on occasion, aptly modified them to fit their own cultural geographies. The familiar theme of the dichotomy between center (civilization) and peripheries (wilderness), so dear to the likes of Lady Nijō and Michichika, reappears for instance in the 1639 diary of Lady Nakagawa, the Edo-based wife of Nakagawa Hisamori, lord of Oka domain (in Kyushu). This time, however, it is Edo that embodies the civilized center and the safe haven to which travelers should return. During a trip to Ikaho hot springs Lady Nakagawa relived the emotions of the Heian courtiers tossed out in the wild, traveling across a space that she unmistakably identified with the boondocks and associated with discomforts and inelegance.¹¹⁰ As she finally made her way back into the safety and glorious pomp of the city, Lady Nakagawa saw Edo as the epitome of civilization and elegance, with its "rows and rows of eaves from beautiful houses, the daimyo residences, inlaid with silver and gold; the market town, where treasures not only from Yamato but also from Korea and China are on display in large numbers; and the crowds of people who parade back and forth."¹¹¹ Like Michichika, who upon reentering Kyoto had breathed a sigh of relief ("we felt the capital drew nearer and nearer and the hardships of travel were gradually forgotten"),¹¹² so did Lady Nakagawa feel elated once Edo was in sight: "Now more than ever I realized I was no longer looking at a mountain village. These are truly times of wealth for the country and of prosperity for the people. Even during this trip I did not encounter any dangerous individuals along the road. The realm *(tenka, amegashita)* is at peace. Taking comfort in the idea that I live in exceptional times, I happily returned home."¹¹³

Also based in Edo was the samurai Toda Mosui (1629–1706), who in the 1680s set out to compose a guide to the must-see sites of the city. While, as Jurgis Elisonas points out, most guides to the famous sites of Edo were, in the seventeenth century, only slightly modified versions of works originally written about Kyoto,¹¹⁴ Mosui's *A Sprig of Purple (Murasaki no hitomoto)* actually dignified the sites of Edo as having a value in themselves. The work was completed in 1683, but, perhaps because commercial publishing had yet to come of age in the city, it only circulated as a manuscript and did not make its appearance on the market until a good two centuries later.¹¹⁵ As we shall see in Chapter 5, it would take a radical reinvention of the concept of "famous place" and the infusion of commercial tones to supplement the lack of *utamakura*-like nuances for the sites of Edo to eventually find their place on the maps of recreational travelers.

SINCE THE EARLY Edo period the road appeared laden with material reminders of a fierce tug-of-war among discourses; mile markers and billboards, gates and purification pools, monuments and checkpoints accumulated by the roadside in a cacophony of claims and symbols. Areas of competence were seized by either placing man-made artifacts or by attributing meanings to already existing natural features. The spatial interpretations and representations of religious and lyrical discourse more or less directly challenged the monopoly that the Tokugawa strove to enforce upon the landscape. By complicating the picture, they paved the way for alternative modes of engagement with the spaces of travel. While the authorities attempted, with a deluge of ordinances and a clever use of cartography, to monopolize mobility by imposing clear and linear directions, the complex nuances created by the proliferation of interpretive frames empowered travelers with the ability to choose, as they could make of Fuji a distant fixture of the road, a worldly projection of heavenly spheres, or an access point to the misty atmosphere of Narihira's "Heianscape." And choose they did. Returning home to Ōmi after his visit to Edo in 1865, Nishikiori Gobei Yoshikura included in his travel jottings a sketch of Mount Fuji as he saw it: a snow-capped mountain surrounded by other peaks and by beautiful trees. In Gobei's rendition, the mountain is worthy of note by virtue of its natural beauty and because, as he annotates, "in the heart of the mountains around here they breed horses for the government."[116] Gobei saw Fuji through the lens of his personal experience both as a local representative of the Edo authorities (the reference to the horses bred for official use) and as an individual traveler who simply enjoyed the peak as a pristine marvel.

By choosing their own interpretations, wayfarers like Lady Nakagawa in the seventeenth century, Arakida Reijo in the eighteenth, and Gobei in the nineteenth established a personal interaction with the spaces of travel—spaces that, as the journey progressed, manifested themselves as more and more open to creative constructions. As will become evident in the following chapters, such malleability empowered travelers not only to reinterpret the significance of each location, but also to question and redefine some of the rules of engagement that purportedly defined the modes of travel.

CHAPTER 2

At the Intersection of Travel and Gender

Item: In the past years we voiced our intention to forbid the lodging of females in temples and monks' residences. However, in these days we have heard that [the temples] are disorderly. Therefore, from now on the path [set by] the previous provision should no longer be disregarded. The rigid rule [stipulates that] no relatives—including one's mother and elder or younger sisters—are allowed within temples, halls, and monks' quarters. We hereby reissue the order, which all should studiously obey.
—"Official Memorandum on the Prohibition to Lodge Women in Temples, Halls, and Monks Residences" (1688)

We are confronted not by one social space but by many.
—Henri Lefebvre, *The Production of Space*

GENDER, ALONG WITH status, was one of the coordinates that defined a person's place in Edo society. It was also one of the parameters that determined one's ability to be mobile and to access specific spaces. Chapter 1 has shown how, across interpretive frames, standards evolved, locations rose to prominence, and the centers of today were not immune from becoming the peripheries of tomorrow. The continuous remapping of space and redrawing of boundaries, I suggested, made landscapes into multilayered entities, so much so that the same site could simultaneously embody a political statement, a cosmic diagram, and a cultural paradigm. In the flexible spaces that emerged from this juxtaposition of meanings travelers found unexpected loopholes to circumvent the logic of officialdom. Gender was one of the platforms where theories and practices met and clashed more stridently.

While gender-based considerations pervaded the debate on mobility in the Edo period, the existence of malleable landscapes rendered the enforcement of official directives on the topic discontinuous and heterogeneous at best. Political discourse mapped the spaces of travel by intersecting the parallels of gender with the meridians of status, devoting great attention to the distinction between male and female travelers, between individuals of high or low standing, between active players and simple pawns in the economy, and between involved or relatively disengaged members of society. Along the roads, however, some of these theoretical distinctions became less clear, or were defined differently. Where political necessities drew lines of separation, actual practice blurred them; where the eyes of administrators were blind to differences, common sense distinguished them clearly.

Sacred areas—the compounds of temples and shrines, circuits, and the slopes of numinous mountains—were one of the grounds in which diverging interpretations proliferated and disjunctions emerged more clearly. Managed by the religious establishment and not infrequently kept in check by the government, these locations were also among the most popular travel destinations. Women, too, made their way into these sacred spaces despite an array of regulations and unwritten traditions that dictated otherwise. The fluid spaces of religious complexes and the debate on gender that ensued therein offer an excellent case study for examining some of the practical implications that the overlapping of discourses had for travelers. On one side, the Tokugawa authority worked to impose order onto the space of the sacred either directly or by means of local administrators and domain lords. On the other, temples and shrines managed their territories and those of affiliate local centers independently, superimposing their own rules and regulations. At times they agreed with the ordinances emanating from officialdom, but just as frequently they did not. In regulating gender, movement, and order within sacred territories, the logic of officialdom had to come to terms with a formidable adversary, the logic of compassion.

Gender and Mobility in the Edo Period

In the course of the Edo period the types of female travelers grew significantly not only in number but also in variety, as women from all walks of life took to the road for increasingly diverse reasons. Existing travel records composed by women in the years between the triumph of Ieyasu at Sekigahara (1600) and the beginning of the Genroku era (1688–1704) are limited to the memoirs of lords' wives and daughters en route either to Edo to serve as hostages, to hot-spring resorts to heal alleged ailments, or to the residences of their prospective husbands after a marriage had been arranged.[1] In a study of road maps produced shortly before or at the beginning of the Genroku era, Fukai Jinzō indeed laments that virtually no female traveler is represented and explains the absence as "an indication that at the time there were very few women who took to the road."[2]

The 1690s kicked off the birth of the floating world culture and the celebration of townspeople's values ballyhooed in the pages of woodblock prints and popular literature. Associated with such transformation was a certain degree of urban prosperity coupled with a growing sense of stability and order. Opulence and security ensured the diffusion of a culture of leisure that came to inform the lives of women as much as it did men's. Within a few decades, women travelers were making more frequent appearances in the official records. A document produced by the checkpoints of Hakone and Nebugawa on 1715/9/23, for instance, reveals that in the second month of that year alone a total of forty-nine women had transited through the two barriers.[3] Of the 171 travel permits collected therein in the span of five months, 167 had been issued for female travelers.[4] As women traveled in larger numbers, their categories became more diverse. By 1721 the authorities acknowledged that "recently in the cities the number of people who on a daily basis request travel permits for women has grown," coming to include "even lower classes and servants" *(suezue karukimono mademo)*.[5] Surviving travelogues from the eighteenth century include the recollections not only of lords' wives, but also of townswomen and poetesses on the road for cultural and recreational purposes.

Official records and court cases of the seventeenth and eighteenth centuries also mention with increased frequency the journeys of female villagers. In the spring of 1799, for example, three women from Shinano Province departed in the midst of great excitement to visit a much advertised public display of sacred images at Zenkōji. These faceless travelers will forever remain anonymous, identified in the records of legal discourse simply as complements to male figures: the wife of Komanosuke, the wife of Tadazaemon, the daughter of Unosuke. But at least we know their story. On their way home the three boarded a ferry on the sixteenth day of the fourth month. Overcrowded with pilgrims, the ferry capsized, and over ninety people perished of some one hundred on board. The wife of Komanosuke, the wife of Tadazaemon, and the daughter of Unosuke were among them.[6]

A consideration on the nature of sources is here warranted. In the vast majority of cases, women remained invisible travelers in the eyes of history because their journeys simply did not leave any paper trail behind. Unless a traveler composed a diary that survived the wear and tear of time, unless she (or he) filed a petition to obtain a passport, made a recorded donation at a temple, inscribed her (his) name onto a memorial stone, or, as in the case of the three unfortunate women from Shinano, became the subject of an official investigation, it was as though the journey never happened. We shall never recover the stories of these true invisibles—the vast, silent majority. At the same time we are left with the task of investigating and explaining the movements of that diversified and dynamic minority of women whose experiences we do know about, particularly because in many cases their journeys occurred despite and in opposition to the dominant ideology.

Paradoxically, the appearance along the highways of crowds of female travelers from all social backgrounds accompanied, and arguably nullified, the government's conscious effort to remove women from the scene. In the eyes not only of the authorities but also of many communities the notion of a woman detached from her designated social niche—a niche carved between motherhood and family obligations and, for women of commoner stock, child rearing and work in the farm or shop—was interpreted as a threat to stability. An often quoted official circular *(furegaki)* of the Keian era (1648–1652) proclaimed, "Women that drink a lot of tea, go on tours and take too many excursions shall be divorced."[7] Echoing a similar attitude against female mobility were the words of *The Greater Learning for Women* (*Onna daigaku,* 1672), a work inspired by the writings of Kaibara Ekiken (1630–1714): "Of tea and wine she must not drink overmuch, nor must she feed her eyes with theatrical performances, ditties, and ballads. To temples (whether Shinto or Buddhist) and other like places where there is a great concourse of people, she should go but sparingly till she has reached the age of forty." The manual also added that "without her husband's permission, [a wife] must go nowhere," for she should "be constantly in the midst of her household, and never go abroad but of necessity."[8] The desire to protect women from the dangers of the road only mildly tinged the multifaceted reasoning behind the attempt to keep them immobile and constrained in a world that progressively called for, and enticed to, mobility.

Traditional expectations and etiquette obliged women of samurai status to remain relatively confined, venturing out only on special occasions such as weddings, funerals, service obligations, or major festivals, and always accompanied by a retainer, an attendant, or a companion.[9] It was one otherwise unspecified "unavoidable business" that brought the daughter of Okuhara Sadayū, a retainer of the lord of Sekiyado (in Shimōsa), to Edo in the eighth month of 1834. When she came to the post station of Senjū, however, officer Nakane Sakuzō asserted that "women do not have businesses" other than transfers, adoptions, and marriage, thus insinuating that her journey to Edo was motivated by sight-seeing purposes, most unbefitting for a lady of her rank. He therefore refused to provide her with porters. The refusal of the bureaucrat irritated Sadayū, who filed a complaint with the Finance Magistrate. An investigation followed, during which both the assistant of the local intendant (*daikan*) and the local wholesaler (*ton'ya*) were summoned and questioned. Eventually, the Magistrate's office issued a statement reprimanding the officers, enjoining that similar incidents not happen again, and demanding that apologies be sent to Sadayū.[10] The clash between Sadayū's daughter and the authorities suggests that female travelers of samurai lineage were bound to meet with difficulties and suspicion even when they journeyed for perfectly legitimate reasons.

The overzealous guard at Senjū, however, was not entirely in the wrong. He was simply operating under the common notion that young women of good families would leave their house for the first time when they traveled to the residences of their prospective husbands. Although in most cases the distances were not so far as to characterize the experience as a full-fledged journey, in some instances young girls traveled to relatively distant regions. The daughter of a senior retainer from Aizu domain, Fujiki Ichi (1687–1719), better known by her Buddhist name, Jugen-in, was only fourteen when she departed from Kyoto to marry Kishi Masatomo, retainer of Kurume domain in Kyushu.[11] In the 1770s the daughter of the Minister of the Right (*udaijin*) Kazan'in Tsunemasa traveled to the far north after being betrothed to the lord of Matsumae domain, in Ezo.[12] These types of travel were acceptable, for they occurred in compliance with orders from above and served the ultimate political purpose of household preservation or alliance by marriage. As such, they did not pose a threat to the status- and gender-based power inequality of the Tokugawa order.

The tightly knit network of checkpoints also helped to implement the government policy on travel and gender.[13] In the early years of Tokugawa rule, Ieyasu and Hidetada had complemented the old, preexisting barriers with new ones created to increase controls over strategic routes. On 1601/7/19 Ieyasu ordered the creation of the Imagire (Arai) checkpoint, while in 1614 Hidetada issued an edict requesting the establishment of more barriers along various roads so that "people without passports would not transit."[14] As mentioned in the previous chapter, at this early stage the function of barriers was primarily to assert at a physical level the ever-present authority of the government and to enforce its status-based policy on movements, a policy that tended to privilege the beneficiaries of the shogun's red seal. Although gendered considerations did not become paramount until a few decades later, the authorities focused on female travelers from early on simply because a woman removed from her household raised a sort of natural suspicion. In 1616 an ordinance forwarded to sixteen ferry services in the Kantō area requested that "*women,* individuals with wounds, *and other suspicious elements* be held at the wharf and immediate notification be sent to Edo."[15] Women necessitated passports and detailed travel documents from the early years of Tokugawa rule. When the lord Matsudaira Muneyo received the order to transfer from Echigo to Mikawa in 1619, for example, he had to obtain a passport in order for fifteen female members of his family and entourage to travel.[16]

Under the third ruler Iemitsu (r. 1622–1651) the gendered character of checkpoints began to take on a more evident shape. In 1625 the office of the Road Magistrate forwarded its guidelines to all barriers specifying that palanquins carrying women were to be checked by female inspectors, or *aratameonna*. No class distinction was made, but it was implicit that only women of high rank would travel in such style. The same ordinance also reemphasized the status consciousness of the rulers, in that it granted special exemptions from inspection to domain lords, imperial princes *(monzeki)*, and court nobles *(kuge)*, unless they looked somewhat suspicious.[17]

Following the institutionalization of the alternate attendance system in 1635 the gender-related purpose of barriers increased, as by then the Tokugawa needed a certain category of women, the hostage wives of the domain lords, to remain sedentary. The movements of these strategically relevant pawns represented a potentially destabilizing factor, for the lords' wives and daughters constituted one of the Tokugawa's main insurance policies against seditious plots and rebellions. These women were valuable in the eyes of the Tokugawa, not as individuals, but by virtue of their association with a specific man and household. As extensions, appendages of their husbands or fathers, these female hostages of high stock served the purpose of keeping the male figures in check and of guaranteeing order.

By way of preserving such order, the necessity arose to further curtail women's mobility by revamping the role of checkpoints as ubiquitous enforcers of the government's policy on travel and gender. The first draft of the *Reminder on What Must Be Included in a Woman's Travel Permit (Onna tegata kakinoserubeki oboe)*, issued on 1661/8/1, established that women's passports were to contain specific details regarding their bearers' identity.[18] As the typologies listed therein suggest, passports became effective indicators of the women's strategic worth in the maintenance of Tokugawa stability. Such worth, predictably, was measured by a woman's association to a male figure. Adult women *(onna*, literally meaning "women" but in most cases best rendered as "wives") saw the foundation of their identity and the very meaning of their existence summarized, in legal discourse, as their being the dependents of men.[19] As such, they entered into an unequal relationship with established pillars of the social order—the lineage, the economic unit, and the family—separation from which was deemed most destabilizing. For the same reason, women who could not claim a direct relation to a man—nuns *(zenni, ama, bikuni),* widows (known as *kamikiri* because they cut their hair but were not ordained nuns), and unmarried girls *(koonna)*—were officially separated from the women who played crucial roles in the economy of household, lineage, and power balance. The same *Reminder on What Must Be Included in a Woman's Travel Permit* also identified as nonstrategic travelers those women who were pushed to the fringes of society and of the economy by reasons other than widowhood, tonsure, or unmarried status, which included the mentally unstable *(ranshin no onna)* and convicted criminals. This last category, the reminder specifies, applied also to men, as the marginality associated with crime overshadowed gender-based differentiations.[20] (The elimination of gendered criteria eventually generated confusion: an early nineteenth-century document on the transit of women at Nakada [Fusagawa] barrier had to specify that female criminals—lit. "women in bonds," *nawatsuki onna*—were indeed to be treated "in the same manner as male convicts"— *otoko towarebito dōyō.*)[21] Gendered lines of demarcation, in other words, were only visible and necessary within the confines of the political, social, and economic order; when an individual ceased to produce (children, goods, or stability), all distinctions became void.

Despite the care exerted in defining a separation between *onna* and *koonna,* age did not constitute an indicator of socioeconomic value and remained subordinate to marital status. The 1661 *Reminder on What Must Be Included in a Woman's Travel Permit* initially defined *koonna* as girls "between one and fifteen years of age" wearing a kimono with long, open sleeves *(furisode).* However, when the ordinance was reissued on 1686/7/12, age was no longer mentioned and girls were to be considered *koonna* for as long as they dressed in a *furisode,* that is, remained unmarried.[22] Specific visual markers— most notably shaved head, short hair, or sleeve length—served to establish the status of female travelers at checkpoints, as Inoue Tsūjo (1660–1738), the most famous victim of checkpoint bureaucracy, well captured in a poem:

Tabigoromo	Travel outfit:
Arai no seki o	as I crossed
koekanete	Arai barrier
Sode ni yoru nami	I resented my status
mi o uramitsutsu	because of my sleeves alone.[23]

The identification of female immobility with order emanated from a central political discourse and extended through the more peripheral branches of power, as the 1666 ordinance issued by Kyōgoku, Protector of Tango, seems to suggest. The document deals with the punishment for crimes committed by various categories of individuals, all classified according to their place in the economy. Examples include retainers, merchants, and farmers who failed to pay their tributes. Among other provisions the document stipulates that "retainers cannot inherit [their position], and their wives and children shall remain within the domain and cannot leave."[24] Although no further explanation is offered, the inclusion of such a clause in a list of rules aimed at protecting order and economic balance helps to sustain the argument that immobile women were seen as the foundation of stability at various levels. This association proved to be not only widespread but also enduring. In 1806 an edict was issued in Akita domain to regulate pilgrimage. The ordinance drew a clear line of distinction between townspeople and farmers, who had to meet different requirements and appeal to different authorities in order to receive permission to travel. All differences notwithstanding, the document made it clear that women need not apply, as both the section on urban commoners and the one on farmers end with the caveat, "Under no circumstances are women permitted to leave the province."[25]

Not unlike the maps of officialdom, which focused on the symbols of Tokugawa authority and ignored or minimized elements of the landscape less pertinent to the rulers' power strategy, the travel legislation of the Tokugawa also tended to target the movements of individuals connected to the government's quest for order and to all but disregard figures it considered marginal, if not flat-out irrelevant, as being of political, social, or economic significance. When it came to gender and movement, the edicts addressed to checkpoints show a great deal of concern with the difference between unmarried girls and wives, but rarely, if ever, do they draw a line between adult males (*otona*, or simply *otoko*) and boys (alternatively called *wakashu, yakusha no kodomo,* or *shōjin*), although they too constituted a segment of the traveling population. Gregory M. Pflugfelder indicates they were relatively mobile, arguing that "their peregrinations took them all up and down the archipelago."[26] However, the ordinances regulating travel thoroughly ignored the legal position of young boys and failed to devote any particular attention to the way in which their special identity—arguably defined by strong feminine elements—intersected with the government's gendered policies on travel. When confronted with their presence, legal discourse tended to conveniently treat boys the same as full-fledged adult males. The edicts of officialdom glossed over ambiguous youths caught between genders as much as they did over the "midway villages" suspended between one official post station and the next. In both cases, only when threats to the public order or to the economy arose did the authorities take action.

Inevitably, the lack of detailed legislation on the subject clashed with the reality of a system where mobility was regulated on the basis of gender. Dressed in feminine, often flowery robes, young boys could easily be mistaken for girls at a first glance, although the sword they carried and the traditional haircut they sported suggested otherwise. Whenever these borderline figures ventured into the rigid spaces of legal discourse, most notably the compounds of barriers, misunderstandings were bound to result. A famous and frequently reproduced nineteenth-century woodblock print of Arai checkpoint perfectly illuminates the confusion that must have troubled many a barrier guard. The print depicts a female inspector, magnifying lens in hand, squatting before a young boy. The boy's robe is open at the front, clearly indicating that she is about to examine his genitals.[27] Shock value and parody aside, it is especially significant that, in the illustration, a woman rather than a male sentinel has been charged with inspecting the boy. Female inspectors were traditionally employed at barriers to deal with female travelers, whom they searched thoroughly. Evidently the boy's partly feminine and partly masculine appearance had created a nebulous area in the otherwise well-spelled-out inspection procedures.

Further evidence of confusion about the treatment of young boys at checkpoints is an inquiry sent out by the superintendent *(rusui)* on 1821/11/10. The query regarded a youngster by the name of Hori Kichisaburō. Aged fourteen, he still wore his forelocks, traditional markers that identified him as a *wakashu,* yet, to the superintendent's bewilderment, his hair was also partially arranged in the style of adult males and he carried a spear.[28] Foreseeing trouble, the superintendent's office petitioned a higher authority asking for clarification on "whether it is fine to treat individuals with and without forelocks in the same manner once they transit through the barriers at Hakone and Imagire." Government authorities investigated the case and concluded that, as a general rule, no specific distinction had to be made between adult and young males ("both individuals with and without forelocks shall be treated in the same manner").[29] Although legislation did not deem it necessary to draw a line between young and adult males, unwritten rules and the common perception that boys were other than men had nonetheless prompted the superintendent to demand elucidation.

If the laws of the government made no room for young boys, popular lore, on the other hand, made of the dichotomy between them and adult men one of its favorite themes. In the works of novelist Ihara Saikaku (1642–1693), as well as in countless erotic prints of the period, young boys emerge as thoroughly feminized figures and as the objects of adult male desire. Their classy and feminine refinement is a corollary to their youth. Although no specific age limits were set in the definition of boyhood (nor for entrance into adulthood), the time inevitably came when young males, "no matter how cute, [would] end up becoming uncouth men *(ki otoko),*" as Saikaku put it.[30]

While official and popular discourses took different stances on the roles and identities of young boys, in other cases their respective takes on gender and mobility seemed to converge. Communities often sided with officialdom in identifying mobile women as a menace to order. With a few exceptions, a woman who chose to remove herself from the traditional roles to which society had assigned her automatically threatened the delicate stability of the household, the village, or the family business. This explains, for example, the strenuous resistance to the practice of unauthorized pilgrimage *(nukemairi)* mounted not only by the authorities, as one would expect, but also, and more surprisingly, by families and peers of the fugitives. The case of Masa provides a fitting example. In 1855 Masa had left for Ise after entrusting her chores to her brothers-in-law. Soon, rumors that she had run off on an unauthorized pilgrimage started circulating, upsetting her "merciless landlord." Worried about his anger, Masa finally decided to return home. "Since she is a woman, maybe the anxiety over her absence is not without reason," commented her nephew, confirming how sometimes social expectations at the immediate family or community level opposed the idea of female mobility more effectively than legal codes emanating from above.[31]

Women of lower social stature, though less bound by strategic considerations than their aristocratic counterparts, were still expected to conform to family obligations. Economic concerns bound them to the household as tightly as norms of etiquette confined ladies of rank. The wives of merchants often doubled as business partners, while the wives of tenant farmers were essential in completing agricultural tasks and, particularly after the second half of the eighteenth century, in sustaining cottage industries. Tradition and expectations, however, evolved with time and eventually made room for some degree of freedom. In the course of the nineteenth century the women of the wealthier rural elites enjoyed a good degree of autonomy and mobility and were in fact encouraged to travel, for, as Anne Walthall observes, "pilgrimages functioned as a finishing school for young women unable to avail themselves of service in the mansion of the daimyō."[32] The Echigo rural entrepreneur Suzuki Bokushi (1770–1842), for example, did not disapprove of his sister's unauthorized journey to Ise, for not only did it serve as an educational experience, but it also helped maintain strong ties with family members residing in other villages or provinces.[33]

Religious journeys in general presented would-be travelers with a great opportunity to challenge the government's rules on mobility. The authorities were cautious not to place too many limitations on what was de facto "a sacred act."³⁴ Consequently, they were willing to allow for exceptions to their policies on travel, gender, and status when the gods were invoked. Edicts of 1601 and 1602, for instance, instructed checkpoints to allow pilgrims to Mount Minobu, men and women, to transit without inspection for three days in the tenth month.³⁵ The government did, to a certain degree, extend its gendered policies on movement to the spaces of the sacred, but the religious establishment quickly and effectively reclaimed much control by contrasting the logic of order with the logic of compassion.

Let There Be Order: Gender and Sacred Spaces in the Eyes of the Authorities

Historically independent and fiercely assertive, religious institutions had suffered a severe blow delivered by the hand of General Oda Nobunaga (1534–1582) in the late sixteenth century. In 1571, determined to crush militant monks who hindered his ambitious plan of territorial reunification, Nobunaga had attacked the complex atop Mount Hiei in Kyoto, slaughtering its monks and leveling its buildings. His reasoning, as contemporary sources indicate, was that the monastery threatened "the maintenance of law and *order* in the country."³⁶

The preservation of order remained the fundamental goal of Tokugawa policies. In the early seventeenth century the memory of the problems caused by gangs of armed monks was still fresh, motivating the government to keep an eye on signs of trouble issuing from religious compounds. There, neither fighting nor disorderly conduct would be tolerated, "because temples are places for praying for the peace of the nation."³⁷ Through laws rather than direct military action the Tokugawa worked to stifle whatever authority and autonomy the sphere of the sacred had preserved and tried to reclaim. Decades before the post of Magistrate of Temples and Shrines *(jisha bugyō)* began to be assigned on a regular basis (1635) the Tokugawa government started issuing edicts on the management and regulation of religious spaces.³⁸ Some ordinances, such as *Laws for Mount Kōya (Kōyasan hatto)* of 1601, *Laws for Ise Shrine (Ise jingū hatto)* of 1603, or *Laws for Asakusa Temple (Sensōji hatto)* of 1613, were directed at specific institutions, while others targeted general religious currents (*Laws for the Tendai School of the Kantō [Region],* or *Kantō tendaishū hatto,* 1613; *Various Laws for the Shingon School,* or *Shingonshū shohatto,* 1615; *Laws for Mountain Asceticism,* or *Shugen hatto,* 1613). The edicts to suppress Christianity also fall under this category.³⁹ The early legislative efforts of the Tokugawa aimed not only at the preservation of peace but also at the demarcation of clear borders and areas of competence.

Even when dealing with the sacred the Tokugawa could not afford to ignore the question of gender. In formulating their policies regulating order in religious spaces they applied the equation between female immobility and the upholding of the status quo. Political discourse was concerned with keeping the peace far more than it was with safeguarding the vows of celibacy taken by the clergy. Moral concerns about impious behavior on the part of the monks did exist, but always within the context of the preservation of order, as temptation and lust were likely to generate disorderliness. Female pilgrims were not discouraged from visiting sacred sites altogether, but overnight stays at temples and shrines were strictly regulated. The *Laws for Mount Tōei (Tōeisan hatto)*, issued by the government in 1654, banned women from spending the night in the Ueno premises of the "Mount Hiei of the East."[40] A similar notification appeared in the 1655 *Stipulations for Mount Nikkō (Nikkōsan jōmoku)*. In neither case, however, did the authorities attempt to outlaw women's pilgrimages to the sites. The 1655 ordinance, for instance, specified that "Women *(fujin)* and nuns may not access the monks' quarters. It goes without saying that they may not be given shelter. Pilgrimage routes going through monks' quarters are an exception."[41]

As potential sources of disorder women were grouped in the same category as masterless samurai *(rōnin)*, ne'er-do-wells, and other such troublemakers whom temples ought to keep at bay. An edict of 1660 sent to Hōraiji (Mikawa Province) stipulated that masterless samurai, suspicious individuals, and women were not to be given asylum. Female pilgrims *(sankei no nyonin)*, again, represented an exception.[42] By virtue of the same logic, certain edicts even listed women alongside fish and fowl (i.e., forbidden foods) as things best kept off religious compounds as they constituted too great a cause of temptation for the monks.[43]

Various attempts on the part of the authorities to regulate the presence of women in religious compounds (often without distinction between pilgrims and other visitors) followed in the course of the eighteenth and nineteenth centuries, an evident signal that such spaces remained vastly contested and their grounds open to interpretation, as the following 1718 reminder exemplifies:

> Reminder
> Item: we hear that there are temples and monks' residences that give shelter to nuns and women. We firmly order to reject [such practice]. We issued [similar] ordinances in the past, but these days they are taken arbitrarily and we have

heard that, in disregard of such orders, temples host nuns and women. This is outrageous. In increased compliance with past regulations *all women (nyonin issai)*, even relatives, should not be given shelter. Of course, secondary temples and branch temples shall be investigated by the headquarter temple.[44]

Aware that temples had traditionally provided the ideal venue for the long-established practice of same-sex liaisons between monks and acolytes—another source of promiscuous hence destabilizing behavior—the Tokugawa had in fact attempted to put a cap on the interaction between members of religious congregations and outsiders of both sexes earlier on, with this ordinance of 1665/7/11:

Item: it goes without saying that those who are not family members as well as acquaintances and women cannot be given shelter in the temple halls or in the priests' quarters. However, already married individuals shall be considered separately.[45]

The edicts promulgated in the seventeenth century had yielded little to no results in this department, therefore in the eighteenth century the Tokugawa attempted many times over to reinstate the point. Issued and reissued at various times, *One Hundred Provisions (Osadamegaki hyakkajō)* included a chapter on the punishment of clergy who engaged in romantic liaisons with women or young acolytes. According to the provision, head monks involved in illicit affairs would face exile, while acolytes would be put in stocks and punished according to the regulations of the temple under which they served.[46] The incessant reissuing of such edicts is in itself a testament to their ineffectiveness. Perhaps acknowledging the futility of its proclamations, the government tried to appropriate the language of religion and, in 1829, condemned promiscuous relations between monks and women as "a breach of the [Buddhist] commandments."[47]

The quest for order was only one of the many motivations behind the Tokugawa's frequent intrusions into the spaces of religion. The political control of religious space served also to reinforce certain basic notions of gender discrimination that sustained the unequal system envisioned by the legislators. When on 1684/3/1 the Tokugawa established a religious calendar for the purification rituals that followed childbirth or death, they crafted a clear hierarchy based on gender. Daughters, even the eldest siblings, ranked lower than their younger brothers. Women were assigned mourning and purification cycles that were twice as long as men's, as a wife was to mourn her husband's passing for thirty days, while half the time, fourteen days, sufficed for a widower. After the birth of a child, a mother was to refrain from entering sacred spaces for thirty-five days; a father, only for little more than half the time, twenty-one days.⁴⁸ The government's hierarchy of pollution mirrored and reinforced its gendered construction of an orderly society and household, where a woman was worth roughly half a man.

Compassionate Pragmatism: Gender and Sacred Spaces in the Eyes of Religious Institutions

The attempts of the Tokugawa to regulate the realm of the sacred were often ineffective because religious institutions could present their spaces as otherworldly and above the law. By raising the banners of sacredness and compassion, temples and shrines could alter or nullify the rules of the Tokugawa, and could do so with a good degree of immunity. So pervasive and respected was the authority of the sacred that even the representatives of officialdom found themselves at a loss when asked to choose between the laws of the rulers and the exceptions of the gods. Takeuchi Makoto has shown how the authorities tolerated scuffles, acts of collective violence, and even pillaging as long as they occurred during religious festivals. Normally the government did not allow similar acts to occur under its watch, but the time apart of the sacred created a convenient loophole that the population eagerly exploited.⁴⁹ The ambiguity of the sacred also interfered with the management of movement. In 1768 the officers of Kiga barrier sent an inquiry asking the senior council *(rōjū)* whether extraordinary arrangements were to be made for women directed to Ise, to the Western Provinces pilgrimage circuit, or on a countrywide tour of the one hundred stages of Kannon.⁵⁰ Their indecision speaks clearly about their inability to trace a clear-cut boundary in a space made open to interpretation by the overlapping of discordant logics.

Much like the government, religious institutions also drafted laws to safeguard their own stability. On the surface many seemed to share with the legislators the fear that the physical presence of women within their precincts, particularly after dusk, would generate trouble. Acting possibly out of fear of intervention by the authorities, religious administrators saw in the prevention of disorderly occurrences a key to self-preservation. Pragmatism and prudence demanded that, every now and then, the quest for autonomy take a back seat to compliance with certain standards expected by the government. Ishiyama Temple, for instance, issued its own set of regulations on 1609/2/18 and forwarded them to its subsidiary branches. The list included bans on distractions of various kinds—from food to women and recreational games—all of which were somehow synonymous with temptation and, consequently, with disorder:

> Item: Fish, meat, and the five pungent plants shall not be brought inside the Sakura Gate.
>
> Item: Pilgrims, men and women alike, shall not access the temple grounds without reason.
>
> Item: After dusk, the pilgrimages of women *(nyonin no sankei)* are not permitted.
>
> Item: *Kemari* and other such recreational games are forbidden within temple grounds.[51]

On the second month of 1658 Kongōji on Mount Amano, in Kawachi Province, also issued a list of general rules regarding the administration of, and proper conduct in, its compounds. Among them, one established that "Women, old and young alike, are not allowed to approach the monks' quarters on the mountain. Women paying a religious visit, after entering the Hall and bowing to the Buddha, must on the same day go outside the Great Gate and leave the mountain. It is not appropriate for them to stay after dusk."[52]

The compliance of religious institutions with the plan for order drafted by the Tokugawa, however, stopped here. Beyond their own thresholds, shrines, temples, and sacred mountains managed space and gender autonomously. While both political and religious discourses, by and large, originated from the premise that the female body was a source of potential destabilization, their lines of reasoning differed dramatically. Historically, religious discourse had called upon notions of pollution and karmic inferiority, rather than on the potential for social turmoil or rowdy behavior, to erect gendered barriers around its spaces and to create zones that excluded women altogether *(nyonin kinsei)*. Suzuki Masataka traces the origins of such women-free zones to four distinct trends: the Shinto aversion to blood defilement, the Buddhist association of women with bad karma, a pervasive contempt for women in Buddhist scriptures, and local folk traditions.[53]

Shinto and Buddhist institutions provided plenty of theological justifications for the exclusion of women from their premises. Both shared revulsion for the association between the female body and blood contamination.[54] Though it ultimately offered the hope of salvation, the *Blood Bowl Sutra (Ketsubonkyō)* of Buddhist tradition described rather graphically the infernal punishments awaiting the women who "polluted the deity of the earth" with the blood they lost at childbirth and the women who washed their blood-stained garments in rivers whose water was "used to make tea to serve the holy men."[55] The general notion of an innate inferiority in women had also permeated Buddhist tradition for centuries. Such inferiority did not stem from their subordinate role to men in the economy of the household and society, as political reasoning had it, but was rather the result of an intrinsic karmic inadequacy that made them unfit to access many sacred areas.

Like many other sacred mountains, Mount Kōya in the Kii peninsula defined specific points along its slopes beyond which women were not supposed to tread.[56] As a 1672 guide specified: "Since its origins Mount Kōya has been off-limits to women. Since they are bound by the thick clouds of the Five Hindrances and cannot achieve Buddhist knowledge because of the menstrual cycle, they cannot cast their shadow on this mountain. But if by any chance they do step in, they are not allowed to cross over to its distant summit, nor to visit its various locations or set foot inside the precincts."[57] The same guide also added: "On the slopes of this mountain numerous areas are reserved for the practitioners. Hence it goes without saying that women and other creatures such as cows, cats, monkeys, wild boars, white herons and chickens are warned to keep off. [. . .] This mountain is not a place for women."[58]

Tales of the Shinto tradition were equally keen on emphasizing the necessity to remove polluted female bodies from sacred spaces. *Records of the Miracles of Ise Shrine, A Sequel (Ise daijingū zoku shin'iki)*, a collection of anecdotes produced by the Ise clergy in conjunction with the 1705 mass pilgrimage to the shrine, included the story of a female pilgrim who, upon reaching Yamada, mysteriously fainted. All attempts to revive her failed. The cause of her fainting became clear when it was discovered that she was menstruating. She had entered a holy space ignoring the taboo on pollution, "thus offending the gods" *(kami no toga nari)*. Carried back across the Miya River at a safe distance from the sacred area of the shrine, the woman quickly regained consciousness.[59] The gods were no longer offended.

In the course of the Edo period a great many women ran up against the constantly refurbished barriers of religious landscape. In 1777 Arakida Reijo came to Mount Shosha, near Himeji, but had to give up on the idea of visiting the numinous mountain: "We wanted to visit Shosha Temple, but we heard the mountain was off-limits to women, so we went to Hiromine instead," she writes.[60] Only seven years before her another woman, the samurai Shinkō-in Myōjitsu, had also made her way to the same complex, commenting that the ban on women "caused trouble" and labeling it "miserable."⁶¹ In 1792 Yamanashi Shigako (1738–1814) stopped short of Mount Akiba's main gate:

> Since women are not allowed to proceed any further I [stopped and] worshipped there. I was so grateful I even shed some tears. An old man with a fan in his hand told me about the so-called Wheel of Five Hindrances *(goshō guruma)*. He explained that women must by all means turn it, [...] [if they do so] they will not suffer. [...] I turned the wheel three times and descended from the mountain.⁶²

Various other sites enforced policies of gendered exclusion. In 1862 Matsuo Taseko (1811–1894) was asked to leave the precincts of Arashiyama in Kyoto, while only three years before Kurosawa Tokiko (1806–1890) had been prevented from accessing the inner shrine on Mount Togakushi.⁶³ In 1855 the mother of scholar Kiyokawa Hachirō could not enter Mii Temple in Kyoto, was kept off Mount Shosha, and could not walk past the second hall at the Mount Hiei complex. Recalling the troubled history of the temple, her son ironically commented, "with all the selfish misdeeds [the monks of Mount Hiei] have perpetrated in the past, it is ridiculous *(warau beki nari)* that now they forbid access to women."⁶⁴

The creation, within the space of the sacred, of restricted areas where rules based on theology prevailed helped to reinforce the notion that temple and shrine compounds existed apart from, and above, the laws of officialdom. This, along with a general will to preserve tradition, may explain the adherence of certain establishments to the practice of excluding women in a day and age when female travelers had become increasingly ubiquitous.⁶⁵ By fencing off areas for adepts only, temples and shrines asserted themselves against the interference and policing of the authorities; Nam-lin Hur, for example, argues that the creation of no-kill zones served as an expedient for religious institutions to claim property over space and to challenge direct interventions by the government.⁶⁶ Torii and gates not only marked the symbolic access to a time and space of the sacred, they also served as veritable territorial borders. The itinerant nun Kikusha-ni clearly perceived their function as thresholds into areas beyond the reach of officialdom. In 1812 she visited Manpukuji in Uji. With its Ming-style architecture, the temple visually proclaimed its distinctiveness.⁶⁷ Enraptured by the sense of otherworldliness generated by both architectural style and religious aura, Kikusha-ni condensed in a haiku the complexity of a landscape where territorial claims were juxtaposed, where the immobility of a mountain's peak contrasted with the hubbub of human activities at its foot, and where gates fenced off the spaces apart of the sacred:

> *Sanmon o*   Step outside the mountain gate
> *dereba Nihon zo.*   and you are back in Japan.
> *Chatsumi uta.*   The songs of tea pickers.[68]

Religious establishments succeeded in delineating their own areas of competence because they blurred the rules of order with the halo of compassion, a line of reasoning against which political authorities had little recourse. When mercy was invoked, temples and shrines became able to act independently from, at times in fact directly against, the regulations of the government. The Tokugawa, for instance, repeatedly demanded that female entertainers and prostitutes stay out of religious establishments to prevent disorderly conduct.[69] Public peace, they believed, was best kept by confining prostitutes to the government-approved pleasure quarters. However, the laws of compassion made it possible for religious complexes to ignore the government's requests. Nam-lin Hur cites one such instance in 1812, when Asakusa Sensōji allowed the Yoshiwara prostitutes displaced by a fire to set up shop temporarily in its precincts. At least seven other times before then room had been made to accommodate Yoshiwara courtesans within the temple grounds.[70] By virtue of the same logic, other such undesirables of official discourse—masterless samurai, vagrants, the destitute—also found refuge in the spaces of the sacred. Early Edo fiction, for example, mentions groups of outcastes *(hinin)* camping out under the eaves of Tōkaiji in Shinagawa.[71] In the late nineteenth century, the rascal samurai Katsu Kokichi (1802–1850) also turned to religious institutions for help in times of trouble. In Ise he received accommodation, food, a hot bath, amulets, and emergency money; when he lay ill in a pine grove in Yokkaichi it was a generous priest who brought him straw pallets and daily meals. Once Kokichi had recovered and was able to depart, the priest offered him a sedge hat, straw sandals, and one hundred copper coins for the road.[72]

Having created relatively autonomous spaces, temples and shrines could manage them as it best fit their interests. The ability to self-regulate access to their precincts allowed religious institutions a degree of pragmatism and flexibility when it came to gender-related issues. Never underestimating the economic benefits of pilgrimage, most shrines and temples then wisely opted to allow visitors of both sexes into their precincts. Donations, after all, knew no gender. The economic benefits of travel functioned as powerful incentives against gendered theories of discrimination, a trend that became ever more evident as the money-based culture of the floating world came of age in the eighteenth and nineteenth centuries. A document of 1771 from Shōfukuji in Koyama village (in modern-day Shizuoka Prefecture) records a hefty offering of five golden *ryō* and 842 silver coins donated to the temple by a confraternity of women *(nyonin kō)*.⁷³

Aside from being generous contributors, female pilgrims turned out to be exceptional customers as well. In 1862 Konno Oito, a merchant's wife, spent over one *kan* and six hundred *mon* in one single day at Mount Haguro. The entrance fee to the mountain came up to two hundred and two *mon* (for her and her travel companion, also a woman), on top of which she added fifty *mon* for a guide, one hundred *mon* for a tour of every hall, six *mon* for candles, fifty for souvenirs, and one *kan* seventy *mon* for the performance of sacred rituals. Straw sandals, fees to convert paper certificates into cash, and refreshments added to the cost.⁷⁴ Although an exact comparison with the spending habits of men is difficult, one may cite the example of Emontarō, a man from Hiyomo village (in modern-day Gifu Prefecture) who traveled to Ise in the same year as Oito and who, like her, kept a detailed record of his expenses. Emontarō spent money chiefly on tolls, accommodation, and sake. On 1862/11/23 he visited Ise Shrine and other sites in the vicinity, but at the end of the day he had only spent five hundred *mon* as an offering to the local clergy—less than one-third of Oito's overall expenditure during the Haguro visit. He does not record buying any souvenir, ritual implement, or "extra" service.⁷⁵

Consequently, religious institutions hardly ever enforced theological arguments to ban female visitors from their premises altogether. Even when adherence to tradition demanded the maintenance of a women-free zone, shrines and temples made partial access possible by erecting appropriate facilities known as Women's Halls *(nyonindō)*. Suzuki Masataka refers to these spaces, usually located within the compounds, as decentered projections of the main sites of cult.⁷⁶ In other cases, religious institutions created special times apart when gendered restrictions were momentarily lifted. Mii Temple in Kyoto did not normally allow women into the inner hall, but an exception was made once a year, on the sixteenth day of the seventh month, as a late Edo traveler recounts.⁷⁷ Some temples with a reputation for inflexibility even turned a blind eye to, and quietly tolerated, intrusions of women into their no-access zones, if we are to believe Konno Oito. In the course of her 1862 journey she entered the precincts of Mount Kōya. Instead of stopping at the Women's Hall, she hired a guide and climbed all the way to the summit. Her purchase of an amulet against menstrual defilement while on the premises indicates that she was not the only woman silently allowed to trespass into the sacred space, and that the complex, in the nineteenth century, housed businesses that catered specifically to female visitors.⁷⁸ During her visit Oito even stayed at a facility run by the local monks. Between access fees, compensation for the guide, generous offerings, accommodation, and the purchase of various ritual implements, she ended up leaving a significant amount of money on the mountain.[79] All taboos associated with the female body notwithstanding, by the nineteenth century "the power of money had blown away any objection pertaining to gender" even on the slopes of Mount Kōya.[80]

Examples of accommodation toward and even active search for female visitors on the part of religious institutions in fact abound. In 1770, fulfilling a lifelong dream of paying homage to the graves of her ancestors, the merchant's wife Suzuki Mihoko came to Kōtokuji in Kawagoe to a warm reception on the part of the local clergy. In her journal Mihoko describes her entrance into the temple grounds: "I hear that once one passes through the mountain gate, the inner gate is usually closed; however, today they are expecting me and have kindly arranged to leave it open." The monks came out to welcome her and entertained her "a great deal." A young acolyte gave her a tour of the complex. "As we passed by the Scriptures Hall the monks were happy to entertain us and I intently listened with nostalgia to stories of the days of old."[81] Even Mount Fuji, whose summit remained officially off-limits to women through 1860, managed to send mixed signals when it came to female patrons.[82] The first access point to the peak, the Murayama gate (originally founded in the twelfth century), had strong *shugendō* overtones that made it difficult for women to gain entry into the area. According to Miyata Noboru, however, the other gates were more porous and it is conceivable that women did enter the complex through them from very early on. Though banned from the peak, women enjoyed free access to the caves on the slopes of the mountain, for the caves were traditionally identified with wombs and associated with the cult of safe delivery.[83] Since at least the late eighteenth century women had been permitted to climb all the way up to the third of Fuji's ten stations or stages (*gōme*), at 1,720 meters above sea level. Moreover, as Miyazaki Fumiko has demonstrated, *nyonin kinsei* restrictions were periodically lifted every sixty years, in the Year of the Monkey Elder Metal (or *kōshin* years).[84] Suzuki Shōzō, who visited the mountain in 1828 (not a *kōshin* year), joining a coed crowd of 318 devotees, provides us with evidence of Mount Fuji's partial openness to women. At the residence of their spiritual leader, where all pilgrims gathered before the ascent, Shōzō estimated that about seventy of the three hundred people present were females.[85]

Particularly in the second half of the Edo period, the complex vigorously sought the financial support of men and women alike. After the mid-eighteenth century the clergy of Yoshida (one of Fuji's gates) explicitly endorsed female pilgrimage, even petitioning the Magistrate of Temples and

Shrines to loosen the requirements for women's passports.⁸⁶ When, in 1808, Sengen Shrine found itself in dire need of cash to rebuild its roof, it did not hesitate to call on all followers for donations. The plea, sent by the head of the shrine complex to Osano, Protector of Echigo, exalted the manifold virtues of Fuji's female deity, Konohana Sakuya Hime. She was simultaneously identified as the protector of silkworms, pregnancy, domestic harmony, and agriculture, which made her appealing to both sexes:

> [The shrine's] deity is Konohana no Sakuya Hime no Mikoto, wife of the grandson [of Amaterasu] Amatsuhiko Hikoho no Ninigi no Mikoto. [. . .] Everyone knows this is a sacred mountain. Moreover, the spirit of Sengen [Shrine] became a female body and bestowed upon us the arts of weaving, spinning, unreeling cocoons, cutting, and sewing. She is also known as the ancestral spirit of sake brewing, who produces sweet sake with the crops from the fields. She keeps thieves and fires away. In addition, this is the spirit who places the utmost importance on the safety of delivery in order to bestow wise children who will continue the family line. For this reason the prayer to the deity is as follows:
>> Of the people in the country, those who have no heir pray to You daily so that You may bestow a successor. Should an heir be born, may You ease the pain. Protect the seed in my womb, let it be as peaceful as Your spirit.
>
> [. . .] Pray before the deity for peace and safety in the realm, for the regularity of winds and rains, for the fertility of the crops, or if you wish for divine intervention when you desire a successor to continue your family line.⁸⁷

While the shrine never went so far as to officially grant women access to the peak in return for donations, its explicit inclusion of women among the beneficiaries of the deity's compassion reveals how many sacred spaces pragmatically negotiated between their own tradition (often inclusive of *nyonin kinsei* elements) and their pressing financial needs.

The art of mediating between traditional principles and economic reality also informed the Shikoku circuit. In the late seventeenth century, a guide penned by a monk offered a substantial ray of hope to women interested in touring the lengthy eighty-eight-site circuit though still conscious of the association between female body and defilement. *Road Map for the Shikoku Circuit (Shikoku henro michishirube)* records a legend according to which a woman completed the tour while remaining unpolluted throughout the entire process ("her monthly hindrance did not manifest itself").⁸⁸ Since the twelve-hundred-kilometer circuit could conceivably be completed in one month, the occurrence did not necessarily stem from a supernatural force. Its characterization as a numinous event, however, effectively advertised the wondrous powers of the sacred landscape on the one hand, and its acceptance of women on the other.

While in reality certain temples along the route remained off-limits to women,[89] many more in the course of the Edo period lured female parishioners with target-specific promises: bestowal of children, protection during pregnancy, and the promise of a safe and painless delivery.[90] Kōenji (stage no. 61), for example, developed specifically as a center for maternity cults. According to a legend, the saint Kōbō Daishi, to whom the entire Shikoku route is dedicated, was in the Kōenji area when he noticed a woman in labor. By promptly easing her pains, he permanently consecrated the site to the cult of easy childbirth. Outside the circuit proper, between stage numbers 71 and 72, at Iōzan in Sanuki, women would pray for Yakushi to bestow them with milk. Other temples in the area attracted women by offering treatments to ward off bad luck after childbirth.[91] The strategy of harmonizing ideals of mercy with pragmatic financial needs—what we may call compassionate pragmatism—ultimately paid off, as more and more women recognized in the Shikoku circuit a relatively friendly space. On average, during the Edo period one in every four travelers along the eighty-eight-stage route was a woman.[92]

IN ITS ATTEMPT to simultaneously regulate mobility, status, and gender, Edo officialdom erected barriers that, in the name of autonomy or of economic necessity, religious discourse helped to topple, thus reinforcing the idea that certain spaces existed across multiple frames of interpretation and that the closed doors of one discourse were the open gates of another. In the malleable spaces that formed at the convergence of competing logics, travelers, including women, saw an opportunity to select the interpretation that fit them best. They learned to define their experience through the most convenient paradigm, often situating themselves in the borderlands where discourses intersected. When religious and political forces faced off, blurring each other's boundaries, travelers became empowered to stray. In Shikoku many stepped out of the officially designated sequence of the circuit, charting itineraries that reflected their individual interests.[93] As Ian Reader has compellingly demonstrated, the landscape of the Shikoku pilgrimage was (and still is) "a moving text that is constantly being rewritten."[94] The same, in fact, held true for all Edo period travelscapes.

Contested and flexible spaces opened the doors to possibilities otherwise denied. Numerous women took to the road in the Edo period exploiting the polysemy of the landscape. The many disjunctions between theory and practice allowed them to negotiate their position, while the competition between opposing logics empowered them to justify their mobility by presenting parameters such as compassion and faith that the authorities were hard put to contest. As they turned their eyes to the open road, women also discovered that the malleable spaces of travel allowed for more creative avenues in their quest for freedom. They discovered the art of re-creating identities.

PART II

Re-creating Identities

CHAPTER 3

Women on the Road
Identities in Motion

> ...the journeys of women are secret, necessitated, or accomplished through the agency of men.
> —Eric J. Leed, *The Mind of the Traveler*

> Women's lives are much too limited, or else too secret.
> —Marguerite Yourcenar

> Being a woman entails so many obstacles.
> —Inoue Tsūjo, 1681

THE TENSION between a legislation that wanted women immobile and common practices that increasingly suggested otherwise created gray areas within which women of all social levels became able to negotiate the arguments of official discourse that prevented them from taking to the road. Along the roads and across the travelscapes of Edo Japan travelers attained a momentary respite from the ordinary;[1] women in particular experienced a brief yet forceful sense of autonomy, and even liberation, as they temporarily "manipulated the dominant tradition to free themselves."[2]

This section concerns itself with the two-tiered process that, out of "re-created spaces," generated the dream of re-creating identities. The malleable spaces of travel sustained many women's attempts to redefine their personas. Along the road women could subtly call into question some of the parameters by which their lives and roles were delineated and could rearrange them along different trajectories in the pages of their memoirs (the subject of Chapter 4). Before they could accomplish this, however, they needed to find a way to detach themselves from the spaces they had been permanently assigned. This was no easy task for, as Chapters 1 and 2 have shown, both legal codes and social expectations tended either to confine women or to regulate their movements meticulously. Since the seventeenth century the government had ordered women in motion to make themselves immediately identifiable: "People of high and low [rank] traveling on a palanquin must open the palanquin door. Pursuant to the regulations of barrier officials, palanquins transporting women shall transit after being inspected by a woman," wrote the [Road] Magistrate to the officials of Arai checkpoint in 1666.³ Even as late as the nineteenth century, moralistic texts exhorted women to deport themselves along the road with the same propriety and restraint they were expected to display at home, as an 1819 work exemplifies: "It is in the way one walks that we see a person's quality. [...] Along the way, do not glance to the side and do not stare at other people. Nothing is worse than whispered laughs with other women. It is advisable to walk in a modest fashion."⁴

To these enduring attempts to micromanage their movements many a female traveler responded with subterfuge. The ways in which women chose to manipulate tradition to achieve liberation varied according to status. The wives of domain lords and powerful retainers were generally more limited in their ability to disentangle themselves from duties and expectations, but often took advantage of the changes brought about by widowhood to become nuns and acquire freedom. Other women chose a different avenue to reinvent themselves and became entertainers. Female commoners were normally less constrained, but those who were forced to travel surreptitiously usually found in the alteration of their appearance, in the choice of alternate routes, or in the anonymity of large crowds a more convenient means to travel and, in some cases, even to be ostentatious.⁵ By exploiting the possibilities embedded in bodies, movements, and narratives, women became able to compensate some of the limitations to which they were subject at home. At the same time, certain trends and dynamics were not new and can be traced to as far back in time as the Heian period (794–1185). The identification of personal narratives, the body, and the road as sites where the rules of normalcy could be bent, where power relations could be called into question and transformations effected, had profound historical roots that are worth retracing, if briefly.

Bodies, Movements, and Narratives: Women's Quest for Agency in Ancient and Medieval Japan

In the Heian period the political and cultural universe revolved around the imperial court of Kyoto. Though excluded from the affairs of state, the women of the court played a key role in the contemporary literary circles. They crafted their own writing style, fittingly known as "women's hand" *(onnade),* with which they produced many a classic of Japanese literature.

Silently yet efficiently, they pulled a great many strings in the elegant microcosm of the palace. During this age, defined predominantly by refinement and femininity, the female members of the court enjoyed numerous opportunities to assert their agency. They did so not only through outstanding literary feats but also by using their tastefully clad, conspicuously concealed bodies as sites of empowerment. As Ivan Morris observed, aristocratic women of the Heian period lived slow-paced lives in a state of semi-obscurity and almost complete concealment.[6] Such self-imposed cloistering did not constitute a limitation, but rather a means by which the ladies of the court could surround themselves with an aura of mystique. Confinement, inaccessibility, and invisibility generated awe and respect, as the words of Tō no Chūjō in the eleventh-century novel *The Tale of Genji* illuminate: "When a girl is highborn, everyone pampers her and a lot about her remains hidden, so that she naturally seems a paragon."[7] Empowerment came not from straightforward rejection of the status quo but from the clever exploitation of its lights and shadows.

If they chose to do so, female courtiers could be remarkably mobile. Though on paper they tended to dismiss the roads as spiraling paths to the wasteland of boorishness, in reality they frequently ventured out. Save for the taboos on unlucky days and directions that, though occasionally gender-specific, ultimately affected everyone, they were not bound by any particular restriction. Once they made the decision to step out of the court, Heian noblewomen effectively managed to turn their outings into what Barbara Ambros has called true "displays of power and status." The elegant carriages in which they journeyed symbolized their privileged position vis-à-vis the less affluent. At the same time, Ambros explains, by generating a void in the tightly knit fabric of court society, noblewomen in motion gained the upper hand in their relations with men, who reacted to their absences by desiring them more.[8]

Few women outside the precincts of the palace, however, enjoyed such privileges. Most ordinary women spent their lives working and breeding and, as Ivan Morris put it, "died at an early age, without having given any more thought to material independence or cultural enjoyments than to the possibility of visiting the moon."[9] Aside from the courtiers, only a handful of self-assertive women who claimed agency by means of their bodies traveled the roads: they were the itinerant performers known as *asobime,* or *yūjo*.[10] The literature of the time depicts them as mobile and relatively unconstrained.[11] En route to Izumi, the daughter of Sugawara no Takasue (1008–after 1059) encountered a group of *asobime* who "hid their [faces] with fans and sang songs," and found them "moving."[12]

Fairly privileged and wealthy, the *asobime* established and maintained connections with powerful figures well into the medieval period (twelfth to sixteenth centuries), when they gained admission into the circles of the military elites while keeping their ties with the aristocracy.[13] As Hitomi Tonomura has observed, entertainers were geographically and socially mobile, for they "traveled between the world of commoners and those who lived 'above the clouds.'"[14]

The independent *yūjo* of the medieval period represented the exception rather than the rule. The ability of women to claim agency while playing in tune with the conventions of official discourse decreased by the late twelfth century. Particularly after the Genpei Wars (1180–1185), women were removed from the public scene as a result of various socioeconomic changes, most notably the emergence of the male-based household *(ie)*, the gradual transition in marriage practices from "wife visiting" *(tsumadoi)* and "taking a husband" *(mukotori)* to "taking a wife" *(yometori)*, and the progressive loss of inheritance rights that women had been granted in the Heian period.[15] Especially hard hit were the women of the samurai class and the female members of the aristocracy, whose narratives, once so creative and assertive, began to fade into perfunctory acts of record keeping.[16] Female bodies also metamorphosed from sites of mystique to objects of contention and contempt; displaced by the new marriage patterns, they were exploited as instruments of sociopolitical preservation. As Hitomi Tonomura points out, men needed, sought, and defended female bodies to secure the continuation of their bloodlines while ironically reviling them for the very same reason, as childbirth, with its "visible flow of blood and high risk of death," generated "a liminal sphere of unpredictable forces that must have invited male fear."[17]

In a trend that continued into the early modern period, only certain female figures remained seemingly immune to the sweeping changes that altered the lives of aristocratic and samurai women. By virtue of their peculiar roles outside the economy of the household and of society in general, religious figures and itinerant performers who consciously created for themselves an identity as "people apart" sidestepped the constraining rules of the medieval age and crowded provincial roads and city streets.[18] At the opposite end of the spectrum, and for entirely different reasons, other remarkable changes of the age benefited certain members of the commoner class.

In the religious sphere, the egalitarian approach of Amidism and the teachings of Dōgen (1200–1253), who had promoted the equality of the sexes in all religious matters, made it possible for commoner women to attend events organized by religious associations—albeit with more limited roles than the male members.[19] By the thirteenth and fourteenth centuries, the increase in agricultural productivity and the development of commercial exchanges resulted in the active participation of more men and women in an array of economic activities. Unlike entertainers and nuns, who had chosen to take exception from the conventions of society, female merchants constituted a productive and well-integrated segment of the economic fabric. Their movements did not challenge or threaten stability and neatly fit in with the status quo. Traveling to city markets to sell produce from their farming or fishing villages or, like the famous ōharame, carrying firewood from the mountain village of Ōhara to Kyoto and throughout the Kansai region, these medieval female travelers hardly conceived of their journeys or of their bodies as platforms for making a statement about agency and autonomy. Like all other traveling merchants, the katsurame who supplied the capital's markets with fish from Katsura simply traveled to fulfill an economic obligation. While they may have failed to see any exceptional element in their daily routines, a confined female aristocrat who caught a glimpse of the katsurame at work thought them unique enough to deserve an entry in her diary. The author of *The Diary of Lady Ben (Bennonaishi nikki),* a chronicle of life at court between 1246 and 1252, describes the arrival at the palace of a group of five or six katsurame carrying baskets filled with freshwater trout *(ayu)* as an event of remarkable interest and as a "rare sight" *(mezurashiki sugata)* for the secluded courtiers.[20]

It would not be long, however, before some among these traveling merchants took notice of the possibilities embedded in the body and in the open road. When a decree prohibiting the killing of living creatures in the rivers of the capital was issued in 1284, the existence of the katsurame underwent a thorough transformation. The very foundation of their living undermined, they took on a new identity as traveling courtesans. Their appearance changed accordingly, evolving from practical to refined, as they donned white robes and began wearing elaborate headgear.[21] Moving from place to place, they performed at banquets in return for monetary compensation. Under the surface, however, they maintained a link to their former profession. At New Year and on the seventh month they would pay homage to local temples and offer fresh fish to the deities. Still active in the Warring States (1490–1590) and Edo periods, they were invited to weddings, military drills, and childbirths to ensure good luck and success. Legend has it that both Toyotomi Hideyoshi (before launching the Korean expeditions in the 1590s) and Tokugawa Ieyasu (prior to the battle of Sekigahara, 1600) invited katsurame to their headquarters.[22] Through a metamorphosis of their bodies and a reconceptualization of their movements, the katsurame thus succeeded not only in reinventing themselves against a law that nullified the foundation of their original identity, but also in crossing the line between outsiders and insiders. Once peddlers glanced at from afar by bored courtiers, they became intimate acquaintances of the great power players of the age.

Equally mobile and familiar with the high spheres of power were the itinerant puppet players and musicians known as *kugutsu*. Documentary evidence traces their presence to the Heian period when, as *Chronicles of Springtime (Shunki)* reports, they entertained statesmen and ministers.[23] *An Account of Puppeteers (Kairaishi no ki)* by Ōe no Masafusa (1041–1111) portrays them as nomads, with men devoted to hunting and women to entertainment and prostitution: "they do not subject themselves to prefectural officials, none of them is a regular dweller, and they are naturally equivalent to 'drifters.'" Similarly, a Chinese poem composed by Fujiwara no Shigeaki (n.d.) offers a portrait of the *kugutsu* as marginal figures disengaged from social conventions:

> Those called kugutsu, where are they?
> They are always on the move, they never have leisure to think.
> At the outskirts they move from place to place, they have no fixed dwelling;
> in their travels they sell their charms, longing for success in bed.[24]

Despite their characterization as drifters, the *kugutsu* were well connected with the higher echelons of society. As they traveled to the palaces and houses of nobility they were welcomed with quasi-regal treatment, so much so that not a few local villagers began to resent their visits, for they proved exceedingly burdensome in terms of levy and taxation.[25] Official records indicate that the *kugutsu* were also consciously assertive and able to exploit the law to their own advantage, filing complaints and promoting lawsuits.[26]

FOR A GREAT many women across the social spectrum, and particularly for women of high status, nunhood had traditionally provided an acceptable release from social expectations and a considerable degree of freedom.[27] As Hitomi Tonomura notes, the demand for nunneries grew substantially from the thirteenth century in a trend explained, at least partially, by women's quest for spaces where they could counterbalance the extensive loss of rights they were experiencing in the age of warriors.[28] After having spent the better years of their lives as wives and borrowed wombs, many widows eventually withdrew from the world, shaved their heads, donned religious robes, and renounced their sexuality. As a radical and often permanent alteration of one's identity, the act of taking the tonsure in fact opened a great many doors into that very world that was purportedly rejected. Recent studies have emphasized the direct relation between hair length and status (the longer the former, the higher the latter), demonstrating how the act of shaving one's head served as a powerful signifier of a woman's alteration, if not complete loss, of her social coordinates.[29] James C. Dobbins has also argued that the tonsure effectively blurred gender boundaries between men and women; the fact that both priests and nuns shaved their heads created what he calls "a certain degree of sexual indeterminacy."[30]

The nun, having given up her place in society, was a renunciant in the true sense of the word. Full-fledged nuns who had completed the entire set of ordination procedures (inclusive of the administration of hundreds of vows) frequently headed for the cloister. Other women, however, opted for alternative forms of nunhood, still requiring celibacy but overall involving fewer vows and, in some cases, only the partial trimming of their tresses.[31] As an alternative to the seclusion of the nunnery, not a few of these renunciants chose to live a life of wandering. Generally considered unbefitting and unsafe for the women (wives) who kept their place in society, travel suddenly entered the range of possible and acceptable activities once the transformation into nun was completed. Not unlike entertainers, nuns were also allowed privileges normally denied to most women, as their state of "indulgent disengagement, lamented but not punished" came with an enviable set of freedoms.[32] *Shirabyōshi* (dancers), *bikuni* (nuns, particularly from the Kumano region), *goze* (blind nuns/singers), and *miko* (female shamans) are indeed among the most recognizable travelers of the medieval period.

The case of the nun Abutsu (Abutsu-ni, 1233?–1283) suggests that medieval religious figures enjoyed a remarkable degree of freedom of movement. Abutsu had resolved to take the tonsure at a young age after an unfortunate affair with a nobleman above her rank. In *Fitful Slumbers (Utatane)* she describes the exact moment when she cut her own hair: "I felt happy when my hand found in the dimness the scissors and box lid I had prepared that day. Yet, as may be imagined, I could not help feeling anxious as I gathered my hair in my hand."[33] Her first long trip as a nun, whose details she includes in the same work, took her to Tōtōmi Province. Distressed by the distance from the capital, she soon decided to make her way back to Kyoto. Already she was beginning to feel an "urge to drift off like the floating reeds."[34] Many years later, in 1277, Abutsu journeyed from Kyoto to Kamakura to settle a pending inheritance dispute before the court. She traveled in the company of a mountain ascetic and composed her most famous memoir, *The Diary of the Waning Moon (Izayoi nikki)*.

Both times Abutsu proved herself an acute observer of country roads, able to vividly describe the "shouting and hullabaloo" at river crossings, the crowded post towns where finding accommodation for the night became a small ordeal, the loud noises that prevented guests from resting, and even the foul-smelling lodgings with which travelers had to put up.[35] Particularly during her later journey Abutsu did not shy away from interactions with others, happily meeting with the children and grandchildren of old friends in Hamamatsu, asking explanations regarding place-names, or querying on the mysterious disappearance of the famous smoke rising from Mount Fuji. In *The Diary of the Waning Moon* she captures the readers' sympathy for her human dimensions, for she is never afraid to reveal her intimate thoughts, to confess to mood swings, and to share personal details about her health problems.

At roughly the same time another famous traveling nun took to the road: Lady Nijō. After taking her vows in 1289, Nijō visited a number of locations throughout the Eastern and Western Provinces, including Kamakura (Sagami), Zenkōji (Shinano), Asakusa (Musashi), Ise, and Nachi (Kii). Although she admits to having left the capital in order to hide from the sorrows of the world, her travels are marked by a degree of autonomy and visibility that only her status as a religious figure made possible. Nijō changed her itinerary on the spur of the moment and made impromptu travel plans—the casual encounter with a group of ascetics who told her the Great Shrine was but a short ferry ride away inspired her to visit Ise: "I was so happy [to hear about it] that I decided to go."[36] Her ability to move freely around the country puzzled ex-emperor Go-Fukakusa, who commented: "For men it is normal to travel to the East and even to China, but women face countless obstacles and cannot embark on the same type of ascetic journeys. [. . .] You could not possibly have traveled alone."[37] But travel alone she did, at least on most occasions. During the trip from Kamakura to Zenkōji, Nijō became so annoyed with her group that she deliberately decided to stay behind, her travel companions' anxiety notwithstanding. Alone she visited Nara—"I went there all by myself" *(tada hitori mairite),* in her words.[38]

Having stepped out of the web of social obligations by taking the tonsure did not make Abutsu and Nijō immune to all rules, however. Whenever the possibility of clashing with officialdom arose, they took care to avoid confrontation. Nijō chose to modify her route in order to spare herself the headache of a certain checkpoint whose guards notoriously made it difficult for travelers to obtain permits,[39] while Abutsu endured (and recalled in verses) an unpleasant encounter with the sentinels at Fuwa:

Kakikuratsu	Under a dark sky,
yuki ma wo shibashi	while waiting for a break
matsu hodo ni	in the snowfall,
yagate todomuru	a man detained us—
Fuwa no sekimori	the barrier guard at Fuwa.[40]

These minor incidents aside, Abutsu and Nijō unquestionably benefited from the freedoms that came with the vows. The case of Lady Nakatsukasa (Fujiwara Keishi, daughter of Takakura Nagatsune), on the other hand, shows how for the court ladies of the medieval age the evolution from a predominantly feminine to a predominantly masculine society had closed many doors and curtailed a good degree of mobility. To Keishi, an occasional recreational outing was a surprise-filled rarity. In 1284 she took a short boat journey to Amagasaki and later visited Nara and Hatsuse. Curious about the world outside the court, she has left us a fascinating description of the sceneries and landscapes she observed ever so keenly.[41] The transition from feminine to masculine had thus reversed the terms, immobilizing the once free and assertive court insiders and granting mobility to some of the outsiders instead.

Increasingly subordinate to the demands of a male-oriented society, in the late medieval period the wives and daughters of warriors saw their freedom and agency further curtailed by a growing array of limitations and impositions. The legal codes of the Kamakura period were rewritten in the fifteenth century in an effort to further control, restrain, and punish the female body. While the original laws drew a conceptual distinction between adultery and rape (though, ultimately, the punishment for the woman would be the same), after 1479 the new codes glossed over the point altogether, lumping consensual and forced intercourse under the general umbrella of extramarital sex and granting the offended husband permission to kill his wife in revenge.[42] The same codes also contributed to the physical confinement of women. One stipulation warned that "should a woman be caught strolling around, her family members will be confined into the house for a period of one hundred days."[43] In light of such efforts to control and constrain women, scholars have contended that the Muromachi period was an age when women of high social standing enjoyed a solid basis of authority within the household but, with rare exceptions, "became increasingly invisible outside of it."[44] There is little doubt that the catastrophic disorders of the Ōnin era (1467–1477), during which Kyoto and its surrounding areas were ransacked and burnt to ashes, created an environment in which few besides well-armed warriors and wandering ascetics who placed no value on life dared to venture. Although a few examples of travel diaries composed by men in this day and age have survived, circumstances made it nearly impossible for most people to travel.[45]

Marked by general instability and widespread warfare, the years of the Warring States further impeded people from taking to the road. With the country fragmented into a series of scattered and reciprocally hostile domains, most roads and bridges fell into a state of disrepair. Domain-run checkpoints *(bansho)* hindered or nullified altogether the notion of freedom of movement.

The turmoil of the age and the minimal authority granted to women ensured compliance with the rules of confinement, silence, and immobility. As a result, few women traveled and few raised their voices. Iwasa Miyoko has drawn attention to a long hiatus in the production of female travel diaries between the fourteenth and the seventeenth centuries.[46]

With the centralization of political power in the hands of the Tokugawa and the obsessive quest for order they had initiated since the seventeenth century, the identification of female travel with a potential threat to the newly created and strenuously defended stability became an explicit concern of the legislators. The degree of surveillance intensified, prompting the necessity for continuous expedients on the part of women who wished to be mobile. As in the past, the ways in which a woman was able to manipulate legal and social restrictions largely depended on her status.

The Cicada That Discarded Her Skin and the Woman Who Crossed the Line: Women of High Status and Travel

Edo period aristocratic and samurai women—a term broadly applied to the mothers, wives, daughters, and even close female attendants of lords, retainers, or governmental officials—still had to abide by the traditional rules of elegance according to which grace and charisma necessitated a good degree of invisibility and confinement. The equation of mystique with elusiveness, which found a historical precedent in the lifestyle of Heian courtiers, had not been forgotten centuries later. "It is a habit, when one yearns for the past and admires refinement *(miyabi),* to hang up the lattices," commented Tsuchiya Ayako, a magistrate's wife, in 1806.[47]

This equation applied to everyday life as much as it did to special occasions, including journeys. Whenever on the road, men and women of aristocratic or samurai lineage traveled inside enclosed palanquins *(kago),* as their station in life demanded.[48] As only those who commanded a large amount of resources could travel in pomp, the palanquin served first and foremost as a material display of wealth and status. Palanquins were also meant to provide comfort and protection from the elements, but because carriers could only lift and maneuver small *kago,* limitations in size de facto forced the passenger to remain constrained in a cramped space for hours on end. For women in particular, the palanquin also functioned as a useful device for leaving their residences and traveling. At closer inspection, however, what could have been an instrument of liberation was in fact the ingenious expedient by which, even while outside, women were still kept inside—sheltered and immobile.

What enclosed palanquins re-created was no less than a miniaturized version of the cloistering that samurai and aristocratic women experienced on a daily basis. A secluded cell, the palanquin prevented its passengers from interacting with the outside world, effectively serving as a portable "module of imprisonment."⁴⁹ In her travel memoir Ayako recalls the day she left for Izumi Province as part of her husband's retinue. Soldiers and attendants lined up on both sides of the procession while she "was pushed into the dark palanquin, and the sunlight turned dim." Although she resented the practice, she did not openly voice her complaints: "Thinking this is the Law for us women, I did not say a word."⁵⁰ So, inside the protective shield of the palanquin, women of high status ventured outside yet still remained detached from the world, at times even unable to tell the direction of their movements: "The wind blew fiercely, so I shut the curtains and did not even know where we were going," writes Ayako.⁵¹ Ayako attempted to raise the lattice screens, but because her eyes had adapted to the darkness of her moving cloister she could not focus: "It was all blurred; I could not even tell where we were."⁵²

Inoue Tsūjo, the daughter of a Sanuki samurai en route to serve under the mother of her domain lord in Edo in 1681, had also traveled inside a palanquin. Isolated from the outside, all she noticed, with a hint of melancholy, was the moonlight filtering through the screens.⁵³ On her way home eight years later, Tsūjo was still looking at the world through the screens of a palanquin. At Kiyomi Temple she wrote: "I heard that the view was splendid, but the ascent up to it was hard, so I looked in from the gate, peeping through the palanquin shutters."⁵⁴ What external observers may have perceived as a symbol of wealth to many a female traveler was but a gilded cage, an "empty, uninhabited palace" inside which, as Ayako lamented, "my spirit is not different from that of a prisoner."⁵⁵

Was freedom of movement an unattainable chimera for women like Ayako and Tsūjo? In the early modern period the custom persisted for women who had married and raised a family to shave their heads after the death of their husbands, and, as it had in the past, the transformation into nuns offered many of them an opportunity to escape from the prison of conventions. While to many the act of taking the tonsure simply symbolized their new condition as widows and did not imply an end to the connection with their households, to others nunhood led to a complete redefinition of roles and identities, including the possibility of abandoning all family-related obligations. Widowed at a young age, Kikusha-ni, the daughter of a samurai from Chōfu (in Nagato Province), embraced the teachings of the True Pure Land, took the tonsure, and began a life of wandering. At the onset of her travel memoir, *Plucked Chrysanthemum* (*Taorigiku,* 1812), she recalls the steps that led her to nunhood: "I adopted the son of a relative, entrusted him with the family affairs, and took leave from this floating world. The day I thought I wished to see every famous nook and corner under heavens and pay homage to [every] shrine and temple, I just took to the road, all by myself."[56]

Her decision to "brush off the dust of the floating world" entailed an almost immediate release from her responsibilities. Kikusha-ni thus became able to travel instantly (in her own words, "just like that," *sono mama ni*) and without the need for such status markers (and symbols of surveillance) as a retinue, a palanquin, or a queue of attendants. A few days after her departure she came to Seikōji in Hagi and wrapped up her transformation by shaving her head completely. She then began a series of peregrinations that combined religious achievements and the pursuit of educational goals, as she journeyed to mingle with literati and art masters of every region and to perfect her poetry skills. Kikusha-ni traveled extensively, composing verses and immersing herself in numerous local cultural circles, experimenting with tea ceremony, painting, the art of combining fragrances, and music. She described herself as a "wandering body" *(unsui no mi)* whose journeys were not regulated by preestablished itineraries or planned destinations. "I have made of myself a drifting cloud in the wind," she wrote. "I do not plan where to go, nor do I establish a day for my return." Released from society by virtue of her new identity, she became able to journey unhindered by the degree of control reserved for laywomen of her status. Upon transiting through the much-feared barrier at Hakone, for example, she lightheartedly sang, "Violets: / I carry them in my hand / as I cross the barrier's gate." Having managed to re-create herself completely, Kikusha-ni saw herself as "a cicada that has discarded her skin."[57]

As Abutsu and Nijō had experienced centuries before her, Kikusha-ni also understood that nunhood did not guarantee complete freedom of movement. On occasions she too encountered insurmountable roadblocks. At Yanagase barrier she heard she would not be allowed to pass, and at Hosorogi, where nuns were permitted to transit, she was still questioned by the guards ("Knocking / at the barrier's gate: / the chirping waterfowls and I").[58] She also maintained profound obligations toward her parents in Chōfu, and during her journeys she often received correspondence from her father, occasionally interrupting her peregrinations to return home for a while. But not much time passed before she would be "enticed one more time by the gods of travel" and leave again.[59]

Kikusha-ni was a freer woman as a nun than she had been as a daughter or a wife. At the same time, there was a price to be paid for her newly acquired independence, and that price was loneliness. Kikusha-ni quickly realized—and accepted—the fact that solitude would permeate her existence as a body in motion:

Kanko sae	Traveling alone
kikanu hi mo ari	there are days I do not even hear
hitori tabi	the cry of a cuckoo.[60]

Nevertheless, her detached life as a religious figure allowed her to make her own decisions, to leave and return at her own will ("I take pleasure in wandering around the world, and I take pleasure in returning home"),[61] and to pursue her own interests. By taking the tonsure Kikusha-ni had transformed her entire persona and had achieved liberation.

Widowhood and nunhood also opened new avenues for Seigen-in Noriko (1725–1794). Born in Edo as Nabe-hime (or Iku-hime), she was the twelfth daughter of a domain lord with a residence in Shirogane. In 1745 Nabe-hime married Hosokawa Okisato, lord of Uto domain (in Higo Province), and took the name Noriko, by which she is commonly known.[62] As a lord's daughter first, and then as a wife, Noriko obeyed the dictates of the alternate attendance system that required her to serve as a hostage in Edo and was thus unable to travel. A mere ten months after her wedding, however, her husband passed away. Noriko then changed her identity by becoming the nun Seigen-in. She did not embrace the opportunity to travel immediately, but in 1777 she ventured to the south of Sagami Province, and a few years later, in 1782, she set out on a far more engaging trip to her "home" in distant Kyushu. Before departure she required permission to leave on a therapeutic journey to Kyushu's hot-spring resorts. Although an array of much closer facilities existed in the immediate peripheries of Edo—a detail that could hardly have escaped the attention of the authorities—her strategic role had so diminished that she was granted official authorization to travel.[63] Unlike Kikusha-ni, Noriko did not become a wandering solitary traveler. She in fact kept most of her status privileges and habits, traveling as part of a large retinue and covering most stretches of the road, including the tour of the Inner Shrine in Ise, in a palanquin. Vaguely justified by therapeutic purposes and unquestionably made possible by her relative disengagement from the affairs of the family, hers was in fact a sight-seeing tour. Not only did she specifically choose to return to Edo along a different route (the Kiso Road) to maximize the number of sites she would visit, she also regretted, at the end of the trip, not having had time to visit Yoshino and Zenkōji among "the famous sites and places of historical relevance I toured in every province."[64]

Unlike Noriko, other widows-turned-nuns seized the opportunity to leave Edo for good. A childless widow at age thirty-eight, Takako (1787–1870), wife of the lord of Kaga, had also been confined to her Edo residence until she took the tonsure and the religious name Shinryū-in. When she petitioned the authorities to travel to Kanazawa in 1838 she was promptly granted permission. She settled there and never left. The authorities in Edo never required her to return. A childless widow and a nun, she had lost all strategic value as a pillar of order and producer of a family line.[65]

AS MENTIONED EARLIER, a second avenue for the reconfiguration of a woman's identity was provided by as dramatic a metamorphosis as that brought about by tonsure. By becoming an entertainer, a woman acquired the special status of "person apart" (as the *shirabyōshi* Takejo put it), less scrutinized and more able to move about.[66] Takejo (n.d.) traveled from Nagoya to Edo in 1720 and left a diary titled *Record of a Journey Taken in the Year of the Rat (Kanoene michi no ki)*. At the onset of her work Takejo subtly hints at her special status and at the freedom of movement it entailed: "Even though the writings of old say that women do not cross the line *(sakai o koezu)*, that may be true for the elegant people. Fishermen's children, with nowhere to go, entrust themselves to the lure of the currents, drifting east and west. . . ."[67] Takejo here directly links her ability to move to her newly acquired identity as an entertainer: fisherman's child *(ama no ko)* was a metaphor for prostitute and, not insignificantly, was also homophonous with a word for nun. She draws her imagery from two poems featured in famous anthologies of the past, *Collection of Ancient and Recent Poems (Kokinshū)* and *New Collection of Ancient and Recent Poems (Shinkokinshū)*:

Shiranami no	I am a fisherman's child:
yo suru nagisa ni	I spend my life
yo o sugusu	near the wave-beaten shores
Ama no ko nareba	and have
Yado mo sadamezu	no fixed dwelling[68]

and

Wabinureba	I have sunk to the
mi o ukigusa no	bottom and like the rootless
ne o taete	shifting water weeds
sasou mizu araba	should the currents summon me
Inan to zo omou	I too would drift away.[69]

Born into a samurai family, Takejo thus became "rootless." In her narrative she celebrates her release from the group of women who are caught in the grip of Confucian tradition ("the writings of old") and, immobile and submissive, "do not cross the line." That her marginality as a detached member of society allowed for freedoms not commonly granted to other female travelers becomes clear once she comes to Hakone barrier. She writes: "It has been established that the likes of prostitutes and itinerant entertainers are people apart *(hito no hoka naru)*, so I was let through without the slightest hindrance *(hisasaka no sawari mo naku)*. Should I be glad? Should I be saddened? I cannot say."[70] Women of high status who stepped out of society by becoming nuns or entertainers used their new identities to acquire a much broader latitude in their movements. They cleverly manipulated existing customs, ultimately finding an avenue of release from social obligations and a way to "cross the line" between inside and outside.

Eluding Scrutiny by Dressing the Part: Female Commoners and Travel

An effective way for female commoners to attain almost complete freedom of movement was to become mothers-in-law. As Nagashima Atsuko has shown, the transfer of authority that occurred with the acquisition of a daughter-in-law realigned a woman's position within the household, releasing the mother-in-law from the bulk of family obligations and enabling her to leave the house more often and for longer periods of time. Nagashima's study of the Sekiguchi, a family of rural entrepreneurs and village elders from Namamugi village (Musashi Province), shows clear patterns in the outings of the family women in the first half of the nineteenth century. As long as the mother-in-law, Orie, was healthy and able to travel, the daughter-in-law, Oie, rarely left the house. Between 1806 and 1813, for instance, Orie, by then a widow in her sixties, traveled thirty-seven times (187 days in total). In the same time period Oie, the thirty-something mother of five, went on only two outings and was absent from the household for no more than seven days. Only with Orie's decline in health around 1814 did Oie start to leave the house more often.[71]

Whereas aristocratic and samurai women could exploit their widowhood as a way to disengage themselves from the net of societal ties and gain a chance to become mobile, for the young wife of a farmer or of a townsman the passing of her husband often increased the burden of obligations. Once widowed, Kuwahara Hisako had to take full charge of the family business, a rice shop, while raising three children. It was not until 1841, at the age of fifty (fifty-one by Japanese counting), that she became able to travel to Nikkō for five months in the company of her friend Oda Ieko (fifty-three at the time), two other women, and three men.[72] The examples of the Sekiguchi women and Hisako also show us that opportunities to travel were likely to come at an older age for most women. In this respect it is worth mentioning that among the 133 female authors of travel diaries examined by Shiba Keiko (aristocrats and samurai, but also commoners) the vast majority (61) took to the road between the ages of forty and fifty-nine.[73]

Not all women, however, could wait to acquire mobility along legally defined and socially accepted lines. When the lack of official transit permits forced them to travel surreptitiously, some female commoners acted on their bodies to effect transformations that would enable them to elude surveillance. Temporary but drastic changes of appearance were among the most common methods resorted to in order to acquire mobility when mobility was not an option. Already in the late seventeenth century, novelist Ihara Saikaku fantasized about the link between the manipulation of one's appearance and freedom of movement. In one episode from *The Life of an Amorous Man* (*Kōshoku ichidai otoko*, 1682) Saikaku makes a passing reference to certain "ambiguous women" (*ai no onna*, lit. "women in between") who donned men's outfits to increase their chances to travel and to enjoy more safety along the road. By looking and acting like men, even going as far as carrying a sword, Saikaku's ambiguous women empowered themselves to move from temple to temple and, as Saikaku himself put it, to "become free" (*jiyū ni narinu*).[74] Even the female protagonist of another popular work by the same author, *The Life of an Amorous Woman* (*Kōshoku ichidai onna*, 1686), slips into a full man's outfit (complete with two swords), shaves her hair to look like a boy, and fakes a man's voice in order to take on the semblance of a young masterless samurai, believing that such camouflage would enable her to move out and about "even at noon, without hiding from [other] people."[75]

It is highly probable that a combination of poetic license and of marketable erotic fantasies induced Saikaku to entice his readers with the image of gender-defying women. Still, the attempt of the masterless samurai Heizaemon to cut his nine-year-old daughter's hair and dress her up as a boy in order to cross Hakone and Arai barriers,[76] and the successful mission of a twenty-five-year-old woman named Tatsu, who defied the precepts of *nyonin kinsei* by climbing to the top of Mount Fuji in 1832 disguised as a man,[77] suggest that for certain female travelers the impersonation of males was in fact within the realm of possibility. The body, in this case, became a means of achieving mobility by way of an ad hoc act of gender reconfiguration.

Other women resorted to camouflage, not to conceal their gender, but to deflect attention by creating a false impression about their social worth. In this case they dressed as nuns. Such was the case with a woman from Shimoimai village in Kai Province who had taken to the road in 1681 following her eleven-year-old son, Ichimatsu, on an unauthorized pilgrimage. Before stepping into the compound of the Kiso Fukushima checkpoint, the two had shaved their heads—he to look like a young acolyte and she like a nun—in order to be granted easy transit. Their plot failed and they were arrested.[78] As the case suggests, commoners of both sexes donned fake religious robes in the hope of deceiving the eyes of the authorities. Only four years after Ichimatsu and his mother tried to pass for an acolyte and a nun, two men, Shirōbei and Rokubei, were caught (on two separate occasions) while attempting to cross a checkpoint without the appropriate travel permits and disguised as Buddhist monks. Arrested, they pleaded guilty to the accusations and were sentenced to death.[79] These unsuccessful schemes confirm that many a commoner saw in the impersonation of disengaged figures a viable option to bypass existing rules and attempt to elude surveillance. Unlike the transformations of nuns and entertainers, however, this means was purely practical, confined in time, and illegal.

Subterfuges of this kind tended to peak during certain religiously charged events such as mass pilgrimages to Ise *(okagemairi* and *nukemairi)*.[80] On such occasions some of the women who defied the authorities by impersonating men fully exploited the above-the-law nature of the sacred and explicitly— even blatantly—flaunted their masquerades, as a record from 1830 reveals:

> There were about fifty young women from Osaka, each carrying a ladle [to collect alms]. The blackening had fallen off and their teeth were white. They were all clad in the same outfits with white leggings on their shins. They wore male pongee clothes and pulled up their cuffs with velvet sashes used by men. They also wore silk crepe loincloths and tied their hair in a knot, like men. They hooded their heads with bleached cotton towels and wrote *Okagemairi* on their hats. Each carried a banner that proclaimed "Runaway Pilgrim."[81]

What enabled these women to openly proclaim their status as runaways while parading in men's attire was, first and foremost, the virtual immunity they were granted by presenting their actions within the framework of religion. At the same time, however, not all pilgrims who camouflaged themselves got away with it, as the case of Ichimatsu and his mother demonstrates. What further empowered the fifty Osaka women to be so assertive was the fact that, unlike Ichimatsu and his mother, they were traveling as part of a

large group. Often associated with religious confraternities, group travel not only rendered a journey safer and more feasible from a financial standpoint, but also offered the advantage of virtual anonymity. No one of the fifty Osaka cross-dressers strikes the chronicler more than the others, for "they were all clad in the same outfits." Likewise, none of the innumerable women whose trip to Enoshima is captured in Andō Hiroshige's *Illustration of the Crowds of Pilgrims Going to Enoshima, in Sagami Province, for the Benzaiten Exhibit* (*Sōshū Enoshima Benten kaichō sankei gunshū no zu,* ca. 1850, Figure 8) stands out for the very same reason: the individual virtually disappears in the mass of identically clad people.

As the fifty cross-dressing pilgrims from Osaka demonstrate, moreover, the ability to hide behind the protective shield of the group even empowered women to become ostentatious and loud, utterly ignoring the precepts outlined in the nineteenth-century educational textbook cited earlier, according to which "it is in the way one walks that we see a person's quality," therefore "it is advisable to walk in a modest fashion."[82] The Edo merchant Senkaku Tōshi had the opportunity to notice just such a bold behavior while touring Enoshima in 1809. Upon approaching the cave of the goddess Benzaiten,

Fig. 8. A boisterous crowd of anonymous women. Andō Hiroshige, *Illustration of the Crowds of Pilgrims Going to Enoshima, in Sagami Province, for the Benzaiten Exhibit (Sōshū Enoshima Benten kaichō sankei gunshū no zu)*. Courtesy Library of Congress, Prints & Photographs Division (reproduction number LC-DIG-jpd-00058).

he came across "a large and showy *(hanayaka naru)* crowd of women, all dancers and geisha from the Kutsuwaya in Yotsuya. All these young ladies on a pilgrimage invaded the road in their gaudy outfits and created a bustle, which is amplified since we are on an island."[83] The fact that the women who crossed Senkaku Tōshi's path were entertainers certainly explains their flashy appearance, and the extra-normative character of the sacred helps justify their assertive demeanor. At the same time one cannot overlook the fact that their traveling as part of a large group further enabled them to escape scrutiny as individuals and, consequently, to act without restraint.

Runaways who journeyed alone or in smaller groups, by contrast, generally chose to keep a low profile. Following their departure, few of the people who had taken off without permission were as flaunting as the fifty *nukemairi* pilgrims from Osaka or as daring (or foolish) as Ichimatsu and his mother. The majority of runaways in fact steered clear of barriers and traveled along trails that were only mildly supervised by the eye of the authorities. Such hidden roads *(nukemichi)*, winding paths that bypassed areas of direct government surveillance by circumventing official barriers, made their appearance in the middle of the Edo period in reaction to the increase in the number of female and/or illegal travelers, which prompted the Tokugawa government to introduce a proliferation of checkpoints.[84] Because in general terms women were subject to more limitations than men in their movements, they frequently availed themselves of these trails, so much so that many came to be known as "women's roads" *(onna no michi)*. Travel along women's roads was accomplished with the complicity of conniving innkeepers or local guides. So widespread and inventive were the activities of these smugglers of women that a 1796 satirical poem *(senryū)* punned:

Tōrinuke	NO TRESPASSING—
muyō de tōrinuke	Thanks to the sign, you find
ga shire	a shortcut.[85]

According to the law, women caught bypassing an official checkpoint would be taken into custody and, in the best-case scenario, sold into servitude. On 1688/9/4, for example, a wet nurse by the name of Tan was arrested for avoiding the Ichikawa checkpoint and was sentenced to serve under a certain Madoka Yasuzaemon.[86] In 1696 another woman, Yasu, ran away from her master without permission and sneaked past the same checkpoint. Arrested, she recounted the details of her escape, including a colorful and dramatic description of the flight. She had met with her accomplice, Hanzaburō, at sunset "by a nameless bridge in the vicinities of the mansion of the Hida lord" in Edo. The two had fled together, resorting to various expedients to make their way to her home province of Kazusa. At a pier they begged the ferry captain to allow them on board. "In the deep of the night," Yasu recalls, "we crossed over to the edge of the fields." In Funabashi they decided to rent two horses; they had no money, so Hanzaburō convinced Yasu to offer her sash in lieu of a payment. They rode to their destination, arriving around midnight. They did not try to find accommodation at an inn and, as Yasu put it during her interrogation, "dawn found us on the front porch of a store." When questioned by the investigators, however, Hanzaburō denied any involvement and accused Yasu of having fabricated the entire story. The two were imprisoned as the investigation continued. Finally, Yasu confessed to having made up the details of the flight and took full blame. Hanzaburō was pardoned unconditionally and sent back to his employer, while Yasu, guilty not only of trespassing but also of lying to the authorities, was sentenced to death on 1696/11/6.[87] The cases of Yasu and Tan indicate that punishment for barrier trespassers was harsh and swift in the seventeenth century. In the second half of the Edo period, however, barrier guards would usually turn a blind eye on illegal side roads.[88] A case in point is the lackadaisical comment Takazawa Jirōshichi, a village officer from Echigo Province, made in his

1774 diary in regard to the Ichifuri barrier: "There is a checkpoint here and women are not allowed through the barrier. So they circumvent it by taking a boat at Aisaki beach. It costs thirty *mon*."[89]

Whereas the use of illegal roads served as a way to challenge or bypass the rules of official discourse, the same travelers who did not think twice about hiring a guide to be taken around a checkpoint did not question, or attempt to defy, spatial hierarchies generated by other discourses. In 1863, Miyake Yae and Yoshiemon, two farmers from Sekigahara, blatantly disobeyed the rules of the Tokugawa not only by taking off on an unauthorized pilgrimage but also by illegally circumventing the checkpoints at Sekigawa and Ichifuri: "We hired a guide at the inn and, at night, we sneaked through a hole in the fence *(inukuguri)* and passed the checkpoint." When they reached Yanagase barrier without the appropriate permits they simply bribed the guard. For all their indifference to the laws of the government, Yae and Yoshiemon showed a profound respect for the dictates of the sacred. When they reached Tateyama, they obediently abided by the rule that required female visitors to remain outside the precincts of the mountain. "Tateyama is off-limits to women, so while I climbed [the mountain] my wife Yae stayed at the Kiyogura Temple lodgings," recalls Yoshiemon.[90] Even travelers of low status such as Yoshiemon and Yae, in other words, demonstrated an acute awareness of the multiplicity of discourses and spatial hierarchies intersecting over the landscape and consciously selected which to respect and which to defy.[91]

IN A SOCIETY that, aside from the web of institutionalized surveillance, had developed a sublime taste for visual representations, peeping, and fantasizing (the leaps of the imagination devised by Ihara Saikaku come to mind), it is not surprising that the objects of such often unsolicited scrutiny sought to escape it by altering or disguising their appearance.[92] In this respect, travel often entailed acts of subterfuge against the rules emanating from the central authority and its bird's-eye gaze over the landscape (Figure 3). As official discourse tended to present women as immobile appendages of men and to value their existence in terms of the degree of their involvement in an economy of submission, more and more women began to see their bodies and their movements as sites of contestation and as platforms for temporary liberation and even audacious acts of self-assertion. Enabled to take to the road by the availability of contested spaces, overlapping discourses, and cleverly manipulated identities, early modern female wayfarers thus set out on their journeys toward re-creation. Their presence along the roads may have been tightly regulated, but, as the next chapter will illuminate, it was precisely on the roads that their true colors began to show far more vividly.

CHAPTER 4

Palimpsests
The Open Road and the Blank Page

> Different Ways of Speaking:
> The speech of men and women.
> —Sei Shōnagon, *The Pillow Book*

> Most things produced in the world that are called *monogatari* [tales] or *sōshi* [books in Japanese] come from the hands of women. For this reason, their language is full of flattery and strained laughter; they show no principles of instruction or admonition. One sees only attractively made-up forms, and does not hear a bold, manly style. One is troubled by their busyness, lost in their complexity. They run to the vulgar, or degenerate into lies. All of them are this way.
> —Hayashi Razan, *Tsurezuregusa nozuchi*

ON THE ROADS of Edo period Japan travel simultaneously offered a chance for recreation, in the leisurely connotation of the term, and for re-creation (that is, the regeneration or reinvention of one's persona). The open road and the blank page of the memoir aided travelers in the art of reinventing themselves, for both areas opened in endless directions, both required personal choices, and both inspired the proliferation of individual constructions and hierarchies. The combination of a detachment from the everyday (the journey) and a creative cultural act (the composition of a diary) offered the possibility of modifying roles and identities by tweaking concepts of gender and status (in both the social and professional sense) that defined the individual at home.

By acknowledging that diaries, far from being neutral chronicles, were texts in which identity was created, asserted, and debated, I suggest that the appropriation of landscapes by means of the brush empowered the authors of travel narratives to either fine-tune or completely redefine their personas.[1] Specifically, the association with literary precedent allowed women of high status to affirm their identity as members of the elite and aided the female members of the literati *(bunjin)* circles in defining their professional worth as the transmitters of a respected cultural tradition. The art of winking at the classical past and of recuperating it through citation, imitation, or various forms of allusive variation *(honkadori)* had a long history and a well-recognized social function. Poetic circles formed communal units where bonds—horizontal ones with peers and vertical ones with the hallowed past—were created through lyrical skills. With the expansion of literacy in the second half of the Edo period, wealthy farmers and townspeople, too, began to see access to the lyrically charged spaces of travel as an opportunity to attempt a dialogue with the revered cultural icons of antiquity. The boom of the publishing industry (discussed in more detail in Chapter 5) popularized the classics and made them available across the social spectrum, enabling commoners to partake in a divertissement thus far exclusive to members of the sociocultural elites. Educated engagements with the landscape gave travelers of commoner stock an opportunity to bypass, if only for the duration of the journey, some of the status- and gender-based obligations to which they were subject on a daily basis. Travelers of both sexes partook in the literary manipulation of spaces and selves. While for men this was one among many avenues of recreation (and re-creation), for their wives and daughters literary travel represented a far more precious and rare opportunity to reimagine their roles, one they exploited ever so eagerly.

Travel Diaries as Texts of Identity

Because travel writing is a form of autobiography, the very parameters that define a person's identity inevitably reverberate in the pages of travel accounts. In penning their memoirs, early modern travelers resorted to forms of expression shaped by gender and status, creating what anthropologist Dorinne Kondo has called "languages of identity and inequality."[2] In interviewing male and female employees of a Shitamachi confectionery Kondo noticed how gender molded their stories of work. While the male artisans' tales were constructed around a "linear scenario," women's accounts appeared "fragmentary, almost contingent" and thoroughly devoid of a master narrative.[3] Although Kondo's study focuses on modern-day artisan practices, her findings offer an interesting parallel with the experience of Edo period travelers. Both Kondo's pastry confectioners and the early modern authors of travelogues considered in this study engaged, through a conscious choice of narrative techniques, in a "culturally specific [...] production of selves."[4]

The art of diary writing was unquestionably a gendered one. Men and women approached the blank page along different avenues, traced different characters with their brushes, represented landscapes in different tones and colors, and engaged with their readers in dramatically different ways. As he jotted down the notes of his trip to Mount Fuji in 1768, the samurai Ikegawa Shunsui explained how pilgrims who needed to relieve themselves on the slopes of the sacred mountain would receive permission to do so from the local temples so long as they washed their hands with a special type of water sold by the monks.[5] When another samurai, Sakai Hanjirō, recorded his visit through various renowned locations in Edo in 1860, he spared the reader no detail, even informing his audience of how he accidentally stepped in dog excrement in the Shiba residence of the Satsuma lord.[6] The Confucian scholar Kiyokawa Hachirō infused the record of his 1855 journey with mentions of his stomach problems and the unpleasant side effects of the summer heat that made sweat pour out of his pores "like a waterfall."[7] Few of the women who traveled at the same time as Shunsui, Hanjirō, or Hachirō ever peppered their memoirs with such dosages of scatological and physiological detail. For the female authors of travel journals, refinement was the name of the game; in penning their travelogues they generally employed expressions, references, and rhetorical techniques of great subtlety, along with a great number of quotations from poetic anthologies and landmark works of the Heian period. Though, as always, exceptions do exist, more often than not women shunned direct involvement or confrontation with the subjects of their writings and chose to conceal their opinions behind the veils of literary tradition.

Women's elusive stance is in part attributable to the medium in which they recorded and communicated their thoughts. The diary format (of which travelogues are arguably a subgroup) had been for centuries one of the media, if not *the* medium, female writers were expected to utilize. There is no question that, as a genre, diaries involved a specific set of rules that guided choices in narrative styles, language, and the interaction between author and readership. Diaries, at least the ones written in Japanese, had historically served as elegant receptacles for personal experiences and intimate thoughts and, private as they may appear, were in fact social objects meant to be shared with one's peers.[8]

Because diaries were frequently interlaced with verses, the conventions of poetry also guided the brushes of travelers. Precise rules spelled out the modalities of poetic interaction with space. Outlined in the days of old and transmitted across time, they specified what a cultured traveler was expected to see, and where. Old treatises in the league of Fujiwara Tameaki's *Bamboo Garden Collection* (*Chikuenshō*, 1285), for example, specified that, "In composing poetry on Naniwa Bay, one should write about the reeds even if one cannot see them. When it comes to Akashi and Sarashina, one should compose so that the moon shines brightly even if it is a cloudy evening. As for Yoshino and Shiga, one composes as if the cherry trees are in full bloom even if they are already scattered."⁹

To such genre imperatives gender added more rules of propriety; so while men like Hachirō, Hanjirō, and Shunsui did not hesitate to draw on down-to-earth themes and wink at prosaic details, most women aimed at total sophistication, profusely apologizing for "putting together clumsy lines" that "may make people laugh."¹⁰ Such form of literary conceit may have been heartfelt, but one suspects it could also have been an attempt to emulate Heian period courtier Sei Shōnagon, who with a similar act of contrition had signed off on *The Pillow Book*. The female authors of travelogues tended to appeal to the authority of classic literary tradition to a far greater extent than their male counterparts and, in many cases, to write Edo space as an adaptation, if not a direct projection, of the Heian landscape. Lowbrow tones à la *gesaku* (the comic fiction of the Edo period) and dry humor found little room in the pages of women's travelogues once the combination of gender and genre was completed.

Infused with echoes of the classics and permanently enveloped in the mists of Heian, countless women's travel narratives of the Edo period strike the modern reader as ethereal—at a first glance, in fact, as scarcely genuine, a bit contrived, and utterly frustrating to the historian in search of "tangible" information. Far from being grounds for their dismissal as sources of historical investigation, however, women's preference for intangible lyrical subtleties speaks clearly about their attempts to utilize the blank page as a way to rewrite their lives. While obeying the dictates of genre and gender, some women turned extreme lyricism to their advantage, transforming it into an act of self-assertion. What on the surface appears to be a case of passive adherence to preestablished canons can in fact be read as a deliberate choice that ultimately helped female authors raise their voices. Many of the women considered in this study refined their skills at writing because they sensed that, as Anne Walthall has clearly articulated, "poetry makes a performative break with everyday speech. In so doing, it makes room for voices otherwise marginalized."¹¹ The frustrated historian soon finds out that the "clumsy lines" and the ephemeral quality of early modern women's narratives are in fact the clever expedients some women used to define their identities while reclaiming centrality and agency.

Written works other than poetry-infused travelogues, it ought to be noted, offered women in search of an outlet just as effective an opportunity to question their roles, display their literary knowledge, and forge a bond with the revered literati of the antiquity. At age seventy-seven Kutsukake

Nakako (1749–1829), the wife of a Shinano merchant, wrote a story titled *Tale of a Misty Moonlit Night (Oboroyo monogatari)*. The plot centers around a dream in which Nakako herself meets such cultural icons of past and present as (among others) belles lettres connoisseur Kamo no Mabuchi (1697–1769), the medieval itinerant poet Saigyō (1118–1190), seventeenth-century *haikai* master Matsuo Bashō, and poetry collector extraordinaire Fujiwara Teika (1162–1241)—a literary hall of fame that well expressed her aspiration to partake in a larger-than-life cultural tradition.[12] Other women exploited the blank page to reinvent their identities even without the support of the open road. As Bettina Gramlich-Oka has argued, writing helped Tadano Makuzu (1763–1825) "raise her voice in the public space defined as a male domain." By exploiting the potential embedded in the blank page, Makuzu "not only established her identity; more precisely she redefined it," to the point that novelist Takizawa Bakin (1767–1848) could not help but notice (albeit belatedly) the "manly spirit" *(otokodamashii)* that infused her polemic and somewhat iconoclastic works.[13] Poetess Nozawa Ukō, a disciple of Matsuo Bashō, also transcended gender barriers by means of the brush. As Makoto Ueda has pointed out, Bashō "treated her as a poet above all and gave her exactly the same kind of advice he would have given a male student." Shiba Sonome (1664–1726), another woman who studied under Bashō, also thought of herself as a *bunjin* before she thought of herself as a woman. She would not tend to her chores until her poetry work was completed, at times even leaving the dirty dishes in a tub for days on end.[14]

Men, for their part, had a linguistic option that was rarely available to members of the opposite sex. Sino-Japanese *(kanbun)*, the distinctive language of male writing, was used to produce both official documents and narratives free of emotive involvement, as *Tosa Diary* author Ki no Tsurayuki (883–946) well knew when he defied gender barriers and impersonated a woman in order to avail himself of the emotionally charged medium of *kana*-based Japanese. As Herbert Plutschow noted in reference to the medieval period, the degree of a traveler's detachment from or involvement with the landscape was often mediated at a linguistic level by the possibility of being able to choose between Chinese or Japanese.[15]

In the Edo period, the conscious choice to write in *kanbun* for a woman implicated a deliberate incursion into male territory. It also served as an unmistakable reminder of the porous nature that gender barriers acquired on such flexible platforms as the open road and the blank page. Hara Saihin (1798–1859), daughter of Confucian scholar Hara Kosho, interlaced her travelogues *(Diary of an Excursion to the East* and *Scattered Notes of an Excursion to the East)* with prose and verses in Chinese. While the latter were not especially unusual, the former constituted a bit of a novelty.[16] The adoption of *kanbun* was in fact but one of the many expedients through which Saihin challenged her identity as a woman. Not only did she never marry, she also appeared reluctant to use cosmetics and never cared for fancy hairdos, with the almost expected result that not a few among her peers perceived her as a sort of tomboy. A scholar who worked with her father wrote about Saihin, "She is an extraordinary woman, quite a match for any man. She even drinks like a man." For her part, Saihin confirmed her iconoclastic stance against gender-imposed roles when she declared, "I intend to go my own way as a person rather than as a woman."[17] Precisely because it was so inextricably entwined with gender, the art of writing offered an ideal platform where certain dogmas and boundaries could be put up for discussion.

Engendering Visions: Men, Women, and the Recovery of a Travelscape's Past

Through the comfort and validation of tradition, travelers of both sexes traced familiar coordinates in an otherwise foreign space, using quotation as a way to domesticate and attribute meaning to the unknown. Drawing on an established heritage, travelers superimposed recognizable images onto unfamiliar terrains, effectively mediating between the "personal" (hence predictable) and the "extraneous" (hence potentially volatile). At the intersection of travel and gender, however, the same site could assume peculiar and even strikingly contrasting nuances when seen through the eyes of a man and of a woman, and re-presented through their respective brushes. From time to time gendered criteria seemed to guide wayfarers in selecting among the array of historical and literary memories associated with any given landscape. Though most men poached freely in the preserve of the past, roaming from visions of Heian to glimpses of the age of warriors, some male travelers gave decidedly masculine slants to their recollections. Some women, on the other hand, seemed to be more selective, and appealed if not exclusively at least more frequently to the Heian age and its tradition of relative feminine authority.

Utsunoyama in Suruga Province offers a case in point. When crossing the mountain's steep and dangerous pass many Edo period travelers found comfort in the notion that, in the days of old, as illustrious a traveler as Ariwara no Narihira (the hero of the tenth-century classic *Tales of Ise*) had trodden the same path, "dark, narrow, and overgrown with ivy vines and maples."[18] The wife of Nagoya domain lord Tokugawa Yoshinao (ninth son of Ieyasu) traveling to Edo in 1633, a fifty-two-year-old woman from a family of domain retainers journeying from Edo to Kumamoto in 1782, and the wife of a magistrate en route from Edo to Izumi in 1806 all evoked the ghost of Narihira along the ivy-covered Utsunoyama road.[19] Treading the same path in 1720, the entertainer Takejo failed to explicitly mention the ivy path, but still managed to bow to the illustrious literary precedent. Coming across a pair of itinerant pilgrims, she writes, the thought crossed her mind to entrust them with a letter.[20] The parallel with *Tales of Ise,* in which Narihira encounters a wandering monk in the same location and gives him a message for a lady in the capital, would not have been lost on any reader of the time. Male travelers, too, used *Tales of Ise* as a reference. During his 1750 journey to Atami, for instance, Master Hōkei (Hōkei-shi), the younger brother of Shinto leader Kikkawa Koretaru, likened his encounter with a traveler in Ogasawara (Kai Province) to Narihira's encounter with the monk on Utsunoyama; while seventeen years later, in 1767, samurai and geographer Nagakubo Sekisui (1717–1801) explicitly alluded to the ivy-covered path while crossing Utsunoyama on his way to Nagasaki.[21] Others, however, opted to validate their experience by a different set of associations. Along the same path where seemingly all women and most men envisioned Narihira, for example, Kiyokawa Hachirō conjured up less lyrical, more action-packed images of military deeds. To him, Utsunoyama was first and foremost the site where warrior Yui Shōsetsu (1605–1651) had tried to keep the daimyo of the Western Provinces at bay.[22]

Regardless of their location, virtually all sites had the potential to evoke gendered recollections. Even in an area such as the Kinai region, which more than any other was prone to being transmuted into a classy Heianscape of sorts, Kiyokawa Hachirō remained focused on military actions, battles, and medieval vendettas. The road between Nara and Kyoto becomes, in his account, "truly the stage of many an old battle," paved with memories of the Genpei Wars and of the Nanbokuchō period (fourteenth century). Instead of Narihira and Genji, his visions included Kusunoki Masashige (1294–1336) and Emperor Go-Daigo (1288–1339), whose deeds alone qualified certain areas as "absolute must-sees" *(kanarazu ki o tome mirubeki nari).*[23] Visiting Suma (Settsu Province) in 1777, a female traveler remarked that "since time immemorial this has been a famous place" and made it a point to visit Suma Temple and "the remains of the house where Genji the Shining Prince lived [while in exile]."[24] Two years later, a male visitor, writer Ueda Akinari (1734–1809), also connected Suma to *The Tale of Genji,* but with a more critical attitude—he warned that the novel had "no historical truth" and was to be read "for entertainment only."[25] A similar hint of skepticism toward the authority of the Heian past appears in the notes of scholar Furukawa Koshōken (1726–

1807), who arrived in Suma in 1783. Koshōken showed awareness of the literary precedent embedded in the landscape but at the end of the day was far more impressed with the natural setting of a nearby beach.[26] Despite the traditional association between the site and the exiled literary icon, while on location in 1855, Hachirō caught no glimpses of Genji's ghost and directed his attention to the military enterprises of Taira no Atsumori (1169–1184) and to the epic clash between the Taira and the Minamoto at nearby Ichinotani.[27] Similarly, the samurai Kawai Tsugunosuke (1827–1868), who visited Suma in 1859, did not elaborate on the site's connection to the exile of the Shining Prince. He briefly glanced at Suma Temple from afar and only cared to visit the graves of Taira no Kiyomori, Atsumori, and Tadanori.[28]

One may argue that travelers were often overwhelmed by the sheer number of historical and literary suggestions available at certain sites and simply picked some at random. While that may sometimes have been the case, it is also undeniable that some of the wayfarers considered in this study display a keen awareness of the gendered character of the past. They readily acknowledge it and openly confess that they chose their recollections accordingly. Kiyokawa Hachirō once again offers a poignant example. Central Japan reverberated with glimpses of Takeda Shingen's (1521–1573) battles against his archenemy Uesugi Kenshin (1530–1578). While transiting through the area, Hachirō did not have time to stop for a moon viewing along the Kiso Road but still managed to "inspect rather carefully the battlefield at Kawanakajima"—one of the many stages of the conflict between Shingen and Kenshin.[29] What Hachirō looked for in central Japan—as in many other places he visited—were, undeniably, visions of a somewhat masculine military past. As he himself tells us, giving his reasoning a remarkably gender-specific tone, "If you are a man *(danshi naraba)*, this is the kind of place you must see and pay attention to."[30] Conversely, when a female traveler, Tsuchiya Ayako, arrived at Owari in 1806, she acknowledged that the region had been the site of a great many battles of old, but quickly added, "these are topics women know nothing about, so I will leave it at that."[31] Women's preference for the Heian past may have been influenced not only by the accessibility of texts composed in "women's hand" but also, possibly, by an implicit identification between the Heian period and female agency. It was precisely this association that may also have motivated early Edo period Confucian moralists and sinologists to attack *The Tale of Genji* and *Tales of Ise* as lewd, immoral, and overall unsuitable for women.[32]

Though prominent among women writers, the tendency to see space through the lens of lyricism was by no means exclusive to Narihira-loving, Genji-worshipping female wayfarers. One need only mention Matsuo Bashō, arguably the most famous Edo period traveler, to fully comprehend the devotion with which the educated brought to light the historical and lyrical dimensions of any given landscape.[33] As extraordinarily talented as he was, Bashō was not an exception, for poaching upon the literary past attracted a number of other male authors. The journey to the far north that the Edoite Tomita Koreyuki and his companion, the monk Yamakage, began in the spring of 1777, for example, was specifically motivated by their desire to visit an array of locations made famous by art and poetry. Koreyuki's travelogue includes numerous references to the medieval itinerant monk and poet Saigyō, uses terms that pertain to the world of Heian aesthetics (the "melancholy of fleetingness," for instance), and recounts a great many historical anecdotes and tales of local lore.[34]

On occasion, less erudite male travelers, as well, would garnish their works with a stylish footnote or two. While he tended to look at the world through the practical eyes of a merchant, Nagoya retailer Hishiya Heishichi (n.d.) was not completely immune to the allure of literary references. On the road he composed his own verses and quoted from such classics as the *Anthology of Ten Thousand Leaves* (*Man'yōshū,* ca. 760), the *New Collection of Ancient and Recent Poems* (*Shinkokinshū,* thirteenth century), and even from Bashō himself.[35] To Heishichi, however, literary interludes represented but a marginal part of a more comprehensive travel experience. Rather than veiling his scenes in the thin mists of the classical past, Heishichi has left us a portrait of a bustling, lively Edo landscape, a space where people ran to and fro, boats delivered goods, shops advertised local specialties, and merchants conducted profitable businesses. One may argue that Heishichi felt no need to re-create his identity completely by wearing the imaginary robes of a poet of the antiquity or a courtier, simply because as a man (and a wealthy textile retailer no less!) he wore fairly comfortable clothes already.

Overall, the ability to cite from pertinent classics empowered travelers of both sexes to bask in the glow of literary tradition, as the diary compiled by Mukai Kyorai and his fifteen-year-old sister, Chine, reveals.[36] The two left Kyoto in 1686 headed for the Great Shrine of Ise. The son and daughter of a Confucian scholar, Kyorai and Chine were well versed in the classics, and travel provided them with the opportunity to display their erudition. As their status and education demanded, they frequently employed conventional imagery from poetic anthologies of the past to transfigure both the time and the space of their journey into quintessential poetic concepts. Although they departed in the fall, they never directly mention the season. Instead, they resort to a sequence of visual suggestions drawn from the heritage of poetic tradition, hinting at the time of the year by the extensive use of evocative terms commonly associated with autumn—fog, wild geese, clover, and deer, among others.³⁷ It is through poetry that Kyorai and Chine obliquely and elegantly set the seasonal coordinates:

Ise made no	Wild geese this morning:
yoki michizure yo	good travel companions
Kesa no kari	on the way to Ise.

Space is also translated in lyrical terms through the use of poem-pillows *(utamakura),* place-names that elegantly allude to precise locations by association. The itinerary through the provinces of Ōmi, Yamashiro, and Ise is transfigured into a passage from symbol to symbol: Nio no Umi (a traditional poem-pillow for Ōmi), Shirakawa (indicating Yamashiro), and Suzuka (a signifier for Ise). The gender-directed associations of Hachirō and Ayako on one side and the coauthored work of Kyorai and Chine on the other confirm that the open road and the blank page were flexible areas where travelers could either polish their gendered differences or overcome them altogether by finding common ground in the embrace of literary heritage.

Gender, however, was not the only factor that inspired the writings of Edo period travelers. The purpose of establishing an intertextual correlation between one's diary and the classics varied also on the basis of occupation and status. Among women of the social and cultural elites, ability with the brush was a prerequisite to consolidating one's place and validating one's role at the center of one's social and cultural universe, while among authors of lesser stock it helped to reshape and reinvent identities altogether.

Confirming Identities through the Written Word: Samurai and Literati Women

Elite women on the road often used the written word to validate their spatial and social hierarchies. In 1639, only four years after the alternate attendance policy had become fully official, the wife of Nakagawa Hisamori, lord of Oka domain, left Edo to visit Ikaho. Her journey to the hot-spring resort may have had therapeutic purposes or may have been, as was often the case with confined wives of lords, a convenient excuse to obtain permission to leave Edo. Whatever the case, Lady Nakagawa chose to commit her experience to paper as a thoroughly cultural mission and concocted a Heian-mediated rendition of her adventure. The opening of her *Record of [a Trip to] Ikaho (Ikahoki)* is, in language and format, a declaration of dependence on the validation of the classics: "People have traveled to a place called Ikaho attracted by its hot springs. They have come back and recounted all the fascinating things [they saw] in the mountain villages. I wanted to see for myself, I wanted to experience that world. At the same time, I craved to see the myriad of flowers on the Musashi Plain. In mid-autumn, when the moon still lingered in the early morning sky, I arose with the dew and departed."[38]

These first lines immediately draw the reader into a narrative time and space far removed from the Edo period. The world that Lady Nakagawa declares she wished to experience at the outset of her memoir is, one suspects, not so much that of her own day and age as the world of courtiers and literary icons of earlier times. Her allusions to the flowers of the Musashi Plain, the dew, and the autumn moon also set the mood for a lyrically infused atmosphere. The Chinese bellflowers *(kikyō),* miscanthus reeds *(karukaya),* yellow-flowered valerian *(ominaeshi),* pampas grass *(hanasusuki),* and gentians *(ryūtan)* Lady Nakagawa describes in her diary were all recognizable lyrical tropes that helped her to establish a connection with the poetic anthologies of the past.[39]

The spirit of Narihira in particular looms large in Lady Nakagawa's understanding of the road from Edo to Ikaho. At Mount Asama, upon whose slopes the gaze of Narihira had lingered centuries before, Lady Nakagawa abides by the rules of lyrical travel and comments, "Today, the smoke billowing from Asama peak celebrated in the verses of Ariwara Chūjō [Narihira] [. . .] is not visible."[40] Through this comment Lady Nakagawa displays literary sophistication and affirms her worth by creating an instant connection between her time and the glorious days of the Heian court.

Topographical inconsistencies did not deter our traveler in her pursuit of lyrical interludes. Banished from the imperial capital for having an inappropriate affair, Narihira had traveled from the core of courtly refinement, Heian (Kyoto), to the remote eastern regions. Our lady, on the other hand, set out from that very East the Heian courtiers abhorred and journeyed from a castle town rising out of a swamp to a hot-spring resort. In spite of the obvious discrepancy between the two experiences, she nonchalantly presented her journey as a mirror of Narihira's "descent to the East" *(Azuma kudari)*. Like Narihira's, Lady Nakagawa's trip involves detachment from a radiant center (not Kyoto but Edo) and descent into the unknown wilderness of the peripheries, which she appropriately labels "the deep East" *(Azuma no oku,* akin to "the middle of nowhere"). Lady Nakagawa frames her adventure around the dichotomy between urban and rural, between familiar comforts, splendor, and beauty on the one side, and alien hardships, gloom, and inelegance on the other: "In the detached cottage there was an old woman wearing some sooty cotton headgear and layers of old-looking robes. Her hands were pulled back inside the sleeves and she appeared ashamed of her own boorishness."[41] As her unsympathetic portrayal of the countrywoman indicates, the antithetical juxtaposition of center and periphery not only functions as evidence of Lady Nakagawa's proximity to the cultural elites but also sustains her construction of a social hierarchy. The diary, in other words, becomes a pretext to reassert her superior stance vis-à-vis the unrefined boors she encounters along the way.

Not unlike Narihira, who in Michinoku had come across "the wife of a commonplace fellow" and had realized "to his surprise that she was not at all the ordinary sort of person he had expected,"[42] Lady Nakagawa does make room for the serendipitous discovery of beauty, culture, and refinement in the backwoods. At an inn, for example, she notices the owner's young daughter, "a beautiful little girl with charming eyes and lips." Enthralled by the sight, she wonders whether "even in the middle of nowhere *(Azuma no oku)* there can be such beauty." On yet another occasion an innkeeper produces, much to our traveler's amazement, copies of three famous poetic anthologies of the past. Faced with such an unexpected gleam of sophistication, Lady Nakagawa declares, "even these mountain peasants have a heart" *(kakaru yamagatsu mo kokoro wa arikeri).* In Lady Nakagawa's construction of social, cultural, and spatial hierarchies, access to and familiarity with the classics could bridge the gap between center and periphery on the one hand and between commoners and elites on the other. By the same token, the ability to perceive the lyrical subtleties of seasonal and natural phenomena, topics par excellence of classical poetry, also had the power to humanize otherwise worthless common folks, as the following verses, which Lady Nakagawa finds etched on a tree and incorporates in her diary, demonstrate:

Toshi nami no	This maple
tatsu to mo shiranu	infuses spirit
yamagatsu ni	in these mountain folks
kokoro o tsukuru	who otherwise would not even notice
momiji nari keri	the passing of time.[43]

But in the middle of nowhere these glimpses of elegance were few and far between. Lady Nakagawa's journey could only function as a perfect mirror of Narihira's if the peripheries were ultimately represented as forlorn wastelands where only distant and feeble echoes of refinement could be heard. Unable to match the perfect luster of the city, rural beauty had to remain imperfect, slightly tainted. The paradigm, in this respect, was once again *Tales of Ise*. The woman Narihira encounters in Michinoku turns out in the end to have "the heart of a simple rustic."[44] Likewise, the charm of the girl who had caught Lady Nakagawa's eye at the country inn is flawed because "the white robe she wore was untidy and she came running through the door." Even the cultured innkeeper who had surprised Lady Nakagawa with not one but three poetic anthologies ends up being surrounded by nothing but simpletons. After being shown the three collections, Lady Nakagawa asks for a copy of *The Tale of Genji,* to which an attendant replies: "What did you say? Genshū? That is quite an unusual name. [. . .] That is a person's name, right? Or is it a type of container? No, it is the name of a Buddhist monk. I know I have heard it somewhere." Lady Nakagawa's excitement instantly turns into amusement, and her final assessment of the experience is a condescending "We had no shortage of laughable moments."[45] The imperfect quaintness of the peripheries effectively reinforces, by contrast, the flawless glow of the center. Travel writing, elevated to the rank of lyrical exercise and transfigured into a form of sociocultural mapmaking, allowed the likes of Lady Nakagawa to affirm their status as members of an educated, powerful, and—at least to them—central elite.

EQUALLY INTENSE, the professional literati's interaction with lyrical heritage served a dual function. While keeping a tradition alive, it also defined the authors as skilled men (or women) of letters, worthy of admission into prestigious cultural circles. To the aspiring members of the literary elite, invoking the blessing of lyrical lineage was an imperative. As Steven Carter observed, doing so in the context of travel constituted a sort of professional rite of passage. The authors' competence was tested through the process of proving themselves capable of instantly recovering a site's literary precedent.[46] The implications were professional as much as they were social, for authors solidified their membership in the inner literary circles by the simple act of searching for validation in the same cultural direction as had their predecessors and peers. While visiting Enoshima, for instance, both the lord Tokugawa Mitsukuni (1628–1700), a man of letters and member of the Mito branch of the Tokugawa family, and the Edo poet Hakuei quoted in their travelogues the same verses attributed to recluse-author Kamo no Chōmei (1155–1216).[47] Their simultaneous recognition of a common literary model bridged the seventy-year span that separated their individual journeys (Mitsukuni traveled in 1674, Hakuei in 1744) and, at the same time, sanctioned their belonging to a timeless community of scholars.

Because literary groups included men and women alike, it is not surprising that female literati would strive to unearth the poetic past of landscapes just as eagerly and zealously as their male colleagues. On 1777/2/9 Arakida

Reijo and her husband, Ise Shrine priest Keitoku Ietada, set out on a two-month journey that would take them to Kyoto, Osaka, Suma, Yamato, and Nara. The feast of lyrical and historical assonances available in the region made Reijo feel slightly overwhelmed. "Before our eyes, famous location after famous location. I cannot begin to say how blessed this place is," she wrote on Mount Yoshino.[48] It was in the course of this journey that she used her memoir and her educated engagements with the travelscape as ways to claim her identity as a transmitter of literary tradition.

Born in Ise Yamada, at age thirteen Reijo had been adopted by Arakida Taketomo, a priest of the Outer Shrine. Despite its prevalent role as a religious center, in the second half of the eighteenth century Ise also thrived as a cultural microcosm. Philologist and nativist scholar Motoori Norinaga (1730–1801, two years Reijo's senior) headed his prestigious school in nearby Matsusaka, while at the same time the rival school founded by Ise priest Arakida Hisaoyu (1746–1804) thrived in Yamada.[49] There is no record of Reijo ever having met the two cultural icons in person, though we know she did have a brief exchange of opinions with Norinaga—he disapproved of her drawing on Chinese sources and she replied by calling him, among other things, a "phony."[50] Be it by way of praise or of criticism, Reijo unquestionably benefited from the intellectual effervescence of the area around Ise. Because of her husband's position, moreover, she was granted access to the Miyazaki Bunko, a library for the use of the local clergy. The support of her adoptive family first and of her husband later also played a key role in her formation as a scholar. Reijo, in short, grew up and lived in an environment that nurtured her intellectual aspirations.

Themes and images of classical literature profoundly influenced Reijo's works, from her historical novels to her poetry, from her scattered literary jottings *(zuihitsu)* to her travel memoirs. In this case the display of literary knowledge served the purpose of solidifying Reijo's identity as a woman of letters, a goal she achieved with a mixture of consummate proficiency and great subtlety. During her 1777 journey, for example, Reijo came to an unstable log bridge in Kiso. In her diary she recounts how, in order to muster up the courage to cross over, she "thought of it as if it were the Suzuka road." "As for the roar of the river running below," she adds, "I thought of it as the melody of a koto."

Koto no ne ni   A mountain torrent
kore mo ya kayou   runs underneath
marukibashi   the log bridge
shita ni nagaruru   I crossed
yamakawa no mizu   to the sound of a koto.[51]

By detailing the way in which she defeated adversity by calling upon literary themes Reijo celebrated her identity as a poet. Not only did she succeed in evoking the image of a location made famous by poetry (Suzuka, a lyrical symbol of Ise Province), she also demonstrated her familiarity with the long-established tradition of using verses as amulets. Poetry making had long served the ritual function of generating the illusion of a safe passage into the unknown, acting "as a charm for the spiritual as well as the physical safety and well-being of the traveler."[52] In this respect the farewell poems of the *Man'yōshū,* virtual talismans whose messages generated a sense of reassurance and protection ("Travel safely and be fortunate!"), had set a solid precedent.[53] As an educated wayfarer Reijo knew this all too well and, in her inventiveness, she actually paid homage to tradition.

Reijo crafted her persona as a literary traveler also in preparation for her second major journey, which took her from Ise to Kyoto and other sites of the Kansai region in 1782. Even on this occasion Reijo valued poetic opportunities as chances to prove herself worthy of inclusion in the literati society. Near the village of Ōno she and her husband followed the road to a Miroku statue only to find out that, as the "narrow path shaded by the gorges went around and into the deep heart of the mountains, [. . .] all signs of human presence disappeared. No longer did we hear the birds cry. The cliffs echoed the roar of a river flowing through the wild gorges." The true literary traveler, Reijo saw this as an opportunity to compose a poem to capture the moment:

Michi mo nashi	The path has disappeared.
tsuyu nomi musubu	Scooping up nothing but dew,
haru no kusa	springtime grasses.[54]

The ability to translate situations into verses needed to be complemented with a flawless understanding of the cartographies of lyricism. Reijo does not disappoint in this respect either. Overall, her writings reveal the extent of her knowledge and her ability to navigate the waters of poetic citation. Her mention of "the Shiga Pass of the old days" suggests that she recognized the literary pedigree of the site. Coming down the same pass, she recalls "that old poem about the wind in the deep mountain river."[55] The reference is to the verses Heian period poet Harumichi no Tsuraki (?–920) had composed about the same site:

Yamagawa ni	The autumn leaves are
kaze no kaketaru	unable to resist the
shiragami wa	current flowing past

nagare mo aenu	the weir built by the wind
momiji narikeri	in the deep mountain river.[56]

Likewise, her description of a cloud-veiled Mount Ikoma winks at *Tales of Ise* and at *Shinkokinshū,* both of which contain lyrics that celebrate the very same site,[57] while the sight of Nunobiki Falls triggers memories of "the words of those [who saw it] in the past."[58] The legacy of the classics resurfaces as she crosses Aoyama on 1782/3/9 and writes, "As I saw the flowers blooming on all the trees around me, I was moved [by the ephemeral]."[59] Her perception of the "melancholy of fleetingness" reveals once again Reijo's indebtedness to the classic tradition, which had made of this notion one of its key themes.

Reijo's recovery of the past was, in general terms, as utilitarian in purpose as Lady Nakagawa's. In Reijo's case, however, it was not motivated by the will to make a statement about social hierarchies, as by the professional imperatives of the literati. Before being a woman, before being the member of a family associated with a religious "center," Reijo saw herself as a *bunjin* and organized her geocultural priorities accordingly. As a woman of letters she was expected to reclaim every bit of historical and poetic memory embedded in the landscape, masculine echoes of warrior glory and feminine hues of aristocratic heydays alike. Reijo delivered, recovering glimpses of Saigyō and of twelfth-century samurai Taira no Yasuyori, of "the plum tree [that filled] the quivers of the Minamoto clan's warriors" in Ikuta no Mori, of medieval warriors such as Minamoto no Yoriyoshi, Yorinobu, and Yoshiie in Sakai, and of "the vestiges of Prince Shōtoku's days" in Nara.[60]

In Reijo's writings rarely do the peripheries assume the negative connotations that travelers like Lady Nakagawa attributed to them. Even in the boondocks Reijo always finds a warm human element that enriches her experience. Of the village of Ishitsu, near Sakai, she writes, "this is very rustic, there is nothing amiable, and yet the innkeeper is such a compassionate person."[61] Whereas the dichotomy between urban and rustic had impelled Lady Nakagawa to buttress her affiliation with a glitzy center, for the men and women of letters the same contrast underscored the lyrical potential of forlorn, dilapidated sites. It was before abandoned moss-covered monuments that Reijo and her fellow *bunjin* most effectively identified themselves as mediators between heritage and novelty, past and present. Matsuo Bashō, the exemplary traveling poet of the early modern period, had paved the way for the practice of savoring decay in his numerous poetic diaries and his famous history-filled verses ("A thicket of summer grass / is all that remains / of the dreams and ambitions / of ancient warriors").[62] Reijo followed suit. Visiting

Tenma Shrine in Naniwa, she noticed "a series of stone monuments lined up one after the other" and, like Bashō, infused them with the power to open a doorway into the past. "These are the spirits *(kami)* of the men who lost their lives on the battlefield," she wrote, adding:

Na zo nokoru	The lords whose names still
nushi wa mukashi no	remain: once upon a time
haru no yuki	a springtime snow.[63]

Touring Kyoto's sites in 1777, Reijo rejoiced at the number of locations reverberating with mirages of history and exclaimed, "I truly believed I saw the past." To her, the glory of the Silver Pavilion stemmed from its value as a gateway into history; the patina of time only enhanced the site's enduring appeal ("this place's fame goes back a long time"). "It is extremely beautiful," she remarked, *"and covered in the dust of time."*[64] The insistence upon the possibility of creating a connection between past and present through poetry is a recurrent theme in Reijo's travelogues and an explicit assertion of the literati's role as preservers of an invaluable heritage.

Where Lady Nakagawa had described with pomp and circumstance her reentry into the splendor of the city, Reijo came to the end of her 1777 journey with a mixture of joy and nostalgia. The road and the travelogue had allowed her to practice, justify, and glorify her art and, by extension, her professional persona. Crossing the Miya River toward Ise, she looked at the opposite bank and felt overcome by "an uncommon mood." As the sun set behind the trees, the last blank page of her memoir waited to be filled. Reijo's final words celebrated travel as the ideal platform for the literati to connect ephemeral poetic images and actual sites:

Kage takaki	One tree on the peak
mine no hitoki wa	casting a long shadow
tabibito o	is the spot
matsu shirushi to mo	where travelers pine.
kyō koso wa mire	Today I saw it.[65]

Writing Escapism: Educated Townswomen on the Road

In the second half of the Edo period, commoners became exposed to the literary pedigree of famous sites through the filtered versions of the classics featured in popular literature and gained access to a poetic tradition that had thus far largely eluded them. As a result it became increasingly commonplace for sightseers of more humble origins to fashion themselves as cultured travelers and for their memoirs to be infused with elegant citations. The era that had begun with a restricted elite of courtiers, warriors, and literati composing elegant memoirs to affirm their worth rapidly evolved into a time when commoners, too, traveled the road of education toward the goal of erudition.[66] With such expansion in the pool of cultured wayfarers the function of the engagement between visitors and landscapes underwent a transformation. For the townspeople and other travelers of commoner stock, diaries often served as instruments of escapism. Those who learned to connect the past and present of certain sites could, like the members of the social and intellectual elites, look down on the unsophisticated.[67] Proficiency with the brush enabled educated commoners to take a symbolic step up the social ladder by associating and in some cases even identifying themselves with prominent literary and historical figures of the past.

Women, again, seemed particularly active in this respect. The composition of poetry-infused diaries allowed them to latch on to a tradition shaped by female courtiers and, by extension, presented them with the possibility of reimagining their place in society. With the exception of the professional literati, men did not pursue this re-creational avenue as eagerly, for, as Anne Walthall has noted, they "could compartmentalize their identity by using different names for their political, familial, and aesthetic activities, putting them on and taking them off like clothing."[68] Men's spaces, in other words, were already sufficiently flexible and allowed for a certain margin of agency. Wealthy townsmen, for instance, found an immediate, convenient, and satisfying avenue to re-creating their personas beyond the gates of red-light districts, where money eclipsed status in mediating access to services. Within the precincts of entertainment quarters the visual distinction between commoner and samurai ceased to exist, for all weapons were left at the gates and ostentation in clothing did not necessarily indicate superiority in status. The pleasure quarter was, in this respect, just as great an equalizer as the open road and the blank page. Where money talked the townsmen ruled, as chronicler Miura Jōshin noted when he observed that the women of the pleasure quarters would "see anyone for the right price, regardless of their high or low status."[69] Paragons of sophistication, high-level courtesans could also assert their agency in the space of the red-light district (for instance, by refusing to serve certain customers). For all other townswomen, precluded from enjoying the status-bending atmosphere of the licensed quarter, the detachment provided by literary travel remained one of the few available outlets for personal re-creation.

Some scholars have emphasized the impact that the rapid changes associated with the crumbling of the Tokugawa order in the mid-nineteenth century had on the ability of women to embrace new roles.[70] Evidence from travel memoirs, however, suggests that, by exploiting the many possibilities of the open road and the blank page, female wayfarers had devised opportunities to quietly manipulate their social coordinates well before the collapse of the Tokugawa. Even during times of relative political stability travel carried one into an extraordinary space and time, an ideal platform for envisioning change. For early modern female travelers, the faint recollection of an episode from *The Tale of Genji* or of a verse from celebrated poetic anthologies of the past could signify the difference between "just" seeing and actively engaging, between being a spectator or an actor on the stage of self-validation. To borrow the words of Michel de Certeau, educated townswomen of the Edo period elevated their narratives to "the art of making a *coup*."[71]

It was indeed by means of forays into the past that Yuya Shizuko (1733–1752), the daughter of a merchant and purveyor to the government from Edo Kyōbashi, staged her coup. Educated under scholar Kamo no Mabuchi, at the age of seventeen Shizuko took the trip from Edo to Ikaho described in her diary, *On the Way to Ikaho* (*Ikaho no michi yukiburi,* 1750).[72] As Lady Nakagawa had done over one century earlier, Shizuko did not present her journey to a hot-spring resort for what it most likely was—a therapeutic trip. Her writing is characterized by the presence of remarkably visionary passages, by the extended use of poetic imagery drawn from the classics, and by a profusion of Japanese-style poetry. The townswoman Shizuko chose to play, on paper, the part of an elegant *bunjin* and occasionally of a quasi-aristocrat.

Shizuko, her mother, and a friend departed on 1750/3/10. The record of her journey opens with verses that include the term "grass pillow" *(kusa no makura)*. Since "grass pillow" was a standard metaphor for travel and for the hardships it entailed, it is not surprising that Shizuko employed such a conventional image at the onset of her work. Hers, however, was more than a perfunctory association: it was a conscious attempt to establish from the start an inextricable link with a poetic tradition that was pervaded with grass pillows as much as it was with other images dear to Shizuko—dew-drenched grasses, mist-veiled plains, and the distant cries of wild geese and bush warblers, to name a few.[73] The arrival at Ikaho, far from occasioning a description of the bathing facilities, provides her with yet another chance to reiterate her connection with the classic tradition by recycling the analogy between cherry blossoms and snowflakes.

Okuyama wa	In the deep of the mountains
hana yori nochi no	when the snow
yuki mo areba	outlasts the blossoms
yuki yori nochi no	I doubt we will see blossoms
hana mo mitemashi	outlast the snow.[74]

A dazzling sequence of codified lyrical images also illustrates Shizuko's departure from Ikaho: blooming wisterias gracing the eaves of the roofs, the cry of the cuckoo *(hototogisu)* intensifying the anguish of separation, and gloomy skies crossed by floating clouds *(ukigumo)*. These conventional tropes served the purpose of sophisticating Shizuko's narrative by hinting rather than expressing and, as a consequence, of elevating both work and author. As in the case of Lady Nakagawa, the practical implications of Shizuko's stay at the hot-spring resort are completely overshadowed by the intent to turn the travelogue into a poetic exercise. As a result, Shizuko makes little or no room for references to everyday activities. The rarefied scenery Shizuko depicts does not include farmers at work in the fields, other travelers marching along the same road, or roadside vendors peddling their merchandise. In her narrative, she removes herself from the reality of her times and sets out to reach not so much the Ikaho of the present as the projection of an evocative poetry-land from the days of old.

The devotion with which Shizuko and her travel companions quoted famous lines and composed some of their own while going to a hot-spring resort underscores the extent to which certain commoners strove to polish their personas on the road and on paper. So deep was Shizuko's identification with her idealized image of the classy, elegant traveler, that at Suieiji she displayed an attitude more reminiscent of Sei Shōnagon (with her contemptuous likening of commoners to basket worms)[75] or of Lady Nakagawa than of a character from the floating world. She writes, "I intended to offer my portable bookcase, but some boorish countrywomen *(inakameitaru onna)* were all standing in that one place. It was noisy and hard to take, so I left promptly."[76] By underscoring the contrast between herself and the group of uncouth women Shizuko determines what constitutes high and low in her social hierarchy and claims a central and superior position therein.

Like that of Lady Nakagawa, Shizuko's narrative, too, can be read as a textual effort to emulate Narihira's descent to the East. On the way home the group reaches Sano no Funabashi, a famous landmark of Kōzuke Province.[77] Here Shizuko notices how disconnected the site is from its lyrical image and concludes that "only the name has survived" *(na nomi nokorite)*.[78] At a first glance one may be tempted to interpret Shizuko's observation as a long-awaited touch of realism: she is finally opening her eyes and describing an Edo period landscape. And yet, the glow of poetic tradition still blurred her vision. Not only was Sano no Funabashi a poetic trope of respectable lineage,[79] it was also an expedient through which Shizuko cleverly, if indirectly, reconnected with the world of Narihira. Many travelers before (and after) her journeyed to Yatsuhashi (in Mikawa Province) only to remark that the irises admired by the protagonist of *Tales of Ise* no longer existed and only the name remained.[80] To the townswoman Shizuko, en route from the hot springs of Ikaho back to Edo, Sano no Funabashi may have offered a convenient surrogate of Yatsuhashi and an excuse to indulge in the melancholic transition between the literary past and the reality of the present.

Shizuko's pragmatic manipulation of topography was not an isolated incident. An anonymous female traveler from Edo, probably the member of an affluent mercantile family, traveled to Sagami Province in 1767 to visit the Benzaiten cave in Enoshima.[81] In her writings the anonymous townswoman made no effort to conceal her acute gender consciousness. For example, when a male travel companion judged the Great Buddha of Kamakura against similar statues he had seen around the country, she commented, "I envy him for having visited so many special places, but for a woman this is impossible" *(onna nite areba kahinashiya)*. She was equally aware of her identity as a townsperson. Seeing a group of children on the beach in Kanagawa, for instance, she wrote, "they were country people *(inakaudo)*, so it was quite a novelty." Having acknowledged her gender and status coordinates, she proceeded to transform her journey and her memoir into the instruments of self-aggrandizement. She recorded her experience in a work titled *Diary of the Azuma Road (Azumaji no nikki);* the very choice of the name "Azuma" in the title reveals a deliberate intention to define her work, and by extension her own persona, as grounded in the world of the Shining Prince and of Ariwara no Narihira. The text that follows also confirms her longing for a connection with the classics. While crossing Tsurumi (lit. "Crane View") Bridge, she marveled at discovering that there were in fact no cranes in sight. "I asked whether there was a good reason [for such discrepancy], but nobody knew," she writes, immediately adding:

Inishie wa	Once upon a time
chitose no kage ya	it reflected
utsurikemu	countless images.
Tsurumi no hashi no	Tsurumi Bridge:
na nomi nagarete	all that drifts [under it now] is its name.

In Kamakura she expressed a similar disappointment when the Bridge of Poetry at Egara Tenjin turned out to be smaller than she had envisioned. One cannot but notice that such criticism conveniently served as the vector for a stylish historical footnote on the one hand ("this used to be one of Kamakura's famous ten bridges") and for a clever nod toward the glorious days of old on the other, for also at the Bridge of Poetry, as at Yatsuhashi, Sano no Funabashi, and Tsurumi Bridge, "all that remains is the name."

The townswoman Kikuchi Tamiko (1785–1864), who traveled across Musashi and Sagami Provinces in 1821, also wrote her escape from the ordinary in a travelogue. The wife of a merchant from Edo Nihonbashi, she had chosen her destination "after hearing about it for the longest time in the tales of others." Tamiko, who was well educated, attributed meaning and worth to a site only on the basis of its inclusion (or lack thereof) in the pages of classical literature. In Kanagawa she doubted the authenticity of a mound commemorating folktale hero Urashima Tarō "because no mention of such a monument being located in this area appears in legitimate texts of the past." She attributed value to Koshigoe as "the place where, in the days of old, Yoshitsune's attempt to enter Kamakura was halted," and rejoiced at the sight of Katase and Shichirigahama not because of their stunning vistas but because the sea, the clouds, and the waves "look exactly as [they are described] in the poems I have read."[82]

Tamiko used her ability to retrieve historical or literary precedent to make a statement about (and call into question) her gender and social coordinates. In Kanazawa she confesses her inability to describe the splendor of the famous eight sceneries by claiming, "for a shallow-brained woman as myself, this takes all the heart and all her verbal abilities." What on the surface appears as an admission of inferiority, and based on gender no less, represents in fact a clever act of re-creation. In recognizing her limitations Tamiko established a direct connection with an illustrious (male) icon of the past, the ninth-century artist Kose no Kanaoka, famous for having dropped his brush before the same landscape for the very same reason. There is no question that Tamiko was familiar with Kanaoka's legend, for in the same diary she writes: "Here is the so-called Brush Drop Pine. A talented famous painter of the past, a certain Kanaoka, thought he would depict this scenic view, so he picked up his brush. Amazingly, the scenery changed quickly before his eyes. Realizing he was not up to the task, he ended up dropping the brush."[83] The brush thus became the instrument through which Tamiko engaged in an act of virtual self-identification with Kanaoka. In an instant she bent the parameters that defined her as a merchant and wife by bridging the gap between past and present, between legendary artist and commoner, between man and woman. Through the establishment of a common denominator linking her world to a tradition that resonated with courtly echoes, Tamiko distanced herself from the Nihonbashi shop where she spent most of her days and imagined herself less as the wife of a cotton wholesaler and pawnshop owner and more as a respected cultural icon—no better, but also no less, than a man.

Deference or Parody? Reverberating Echoes or Silenced Voices?

Given the often iconoclastic character of Edo literature, one must wonder whether some of the female authors discussed here were in fact parodying the classics rather than trying to emulate them. A tongue-in-cheek approach to tradition was not at all uncommon in the literary production of the time—and *Tales of Ise* and *The Tale of Genji* were among the preferred targets.[84] The possibility exists, then, that some authors of travel diaries might have in fact been lampooning the past and spoofing its dogmas. The line between deference and parody may be clear in works of fiction bearing such irreverent titles as *The Dog Pillow (Inu makura)* or *Sham Tales of Ise (Nise monogatari)*, but the true intentions of travelogue authors who played with literary tradition are more difficult to assess. When Yuya Shizuko winks at *Tales of Ise* by transposing Yatsuhashi onto Sano no Funabashi, is she "seriously" in awe of a cultural precedent or is she intentionally devaluing it by uprooting it from its original geographical and chronological coordinates? How do we tell calculated mockery from clumsy but otherwise sincere lyricism?

The problem is best dealt with by looking at it from a different angle and asking a different question: is burlesque distortion irreconcilable with the notion that diary writing served as a way for authors to reenvision their roles? The answer, in this case, is no. Parody does not ipso facto rule out re-creation, for it still entails recognition of and homage to a literary precedent, it still necessitates an act of association between past and present authors and, most important, it definitely underscores a good degree of ambition, audacity, and even arrogance on the part of the parodist, who rejects a given order and creates a new one (however topsy-turvy), placing his or her mode of interpretation at the center. Whether by way of emulation or by way of mockery, the aspiring litterateurs of the age managed to set their own rules and to place themselves solidly in the spotlight. But for how long?

As profoundly as these travelers identified their experience with the likes of Narihira or Sei Shōnagon, and as effective as travel was in providing a welcome break from the ordinary, one wonders how far-reaching the consequences of literary re-creation could be. In *Carnival in Romans,* Emmanuel Le Roy Ladurie argues that the space and time apart of the carnival festivities, which are similar to travel in their challenge to normative rules, constituted a learning experience "that entailed the potential for progress."[85] In the same vein, one may wonder whether the effects of re-creational travel allowed for a permanent transformation in the minds of the women who had reimagined themselves or whether the diversion was only temporary. Did the ability to reinvent oneself remain confined to the space and time of the journey, or did the travelers' homecoming coincide with a new beginning of sorts?

As rites of passage into adulthood, certain types of travel had permanent transformative effects. The Nagoya merchant Hishiya Heishichi, for instance, admitted in his 1802 diary that "every journey entails plenty of difficulties. As the saying goes, 'Send a cherished child on a journey.' [...] In all honesty, when I think of all those [hardships], I realize they constitute a good form of discipline."[86] Echoing Heishichi's words, in his 1810 anthology of advice for travelers *(Collection of Travel Precautions; Ryokō yōjinshū)* Yasumi Roan cited the same proverb and pointed out that "travel is a good form of training for young people."[87] Equally permanent was the creation of a lifetime bond among villagers from the northeastern regions who had successfully completed together the long pilgrimage to Ise Shrine. They came to be known as Ise brothers *(Ise kyōdai)* and "were seen as sharing a tie for life."[88]

Nevertheless, the illusion of an extra-normative experience, of a time and place above and beyond the rules of the ordinary was, for many, but a momentary thrill. Travel was addictive (as evidenced by the multiple journeys taken by the same person) possibly because many of its benefits were so fleeting and impermanent.[89] The enthusiastic reception by families and friends upon return, the excitement of distributing amulets and souvenirs, and the emotional recounting of one's adventures were destined to wear off as life as usual reinstated its petty demands. Back in Nihonbashi, the townswoman-turned-cultural-icon had to reacquaint herself with the everyday, with the routine of the shop and household. Travelers then resorted to an array of expedients to leave a permanent record of their extraordinary adventures. The erection of pilgrimage monuments was one such device. Upon completion of their trip, pilgrims would commission memorial stone pillars recording the date and destination of their travels and the names of the participants.[90] Permanently standing at street corners and along main avenues, these pillars literally cast in stone what had been a remarkable but otherwise self-contained event. Travel memoirs served a similar purpose, for they too allowed travelers to commemorate their achievements indefinitely. Even diaries that were not published at the very least circulated among family and friends, forever conveying the emotions travelers had experienced during their journeys.

For the authors of travel journals, going back to the pages of their travelogues after the completion of the journey, adding notes, and perfecting their narratives was standard practice, since it was often inconvenient, if not practically impossible, to compose elegant and detailed accounts while in motion. Shinkō-in Myōjitsu (ca. 1717–?), the wife of a Kyushu samurai, tells of a boat trip during which large waves foiled her attempts to write and made it difficult even to hold the brush.[91] Yasumi Roan included a section on the issue of simultaneous recording (titled "How to Write Diaries While Traveling") in his 1810 *Collection of Travel Precautions,* advising that revision of one's notes after the completion of the trip was indeed the best way to go about diary writing:

> When traveling and visiting famous places and historical sites you will hear about rare things and will see spectacular views. It is then a good idea to make a note in your diary of when and where the sighting occurred, describe it, and, should verses come to mind, be that Chinese, Japanese, linked verses, or haiku, just jot down how they came about, for you will not have time to write them down beginning to end. If you decide to draw a view of mountains and rivers, make a sketch of it as is and, upon return, draw a good quality copy. If you decide to write a perfect poem or to draw a perfect picture while on the road they will be a burden to carry and will not come out as well. This is something to consider.[92]

The act of rewriting diaries served also as a way to better approximate the high standards set by literary tradition and to take yet another step in the direction of the classical past. "In all honesty I reckon that what I say while I travel is noticeably below standard, but since I plan on revising it afterward, I just idly jot things down as is," admits the entertainer Takejo in her 1720 travel account.[93] As commonplace as revision was, however, certain travelers still spent an unusual number of years, often decades, polishing and repolishing their memoirs (Kuwahara Hisako, three years; Oda Ieko, ten; Kutsukake Nakako, twenty).[94] Arguably, theirs was an attempt to rekindle a flame that no longer burnt and to reenter, if only vicariously, the time and space of detachment and re-creation.

Symbolic thresholds were crossed by the act of taking to the road, but under a purely institutional viewpoint the "status" of travelers like Tamiko or Shizuko did not change as a result of their trips. The voices they had raised in their travel memoirs, however, still resonated through the written word. The travel diaries and the poetry *bunjin* composed while touring famous sites served as entrance exams into literati circles and were unquestionably meant for circulation, at least among peers. Other works were eventually published. Kaibara Ekiken, for instance, made a case for the publication of Inoue Tsūjo's diaries with a Kyoto publisher.[95] Takejo's *Record of a Journey Taken in the Year of the Rat* was printed and made available to the general public in 1807 by scholar Shimizu Hamaomi (1776–1824),[96] and, as the 1827 introduction to Kikuchi Tamiko's diary suggests, it enjoyed a good degree of success: "Recently, a work by a certain Takejo called *Diary of the Year of the Rat [sic]* has been praised by famous scholars as an edifying work."[97] Even those authors who claimed that they only wrote for themselves did so more as a form of literary affectation than out of a sincere concern for privacy. Kikuchi Tamiko was one of them. She declared that her memoir was "not intended for an audience. It is written for my diversion alone, so I cannot be blamed."[98] This, however, was simply another means of identifying with a Heian celebrity, Sei Shōnagon, who had concluded *The Pillow Book* with a suspiciously similar caveat.[99] An introductory note to Tamiko's work, dated 1827/4/6 and penned by someone claiming to be a distant relative, suggests in fact that her diary was circulating and being enjoyed by her peers. More important, it confirms that Tamiko's efforts at establishing a bond between her work and the illustrious classics, and between present and past, had worked, and that the diary format was still perceived as the ideal way for women to raise their voices:

> Beginning with *Tosa Diary,* innumerable travelogues *(tabi no ki)* have been written. Even in the past [people] were familiar with the writings of the famous and unequaled poet, master [Ki no] Tsurayuki. As for the works of women, everyone today praises as exquisite the likes of *[Diary of the] Waning Moon* and *Sarashina Diary.* They have been made into books and are of help in practicing *kana* writing. However, these masters were born in the days of old, at the time when the way of poetry flourished; they served at the great court, and only [composed] Japanese poetry *(Yamato uta)* out of everyday topics of conversation and short-lived jokes alike, using pillow [words] to give [their poems] a natural air of elegance. [...] Now, when reading this *Diary of [a Trip to] Enoshima,* one appropriates the spirit and the language of the past *(inishie no kokoro kotoba).* There are many points that catch the eye and it is smoothly written. Women so far have followed this path. Today, those who compose poetry for the first time [...] are startled and become inspired.[100]

Metaphorically, the strokes of the brush on the page mirrored the footsteps left along the road. By looking back at them, either by reading or by retouching the original manuscript, the authors could relive their journey. Journals and memoirs allowed the voices raised in the malleable spaces of travel to come back as reverberating echoes and never to be silenced again. The parting shot in the diary of Inamura Kiseko (1790–1860), a doctor's wife from a family of wealthy merchants who traveled to Hakone in 1842, best sums up the exceptionality of her experience and her attempt to make it resonate forever by sharing it with others in spite of the impermanence of it all:

> I heard the cry of the nightingales with my companions on that gem[101] that is Mount Hakone, and I pacified my heart from all miseries by the flowing waters of White-thread Fall. As I looked at the mountains day and night I established a bond with those friends whose heart, like the mountain spring, is shallow.[102] I think of this with envy. I zealously wrote words that are more flowering than the cherry blossoms depicted on the folding screens at that inn in Miyanoshita, brush stroke after brush stroke, always repeating, "how strange." Those who [reading my diary] felt like they were sharing the grass pillow with me will come to the end of this scroll and think they are awaking from a dream.
>
> | *Katanari no* | They have not yet blossomed |
> | *waka nado kikedo* | and are young, but |
> | *koto no ha no* | their scent |
> | *hana wa nioi no* | will not last long: the flowers |
> | *mijikeru mono o* | of words.[103] |

PART III

Purchasing Re-creation

CHAPTER 5

Print Matters
Popularizing Past and Present

>That's right: unless you're Kita and Yaji from *Shank's Mare,* travel ain't much fun.
>—Jippensha Ikku

HAD THE demanding wife of Nakagawa Hisamori lived in the second half of the Edo period, her request for a copy of *The Tale of Genji* in the remote mountain hamlet on the way to Ikaho might have prompted a positive reply. By then, finding a provincial innkeeper familiar with Murasaki's novel would not have been as hard a task as it apparently was in the seventeenth century. Through the diffusion of printed culture, in the course of the eighteenth and nineteenth centuries the art of recovering a site's past, hitherto largely exclusive to literati, aristocrats, and samurai, became commercialized and popularized to an increasingly great extent, enabling even townspeople like Kikuchi Tamiko to reinvent themselves as cultured travelers. Eyewitness to such democratization of knowledge was Tsuchiya Ayako, the magistrate's wife en route from Edo to the Kansai region in 1806, who noticed how even her attendants could grasp the literary dimension of certain locations along the Tōkaidō. At Yahagibashi, near Okazaki, she remarked that the site "appears in the poems of old days and everyone knows of it, even the servants."[1]

Sustained by a general economic and cultural growth and a sharp rise in literacy rates, the commercial print industry boomed in the course of the Edo period. An ever-growing array of published materials on the theme of travel familiarized many a commoner with the potential embedded in the landscapes. Not a few of them, as Tamiko demonstrates, cleverly exploited this new avenue, becoming enthusiastic participants in the practice of cultured travel as re-creation. Even wayfarers of a certain cultural caliber would in fact avail themselves of commercial guides for reference and inspiration. An erudite man capable of mustering up recollections on his own, Kiyokawa Hachirō did not disdain occasional help from more popular vectors of information. Touring Kyoto during his 1855 journey, he looked for details about the Gion Festival and Hongan Temple in *Illustrated Guide to the Famous Places in the Capital (Miyako meisho zue)*, as he himself admitted.[2]

While advertising the historical, literary, or religious pedigree of famous sites, works printed for popular consumption also contributed to the creation of new spatial hierarchies based on services and amenities. In the nineteenth century, the culture of commercialism was ripe and pervaded actual landscapes as much as their literary or artistic renditions. Wayfarers and armchair travelers alike were exposed to and bombarded by more or less direct forms of commercial advertising. Market-based standards for the evaluation of space entered the scene, enabling prospective travelers to redraw the map once again. The already shifting centers established by poetry, politics, and faith were put up for debate and reshuffled around one more time.

Publishing the Past

A convenient way for literate commoners to acquaint themselves with the history of famous locations was to do so through the explanations and illustrations included in travel guides. Rendered popular and affordable by the adoption of the woodblock in lieu of movable type, travel guides became available by as early as the mid-seventeenth century; by the eighteenth they stacked the shelves of bookstores in Kyoto, Osaka, and Edo.[3] German physician Engelbert Kaempfer (1651–1716) testifies to their early popularity. During his stint in Japan in the early 1690s, he noticed "a poor traveler on foot whet[ting] his appetite by consulting a printed guidebook, which they all carry to find out where these and similar dishes are sold and where they are prepared best and cheapest."[4] Kaempfer himself purchased a few such guides, for in Hakone he writes, "This is an area where my Japanese *dōchūki,* or travel guide, advises the traveler to be careful."[5]

Besides popularizing knowledge about the history of famous sites, this type of commercially published material also helped instill in prospective travelers the notion that most spaces were open to them and, as a consequence, that the (alleged) rigidity of officialdom and certain branches of religious discourse almost always came with suitable alternatives. William Coaldrake has made this point in regard to woodblock prints *(ukiyoe),* arguing that, in depicting the sites and views of Edo, they seized upon certain spaces in the city, "replacing the official metaphor of benign and omnipotent rule with a metaphor of the urban good life."[6] Likewise, using prints and commercial literature as evidence, Marcia Yonemoto has provided a compelling case study of Nihonbashi's evolution from rigid pillar of governmental geopolitics to fluid receptacle of urban values.[7] Guidebooks achieved a similar goal, for in the name of profit they, too, placed ordinary travelers and their needs on a pedestal.

Already by the mid-seventeenth century, decades before Kaempfer's visit, prospective travelers could gather information about the history of certain landmarks from *The Complete [Directory] to Famous Locations along the Roads of Japan* (*Nihon dōchū meisho zukushi,* publisher unknown), a guide that detailed the itinerary from Edo Nihonbashi to the Kamigata region along the Nakasendō and included informative segments on various sites in the Western Provinces.[8] While its approach is mostly pragmatic, with notes about distances, prices, and checkpoints, *The Complete Directory* does not neglect to call the readers' attention to locations bestowed with literary or historical precedent, including for example the site of the Musashi battle fought between Takigawa Kazumasu and Hōjō Ujimasa in the late sixteenth century, a monument to Minamoto (Kiso) Yoshinaka (1154–1184), or locations associated with sixteenth-century lord Oda Nobunaga. Another mid-seventeenth-century guide, *Travelogue* (*Dōchūki,* author unknown, first published in 1655, most likely in Kyoto), propagated information about the celebrated locations along the Tōkaidō (the term "famous site," *meisho,* appears several times). It lists distances and prices while at the same time flagging famous mountains, castles, crossroads to other destinations (the road to Kamakura, the road for Ise pilgrimage from Seki, the road to Fushimi), monuments to historical figures, temples, shrines, torii, Jizō statues, and Kannon halls. Furthermore, *Travelogue* guides its readers to scenic views ("The road, lined up with ancient pine trees by the roadside, runs near the ocean") and to teahouses offering local food specialties.[9]

Seventeenth-century guides, in short, were already conceived of as complete reference manuals. Their goal was not only to list distances and prices but also to offer an introductory-level crash course in educated wayfaring. Nowhere is such goal clearer than in the opening statement of *The Travel Sparrow, A Guide to All Provinces* (*Shokoku annai tabi suzume,* 1687):

> The country of Reed Plains [i.e., Japan] originated long ago at the time when the land was created from above and emerged out of chaos. After the drops from the heavenly spear formed Awaji Island, the time came for men [to inhabit the archipelago]. Since the remote past Emperor Yōmei established the five provinces and the seven roads and Emperor Monmu divided [the country] into sixty-six provinces. In the age of sages, when the land is so stable it no longer moves, I traveled across the various provinces, east and west, north and south,

on land and sea, willing to look in all districts for the rules of the road and for old mementos of famous places. I filled my ink case, pulled the strings of my leggings and sandals, and took to the road. Many decades later I collected travelogues. I looked at these records and reckoned that allowing those papers to pile up in the leather boxes of my family treasures would be narrow-minded. I copied the most important [passages] so they can be taken along on journeys and I now wish to divulge them to the world. To provide guidance to neophyte travelers I thought I would chirp the *Menqiu,* so I entitled this work *The Travel Sparrow.*[10]

Who were the "neophyte travelers" the compiler of *The Travel Sparrow* had in mind? Most likely the educated and those aspiring to hone their skill of connecting present locations to old texts. The author's search for "old mementos of famous places" was indeed of the refined kind, as his use of allusive pillow words (the country of Reed Plains) and his references to the creation myth of the *Record of Ancient Matters (Kojiki),* to Chinese literature, and to Japanese history would suggest. In this respect *The Travel Sparrow* kept its promise, delivering lists of sites of historical interest as well as illustrations of key landmarks. Its map of the famous places of Uji, for example, advertises Uji Bridge as a gateway into history, as a side note informs the reader in search of quick historical references that "Sasaki [Takatsuna] and Kajiwara [Kagesue] crossed this bridge on the twenty-first day of the fourth month of Juei 3 [1184] coming from the south."[11] *The Travel Sparrow* was reprinted in 1696, 1701, and 1720, suggesting that the appeal of informed travel loomed large.

Illustrated Maps of All Provinces Easy to View in Any Order (*Shokoku yasumi kaibun no ezu,* 1685) offers another particularly poignant example of the way in which seventeenth-century guides sustained the diffusion of cultured travel—its introduction proudly boasts that the guide would enable one "to find famous sites, old monuments, shrines, and temples without having to ask."[12] At the same time, *Illustrated Maps of All Provinces Easy to View in Any Order* is also an excellent case study for the way in which the publishing industry of the early Edo period strove to place travelers and their needs on center stage. Entrusted with the task of illustrating the guide, Hishikawa Moronobu (1645–1715) produced images that elevated travelers—literally—above all other elements of the landscape. In his illustrations the road links one print to the next, but rarely does it stand out as the centerpiece. Often it is but an inconspicuous strip of land along which are depicted disproportionately tall travelers that tower over buildings and trees. While the limited possibilities offered at the time by woodblock technology may have played a role in such apparent disregard for scale and proportions, it is also arguable that the human element was meant to be the focal point of these maps.[13] *Illustrated Maps of All Provinces Easy to View in Any Order* thus set aside the theophanies of mandalas and the arid calculations of official cartography to privilege an anthropocentric view where the authors, the characters, and the readers shared knowledge about the road and, in many cases, owned it completely.

What readers learned from this guide was infinitely more than how to reach a certain destination. They learned to take center stage on the road and, ultimately, to manage their movements somewhat freely and independently. As the title of the work implied, the space and time of travel were not meant to be dominated by a fixed narrative or sequence and could be approached "in any order" *(kaibun)*. The term alludes to poetic palindromes *(kaibunka)*—sequences of verses that, when written syllabically, could be read both from beginning to end and vice versa.[14] By extension, the reference is meant to emphasize the free approach of the guide to the spaces of travel and the opportunity for the reader and the wayfarer to decide independently which direction to take. The time of travel could also be organized at the reader's discretion, for *Illustrated Maps of All Provinces Easy to View in Any Order* established its own calendar, which was relatively independent from official and religious dogmas. In the opening section readers found a chart listing a series of inauspicious days for departure, a few for each month of the year. The list, specifies the author, was originally compiled by the Heian period master of divination Abe no Seimei (921–1005). No one was to set out on a journey on any of the unlucky days included therein—indeed, as the guide explains, on those days it was best "to give up entirely on the idea of accomplishing anything." Anthropocentric and creative, *Illustrated Maps of All Provinces Easy to View in Any Order* was also pragmatic, and consequently the author and publisher figured out a way to free their readers from all restrictions. They included a special sequence of verses whose recitation would "ward off evil occurrences" and "turn [a bad day] into a lucky one," thus enabling prospective travelers to depart at their own leisure on any day they wanted—in any order indeed.

ALL THE aforementioned guides were first published before the Genroku era (1688–1704), a time generally associated with the first affirmation of urban commoners' values. That travel and the human element therein would be the concern of commercial publishers before the 1690s attests to the early connection between printed matter, mobility, and recreation. This connection would only deepen with the blossoming of the *ukiyo* culture and its anthropocentric and hedonistic values.

In the second half of the Edo period, as the printed word became "a commodity like any other,"[15] status and wealth were no longer the sole factors that mediated access to knowledge. A relatively large number of commoners—men and women—gained access to reading materials not only by virtue of the surge of the printing industry and the development of circulating libraries but also, and perhaps more important, thanks to the general rise of literacy. Schools in the seventeenth century had catered mostly to samurai and village leaders, but by the mid-eighteenth century schooling had also become available to well-to-do urban commoners.[16] By the time Yuya Shizuko departed on her 1750 journey, people from all social backgrounds could attend small local academies known as temple schools, or *terakoya*. While relatively limited in number and geographical distribution until the early 1800s, *terakoya* spread rapidly across the country in the course of the nineteenth century. Conrad Totman indicates that there were over five hundred such schools before 1803; after 1803 and through the end of the Edo period their number skyrocketed to over six thousand.[17] Though still mostly concentrated in the urban areas, opportunities for learning were not entirely absent in the rural peripheries.[18] Several foreign visitors to Japan in the nineteenth century were duly impressed by the literacy level of the general population and by the fact that even the lower classes had access to texts.[19] Although exact statistics are not available, by the late Edo period the literacy rate in the cities may have approximated an astonishing 80 percent for men and 50 percent for women.[20]

Temple schools introduced both townspeople and farmers to the fundamentals of reading and writing, eventually boosting a remarkable expansion in readership and literacy in general. At the same time their primers *(ōraimono)*, which often reproduced simplified versions of the classics, aided the diffusion not only of literacy but also of literary appreciation. It was through their pages that many commoners caught their first glimpses of hitherto elusive icons such as Ariwara no Narihira and Genji the Shining Prince. Predictably, in a gender-conscious society such as that of the Edo period a subgenre of educational textbooks created exclusively for women also circulated. A limited number of these works promoted the knowledge of classical literature by focusing on the lyrical heritage of famous locations. *Old Courtly Practices for Women: A Thin Pocketbook* (*Onna yūsoku hyōbunko*, 1866), for instance, described Ikuta no Mori as "a place of poetic fame" *(uta meisho)* with "sceneries that trigger memories of the past" *(mukashi no omoi deraruru keshiki nari)*, while *A Japanese Fabric of Selected Principles for Women* (*Onna sen'yō wakoku ori*, 1808) revisited the notion of poetically charged spaces by featuring images of eight celebrated landscapes (Wakanoura in Kii,

Sumiyoshi Bay in Settsu, Akashi Bay in Harima, Mount Yoshino in Yamato, Shiokama Bay in Rikuoku, the Kamo River in Yamashiro, the Mogami River in Dewa, and of course Mount Fuji in Suruga), associating each one of them with famous lyrics.[21] The poetic reference of choice for Mount Fuji fell on the celebrated verses penned by Narihira in admiration of its lingering snows (Figure 9). Already familiar to the wealthy patrons of the seventeenth century who had access to the exclusive cartographies of lyrical space (Figures 6 and 7), Narihira's poem was now theoretically accessible to prospective travelers of more modest means and backgrounds.

Images of Narihira in transit by Mount Fuji—often enhanced by the inclusion of the poem—appear in other nineteenth-century textbooks for the education of women, including *A Treasury of Precepts for Women* (*Onna teikin takara bunko,* late Edo period), *Yamato Library: Teaching One Hundred Poems by One Hundred Poets* (*Oshie hyakunin isshu Yamato bunko,* 1829), and

FIG. 9. Rendition of Mount Fuji's poetryscape in *A Japanese Fabric of Selected Principles for Women (Onna sen'yō wakoku ori),* a nineteenth-century primer for women. From Emori Ichirō, *Edo jidai josei seikatsu ezu daijiten,* vol. 5. Courtesy Ōzorasha.

Crimson Brocade: A Great Treasury of One Hundred Poems by One Hundred Poets (*Taihō hyakunin isshu momiji no nishiki,* 1841). An earlier manual, *Jeweled Camellia: Gleanings of One Hundred Poems by One Hundred Poets* (*Shūi hyakunin isshu tama tsubaki,* 1768), also included the snapshot of a classy courtier enraptured by the spell of the mountain. In this case, however, the man lacks an entourage and is not riding a horse—two attributes commonly associated with Narihira. The verses included at the top of the illustration identify him in fact as the eighth-century poet Yamabe no Akahito.[22] *Jeweled Camellia* thus provided an alternate reference for those wishing to attribute a literary significance to the famous mountain. By means of straightforward visual aids and ad hoc quotations, temple-school primers effectively familiarized women with the many lyrical connotations of the country's travelscapes.

Terakoya textbooks helped to popularize the educated engagements of cultured travelers, not only by directing gazes and prompting recollections, but also by introducing commoners to the art of rewriting space according to uniform poetic canons. Two late eighteenth- to early nineteenth-century primers, *Precious Ancient Bookcase for Women* (*Onna banzai takara bunko,* 1784) and the aforementioned *A Japanese Fabric of Selected Principles for Women,* associated the sight of Akashi Bay with the same verses from the tenth-century *Collection of Ancient and Recent Poems* (*Kokinshū*):

Honobono to	Dimly through morning
Akashi no ura no	mists over Akashi Bay my
asagiri ni	longings trace the ship
shimagakure yuku	vanishing from sight floating
fune o shi zo omou	silently behind the isle.[23]

Both textbooks featured sketches of the bay combined with the verses of old, creating indelible mental images of a rarefied poetryscape, a form of cultural imprinting that was sure to reverberate in the travelers' perceptions and depictions of the site once on location.

By the late eighteenth and nineteenth centuries, travel guides had also reached nearly perfect levels of comprehensiveness in cataloging appropriate literary precedents. *Illustrated Guide to Edo's Famous Places* (*Edo meisho zue,* published in 1836 by Saitō Gesshin Yukinari), for example, is a virtual inventory of every single erudite association a site could possibly trigger. In reference to Kanazawa (Musashi Province), for instance, the guide not only mentions the legend of ninth-century artist Kose no Kanaoka, who had famously dropped his brush before the sublime eight views, but also advertises Kanazawa's connections to Western Lake in China and to medieval poet and essayist Kenkō Hōshi (1283–1350).[24] Direct quotations from the works of early Edo period authors such as the Zen monk Takuan (1573–1645) or Matsuo Bashō also helped the aspiring educated traveler to recollect appropriate lines while on location. The iconic wayfarers of the seventeenth century were thus transmogrified into cultural commodities to provide nineteenth-century townspeople on the road with the elegant references demanded by literary re-creation.

Other late Edo period guides even included parallel depictions of the same site in its contemporary and historical versions. A case in point is Akisato Ritō's entry on Yatsuhashi in *Illustrated Guide to the Famous Sites along the Tōkaidō* (*Tōkaidō meisho zue,* 1791). As Franziska Ehmcke has shown, one of the illustrations captures Yatsuhashi as an eighteenth-century traveler would have seen it—fields, roads, meadows, but no irises. The second image, however, delivers the appropriate historical connection, as it provides a snapshot of Narihira's party enraptured by the gloriously blooming flowers.[25] By including present and past views of the same location, the guide first aided visitors in recognizing the landmark and subsequently directed their gazes step by step in the transition from "now" to "then." Not always spontaneous, at times arguably mechanical and induced by these prepackaged associations, by the late Edo period the art of establishing a lyrical engagement with space had not only been democratized: it had been given a price and put up for sale in bookstores.

GUIDEBOOKS and education manuals were not the only means by which the association between places and poems became part of collective knowledge. Less proficient students, in fact even the almost illiterate, could envision the days of old reproduced in more directly visual media, notably woodblock prints and board games *(sugoroku)*. Particularly after the introduction of the multicolor print in the second half of the eighteenth century, *ukiyoe* became popular forms of expression for artists and of enjoyment for their customers. The great masters of the period mass-produced splendid and affordable woodblocks that celebrated the inherent beauty of everyday life in the floating world. Others, however, looked to famous travel destinations for inspiration and, not infrequently, they incorporated the sites' cultural heritage into their images. This further enabled commoners to see those ghosts of the past that had hitherto been manifest only to the elegant, the wealthy, and the refined.

Keeping alive an association initially familiar to the literati and later popularized even in temple-school primers, *Print of Akashi Bay (Akashi no ura no zu*) by Utagawa Kunisada (1786–1864) portrays a pensive Kakinomoto no Hitomaro, the seventh-century poet to whom a local shrine was dedicated.[26] Hitomaro sits under a tree, gazing intently at the bay while the sun rises on the horizon. As in the *Kokinshū* verses cited above, distant sails are disappearing behind an isle. The print, in other words, captures the instant when Hitomaro—to whom the verses are often attributed—was inspired to jot down his famous lines. It is also a visual rendition of the poem itself, as it includes all the elements of the landscape celebrated therein and makes them immediately available to the general public. By virtue of temple-school primers and *ukiyoe* that perpetuated his connection to Akashi, Hitomaro became known even among nineteenth-century townspeople and merchants as one of the obligatory stylish references to make when on site. To his memory, for instance, bowed a group of sugar industry workers who traveled from Shikoku to Ise in 1848; they "climbed on a hill and visited Gasshō Temple on Hitomaro Hill," where they "worshipped three times Hitomaro Daimyōjin of the first rank and admired the sacred persimmon tree inside the precincts."[27]

Popular pastimes of the Edo period, board games also played a significant role in the propagation of cultural topography. Originally a divertissement for the higher echelons of society, *sugoroku* began to circulate among the general public by the second half of the seventeenth century. Early versions were conceived around the theme of the pilgrim's progress—for instance, the various stages of enlightenment or the path to heaven—but already by the end of the 1600s games celebrating more down-to-earth journeys also entered the market.[28] By the nineteenth century, *sugoroku* utilized all sorts of themes, including cultured travel. *The Board Game of Narihira and the Tales of Ise* (*Ise monogatari Narihira sugoroku,* 1844–1848, illustrated by Ichiyōsei Toyokuni, published by Fujiokaya Hikotarō; 76 x 40 cm) promised to take players along the various stages of Narihira's adventures as narrated in *Tales of Ise.*[29] As in the literary work from which it drew its inspiration, the game, too, starts off with the hunting trip in Kasuga and follows Narihira's odyssey along a sequence of memorable encounters with sites of heart-wrenching beauty, including the iris moor at Yatsuhashi and the lingering snows of Mount Fuji. In the block illustrating the poetic interlude with Fuji, a caption indicates that this is "the road Narihira [traveled] when he descended to the East." We encounter, somewhat predictably, Narihira and his attendant gazing at the peak; by way of quick reference, the famous lines he composed on that occasion are also added to the illustration. The Narihira in question, however, looks suspiciously like an Edo period character and not at all like a member of the Heian aristocracy. He is either an "actualized" version of the hero or a nineteenth-century cultured wayfarer playing the role of Narihira.

Even the words in which he praises the beauty of the view—"Is this a great scenery or what?"—would more likely have come from a man of the floating world than a courtier of the days of old. In language and appearance this board game transforms a literary icon of the past into a veritable Edo period traveler, rendering him less distant and intimidating and, by extension, making the association between poems and places more down-to-earth and approachable for an ordinary audience.

Unveiling yet another layer of meanings hidden in the same landscape (this time without any apparent intent to "actualize" the characters involved), *The Board Game of the Grand Hunt on Fuji* (*Fuji no makigari sugoroku*, 1830s; illustrated by Utagawa Sadafusa, published by Sawaya Kōkochi, 66 x 46 cm) visually recounted the deeds of Minamoto no Yoritomo (1147–1199) and his gang of warriors in the area.[30] Mount Fuji appears in a bird's-eye view at the center of the board, in what corresponds to the arrival square *(agari)*. Also towering in the same square is an earthen embankment erected for Yoritomo to supervise from above the hunt unfolding at the foot of the mountain. All around, samurai scramble into action. The player in this case is able to identify symbolically with Yoritomo, as he, like the famous warrior, has privileged access to a view from the top. By enabling ordinary folks to travel vicariously while impersonating the likes of Narihira and Yoritomo, board games empowered the less privileged to temporarily reinvent themselves. Moreover, as visual vectors of information such as *ukiyoe* and *sugoroku* gained popularity, access to basic information about the land stopped requiring "literacy" in the strictest sense.[31] Half-jokingly but also half-seriously, these printed materials fortified the democratization of knowledge and made informed awareness of the land theoretically possible across almost the entire social spectrum.

THE COMPREHENSIVE printed guidebooks and the *ukiyoe* of the nineteenth century contributed to the democratization of movement in more ways than one. Not only did they index educated references for everyone to consult, they also advanced the process by which the spaces of travel became malleable and open to interpretation. Where official proclamations and moralizing texts declared that women belonged to the domestic sphere, for example, commercial guidebooks in the league of *Illustrated Guide to Edo's Famous Places* responded by pointing out public spaces where female visitors were in fact welcome. Predictably, many such sites included religious establishments that enticed female visitors with promises of easy pregnancy and safe childbirth: examples were Shōjuzan Myōōin in Meguro, whose enshrined deity, Koyasu Kannon, "releases women from complications during delivery";

Fig. 10. Ordinary wayfarers as parodied projections of Narihira. Suzuki Harunobu, *A Parody of Narihira's Journey to the East (Mitate Narihira Azuma kudari),* woodblock print, vertical chūban, 28.4 x 21.2 cm, ca. 1768–1769. Photograph © Museum of Fine Arts, Boston, William S. and John T. Spaulding Collection. Courtesy Museum of Fine Arts, Boston.

Shaku Shrine in Takanawa, where "women who marry late come to pray for marital bliss"; or Myōkenji in Toda, which "distributes amulets for a safe delivery." Aside from locations that aided women in their traditional roles of devout temple-goers, wives, and mothers, however, *Illustrated Guide to Edo's Famous Places* also depicted women out and about, engaged in an array of more leisurely activities, such as admiring the maple trees at Kaianji, shopping for souvenirs at Ōmori village, enjoying the springtime blossoms at Peach Garden (Momozono), and crowding Ueno Park and the banks of the Sumida River for the seasonal cherry-blossom viewing.

Parody-oriented *ukiyoe* achieved the same two-tiered goal of informing about the past while creating a sense that the roads toward re-creation were open for all wayfarers to roam. In Utagawa Toyokuni's (1769–1825) *Segawa Rokō's Descent to the East* (*Segawa Rokō Azuma kudari,* ca. 1807) it is an actor with his entourage—not a Heian courtier—who poses in admiration of Mount Fuji. The actor rides a horse dappled with white polka dots, a comical allusion to Narihira's verses that celebrated the summit of Fuji as "dappled with fallen snow."[32] In a print by Suzuki Harunobu (1724–1770), *A Parody of Narihira's Journey to the East* (*Mitate Narihira Azuma kudari,* ca. 1768–1769, Figure 10), the two onlookers are a young woman and a boy. The woman, pipe in hand, is riding a horse and staring intently at the mountain—her posture and placement in the illustration are clearly meant to allude to Narihira. The boy holds the horse's reins in one hand and a pipe in the other. Unconcerned with the mountain, he is looking at the woman's face.[33] The ubiquity of these tongue-in-cheek references to Narihira's interlude with Mount Fuji indicates first and foremost that by the second half of the Edo period the link between the site and the character rested firmly in the realm of common knowledge, a prerequisite for the public to appreciate the parodic value and humorous content of the prints. At the same time, the placement of ordinary folks within a setting traditionally reserved for an icon of the caliber of Narihira also suggests that on the roads of late Edo period Japan anyone—even actors and women!—could dream of impersonating the elegant literary traveler.

Shops and Sceneries: Commercializing the Spaces of Travel

With its attention to the needs of the individual, commercial publishing also supported a further reconfiguration of the centers and peripheries of travel. Until the nineteenth century the bulk of commercially published materials came from the Kansai region; inevitably, these early works perpetuated the image of the West as the cultural center and identified the East with remoteness and cultural inferiority. Even the first guide to the famous sites of Edo (*Guide to Edo's Famous Sites,* or *Edo meishoki,* 1662, published in Kyoto by Asai Ryōi) had argued, somewhat condescendingly, that "In Musashi / [people] imitated / the manners of the capital / so now they / are courteous."[34] Edo, in Ryōi's work, is still and only "the capital of Azuma"—the wild East.[35] While the prominence of the city as the headquarters of the Tokugawa may have motivated the Kansai-based publishers to produce and market the guide, Edo's lack of cultural clout ultimately undermined any genuine effort on their part to pay it proper tribute.[36] Even the allegedly comprehensive *The Travel Sparrow* was prominently focused on the western provinces, unable perhaps to find much historical or poetic relevance in the East. While Books 1 (from Kyoto to Edo via the Tōkaidō) and 3 (Kyoto and Ise) are filled with information and historical anecdotes, Book 2 (dedicated to the eastern and northern regions, from Edo to Dewa and Nikkō) offers but scanty detail aside from mileage. *Edo's Famous Places: One Hundred Poets, One Poem Each* (*Edo meisho hyakunin isshu,* 1663), penned by Kondō Kiyoharu, did elevate Edo in a lyrical dimension, but even in this case the East was not yet deemed worthy of shining with its own light and emerged only through the reflected glow of Fujiwara Teika's original *One Hundred Poets, One Poem Each,* a revered work of literature made in and for the court aristocrats of the West.[37]

In the second half of the Edo period, however, the East began to claim serious literary attention. On the one hand, the publishing industry had by then established a solid foothold in Edo and the city had finally surpassed both Kyoto and Osaka as a publishing powerhouse.[38] On the other, new expectations on the part of travelers helped place the East more prominently on the map. For a number of wayfarers with minor literary aspirations the new yardstick that measured the space of travel was in fact determined by the booming commercial economy. Even for a scholar such as Kiyokawa Hachirō the commercially savvy East represented the paragon against which the worth of any other site was to be judged: "Osaka may well be one of the three major cities and, when compared to Kyoto, seems like a fine place, but when seen from Edo it is not [a site] people visit and the food is all bad" is one of his plainspoken comments.[39] By the nineteenth century, calling upon Kyoto and the West for self-glorification was certainly still *en vogue,* as the examples of literary travelers discussed in previous chapters demonstrate, but it was no longer a must. In the eyes of many, the Kansai region lost ground when standards other than religious fame, historical prominence, or lyrical clout began to inform travel. As Kiyokawa Hachirō explained: "The western region, once so thriving, has gradually declined. [. . .] Even Kyoto is [characterized] mostly by frivolity and boorish stinginess, most unsuitable for an aristocratic city inhabited by high-ranking officials. [. . .] These days the Kantō region plays the role once that of Kyoto."[40] As a telltale sign of Edo's newly acquired centrality, a great many guides of the nineteenth century— one may cite *Famous Sites of Edo: An Almanac of Flowers* (*Edo meisho hanagoyomi,* 1827), *Souvenir of Edo: A Picture Book* (*Ehon Edo miyage,* published between 1850 and 1868), and *Chronicle of the Year's Events in the Eastern Capital* (*Tōto saijiki,* by Saitō Gesshin, 1838)—began bluntly defining Edo as Tōto, the Capital of the East, either in their titles or in their colophons.[41] In the nineteenth century poetic relevance and historical pedigree still guided the gazes of cultured travelers (who now included educated townspeople), but the democratization of movement and the popularization of knowledge had introduced entirely new elements by which to gauge the value of a site, gradually allowing for less poetically charged and more consumer-friendly destinations to climb the charts. The centers had shifted again.

The trend toward the inclusion of commercial spaces manifested itself in many of the same media that had supported the democratization of literary knowledge: *ukiyoe*, board games, and guides. In Utagawa (Andō) Hiroshige's *Viewing Mount Fuji from a Tea House at Zōshigaya* (*Zōshigaya Fujimi chaya*, Figure 11) from the series *The Thirty-six Views of Mount Fuji* (*Fuji sanjūrokkei*, 1858–1859), the peak that had long served as poetic or religious inspiration to throngs of travelers becomes the focal point of a commercial enterprise—a teahouse. Two women enjoy the scenery. One sits on a bench, smoking and sipping tea (a teacup is placed next to her) under a roof decorated with bright-red paper lanterns. She is glancing over her shoulder to take in the

FIG. 11. Shops and sceneries in Utagawa (Andō) Hiroshige's *Viewing Mount Fuji from a Tea House at Zōshigaya* (*Zōshigaya Fujimi chaya*). From the series *The Thirty-six Views of Mount Fuji,* 1858–1859. Courtesy Library of Congress, Prints & Photographs Division (reproduction number LC-DIG-jpd-01581).

view of the peak. The other woman stands and gazes straight at the mountain, clearly enraptured at the sight. Mount Fuji is here reinvented once again: not only a lyrical landmark, not only the pillar of a cosmic order, the mountain was also a marketable commodity and the backdrop for leisurely interludes sustained by the commercial economy. The relationship of interdependence that, in the cartographies of lyricism, assigned meaning to a landscape by virtue of its connection to an iconic character of the past has now taken a different direction. Businesses have replaced historical and literary figures—it is now shops and sceneries that frame each other and enhance each other's value.

The Board Game of a Pilgrimage and Ascent to Mount Fuji through Its Northern Gate (*Kitaguchi tozan Fuji mōde dōchū sugoroku,* Figure 12) also layered the travelscape with elements of the sacred, the official, and the commercial. While the term "pilgrimage" in the title may suggest an emphasis on the religious theme, the *sugoroku* in fact contains visual and textual

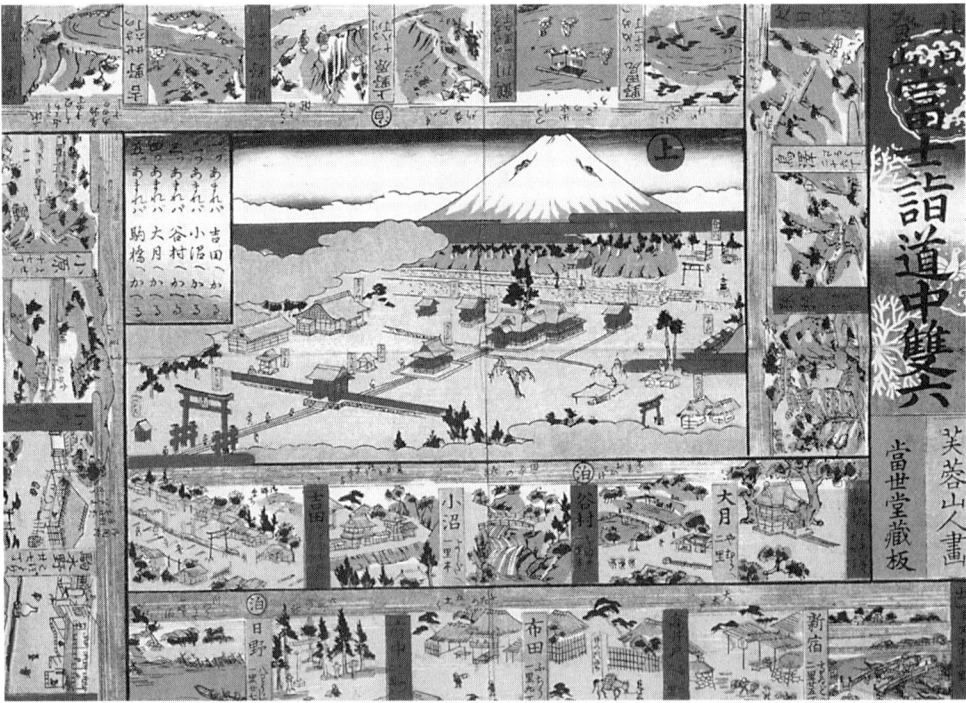

FIG. 12. Spatial architectures in a late Edo period board game. *A Pilgrimage and Ascent to Mount Fuji through Its Northern Gate (Kitaguchi tozan Fuji mōde dōchū sugoroku),* Mizuki family collection. Courtesy National Museum of Japanese History, Sakura, Chiba Prefecture.

information that transcends the sacred. Mount Fuji towers at the center of the board as the final destination for the players-turned-pilgrims. Sites of religious interest and locations made famous by their natural beauty mark the players' advance along the route. In the manner of an actual guidebook, *The Board Game of a Pilgrimage and Ascent to Mount Fuji through Its Northern Gate* displays the distances between its various stages and even relays important (if concise) information on areas of direct government authority (most notably the Suwa checkpoint, or *bansho,* at Uenohara and the Kobotoke barrier near Komagino). The player landing in Komagino would learn an important lesson about the Tokugawa's management of movements, for a note above the illustration reads, "Checkpoint! If you do not have a permit, you go back to Edo"—that is, square one. Finally, the commercial is introduced. The traveler arriving at Yose would be notified of "the local specialty, freshwater trout sushi." Travel guides disguised as playthings, nineteenth-century board games miniaturized the best of the spaces of travel, allowing for instantaneous, time/space-compressed, and vicarious odysseys while condensing multiple layers of meanings into an easy-to-grasp format.

What prints and board games achieved in a compact visual form, guidebooks provided with abundance of detail in a combination of text and images. Skimming through the pages of *Illustrated Guide to Edo's Famous Places,* prospective travelers would become acquainted with the many identities of Mount Fuji, from the numinous to the historical and, of course, the commercial. At a considerable distance from the city (approximately one hundred kilometers, or sixty miles), the mountain was not immediately accessible to the Edoites. Travelers coming from the east would also have had to obtain a permit to clear Hakone barrier, hardly an enticing prospect. Despite these shortcomings, Mount Fuji towered as a visible element of the cityscape and one that made its presence therein more concrete and ubiquitous by means of its numerous replicas. It is to these surrogates that most entries in *Illustrated Guide to Edo's Famous Places* are in fact dedicated. What the guide said of the replicas, however, indirectly spoke about the many identities and meanings of the mountain proper. Readers could learn about Mount Fuji's religious dimension and about the mercy of its deity because the miraculously ubiquitous goddess made herself conveniently available for consultation in a small shrine in town, Fuji Sengen Shrine in Komagome: "Enshrined here is the deity Konohana Sakuya Hime. This goddess performs miracles and is therefore the tutelary spirit of the place. In the past this shrine was located in the backyard of the Kaga lord [residence] in Hongō and was moved to its present location in the Kan'ei era [1624–1630]."[42] Readers could also acquaint themselves with Mount Fuji's historical role as the background to the deeds of warriors: "[Fuji Sengen is] to the right of the Shibō village road, deep in the mountain. It is under the administration of Tentokuji, a Shingon temple in Hodogaya. In the area there is a dark cavern the locals call 'the Fuji cave.' As the story goes, in the days of old the lord [Minamoto no] Yoritomo was hunting at the foot of Mount Fuji when he ordered Nitta Shirō Tadatsune to inspect the inside of the cave. Tadatsune went in, but eventually made his way out."[43]

More important, readers would discover that commercial amenities were also associated with the mountain. At the Fuji shrine in Komagome, the powers of the deity were materialized in the "straw snakes, fans, and five-color nets [. . .] for sale as local specialties."[44] Those unfamiliar with Hiroshige's woodblock print of Mount Fuji as seen from the teahouse in Zōshigaya (Figure 11) were still enticed to admire the peak from the comfort of a commercial facility, as the guide informed them that it was indeed possible to catch a glimpse of the elusive summit while enjoying the services of a Fuji-view (Fujimi) teahouse:

> Far in the distance to the southwest one can see the white peak of Fuji. When the wind sweeps the thin clouds away it unveils the true colors of winter, but then suddenly the view disappears—it cannot be fixed in an instant, it is a view that changes all the time. It is truly a splendid sight.
>
> | *Kiri shigure* | Fog, early winter rain: |
> | *Fuji o minu hi zo* | today Mount Fuji is not in sight. |
> | *omoshiroki* | Interesting![45] |

The accompanying illustration underscores the connection between scenery and shop. On a clear spring day Mount Fuji has appeared, its summit in full sight. A steep road leads the travelers directly to the gates of the teahouse; patrons are arriving on foot and in palanquins and are being welcomed by the staff. The garden overlooks the amazing scenery, with trees offering shade and benches providing a comfortable environment for the clients to sip tea, smoke, and rest. Few of the people included in the illustration, however, seem to be focusing on the stunning view of the famously elusive peak; most display a matter-of-fact attitude, as if from this particular teahouse the sight of Mount Fuji were a given. *Illustrated Guide to Edo's Famous Places* acknowledged and sustained the proliferation of meanings by simultaneously presenting Mount Fuji as a sacred peak, as a source of lyrical inspiration, as a site of historical relevance, and as the focal point of various commercial enterprises.

Whereas political discourse conceptualized the highways as series of official post stations, late Edo commercial woodblocks and literature often tended to present the roads as a series of commodities. Works in the category of Hiroshige's *Famous Products of All Provinces* (*Shokoku meisan,* late 1830s) or Chigata Nakamichi's *Guide to the Local Specialties of All Provinces* (*Shokoku meibutsu ōrai,* 1836) touted the realm as a consumers' paradise, charting its spaces with the help of landmark specialties. It is the lobsters of Kamakura (not its temples or its vestiges of warriors' history), the handicrafts of Hakone (not the checkpoint or the Hakone sanctuary), and the abalone of Enoshima (not its famous shrine to Benzaiten) that justify the inclusion of these locations on the map.[46]

Active participants in the commercialization of recreational travel were also the authors of travel novels. Their works of fiction, often recounting, as noted by Howard Hibbett, "imaginary travels, seasoned with actual place names and a little guidebook detail,"[47] achieved little in terms of accuracy but effectively contributed to the promotion of movement as re-creation. Through parody and humor they celebrated the triumph of the human element over the attempts of official discourse to micromanage travel. At the same time, travel novels reinforced the association between escapism and commercialism both in format (as acquirable objects that could unleash one's imagination) and in content.

In this respect no author was more prolific than Jippensha Ikku. A star in the competitive market of commercial literature, Ikku owed his fame and his livelihood to the success of such classics of travel fiction as *Shank's Mare* (*Tōkaidōchū hizakurige*). The work was released in a series of installments between 1802 and 1811, with a retroactive introduction issued in 1814 and a Kiso Road sequel running through 1822. In the course of their odyssey Kita and Yaji, the heroes of *Shank's Mare,* come across not only a gallery of picturesque characters drifting along the roads of the floating world but also an endless variety of commodities. Some of these products become the centerpieces of hilarious skits in what to all practical purposes seem to be the Edo period versions of (parodied) infomercials. Such is the case, for example, with the yam gruel *(tororojiru)* through which the Tōkaidō post town of Mariko had acquired a certain degree of notoriety among wayfarers. Kita and Yaji's attempt to sample the famous delicacy fails when a fight breaks out between the owner of the teahouse and his wife, who hits him with a mortar, causing the soupy concoction to spill all over the floor. The scene closes with the husband, the wife, and an attendant slipping and falling to the ground as Kita and Yaji give up on their idea and hit the road again.[48] A similar misadventure-turned-promotion occurs in Yumoto, a place famous for its woodware. Here, Yaji attempts to bargain for a discount on a tobacco box originally priced at three hundred copper coins. Smitten with the charming salesgirl, he eventually agrees to pay four hundred.[49] In a humorous key, these episodes effectively advertised the association between certain sites and certain material objects, offering an alternative to the traditional evaluation of a place's worth in terms of religious, historical, or literary pedigree. An exemplary product of the age of commercialism, *Shank's Mare* in fact tends to highlight the tangible amenities of most sites at the expense of their official, lyrical, historical, or religious facets. Kita and Yaji, for example, reach Hakone craving the "sweet sake and fish for which the mountains have been so long famous." The presence of the official checkpoint and of the famous Hakone sanctuary is, in the story, only barely acknowledged.[50]

FOR THOSE who chose to embrace commercialism, travel occurred across a space transformed through consumption, redefined by multiple layers of significance, and reduced to symbols acquirable by everyone. Just when lyrical travel had ceased to be the exclusive preserve of a few, commercial publishing reconceptualized movements and spaces yet again, promoting old and new landscapes by virtue of their services and consumer-friendly standards. Popular printed culture thus readjusted and complicated the parameters that defined the rules of engagement with the landscape, celebrating common folks on a par with literary icons, flatulence with evanescence, and tangible commercial amenities with ethereal sequences of verses. While cultured travelers, the purists of lyricism, remained free to replicate the deeds of Saigyō and Narihira as they wandered about, the characters of the floating world, in search of juicy situations and instant, material gratification, made it abundantly clear that "unless you're Kita and Yaji from *Shank's Mare,* travel ain't much fun."[51]

Late Edo printed commodities simply reflected a larger economic process that had been in motion since the seventeenth century: the steady rise of commercialism. Combined with the democratization of travel, the birth of a consumer culture allowed a number of locations to overcome their exclusion from the maps of legal, religious, and lyrical discourse, for in the geography of the land envisioned by commercial literature entrepreneurial ingenuity could buy an otherwise inconspicuous village the badge of famous site and, with that, a way out of anonymity. It was against this ever-changing background that travelers devised yet new ways of reimagining themselves. As commercial publishing unveiled travelscapes hitherto unknown, new modes of re-creation shaped by the commercial economy began to take shape and proliferate.

CHAPTER 6

Icons of Escapism

Beauty:
a stall selling sweet sake
at the temple gate.
 —Miyake Yoshiemon (1863)

From a world of individuals we have passed into an even more passionate world of symbols.
 —Jorge Luis Borges

FOR THE EDUCATED, writing and quoting provided a way to interpret the landscape through erudition. At the same time, the economic framework within which travel occurred enticed travelers from all social standings to appropriate a site not solely through ephemeral visions of the past but also through the material acquisition of icons. As the Edo period evolved into an age when money mattered more than pedigree, travel offered many a chance for re-creation by means of tangible amenities. The shift toward a more commodified engagement with the landscape was sustained not only by the authors of published materials but also by the locations themselves, many of which reorganized their infrastructure to cater to all types of travelers in what was becoming an increasingly lucrative and competitive business. Temples and shrines were among the first sites to undergo such transformation, but secular facilities quickly followed suit.

Locations made famous by literary, poetic, or historical evocations *(utamakura* and *meisho)* had lured the educated for centuries, but in the Edo period the incitation to discover what novelist Jippensha Ikku would later label "the indescribable pleasures of sea and sky" began also to titillate the spirits of commoners.[1] As a result, not only did new locations become identified as *meisho* but even the good old lyrical sites of the past underwent a makeover of sorts, adding to the patina of the past the luster and glow of presently available, conveniently purchasable services.

Trading Spaces: Old Sites, New Options

For economic reasons, Shinto and Buddhist establishments had been among the first promoters of travel, striving early on to provide an array of diversions for their visitors. A decline in landed power during the late medieval period had forced numerous centers of faith to seek financial support among their parishioners, bringing about the necessity to promote their image in more appealing commercial terms. In order to survive economically after losing its lands to the government in 1600, for instance, the sacred complex at Mount Hiko looked at lay sponsorship. It began coining its own money, which visitors were required to purchase prior to accessing the area, for only Hiko money could be used to pay for lodging, food, medicines, amulets, and entrance fees.[2] The trend toward the commodification of the sacred continued throughout the Edo period and did not escape the eye of many a traveler. In 1692 the Confucian scholar Kaibara Ekiken reported, not without a hint of criticism, that the monks at the Benzaiten grotto in Enoshima (Sagami Province) made a profit by selling "expensive torches to each person that enters the cave."[3] Likewise, when the samurai Ikegawa Shunsui visited the sacred mountain of Ōyama (also in Sagami) in 1768, he scorned the local clergy for "covet[ing] money to a great extent."[4]

Far from being a "pure" act of faith, pilgrimage was an enterprise that required a solid economic infrastructure to pay for advertising, lodgings, and the production and marketing of amulets and charms. Temples and shrines delivered on all fronts, dispatching proselytizers known as *oshi* (or, in the case of Ise, *onshi*) as virtual travel agents, distributing amulets as tangible reminders of the sacred and providing pilgrims with hospitality in their precincts.[5] Each *oshi* controlled a region or area he would tour regularly with the purpose of visiting parishioners, organizing the creation of confraternities, and promoting visits to his affiliate establishment. Equipped with promotional materials such as amulets, souvenirs, and ritual prayer books, the *oshi* would enter rural villages, post mandalas and scrolls depicting the foundation legends of their institution, and make a case for the salvation value of their theologies.[6] Some scrolls contained graphic images of hells and demons, the afterlife punishment reserved for those impious villagers who failed to support the complex. As Mark Teeuwen has argued, parishioners were such a precious commodity that it was not unusual for *oshi* of the same complex to trade, pawn, or purchase each other's areas of competence.[7]

Religious establishments pursued the commercial reorganization of their identity actively and aggressively. Since the medieval period, marketplaces known as *monzenmachi* (or *monzenchō*) had developed around the gates of the major centers of faith. Their growth continued until, in the late seventeenth century, a place like Ise projected the image of a "holy industry," as a foreign visitor, the physician Engelbert Kaempfer, remarked.[8] In the 1690s, when he came to the Great Shrine area, the precincts were indeed mushrooming with businesses. The literature of the time depicts the local *onshi* busily preparing New Year messages to deliver to patrons around the provinces and industriously organizing the tours of wealthy Edo townspeople.[9] A compilation of miraculous stories centered on the Great Shrine and written in 1705 by the Ise priest Watarai Hironori includes cameos of zealous *onshi* providing financial assistance and guidance to destitute visitors.[10] The efforts of this holy industry paid off. Pilgrims purchased strings of coins to use as offering money and sponsored ritual *daidaikagura* dances that generated "mountains of gold and silver" for the shrine.[11]

In the seventeenth century, however, the Ise clergy did not hold a monopoly on the business of faith, for the area around the shrine bustled with profit-seeking priests as much as it did with secular peddlers and entertainers. An illustrated travel guide first published in 1687, *The Travel Sparrow* presents the Great Shrine area through images that include the sacred as much as they do the mundane.[12] Next to a devotee taking cleansing ablutions in the Miya River, the Inner and Outer Shrines, a pilgrim tossing coins from the Uji Bridge, and other such landmarks as Futami no Ura, the Wedded Rocks, and Mount Asama, one can also spot a couple of female entertainers (the text refers to them as "the famous Osugi and Otama") and a shop selling the local specialty, a type of rice cake known as *okoshigome*. Another guidebook, published one year after *The Travel Sparrow,* also advertises Ise as a complex space where sacred acts overlapped with very down-to-earth diversions: "The area covers about three *chō*. There are three or four theaters for *kabuki* and *jōruri,* every other establishment is a large teahouse—there are about two hundred of them. Among them, particularly famous are the Urashimaya, the Waizumiya, the Uraguchiya, the Ebisuya, the Hiragiya, and the Fujiya in Furuichi, along with the Mitsuharaya, the Ōsakaya, and the Kashiwaya in Nakanojizō."[13] Such abundance of entertainment facilities, continues the guide, is a guarantee of "a blast" *(ōsawagi)*.

Ise Shrine is but one example of how religious establishments and secular entrepreneurs vied for a share of the business of faith. In the seventeenth century even the temple-sponsored itinerant proselytizers came face-to-face with creative competitors from the private sector. As early as 1650 the head of the Iwamotoin, a center for the cult of the goddess Benzaiten located on the island of Enoshima, was forced to appeal to the Magistrate of Temples and Shrines to put an end to the activities of local fishermen who were eroding the temple's monopoly by selling amulets and running inns. In laying out his case, he began by reminding the authorities that fishing—as opposed to running hostels—was supposed to be the occupation of the Enoshima villagers. "In the past," he continued, "the entire island was under the rule of this temple [the Iwamotoin] and for such reason fourteen or fifteen of those people, a while back, expressed their desire to distribute Benzaiten's amulets." This, it turns out, was the beginning of the face-off between religious and secular entrepreneurs.

> Because they were allowed [to do so] to a limited extent in certain areas, they have begun making a living out of selling Benzaiten's amulets while at the same time selfishly neglecting their duties to the goddess. As if this were not enough, for the past four or five years they have been running four or five inns. With no distinction for rank, they indiscriminately drag wayfarers [to their establishments] and do not instruct them on how to reach the temple lodgings, so the temple has lost its income. They are a nuisance.

The abbot then outlined the dire economic consequences of such intrusion into the Iwamotoin's business:

> Although Benzaiten has no temple land, for a while we have set up pilgrims at the old monks' lodgings. Thanks to their entrusted funds we have offered lights to the deity and made repairs; the temple has thus survived. Meanwhile, the above mentioned inns prosper and do not direct travelers to our lodgings, so the tributes for the offering of lights are not coming in and we are inconvenienced. [...] The dragging [away] of travelers is the reason for the decline of the complex lodging.

The petition ends with a plea to "summon the five people who run the inns [...] and order them to shut down their businesses" and to "tell those selfish men who distribute amulets and do not perform any service for Benzaiten to provide a service to the goddess."

The office of the Magistrate launched an investigation of ancient records and historical precedents that confirmed the authority of the Iwamotoin over the religious businesses of the island. While he called for the immediate cessation of the local entrepreneurs' illegal activities, the Magistrate also acknowledged the superior quality of the services offered by the secular competitors; he therefore allowed some room for compromise by permitting private inns to accommodate domain lords and high-ranking officials in case temple lodgings proved inadequate for travelers of such stature. Aside from these special circumstances, however, no one was to run inns "secretly" *(naishō nite)* and indiscriminately on the island, and ordinary pilgrims could only stay at the Iwamotoin facility. Finally, amulet distribution could only continue under the condition that those who profited from it also provide public services to the temple.[14]

Faced with the prospect of being cut off from the pilgrimage business, the secular entrepreneurs simply moved around the corner and went to Edo, where they passed themselves off as Enoshima *oshi* and continued to lure customers to their inns. Their ploy was eventually discovered, however, and a new court battle ensued. The villagers lost again, and in 1707 they had to promise the head of the Iwamotoin that they would forever refrain from posing as religious figures:

> Item: We, the inhabitants of the towns at the foot of the mountain in the island [of Enoshima], travel to Edo and pose as *oshi* from the [Iwamotoin] mountain. We give away amulets and sacred images such as those of the goddess [Benzaiten] all over the place, and for this reason you consider us bad. Hereafter, with the exception of those who go to Edo to see friends and pay visits of courtesy, bringing with them souvenirs, we will resolutely put an end to the activity of those so-called *oshi* who go around with amulets. [...]
>
> Item: When visitors go to the temple facility, even if they are friends traveling with us, and even if it is for a brief stop, we will not give them lodging.[15]

As evidenced by the fierce legal battle between real and fake Enoshima *oshi,* throughout the Edo period the ability to control one's share of the market was continuously put to the test. As shrine and temple complexes faced the aggressive competition of private entrepreneurs, they devised surprisingly creative solutions to stay afloat. The Iwamotoin in Enoshima, for example, came up with a rewards program for its customers, distributing a coupon *(kitte fuda)* that would allow them to enjoy special services and benefits while touring the island. Those in possession of the coupon could walk all the way to the altar at both the upper and lower shrines, received a sample of sacred wine to offer to the deities, and enjoyed unlimited access to Benzaiten's cave. In 1809 the Edo merchant who wrote under the pen name Senkaku Tōshi even used the coupon to catch a ferry ride back to the mainland.[16] Nor was the rewards program of the Iwamotoin an isolated case. As an 1802 guide to Shikoku claimed, the religious institutions along the various stages of the circuit would help visitors defray some of the expenses of the trip and, after twenty-one visits, a pilgrim would even receive a personal retreat *(anshitsu)* as a sort of bonus.[17]

By virtue of the creativity of most entrepreneurs, religious and secular alike, countless locations revamped their identity by adding more commercialized and recreational refinements. Like many other religious complexes, Ōyama combined sacredness and commercialism. A convenient network of roads connecting it to every corner of the Kantō region and the widespread promotional activities carried on by its *oshi* made Ōyama a popular destination for Edo travelers. In the summertime, at the peak of pilgrim season, many private houses in the area doubled as inns, undermining, as in the case of Enoshima, a business sector that had hitherto remained the privilege of the local clergy. Many such villagers-turned-entrepreneurs offered to ship and deliver the luggage of travelers headed toward Mount Fuji by means of a service called Fuji Baggage Express *(Fuji kake nimotsu)*.[18] The villages at the foot of Ōyama also offered such amenities as artificial waterfalls, miniature hills for those too idle or too unfit to climb the real mountain, and clusters of top-of-the-line inns.

In Ōyama as in Enoshima, the tension between religious institutions and secular industry prompted many a legal battle. In 1702 the local *oshi* brought to court villagers who disguised themselves as religious figures and surreptitiously distributed amulets. The villagers lost the case, but their businesses were far from dead, because in 1752 the complex filed yet another claim accusing them of running illegal inns, teahouses, and even brothels. Summoned before the authorities, the village representatives denied the allegations, arguing that "those who appeared to be streetwalkers *(tomeonna)* and prostitutes are in fact the daughters and wives of local peasants, hired during the Sekison [Temple] festivities as helpers."[19] Competition pitted not only clergy against secular businessmen, but also village against village. In 1779 a quarrel regarding the monopoly on packhorse fares and the lodging of pilgrims broke out between two settlements located along the Yagurazawa road, one of many roads that led to the mountain.[20] Although it never lost its identity as a center of faith, Ōyama (like Enoshima and Ise) did not escape the great expectations stirred up by commercialism and in the course of the Edo period witnessed a proliferation of businesses in and around the space of the sacred.

In other cases the transition toward the commercial resulted in a forging of surprising alliances between religious and secular entrepreneurs, who found ways to peacefully coexist and share in the profits. Kamakura offers a case in point. An illustrious destination for travelers in search of erudite historical recollections, the former capital of the samurai reverberated with the vestiges of the warriors' golden days, most notably at the Tsurugaoka Hachimangū (site, among other events, of the infamous assassination of the shogun Minamoto no Sanetomo in 1219). It also flaunted a respectable religious identity with the statue of the Great Buddha (cast in 1252), five great Zen temples (known collectively as Kamakura gozan), and various sites associated with Nichiren (1222–1282), founder of the Lotus Sect. Local businesspeople latched on to Kamakura's identity as a religious and historical landmark and created ventures that exploited just such a pedigree. When the samurai Jijūken Ikkishi arrived in town in 1680, for example, he attended a *kagura* performance at the Hachimangū. What on the surface appeared to be a genuine ceremony was in fact a commercial production (no doubt organized with the complicity of the Hachimangū clergy) that commodified the sacred and put it on display. As Ikkishi recounts, "The locals told us that the so-called Shinto priests and acolytes were actually innkeepers from Yukinoshita and their wives. Indeed, among them were also inn waitresses clad in ceremonial robes."[21] The performance, in short, was a contrived version of tradition passed off as the real deal in the name of profit and publicity. At the same time, it was also a symbol of the way in which the partnership between the religious establishment and secular entrepreneurs could foster the development of a creative service industry that facilitated the interaction between visitors and sites. The phony *kagura* enabled all spectators to become exposed to an aspect of Kamakura's heritage. While erudite visitors needed no such mediation to appreciate the religious traditions of the samurai's former capital, the less cultured no doubt benefited from the service.

With the growth of popular travel, the necessity for such mediators became more pressing. An eighteenth-century visitor to the Hachimangū, an anonymous Edo townswoman, noticed a number of local guides (monks and laymen alike) who promised to provide travelers with tales of Kamakura's golden age. Some, as it appears, accomplished their goals with better results than others. One of them, whom the townswoman hired at the Hachimangū, "blabbered about tales of old times. His breath was so bad that [my friend] Yukimasa, disgusted, tried to stay away from him, but the guy zealously walked nestling close, lecturing and sparing us no detail." Despite this unpleasant experience, our traveler left Kamakura a satisfied customer, for, as she recalls, "We visited a number of unique, old places."[22] Once again the culture of commercialism had come to the rescue of ordinary folk in search of a connection with a site's history. When manuals, textbooks, and prints failed to fully inform, tour guides came in and, for a fee, eased a visitor's journey into the past.

In the nineteenth century, commercialism had become a ubiquitous, inescapable, and generally welcome feature of the travelscape. The memoir Nagoya merchant Hishiya Heishichi kept in the course of his 1802 journey to Nagasaki provides an example of how old sites offered, by then, brand new options. While visiting the complex atop Mount Yuka (Bizen Province)

Heishichi partook simultaneously and with equal interest in its religious and secular atmosphere:

> We walked up the slope for about twenty *chō* [1.3 miles], at which point we spotted a beautiful teahouse and went in to rest. The teahouse faced south. We sat down [in a room] covered in brand-new straw mats and were offered tobacco. As we puffed away we took a look [outside]. Before our eyes we saw all the mountains and isles of Sanuki and the castle of Marugame. [...] Before such a spectacular view, one's spirit is rejuvenated. The splendor of the scenery made it hard for us to get back up and on the road, but in the end off we went. [...] We proceeded for thirty-four *chō* [about two miles] and came to the vicinities of the main hall. Two *chō* [two hundred meters] from it stood an imposing stone gate and two *chō* from the gate, on a flat area, some fifty or sixty teahouses and inns lined up on both sides [of the road]. Two or three girls stood at the door of each establishment; each time they spotted a wayfarer they yelled, "Come in and relax. Have something to eat first and then go on your pilgrimage. We have some delicious sake and an array of appetizers. Try our noodles."[23]

Heishichi walked past the lively *monzenmachi* and visited the religious complex. On the way back, however, he made a stop at the Nishiya, "an exceptionally large teahouse" not far from the temple gate, whose girls "are much better than those from the other establishments."[24] Compromising between faith and commercialism, the complex at Mount Yuka allowed for a redefinition, if not a reversal, of the travelers' priorities: "Have something to eat first and then go on your pilgrimage" is how the waitresses of the local inns enticed temple-goers. The portrait that Heishichi has left us exemplifies the new options that were becoming available at old sites. To enter the space of the sacred atop the mountain, visitors had to cross a well-organized space of the leisurely and the commercialistic at the bottom of the hill.[25] Both complemented each other, defining the overall value of Mount Yuka as a nineteenth-century travel destination.

Acquiring Spaces, Purchasing Escapism: The Role of Souvenirs and Specialty Products

Material mementos of one's journey, souvenirs had existed since well before commercialism took root and blossomed in the Edo period. As early as the eighth century Prince Aki, traveling on an imperial visit to Ise, had composed a poem in which he wished "the white surges far upon the sea of Ise" were flowers he could "wrap and bring [. . .] home as a souvenir *(iezuto)* for my beloved wife."²⁶ At roughly the same time, one of the frontier guards whose verses are collected in the *Anthology of Ten Thousand Leaves (Man'yōshū)* wrote:

Iezuto ni	I have gathered sea-shells
kai zo hirieru	to take home as presents,
hamanami wa	though ever higher
iya shikushikuni	the waves beat
takaku yosuredo	on the shore.²⁷

In the medieval period—the year was 1350—the traveling monk Sōkyū came to Sue no Matsuyama, a lyrical site in Rikuzen Province. He thought, "Since it would have been regrettable to pass by the famous Sue no Matsuyama and only glimpse it on the way, [. . .] why should we not look for souvenirs?" and proceeded to gather pinecones and shells as keepsakes. Memoirs themselves were in fact considered precious tokens of one's travels, as Sōkyū explains: "I brought these notes with me to the capital as a souvenir of my journeys."²⁸ The very title of his work—*Souvenir for the Capital (Miyako no tsuto)*—indicates the diary's real function.

By the first century of the early modern period the souvenir industry had gone a long way, and rare were the travelers who would be content to simply collect flowers or seashells to commemorate their journeys. Temples, shrines, and circuits first created the commercialized souvenir by putting a price tag on their amulets. The secular versions did not wait too long to enter the scene. Engelbert Kaempfer describes children selling keepsakes along the streets of Kyoto in the 1690s and adds, "One thing is certain: nobody travels through the city without buying some goods made in Miyako to take home for himself and others."²⁹

Commonly translated as "specialty products," *meibutsu* were locally produced items travelers acquired and brought home as cherished reminders of their journeys. The swords of Kamakura, the wooden handcraft products of Hakone, and the shell-decorated ornaments of Enoshima served the same purpose then as most knickknacks sold in tourist resorts and at airport shops do today. They not only created an immediate sense of "acquisition" of the site but also prompted recollections at home and, in a distilled format, symbolized the successful completion of a tour away from the ordinary. Visiting Enoshima in 1768, Ikegawa Shunsui called the shell-decorated items "the specialty *(meibutsu)* of the island" and observed how they were especially sought after by pilgrims who would "buy them and take them home as souvenirs" *(iezuto)*.[30] Then as now the practical usefulness of these icons was frequently subordinate to their symbolic function as ways to connect with a site, as an episode from Jippensha Ikku's *Shank's Mare* illustrates. Passing through Kazamatsuri, Kita expresses his intention to buy a torch because "They're famous for them here." When Yaji points out that a torch would be of no use in broad daylight, Kita replies, "That doesn't matter. [. . .] You get one and light it."[31] While Ikku's foremost preoccupation here is with the salacious pun upon "lighting" (a torch) and "being turned on" (sexually), the skit also underscores a prevalent attitude among nineteenth-century travelers, the tendency to associate a site with its merchandise.

Along with material objects, gastronomic specialties also offered, literally, a taste of a locale. Dried and pickled products could travel back to the visitors' home province, but as a general rule most local delicacies needed to be consumed on location, where they enhanced the sense of communion with the site. Anticipating the international character of Nagasaki, for instance, Hishiya Heishichi had commented, "Once in town, even the food will be outlandish," immediately identifying the peculiar flavors of the local cuisine with the cosmopolitan nature of Japan's prominent city-port.[32] With his gastronomically oriented expectation Heishichi—perhaps unconsciously—had latched on to a practice that went back a long way. Examples of incorporation through ingestion—that is, of the internalization of a site's essence through food consumption—are included in a work of literature that predates Heishichi's journey by more than a millennium. *Record of Ancient Matters* (*Kojiki*, 712) tells of Izanami's journey to the land of the dead, where she eats "the Hades food" and irreversibly becomes part of that world.[33]

In the Edo period travelers continued to associate spaces with comestibles, but did so mostly—though not exclusively—within the frame of the market economy. Many places that, unlike the *utamakura/meisho* of the past, did not have a strong lyrical, religious, or historical dimension, could still make themselves palatable to the public simply by promoting the right house special, as in the case of Mariko and its yam gruel presented before. At the opposite end of the spectrum, locations with preestablished pedigrees could lose their allure if their cuisine fell short of their reputation. When an exhibit of Nyorai images from Zenkōji came to Kyoto in 1705, the samurai Asahi Monzaemon, author of *Records from a Parrot's Cage* (*Ōmurōchūki*), rejoiced at the realization that he would not have to travel all the way to Shinano to see them. The lackluster flavor of the local cuisine, rather than the length of the trip, was the reason for his elation:

Shinano soba	Soba is the specialty
meibutsu naredo	of Shinano.
nido ideba	I traveled there twice
aji ga waruute	and twice it tasted terrible.
mairare mo sezu	Now I don't have to go!³⁴

Both the Tōkaidō post town of Mariko and the Zenkōji area in Shinano exemplify the extent to which gastronomic specialties became key ingredients of travel culture in the floating world.

Enoshima offers another case in point, for its fame as a destination for gourmands became as remarkable as its prestige in religious, historical, and literary terms. When visiting the island, the educated would often cite the verses ascribed to Kamo no Chōmei that celebrated its religious pedigree and its spectacular natural setting.³⁵ Other visitors, however, chose to celebrate Enoshima's identity in a more commercially mediated fashion through buying the seafood specialties for which the site was equally famous. When the samurai Iwamura Yasuhisa and two of his friends came to the island on the tenth month of 1814, they were eager to sample its fresh fish, an act through which they intended to establish a connection with Enoshima's marine ambience. Unfortunately, the three discovered that inclement winds, violent waves, and heavy rains had kept the local fishermen ashore. They resolved to tour the local markets nonetheless, but much to their chagrin their mission yielded no more than three meager abalone shells. "Truly a shame," commented Yasuhisa. To add insult to injury, the three dined on bamboo shoots in lieu of "the fish with which we ought to have been treated." The irony of being served traditional mountain food while on an island did not escape them, and they composed verses to capture their disappointment: "In the mountains we toasted with fish, now we come to Enoshima and are fed bamboo shoots!" Having identified Enoshima with one of its most recognizable icons, fresh seafood, Yasuhisa and friends viewed the inability of the island to deliver as a failure, for it prevented them from incorporating what they perceived to be the essence of the site. The following day, when they came to a famous fish-shaped rock, one of them sarcastically remarked:

Katsuo naku	Since there is no bonito [on the island]
gyoban no ishi mo	couldn't it be that the fish-shaped rock too
na nomi kana	is nothing but [an empty] name?³⁶

The use—in a gastronomic and commercial context—of an expression reminiscent of the one educated wayfarers frequently employed to underscore their nostalgic yearning for the past ("only the name remains") is especially indicative of the new, commodified ways in which travelers assigned meaning and related to sites. The shortage of fresh seafood in Enoshima was as disheartening to some travelers as the absence of Narihira's blooming irises in Yatsuhashi was to others—in either case they could only acknowledge, some with melancholy, some with irony, that "only the name remained." The inability to establish a gastronomic connection, however, did not completely tarnish our visitors' spirits, for they found other ways to acquire a piece of Enoshima. Noticing a great many stalls selling shell-decorated items, Yasuhisa and friends proceeded to buy "quite a few" trinkets, finally succeeding in forging a money-mediated link with the site.

Aside from material objects and food specialties, there were cases in which potions, ointments, and miraculous panaceas became the defining icons of certain locations. Re-creation, as we shall see in the next chapter, often entailed acts of physical regeneration; in this respect pharmaceutical concoctions that promised to transform or heal the body had the potential to enhance the appeal of certain places. The Tōkaidō post station of Odawara (in Sagami Province) had witnessed its fair share of significant historical events, from the arrival of Hōjō Nagauji (Sōun), who had seized the castle in 1494, to the sieges of Uesugi Kenshin (1561), Takeda Shingen (1573), and Toyotomi Hideyoshi (1590). Among many travelers, however, Odawara was prominently associated with its *uirō,* a miracle drug that allegedly cured an array of ailments. The nun Kikusha-ni turned the Odawara specialty into the centerpiece of one of her poems,[37] and novelist Jippensha Ikku concocted one of Kita's misadventures in *Shank's Mare* around the popular ointment.[38]

Souvenirs not only made sites acquirable and transportable but also facilitated and perpetuated associations between key landmarks and their quintessential characteristics or relevant precedents. The city of Nagasaki in Kyushu provides a case in point. As an international port in an age of tightly regulated contact with the outside world, the city rapidly developed a reputation for being cosmopolitan, if not altogether exotic. The woodblock prints that were sold on location and circulated countrywide marketed just such a notion by featuring the city's Chinese and Dutch residents or by mapping the location of its foreign settlements. The Confucian scholar Furukawa Koshōken, passing by the two-story Chinese residence in 1783, noted how "it is featured in the prints of Nagasaki that are in huge demand, so it is often reproduced. It is a must-see" *(kore o miru beshi).*[39] As Furukawa Kōshoken demonstrates, the evocative power of material objects had the potential to shape and validate a traveler's impression of a site. Countless visitors used artifacts as ways to grasp the meaning of a landscape and to connect with its heritage. While Kōshoken acknowledged the Chineseness of Nagasaki by association with the commercial prints that publicized the city's foreign character, in 1825 a female traveler by the name of Nakamura Ito identified the former site of Hamana Bridge and acknowledged its historical value thanks to its representation in a material icon she already owned: "I looked back, having heard that Arai was once the site of Hamana Bridge. Even today it has retained the appearance of a bay. At home back in Kanda I have a double folding screen that depicts the days of old when the bridge still stood. The illustrations are antique, with wayfarers wearing court ceremonial headgear. Even the landscapes seem of days gone by, although the view is still beautiful these days."[40]

Material icons, quaint keepsakes, and specialized gastronomies could thus take on the function of virtual travel guides, for they too, in some cases, aided travelers in the recovery and acquisition of sanctity, of lyricism, and of history. Enoshima offers once again a fitting example. While inside Benzaiten's grotto, visitors prayed for worldly benefits; outside the cave they could incorporate the goddess's blessings by gobbling down the fortune dumplings *(fuku dango)* that local entrepreneurs sold in makeshift stalls. The fortune dumplings marketed a religious concept *(genze riyaku,* or worldly benefits) in the form of an easily obtainable material object. Emerging from his guided tour of the cave in 1820, the traveling *haikai* master Jippōan, who had already visited the island forty years prior, observed that "the only things that have not changed here are the shell-decorated items and the atrocious fortune dumplings which, now just like then, are sold to visitors against their will!"[41] If longevity is any indication of success, then the peddlers of fortune dumplings enjoyed a good degree of popularity despite the fact that, as Jippōan remarks, they displayed little finesse in shoving their product down visitors' throats.

The merchandizing of divine mercy was by no means exclusive to Enoshima. A similar situation existed in Yoneyama (Echigo Province), where the local temples catered to female devotees by selling them the "Water for a Safe Delivery," and secular businessmen responded by offering rice cakes that would give women strength at childbirth,[42] or on Mount Haguro, where holy comestibles publicized as the "Souvenirs of Dainichi-sama" sold for fifty copper coins.[43]

Sanctity was not the only element of a site's identity to become a commodity and end up for sale on roadside stands. Tachibanaya Buhei, a clever entrepreneur from Enoshima, figured out a way to distill literary prestige into material objects. He first claimed a lyrical pedigree for his inn by enchanting his guests with the tale of how the ocean view from the second floor had inspired no less an author than Ōta Nanpo (1749–1823) to rename the establishment "Tower on the Hazy Sea" (Enparō). Then he turned the quaint—yet ephemeral—anecdote into tangible souvenirs by selling cups inscribed with the evocative name.[44] They may not have known who Ōta Nanpo was, but nineteenth-century travelers to Enoshima could, for a modest fee, own an object that resonated simultaneously with literary echoes and with the lulling sound of the island's waves.

History, too, underwent a similar process of transformation into a marketable commodity. Kogonji, a temple made famous by the grave of imperial loyalist and *Chronicle of Great Peace* (*Taiheiki*, 1372) hero Kusunoki Masashige,[45] put rubbings of the carved tombstone inscription up for sale. "The rubbings of the epitaph composed by the lord of Mito, 'Ah, the grave of Chūshin Nanko,' and the inscription by Shunsui cost one hundred [coins] each, while the rubbings of the epistles and letters of commendation cost fifty each," recorded a visitor in 1848.[46] For travelers in search of historical anecdotes but in need of props, illustrated maps pointing out the old sites of Takeda Shingen's deeds were widely available in Shinano Province, while near Mount Ōe, in Tango Province, a teahouse sold scrolls that depicted Minamoto no Yorimitsu (944–1021) entering the mountain in hot pursuit of a gang of bandits; some represented the event in such a glorious light that Kiyokawa Hachirō was disappointed to discover that the actual mountain was nowhere as tall and lush as its printed version![47] Better yet, near the site of the famous 1184 Ichinotani battle between the Taira and the Minamoto, teahouses sold none other than a culinary rendition of the event. The creative shopkeepers had come up with a catchy, pun-filled slogan that suggested how, by eating their "Atsumori noodles," visitors would in fact be gobbling down a mouthful of history: "Hot (*atsu*) noodles for [Taira no] Atsumori [served] in a huge (*dekkai*) bowl for Mount Tekkai, with a fine (*yoshi*) seasoning for [Minamoto no] Yoshitsune, at a price of sixteen coins, for Atsumori's age."[48]

As commercialism burgeoned and the historical icons of the past became the trinkets and menu items of the present, the modalities of the interaction between visitors and sites also expanded dramatically, taking on new nuances that did not replace but complemented the old ones. In the diaries of the educated, space continued to be measured in syllables and through the intensity of literary echoes. In the nineteenth century, travelers like Ri-in (who visited Kanazawa, Kamakura, and Enoshima in 1855) were still validating and acquiring spaces by means of erudite forays into the days of old. In Kanazawa, Ri-in explicitly presents herself as a knowledgeable mediator between past and present: "Matching [the beauty of] this landscape with a brush is no easy task. I remember that *once upon a time* (*inishie*) Kose no Kanaoka gave up and dropped the brush. [. . .] The name Eight Scenic Views originated *in the past* (*mukashi*), when the Zen master Shin'etsu visited this place and compared it to the eight panoramic views of Western Lake in China. [. . .] [This tree was] planted *once upon a time (inishie)* by the lord Yoritomo."⁴⁹ Other travelers, however, opted for more tangible engagements, sometimes instead of, at other times alongside educated interactions. Visiting Mount Yoshino in 1855, Kiyokawa Hachirō readily acknowledged the variety of icons by means of which visitors could connect with the site—lyrical ("it is not only famous for its cherry blossoms") and historical ("it is the site that more than any other has inspired loyal retainers, hence the connoisseurs of old history make it a point to visit it"),⁵⁰ for sure, but also commercial ("its local specialty is arrowroot starch").⁵¹

Gastronomies and knickknacks provided a convenient way to forge a link with a travel destination for those who did not wish to experiment with the ethereal and often slippery pillow words of poetic travel. Lacking a formal education no longer precluded one from symbolically "owning" a site—all it took now was a string of coins and, sometimes, an appetite. Sayo (or Saya) no Nakayama, for instance, had been for centuries a lyrical landmark of Tōtōmi Province and was celebrated in the verses of poetic anthologies as a site associated with the moon and with the hardships of travel.⁵² Particularly famous was its representation in one of Saigyō's poems:

Toshi takete	Never have I thought
mata koyuru beshi	at my old age
omohiki ya	of crossing you,
inochi narikeri	O Nakayama Hill at Sayo.
Sayo no Nakayama	All comes of fate.⁵³

In a number of travelogues from the late eighteenth and nineteenth centuries, however, the same site is seized upon and digested through a far less ephemeral symbol, its rice jelly cakes *(ame no mochi)*. Along the tortuous mountain pass, Yamanashi Shigako—whose family ran a brewery in Suruga Province—skipped the conventional dramatic tones demanded by literary precedent and composed a lighthearted poem on the site's tasty souvenir:

Hiru naredo	It is noon
na ni au Sayo no	in famous Sayo no
Nakayama ni	Nakayama, and
ima furu ame no	they sell a deluge of rice jelly cakes
mochi o urunari	in the pouring rain.⁵⁴

Shigako, who on other occasions also displayed her prowess as a cultured traveler, confirms that multiple interpretive possibilities were available at any single site. Visitors who passed through Sayo no Nakayama could choose to be enraptured by visions of Saigyō or to be distracted by the scent of rice cakes. To Kiyokawa Hachirō, Sayo no Nakayama presented at least four overlapping identities, all equally legitimate: the historical ("it is also known for its numerous sites of historical relevance"), the folkloristic (the "weeping rock"),[55] the religious (an inscription attributed to Kōbō Daishi), and, inevitably, the commercial (the rice cakes and the beautiful teahouses, which "were all built anew after the [recent] earthquake and are now prettier than ever").[56]

As visitors demanded to access and possess sites by way of tangible amenities, the travel industry responded with a proliferation of merchandise and self-referential simulacra. In late Edo Japan, a traveler's ability to acquire a site by means of purchasable commodities represented an important complement to historical, literary, or religious escapism. Tangible objects and local specialties had become the material equivalents of a quotation, the commodified counterparts of an intellectual, intertextual engagement. Through such commercial icons of escapism the spaces of travel multiplied ad infinitum, becoming domesticated, pervasive, and attainable by way of a simple monetary transaction.

Supply and Demand: Forged Icons and Surrogate Travelscapes

In order to match the rising demand for commodities, many such icons of escapism were in fact fabricated. As travel became increasingly commodified in the late Edo period, surrogates and forgeries helped to sustain the reputation and attractiveness of various sites when original and authentic assets were in short supply or altogether absent. In 1820 *haikai* master Jippōan denounced certain Enoshima entrepreneurs who were importing from Musashi one of their alleged "local" specialties—pickled abalone. He also insinuated that the same could be true of another famed *meibutsu,* the minced bonito of Odawara. Just as artificial, he suspected, were some of the historical artifacts scattered through Benzaiten's cave. While being shown around the site by a guide who pointed at various relics, the master observed: "This side gallery appears to have been excavated artificially [. . .]. Swindlers *(yamashi)* flock to all these famous places and sites of historical interest near Edo and imitations of original works are so numerous that it is hard to believe most of these things [are authentic]."[57] As cynical as Jippōan may have been, his words reveal plenty about the relevance that symbols and simulacra—regardless of their authenticity—had acquired in establishing the overall image of a site.

Even before Jippōan's time certain travelers had developed a flexible, if not iconoclastic, attitude toward the heritage of tradition associated with famous locations. The Edo pharmacist Anjin, who went to Sagami in 1767, was not the least bit impressed when a monk in Kanazawa elaborated on the legend of Kose no Kanaoka, the ninth-century painter who was said to have dropped his brush in awe before the spectacular eight views. While for the educated and the refined recognizing the legacy of Kanaoka by the Brush Drop Pine was an almost mandatory sign of historical knowledge, to Anjin the monk's words rang hollow and did not prompt any foray into the past. One of Anjin's travel companions took notice of his skepticism and wrote, "Anjin says that this [Kanaoka's legend] has been accepted as true since who knows when by the locals and passed on as a tradition."[58] When it did not raise suspicion, the widespread practice of associating sites with icons did at least generate confusion. In the late eighteenth century, Shinkō-in Myōjitsu, a woman of samurai lineage, traveled from Kumamoto to Kyoto. At Enfukuji in Tomo she came across "Bashō's tumulus" *(Basho no tsuka),* but having previously visited another purported "Bashō's tumulus" in Ōtsu, she asked a monk which of the two was in fact the real one *(izure makoto naran).* The monk honestly admitted that the local monument was nothing but a symbolic token of respect erected by admirers of the poet and that there was no evidence of Bashō himself ever having traveled to the site.[59]

John Urry, in regard to contemporary tourism, has defined this cycle of supply and demand for contrived recollections a "self-perpetuating system of illusions."[60] To a certain extent Urry's definition applies also to the forged icons of early modern Japan—they did proliferate and they did purport to generate a (false) air of connoisseurship and a sense of belonging in a foreign space. What Urry conceives of in seemingly negative terms, however, was in fact a vital component of travel in the late Edo period. Some wayfarers may have felt betrayed by forgeries and annoyed by pushy peddlers, but the majority of them sought the chimera of being disentangled from the demands of the everyday and resorted to all means possible to generate just such an illusion. Some opened their minds to the ghosts of the past, but many others opened their wallets and their mouths for the specialty products and tasty treats of the present. Through different means, the erudite and the trinket buyer ultimately strove to achieve the same goal; at the end of the day, the intangible pillow words and poetic citations of the former were just as illusory as the forged artifacts and phony *meibutsu* of the latter.

AS ICONS MULTIPLIED so did famous landscapes, replicas of which were created and advertised all over the country. Sacred spaces in particular were among the most frequently reproduced. Targeting visitors who were unable to afford a trip to the "real" site, various institutions built scaled-down versions of their main complexes in order to attract larger crowds.[61] Many such surrogates were meant to make the experience of religious travel available to all, especially women and children. This was especially true of sites that enforced the *nyonin kinsei* policy. In Kyoto, the Women's Central Hall *(nyonin no chūdō)* at Shiba Yakushi presented itself as a convenient alternative for women banned from Mount Hiei, at least according to a visitor who came to the shrine in 1855.[62] A women-friendly surrogate of Mount Kōya existed also in Iyo Province, between stages no. 65 and no. 66 of the Shikoku circuit. Originally named Konkōzan Senryūji, it was also known as the Mount Kōya of Women *(nyonin Kōya)*.[63] Yet another surrogate of Kōya existed in Edo; known as Kokugenzan, New Kōya, or Mount Kōya of the East, it too made the experience of climbing the sacred mountain entirely available to visitors of both sexes, without compromising the (alleged) integrity of the original site. According to a conveniently crafted creation legend, the founder of the duplicate complex was on the slopes of the real Mount Kōya when, one night, the great master Kōbō Daishi visited him in a dream. The master asked him to retrieve a statue from Mount Tsurugi, in Shikoku. "Your home province is far from my mountain [i.e., Mount Kōya]. Go now and fetch the statue. You must take it back to your home, create a copy of this mountain, and found groups of believers for those women and children who have a hard time coming all the way here on a pilgrimage."[64]

Examples of duplicated travelscapes include not only sacred mountains but also multiple-stage religious circuits. The Temple of the Five Hundred Arhats in Edo simultaneously re-created in a skillfully distilled format not one but three pilgrimage routes: the Chichibu circuit, the Bandō circuit, and the Shikoku route. On the premises, as Timon Screech has argued, "devotees progressed around a miniaturized sacred geography of their land" without strolling too far from the city.[65] It was perhaps its value as a site where cheap and quick escapism became possible that made the Temple of the Five Hundred Arhats—and surely many other such surrogates—a preferred destination for "old grannies and granddads and country yokels," as comic novelist Ichiba Tsūshō put it in 1782.[66] Scholar Igarashi Tomio has made a similar point in regard to the miniaturized versions of the Azuma thirty-three-stage circuit and the Tone thirty-three-stage route built in Ōta (Kazusa Province). Surveying nineteenth-century travel diaries from the area, he noticed how the replicas appealed in particular to the women of nearby villages. While the men from Musashi and Kazusa found it relatively easy to journey as far as the Western Provinces, Ise, and Konpira, women (generally impeded—Igarashi points out—by the dictates of passport and barrier regulations) preferred the comfort and convenience of miniature replicas, which they toured composing verses, paying homage to Kannon, and escaping, however briefly, what Igarashi refers to as "the yoke of feudal society."[67] As artificial as they were, surrogate mountains and small-scale circuits became instrumental in promoting mobility and in offering a temporary sense of liberation from the ordinary.

Nineteenth-century guides to the sites of Edo such as Saitō Gesshin's *Illustrated Guide to Edo's Famous Places (Edo meisho zue)* and *Chronicle of the Year's Events in the Eastern Capital (Tōto saijiki)* list dozens of replicas in and around the city, defining them as "alternate abodes" *(kanjō)* of specific deities, as "identical" *(onaji)* copies, or as "transferred" *(utsushi)* versions of the originals. An Edoite who did not wish to leave the city could still travel across the land by visiting Edo's renditions of Kumano (Kii Province), of Kyoto's Sanjūsangendō, of the Inner and Outer Shrines of Ise, of Kashima and Katori Shrines (in Hitachi and Shimōsa), of the Kamakura Hachimangū, and of the three main sites for the Benzaiten cult (Enoshima, Chikubushima, and Miyajima).[68] Miniaturized copies of multi-stage pilgrimage circuits comprised imitations of the Western Provinces tour (one of which was a conveniently short route of only three *ri* in length—a little over three hundred meters—allegedly founded in 1771 by a Kanda brewer), of the Shikoku *henro* (the eighty-eight-stage Arakawa Kōbō Daishi circuit), and of the Bandō circuit (the copy extended from Yushima, went through Komagome, Nippori, Ueno, Asakusa, and came to an end in Fukagawa).[69] Fudasan Yōbukuji in Nishi Nippori was ambitiously conceived as a copy of the One Hundred Kannon megacircuit that combined Western Provinces, Chichibu, and Bandō. According to *Illustrated Guide to Edo's Famous Places,* the founder, Gikō Shōnin, had decided to create this small-scale version of the pilgrimage route "in order to provide access to the Buddhist faith to those boys and girls who would have a hard time going to the original locations."[70]

The self-referential nature of surrogates multiplied exponentially in the replicas of circuits, where not only the tour as a whole but also each stage re-created an original site. One of Edo's versions of the Western Provinces tour departed from within the precincts of Ōji Sanctuary and ended at Hōjūji in Misaki. *Chronicle of the Year's Events in the Eastern Capital* explained how each stage, including the departure and arrival sites, was in fact an exact duplicate of the corresponding temple or shrine in the original circuit (Table 1).[71] The "system of illusions" generated by the intersection of mobility, commercialism, and escapism was indeed ubiquitous, redundant, and self-replicating, but the success of surrogates and miniatures also indicates that it was a welcome element of travel culture in the late Edo period.

TABLE 1. A surrogate of the Western Provinces tour in Edo. Each stage replicates one individual site of the original circuit (adapted from Saitō Gesshin's *Chronicle of the Year's Events in the Eastern Capital*).

Stage no.	Surrogate's name	Original (province)
1	Ōji Gongen	Mount Nachi (Kii)
2	Komagome Taiunji	Mii Temple (Kii)
3	Nishigahara Muryōji	Kokawa Temple (Kii)
4	Takinogawa Shōjuin	Makinoo Temple (Izumi)
5	Nishigahara Shōrinji	Fujii Temple (Kawachi)
6	Hiratsuka Myōjin Kannondō	Tsubosaka (Yamato)
7	Yanaka Saikōji	Oka Temple (Yamato)
8	Sendagi Kōgenji	Hase Temple (Yamato)
9	Yanaka Tennōjichū Engyōin	Nan'endō (Yamato)
10	Tabata Chūdaiji	Omuroto Temple (Yamashiro)
11	Tabata Fumonji (Saigyō-an)	Daigo Temple (Yamashiro)
12	Takinogawa Yatsumura Jutokuji	Iwama Temple (Ōmi)
13	Shinobazu Anainari	Ishiyama Temple (Ōmi)
14	Ueno Gokokuin	Mii Temple (Ōmi)
15	Sendagi Shōrinji	Ima Kumano (Yamashiro)
16	Ueno Kiyomizudō	Kiyomizu Temple (Yamashiro)
17	Komagome Shindō Shōnenji	Rokuharadō (Yamashiro)
18	Shitaya Jōrakuin	Rokkakudō (Yamashiro)
19	Komagome Yaba Shōsenji	Kōdō (Yamashiro)
20	Tabata Kōmyōin	Zenbu Temple (Yamashiro)
21	Tabata Yorakuji	Anaho Temple (Tanba)
22	Yanaka Chōanji	Sōji Temple (Settsu)
23	Nishigahara Fudōin	Katsuo Temple (Settsu)
24	Sendagi Daibōfukuji	Nakayama Temple (Settsu)
25	Nezu Gongen	Kiyomizu Temple (Harima)
26	Sendagi Seson'in	Hokke Temple (Harima)
27	Nippori Yōfukuji	Mount Sosha (Harima)
28	Komagome Entsūji	Nariai Temple (Tango)
29	Tabata Tōgakuji	Matsuo Temple (Tango)
30	Shinobazu Benten	Chikubushima (Ōmi)
31	Yanaka Kinreiji	Chōmei Temple (Ōmi)
32	Yanaka Kannonji	Kannon Temple (Ōmi)
33	Misaki Hōjūji	Tanigumi (Mino)

The iconic landmark by definition, Mount Fuji, too, generated a myriad of miniaturized copies. By the mid-Edo period the mountain cult was sponsored by some four to eight hundred confraternities in the greater Edo area alone, many of which financed the construction and promotion of replicas.[72] Some appeared relatively late (Saitō Gesshin indicates that the Fuji replica at Fukagawa Hachimangū was built in the early nineteenth century),[73] while others had been in place for quite some time. According to Asai Ryōi's *Guide to Edo's Famous Sites* (*Edo meishoki,* 1662) the Komagome copy had been created sometime in the 1560s, when an unseasonable snowfall blanketed a small hill in the area on the first day of the sixth month (the day on which the real Mount Fuji opened its slopes to visitors). Many saw it as a sign from the gods and erected a small shrine that came to be considered the alternate abode of the mountain deity.[74]

As mentioned before, a journey to the real Mount Fuji was certainly not impossible but, for many an Edoite, a bit demanding in terms of time, money, and energy spent on procuring passports to clear the barrier at Hakone. Because of its harsh terrain and its lingering snows, moreover, Mount Fuji remained off-limits for long periods of time. Even when it was open to visitors, women had only limited access to the mountain. All these factors combined to make trips to Mount Fuji's Edo-based replicas more convenient and rewarding than journeys to the actual site. In offering a long list of Fuji imitations, *Chronicle of the Year's Events in the Eastern Capital* underscores the extent to which some Fuji cult practitioners identified surrogates as perfectly valid alternatives to the original mountain: "Because of its lingering snows, it is usually impossible to climb [the real] Mount Fuji in Suruga Province, and one has to wait for the hot season to ascend. Emulating this pattern, [the devotees] come on a pilgrimage [to its various replicas] on this particular day [6/1]."[75]

By the mid-nineteenth century Fuji imitations had become part and parcel of Edo's cityscape: Utagawa (Andō) Hiroshige I (1797–1858), for example, included the Mount Fuji replica at Meguro in his series *One Hundred Famous Views of Edo* (*Meisho Edo hyakkei,* 1857, published by Uoya Eikichi; see Figure 13). Towering behind the Meguro surrogate, in the distance, is the real Mount Fuji. Through a clever use of perspective, however, Hiroshige makes the Meguro imitation (a hill of about nine to twelve meters in height) appear as tall and imposing as the original mountain. Visitors are portrayed climbing the Meguro Fuji, while others enjoy the beauty of blooming cherry blossoms at the foot of the hill: Mount Fuji's imitation at Meguro thus offered the perfect combination of sacred and leisurely and, in Hiroshige's rendition, was every bit as stately and glorious as the original peak.

FIG. 13. A Mount Fuji surrogate in nineteenth-century Edo. Utagawa Hiroshige I (1797–1858). *Original Fuji, Meguro (Meguro moto Fuji)*, woodblock print, vertical ōban; 36.3 x 24.7 cm. From the series *One Hundred Famous Views of Edo (Meisho Edo hyakkei,* 1857). Photograph © Museum of Fine Arts, Boston, William S. and John T. Spaulding Collection. Courtesy Museum of Fine Arts, Boston.

Like printed materials and tangible merchandise, duplicates facilitated and democratized the acquisition of escapism and of re-creation. Pragmatically, they did not require visitors to travel long distances in order to access extra-ordinary spaces and experience a release from the everyday. To borrow the words of Dean MacCannell, the promoters of miniaturized surrogates, like the peddlers of bogus souvenirs, strove to attract customers with a "staged authenticity" that created the mirage of an almost real experience.[76] A mirage was exactly what travelers demanded and what icons, imitations, and forgeries delivered. The illusory, in fact, even overshadowed the authentic when illustrated maps turned ordinary mountains into lush and imposing peaks, or when printed guides began to publicize certain surrogates as superior to the original sites they replicated because they were easier to access, endowed with more commercial amenities, and surer to offer an immediate gratification. The Mount Fuji at Takada was one such enhanced alternative. As *Souvenir of Edo: A Picture Book* explains, this replica was "not like the other Mount Fuji. Pilgrimage is allowed until the eighteenth day of the sixth month. They sell wheat straw snakes. Merchants come out and put up tea shops, it becomes extremely lively on those days."[77] Enjoyable and convenient, the contrived versions of Fuji were in high demand among the Edoites. As Saitō Gesshin observed, in and around nineteenth-century Edo, the craze for duplicates was such that there were simply not enough hills in town and many of the replicas had to be hastily built by piling up rocks, "for this is the latest fashion of recent times" *(kinsei no hayari nari).*[78]

BY DEVICES such as edible specialties, transportable knickknacks, and duplicated travelscapes, the entire geography of the land and the heritage and essence of its sites became available to travelers from almost all walks of life. A clever business venture, forged icons and miniaturized copies unveil the complexity of the interaction between spaces and the economy and the extent to which mobility had diversified along horizontal (i.e., geographical spread) and vertical (i.e., social types) lines by the late Edo period. The marketing of traditions as trinkets and the use of forgeries and surrogates occasionally prompted skepticism and confusion, but the vast majority of visitors who flocked to see them showed no sign of being bothered by the fact that many sites were nothing but imitations. In 1828, returning from (the real) Mount Fuji to his native Shimōsa, pilgrim Suzuki Shōzō stopped in Kamakura. The main hall of the Hachimangū was not accessible, but Shōzō, at least in his travel memoir, was just as satisfied to have visited a surrogate temporary shrine.[79]

By the nineteenth century, a traveler's immersion in the history of a site and his or her appropriation thereof no longer needed to be effected through cultural prowess: money sufficed. While some scholars have argued that money became a critical mediator between space and time only with the advent of the modern age,[80] it seems evident that, if to a lesser degree, the money economy already informed mobility in the Edo period, defining and redefining the worth of sites while shaping the travelers' perception of, and engagement with, many a landscape. Duplicates and souvenirs joined the other ubiquitous commodities of escapism—travel novels—in partially disconnecting the visitor/reader from the "real" experience and in providing a vicarious, convenient, more manageable, and just as acceptable version of travel and of its backdrop, the flexible travelscapes of Edo period Japan. At the same time, material objects offered an alternative to literary knowledge. Affordable and ubiquitous, they required little or no intellectual effort and guaranteed to connect the buyer with an appropriate cultural precedent or with the very essence of a site's identity. After the journey ended, both memoirs and souvenirs kept the experience alive; but whereas the resuscitated ghosts of Narihira and Saigyō whispered only to the educated from the pages of a diary, the flashy shell-decorated screens from Enoshima remained on display in the traveler's home for everyone to see.

CHAPTER 7

Bodies, Brothels, and Baths
Travel and Physical Re-creation

We are body.
—Caroline Walker Bynum, *Fragmentation and Redemption*

It is by means of the body that space is perceived, lived—
and produced.
—Henri Lefebvre, *The Production of Space*

THE PREVIOUS CHAPTERS have all hinted at the manifold ways in which the body could become a "location of practice and change."[1] The authorities saw in physical attributes, from the shaved heads of nuns or the forelocks of young boys to the wombs of adult women *(onna),* powerful indicators of a person's place, function, and value. The body and its manifold physiological manifestations were also central to religious discourse. As discussed in Chapter 2, the body as a source of pollution mediated a person's ability to access certain Shinto and Buddhist spaces. With rare exceptions, Buddhism traditionally interpreted physicality as a hindrance to the attainment of enlightenment and saw in ascetic practices that manifested disdain for the body (dietary limitations, fasting, immersion in cold water, and tonsure, to name a few) one of the necessary steps toward achieving a detachment from illusion. In areas such as Kumano or the Fuji caves, identified as earthly projections of wombs, space became body and body became space.[2] In another example of the interconnectedness between the body and the sacred, Winston Davis has suggested that ailing parishioners would collect and drink the water from their *oshi*'s bath in hopes of regaining their health.[3] The physical implications of this act are at least threefold. First, the *oshi* could shed some of their ethereal holiness in a corporeal entity (the bathwater); second, the supernatural powers with which religious figures were endowed could be transferred to other bodies (by the act of drinking the bathwater); and third, suffering bodies could recover their strength by such act of incorporation.

Records from the Edo period also shed a light on their authors' profound awareness of their physicality. Anne Walthall, for example, has shown how a female member of the rural elites from Shinano Province merged body consciousness with gender consciousness and regretted having "the weak body of a useless woman."[4] Constantly confronted with physically demanding tasks, travelers were especially inclined to perceive their experiences in bodily terms. In her journal, an anonymous townswoman who visited Sagami Province in 1767 acknowledged the physical limitations that hindered female travelers, noting for example that the absence of ferries at a certain beach "made it hard for us women to cross over." When her party (including travelers of both sexes) decided to visit a cave "located amidst tall, steep mountains," she hesitated: "Climbing to go see it is not something I would want to do. Obviously, the men decided to go." With the help of her travel companions she made her way to the top, but was again confronted with her physical shortcomings when it came time to retrace her steps: "When I attempted to descend, I started feeling dizzy."[5]

Many of the case studies presented in the previous pages indicate that, across discourses, the body was one of the primary sites where rules were imposed; where defiance, contestation, and assertions of individual agency manifested themselves; where change was implemented by external alterations to one's appearance (tonsure, cross-dressing); and where connections were forged by the ingestion of culinary icons. To borrow the words of Marta Vicente and Luis Corteguera, who have looked at examples from the early modern Spanish world, wayfarers acted on their bodies "in a social context, confirming the rules or becoming subversive by defying those rules."[6] At the same time, the cases introduced here reveal how bodies were permeable thresholds that mediated between external spaces and internal constructions of the self. The metaphors that the nun Kikusha-ni chose to describe her release from social expectations clearly indicate how re-creation began with the body. She considered herself a body adrift and a cicada that had discarded her skin.

Given such prominence of the body as a mediator between the self and the environment, it comes as no surprise that acts of engagement with the spaces of travel included also physical appropriations of various kinds. Travel was a thoroughly sensory experience. Vision played a key role in linking visitors to sites, as travelers climbed peaks in search of all-embracing vistas, journeyed to spots from which they could enjoy the best views of famous locations, and strove to catch glimpses of the outside world through the palanquin shutters. Hearing was just as important. In their memoirs, not a few travelers comment on the noises they heard at certain sites or on the eerie silence of others. As she waited for a new permit after having been denied transit at Arai barrier, for example, Inoue Tsūjo filled her 1681 diary with descriptions of the lively sounds of the road and of the calls of wayfarers that she heard from her room at a local inn.[7] Karyō-ni (1696–1771), the widow of a merchant from Kanazawa in Kaga domain, included in her 1750 memoir a paragraph on the deer cries echoing through the mountains at night.[8] Travel entailed an olfactory experience as well. The scent of *uirō* in the air at Odawara became the centerpiece for one of Kikusha-ni's haiku, while the anonymous townswoman who visited the Tsurugaoka Hachimangū in 1767 made it a point to jot down a few lines on the unbearably bad breath of the local guide.[9] As discussed in the previous chapter, local gastronomies effectively offered visitors the opportunity to taste the flavor and even the historical or religious valence of certain sites. Inevitably, the desire to experience physically the novelty of the unfamiliar found a tactile outlet as well, as various opportunities to come into contact with, touch, and be enveloped by a site and its icons became the focus of many a traveler's interaction with the spaces of travel and of their efforts to achieve re-creation. Mediated by commodification and popularized by commercialism, the transformative process that combined mobility and physicality was available at hot-spring resorts and in roadside brothels. The physical removal from the space of the ordinary helped travelers to let go of the imperatives that regulated their lives at home, while the regeneration of the body brought about by immersion in hot-spring waters and by impromptu sexual adventures amplified the sense of metamorphosis they felt as they crossed extraordinary, flexible spaces.

The commodification of recreational travel had generated new material ways of embracing escapism while bringing old ones to new heights. Bodies too, like historical events or heavenly blessings, became acquirable icons and tokens of re-creation, a variation on the theme of *meibutsu*. They, too, could serve as frames of reference to organize spaces and generate hierarchies along priority lines different from the ones introduced so far. To the erotic traveler, interaction (and intercourse) with local prostitutes served a purpose similar to what lyrical or historical recollections did for the educated and what the acquisition of material objects did for other wayfarers in the age of commercialism—it was a way of evaluating the worth, sampling the flavor, and appropriating the essence of an unfamiliar space. The "cartographies of desire" conceptualized by and for the sex traveler measured and mapped the territory with yet another yardstick, eroticism.[10]

Like the brothel, the bath enabled visitors to enjoy a rejuvenating and transformative experience. If movement and travel were metaphors for change in the floating world, so was bathing. From the first bath of a child to the final cleansing of the deceased, life unfolded along a series of ablutions, as novelist Shikitei Sanba (1776–1822) once proclaimed.[11] The immersion of the body in water was invested with a variety of meanings, spanning the religious, medical, and recreational. Not unlike pleasure quarters and sacred mountains, hot-spring resorts were spaces apart with rules of their own and as such offered travelers the opportunity to immerse themselves fully—body and spirit—into their extra-normative atmosphere. Not only geographies and identities, but also bodies were re-created as a result of travel.

Embodying Travelscapes: Prostitutes and the Erotic Traveler

The hedonistic side of Edo culture succeeded in carving out independent spaces where one could momentarily escape the constraints and expectations of the everyday. As mentioned in Chapter 4, for the men who lived in the city the pleasure quarter represented a convenient and immediately available outlet for re-creation, provided of course that one carried enough cash and knew the proper etiquette to gain access into the brothels. As fenced-off sites where the rules of normalcy were relaxed and where social hierarchies were turned upside down, urban red-light districts such as Edo's Yoshiwara were generally perceived as spaces apart, so much so that, as Marcia Yonemoto has pointed out, they were even reimagined as foreign countries.[12] At the same time, however, they were spaces that operated with the government's seal of approval. As removed from the ordinary as it may have felt, sex in the city's licensed quarters thrived under the complacent, approving scrutiny of officialdom.[13] Sex on the road was a different matter altogether. Not only was it farther removed from the city, thus more physically detached from the ordinary for the urbanites, it also occurred outside and against the boundaries of official discourse, which issued countless edicts prohibiting the presence of prostitutes in the inns along the major highways.[14] It was, in other words, a complete departure and disjunction from the everyday, the expected, and the legally acceptable.

In charting the territory, sexual travelers produced eroticized topographies based on the elegance of local courtesans and on the promise of high-quality titillation. Like all other imagined geographies, the maps of pleasure were never absolute. Shaped by personal preference, they made it possible for one man's rousing wonderland to become another man's descent into soporific insipidness. Consequently, sexual centers and peripheries ebbed and flowed continuously in the name of eroticism and (perceived) sophistication. In the late seventeenth century, the Kamigata region loomed large not only in the maps of the educated but also in the cartographies of the erotically inclined. Published in Kyoto in 1688 and penned by Tsuruya Kiemon, Yoshida Rokubei, and Iseya Ichirōbei, *Guide to the Brothels of All Provinces (Shokoku irozato annai)* perused famous pleasure quarters in the cities as well as less glamorous teahouses in peripheral post towns. This guidebook, in other words, aimed at providing sex aficionados with a road map to distinct spaces of pleasure. It listed the names of the girls employed in each establishment, their specialties, the types of food served, and—most important—prices. The guide's journey began in Kyoto, where, according to the authors, the Shimabara stood out as "the headquarters (*honji,* lit. "head temple") of this country's red-light districts." Removed from the city after the 1657 Meireki Fire and relatively inconvenient to reach, Edo's (New) Yoshiwara did not fare too well in the erotic topographies of this seventeenth-century guide, which made it a point to emphasize how little in common Edo's licensed quarter had with the red-light district of "the capital" (i.e., Kyoto).[15]

In the early nineteenth century, some travelers still identified the Kansai with the core of the country's elegance—erotic and otherwise. The Nagoya merchant Hishiya Heishichi, for instance, described the courtesans of Nagasaki as unrefined and utterly strange country girls who spoke with an unattractive provincial accent and who would not stand up to comparison with their classier Kamigata colleagues. Even though the local red-light district reminded him of Osaka's Shinmachi, the similarity ended there, for the girls in the teahouses were in fact "extremely incompetent and completely different *(ōkini koto ni shite)* from those of the Kamigata." Even in Hakata, Heishichi managed to reassert the superior quality of the courtesans from the Kyoto and Osaka area. While he dismissed the local girls as "somewhat inferior" to the ones in Shimonoseki, he found solace in the fact that some of the apprentices "came from the Osaka area, so they are not too bad."[16] Other travelers, however, remapped the cartographies of sexual indulgence altogether, shifting the center toward Edo. Kiyokawa Hachirō, for example, disparagingly dismissed the entertainers of Kyoto and Osaka as "truly incompetent and insignificant, [...] even less interesting than the beginners in Edo," insinuating that their fame was simply due to the poor taste of their customers, "country bumpkins who come into town and do not know any better."[17]

IF RE-CREATION presupposed an engagement with extra-ordinary spaces, nowhere would travelers encounter more outlandish an environment than in Nagasaki, at the crossroad of domestic and foreign, commonplace and exotic. Nagasaki featured prominently in the cartographies of the educated who were drawn there by curiosity or appreciation for Chinese or Western culture. For similar reasons it also carried considerable prominence in the maps of sex travelers, who came to Nagasaki attracted by the Maruyama red-light district. Though legally sanctioned as a licensed quarter, the Maruyama had a distinct edge over similar spaces of government-approved sexual diversion, as its girls fueled unusual fantasies and enticed curiosity for their interactions with the members of the local Dutch and Chinese settlements. Before Hishiya Heishichi visited the city (and, despite his tirade against the girls' incompetence, not a few of its teahouses) in 1802, scores of other travelers had journeyed to Nagasaki only to be distracted by the irresistible allure of the Maruyama. In 1688 Ihara Saikaku, describing the travels of merchants from Kyoto, Osaka, Edo, and Sakai to Kyushu, had ironically commented that "the money from the home provinces would have a better chance of returning safely to its masters if there were no Maruyama quarter in Nagasaki,"[18] while in the 1690s Engelbert Kaempfer had acknowledged the popularity of the Maruyama by claiming that it was "frequented no less than the temples."[19] Receptive to Nagasaki's claim to erotic and exotic fame, the seventeenth-century *Guide to the Brothels of All Provinces* featured a section on the Maruyama, devoting a good deal of voyeuristic attention to the engagements between the local courtesans and the Chinese. According to the guide, every time a Chinese vessel entered Nagasaki harbor, the women of the Maruyama would go out aboard small boats and parade back and forth to welcome the sailors. Repeat customers would be taken directly to the brothels, where they would spend two or three days, and then, "having found solace, they [would] go back" *(nagusame kaeru)*. First-timers, on the other hand, would be welcomed by an interpreter, taken to a separate facilty, served food and sake, and only later be shown to the brothel after they picked a girl.[20]

In the eighteenth century the borderland character of Nagasaki spurred the interest of Furukawa Koshōken, a Confucian scholar who, in 1783, descended upon the city to "investigate its customs," as he prudently put it. Koshōken could not resist the temptation to explain metonymically the cosmopolitan and often rambunctious atmosphere of the city by hinting at the multiethnic clientele of its courtesans:

> Twenty-five prostitutes at a time have permission to access the compounds of the red-haired barbarians [i.e., the Dutch] and of the Chinese. They come and go every single day. Considering that all of them have their own attendants, the result is a considerable chaos. There is a guard at the gate called the "searcher" *(saguri)* who, as they make their way out, has the task of inspecting their robes. However, since they come and go on a daily basis, he just quickly pats their clothes.

> The courtesans loathe going to the residence of the red-hairs and deem it bad for their reputation, but this is a decision of the government so they have no choice but to go. Moreover, the courtesans who go to the [residence of the] red-hairs are those who, in the Maruyama, are not in bad health. When a red-hair likes a courtesan, he gives her all sorts of precious objects. When the elegant customers of the Maruyama become able to do the same, they pay to have the girl released, so she no longer goes to the Dutch compound. As for the red-hairs, if by any chance they find out that a courtesan is having an illicit affair, they strip her naked, paint her entire body with ink, and kick her out at the gate. A local man told me that there have been a few such incidents of girls being kicked out in the past five or ten years. Since it is hard for them to go back to the Maruyama [like that], they hide in the neighborhood, borrow some garments, and make their way back when it is dark.[21]

Having identified Nagasaki as a site of exotic Otherness and clarified its outlandish nature through the image of ill-mannered and generally repulsive foreigners cavorting with reluctant courtesans, Koshōken concluded—at least on paper—that the local customs he had come to investigate were indeed reproachable. Whether he physically engaged with the objects of his inquiry we do not know, for he is careful not to say.

Aside from the seemingly incorruptible Koshōken, however, most male travelers used Nagasaki prostitutes to develop a connection with the city. Sexual engagements helped them establish a specific power relationship with an hitherto unknown body/space, thus empowering the client/outsider to dominate the prostitute/insider and to overcome the sense of disconnect that occurs while traveling away from home. In this respect, intercourse, like the recovery of historical and lyrical precedent or like shopping, facilitated the seizure of the unfamiliar. Hishiya Heishichi experienced and tamed the peculiar essence of Nagasaki through its women. When he first approached the Maruyama prostitutes during his 1802 visit he found them "utterly bizarre" *(ito okashiki)*. Underscoring the equivalence between bodies and sites, Heishichi used the same expression to describe the city itself—Nagasaki too was, at first, "utterly bizarre." As Heishichi gradually became accustomed to the local lifestyle, he began frequenting "the usual tobacco shop" *(rei no tabakoya)* where he would feast and be entertained by dancers and courtesans. They became the mediators between Heishichi and the exotic around him, for it was through them that he progressively internalized the Chineseness of the city: "I am not one to enjoy lust as if I were in the prime of life, but I do find this chance encounter with the different customs of a faraway place to be quite a novelty. Before falling asleep I love hearing a detailed story describing the tastes of the Chinese customers." After five days of frolicking with the courtesans, Heishichi finally declared himself "acquainted with the locals" and decided to leave.²² In other words, once he thought he had grasped the full dimension of the city, Heishichi lost the incentive to interact with the icons of Nagasaki's foreignness and felt ready to move on.

THE EQUATION of travel with a sexual odyssey had long provided inspiration for an extensive literary production and for a great many visual representations. Since the Heian period celebrated literary works had portrayed famous lovers on the road; one may mention the ubiquitous Ariwara no Narihira or the exiled Shining Prince as fitting examples. More befitting the townsmen's spirit of the Edo period were erotic adventurers of a different breed, epitomized by Yonosuke, the hero of Ihara Saikaku's *The Life of an Amorous Man* (1682). In the final segment of the novel Yonosuke sails off toward the elusive Isle of Women, in a glorious departure that not only provided an outlet for travel-based wishful thinking and eroticized flights of the imagination but also envisioned an entirely new type of travel destination, a titillating though entirely fictitious pleasureland. The maps of erotic travel thus included both real and fantastic destinations, for their cartographers looked just as avidly at such imaginary places as the Isle of Women or the Isle of Men as they did at actual roadside brothels. These locations functioned as milestones for the erotic traveler in much the same way as lyrical sites, religious compounds, or post towns marked the pace of the journey for the educated, the pious, or the official wayfarer. Not unlike the earthly manifestations of heavens and mandalas or the lyrical sites where poets engaged in a spiritual dialogue with the literary icons of the past, the landmarks of erotic desire (real and fictitious alike) were idealized projections of individual desires and aspirations. As such, they sustained the proliferation of meanings surrounding places, enhanced the versatility of Edo period travelscapes, and added to the intricate vocabulary of space, identity, and autonomy in the early modern age.

Not only did the commercial publishing industry play a pivotal role in fostering the development of new parameters to value a site, it also gradually pushed sex-based modes of interpretation into the vast realm of public knowledge. In the seventeenth century, innovation came mostly in the form of Saikaku's imagined geographies and in the establishment of a market for guides to pleasure quarters, evaluations of courtesans *(yūjo hyōbanki),* and even diaries of erotic journeys, all of which made their appearance in the stalls of urban bookstores.²³ By the eighteenth century, the erotic cartographies of commercial publishers became even more comprehensive, now also catering to sexual travelers who had little or no interest in women. In 1768, for instance, Hiraga Gennai (1723–1779) produced *A Close Inspection of Male Love: Three Mornings (Nanshoku saiken mitsu no asa),* a guide to the male prostitution establishments of Edo, Kyoto, and Osaka, "featuring a detailed list of all the places for male-male sex across the provinces."[24] Published works of the late Edo period widely fantasized on the theme of the sexual journey, producing anything from guides to the way of the *tsū*—that is, manuals for the pleasure quarter connoisseur—to erotic prints *(shunga)* specifically devoted to the theme of travel,[25] to maps of imaginary lands of pleasure modeled after (and meant to be metaphors for) real licensed districts.[26] Their increasingly flexible attitude toward what constituted a famous site engendered new eroticized icons and facilitated a traveler's ability to connect with any given landscape.

By the nineteenth century, the mapmakers of eroticism had repaved each road with a lush new surface of sexual overtones. Utagawa Kunisada's *Erotic Prints in Fifty-three Stages (Shunga gojūsantsugi),* for example, transmogrified the fifty-three stations of the Tōkaidō highway into the fifty-three stages of sexual encounters.[27] So did *The Fifty-three Stages on the Tōkaidō: A Diary of Rubbing Thighs (Tōkaidō gojūsantsugi hizasuri nikki,* 1855), the ultimate sexual guide to Japan's main highway. Eroticism reappropriated sites otherwise claimed by political, religious, or literary discourse and imbued them with a new, more prurient character. No target was spared (not even the sacred) in this reorganization of the land based on sexual priorities: "Thank goodness on the way to the Great Shrine I gained access to this plump, heavenly cave"; "Among all thirty-three stages this is the closest to paradise, and we partake in the highest of all rewards," reads the dialogue between an Ise pilgrim and a courtesan captured in *A Diary of Rubbing Thighs.*[28]

The same work represents the ever-malleable Mount Fuji in yet another light, surrounded not by poetic mists or merciful avatars but by a titillating halo of sexual innuendos. In *A Diary of Rubbing Thighs* the Fuji caves, generally associated with fertility cults or the adventures of Nitta Shirō as narrated in *Mirror of the East (Azuma kagami),* become the pretext for a crude association between the landscape and female genitals, as the guidebook proclaims, "Rather than a secret tunnel to the slopes of Mount Fuji I'd rather worship your cave."[29] The metamorphosis of Fuji into a catalyst to erotic fantasies does not stop here. Accompanying the entry on the post town of Hara is a small illustration of the mountain, justified, one would imagine, by Hara's fame as a *kaidō ichi,* one of the preferred sites from which travelers could enjoy a view of the peak. The caption, however, marks a dramatic departure from the conventional, as it neither pays tribute to Fuji's lingering snows nor does it wink at the ghost of an enraptured Narihira. More prosaically, it puns on the name of the location by lamenting that sexual arousal can cause exhaustion (dry kidney): "In Hara he is pissed: when one gets hard in Hara, is it hard to piss?"[30]

Religious and historical pedigrees alike are deconstructed and given a whole new spin in this work, as locations become famous for being the stages, not of miracles, poetry writing, or epic battles, but of passionate lovemaking on the part of historical characters. *A Diary of Rubbing Thighs* dwells on the erotic deeds of Oguri Hankan (1398–1464) and his lover Teruta Hime at Yugyōji in Fujisawa, and of Minamoto no Yoshitsune (1159–1189) and his mistress Shizuka—caught frolicking in Fujisawa with the assistance of Yoshitsune's devoted sidekick, Benkei. Equally sexualized are local gastronomic specialties, whose history is dished up with plenty of added spice. Regarding the famous Asakusa seaweed sold on roadside stands in Shinagawa, the guide informs its readers that "The numerous waitresses pull wayfarers [into their inns] and force them to lay with them, day in and day out. Juices flow and fertilize the sea—no wonder the local seaweed is so tasty. The juices that flow out at night, however, stink in the morning, hence the name Asa-kusa [Stinks in the Morning] seaweed." Ariwara no Narihira, the epitome of the refined erotic traveler, could not and did not escape the attention of the authors, who parodied his descent to the East to enliven the story behind the gastronomic landmark of Ōiso: "Here Ariwara [no Narihira], during his descent to the East, hooked up and slept with a female wayfarer. He kneaded her opening till it looked like a millet rice cake. This is, they say, the origin of their specialty product."[31]

In the age of commercialism, travelers could relate to spaces by acquiring referential symbols thereof, and the geographies of pleasure were no exception. In this case, local women (or men, for travelers like Gennai) became the embodiments of travelscapes, the equivalent of local specialties meant to be displayed with a price tag, acquired, and consumed. *A Diary of Rubbing Thighs* suggests a virtual equivalence between the female body and the famed *meibutsu* of Mariko, noting, "When it's time to have sex, the prostitutes sprout out like yams, which also happen to be the local specialty."[32] Equally indicative of such identification between bodies and commodities is a comment Kita of *Shank's Mare* fame makes in Mishima. In search of diversion with a local girl, he inquires about the availability of "that merchandise."[33] The word Ikku puts in Kita's mouth, *shiromono,* refers primarily to objects for sale and items strictly related to consumption, betraying a general trend toward the objectification of bodies among the producers and consumers of late Edo travel culture.

Transformed into local specialties, prostitutes now gave new meaning to already well-known locations. Tōkaidō post towns such as Fujisawa, Shinagawa, Akasaka, Yoshida, and Goyu may have been identified as official relay stations in the maps of the government, but in the eyes of several travelers, writers, and artists of the floating world they were mostly known for their brothels. Andō Hiroshige visually captured the erotic essence of Akasaka and Goyu in his *The Fifty-three Stages of the Tōkaidō Highway* (*Tōkaidō gojūsantsugi,* Hoeidō series). The print of Akasaka depicts the inside of an inn where customers are preparing for the night. One is returning from a bath, another smokes a pipe while a waitress serves him dinner. In another wing of the inn the girls are preparing for work. As Konno Nobuo observed, "the folded mattresses in the room tell in an intriguing and mysterious way what the function of these inn attendants really was."[34] In Goyu the scene is even livelier, as a couple of teahouse girls are forcefully pulling two unwilling wayfarers into their establishment. Works like Hiroshige's woodblocks of Akasaka and Goyu, Kunisada's *Erotic Prints in Fifty-three Stages,* or *A Diary of Rubbing Thighs* seized the strongholds of Tokugawa geopolitical authority—the Tōkaidō post towns—and transformed them into virtual headquarters of the floating world's counterculture by the alternate logics of eroticism and commercialism. By replacing official functions with bodily functions, these guides and prints indirectly questioned the monopoly of the Tokugawa over roads and post towns, presenting the realm not as an orderly structure but as an extended and often chaotic underworld of sensual pleasures.

One may also point out that the 1830s Tōkaidō series by Hiroshige was not conceived specifically with the erotic traveler in mind, as none of the other locations depicted therein is explicitly presented by association with the sex industry (the print of Kanagawa also includes teahouse girls approaching travelers, but they are not the main focus of the illustration). There are sites celebrated for their poetic value (Mount Fudesute near Sakanoshita) and others for their natural sceneries (Hara), for their inclusion in folk legends (the weeping rock near Nissaka), for their connections to government authority (Nihonbashi, Fujieda, Fujikawa, Seki), for their religious landmarks (Fujisawa, Miya), or for their famous specialty products (Mariko, Kusatsu). Hiroshige's choice of eroticism (or flat-out sex trade) as the underlying motif for the prints of Akasaka and Goyu not only speaks volumes about the ability of bodies-as-commodities to shape (or reshape) a site's identity, but also underscores the degree to which, by the nineteenth century, publications intended for the general public matter-of-factly incorporated modes of interpretation based on sex. Eroticism as a frame of reference had become part and parcel of the culture of travel in the late Edo period. By then, criteria based on erotic curiosity had even transcended the boundaries of gender.

Actual intercourse with local prostitutes may have been the preserve of male travelers, but with the gradual transformation of bodies into icons, courtesans and waitresses became must-see elements of the landscape for *all* travelers, not only men, and not only the sexually inspired. The diffusion of eroticized cartographies sustained by the publishing industry, and the establishment of a commonly accepted equation between bodies and commodities, made it increasingly easy and commonplace for female travelers to identify prostitutes with landmarks and to treat them accordingly. In 1775, returning to her hometown of Warabi (Musashi Province) after a pilgrimage to Mount Minobu, Enomoto Myōshin came to Moto Yoshiwara, where the local entertainers caught her attention. She could have chosen to dismiss the encounter and never mention it in her travel memoir; instead, she captured it in a haiku, transforming the local prostitutes into quintessential embodiments of the site's elegance.

Ukareme wa	Entertainers,
Moto Yoshiwara no	are they not the sparrows
suzume kana	of Moto Yoshiwara?[35]

In the Edo period the word "sparrow" *(suzume)* was often used as a metaphor to indicate someone in the know.[36] By extension, it took on the meaning of a mediator between insider and outsider, which was exactly the function Myōshin attributed to the prostitutes of Moto Yoshiwara. A similar response can be found in the verses that the traveling nun Kikusha-ni composed in 1812 while transiting through the post towns of Yoshida and Goyu.

Yo no aji ya	A taste of this world:
Yoshida no hana ni	for the flowers of Yoshida,
hitoya kyaku	a customer for the night.
Furisode no	Caught by the swinging sleeves
Goyu ni hikaretsu	at Goyu:
fuji no maku	a wisteria curtain.[37]

Like Myōshin, Kikusha-ni hints at the fact that bodies could function as entry points into unfamiliar spaces (behind the "wisteria curtain") and as vehicles through which outsiders could get "a taste of this world." Regardless of gender, late Edo period travelers exploited the bodies of prostitutes as a way of seizing and taming the unknown, and did so even without needing actual intercourse.

Some women travelers used modes of engagement with the landscape centered on courtesans and entertainers to subvert existing rules. The daughter of a samurai at the service of the lord Tokugawa Nariaki, Nishimiya Hide

(1834–1912), identified prostitutes as tangible manifestations of a tantalizing, mysterious, and extra-normative space and time. On her way to Mito in 1868, Hide had no choice but to spend the night in a post town notorious for its brothels. Though the members of her retinue hesitated, Hide seemed fascinated by the idea of catching a glimpse of the unknown by observing the local girls. She argued her case: "What do they do by way of entertainment? [...] If it's that *unusual*, it won't hurt to spend a night watching it." Hide's words not only reveal her desire to experience novelty by means of the local entertainers but also challenge established rules of propriety for a lady of her rank—rules her reluctant travel companions well understood and unsuccessfully attempted to enforce. Her wish was eventually granted: the party stayed, and Hide found the experience "most enjoyable."[38] Along the roads of late Edo Japan bodies became landmarks and souvenirs on display for anyone to seize, if not physically at least with the eyes and with the brush. The cartographies of eroticism had become adaptable and tantalizing enough to interest and inform travelers of both sexes in search of a respite from the ordinary.

Physical Regeneration as Re-creation: Travel to Hot Springs

Much like bodies, trinkets, and gastronomies, the bath itself functioned as an instrument for attaining escapism and regeneration in the context of the commercial economy. As Lee Butler observes, the trend to utilize the space of the bath as a site of leisure and "even pleasure" had begun in the late medieval period;[39] by the Edo period, the bath's role as a space apart with the potential to transform the body had grown exponentially. In the realm of nineteenth-century fiction—from Ikku's *Shank's Mare* to Sanba's *The Bathhouse of the Floating World* (*Ukiyoburo*, 1809)—the theme of the bath as a place removed from the ordinary is often played in a comical key,[40] but reality did not lag too far behind. Outsiders truly did experience the impact of regional diversity at hot-spring resorts and public baths, as the case of Aunt Ogasawara exemplifies. A woman of the Mito domain, Aunt Ogasawara visited a public bath in Edo for the first time in the late Tokugawa period. As she walked in, she found a bucket filled with hot water. Thinking it was very much "like Edo townsmen" to pamper their customers, she went ahead and used it. The bucket, however, had not been placed there for her, but belonged to another person. When the mistake was discovered, Aunt Ogasawara apologized profusely in embarrassment, while the Edoites brushed off the incident as trivial.[41] For better or worse, baths and pools—at hot-spring resorts as well as in the numerous inns along the highways—did assume the function of sites where outsiders met with, and literally immersed themselves in, a world apart. Many hot-spring visitors shared with erotic travelers the notion that a physical engagement with space was just as valuable and effective a way to re-create oneself as the acquisition of merchandise or an erudite connection. Not surprisingly, the line of demarcation between these three types of interactions became particularly blurred in the brothels and in the precincts of hot-spring resorts, where bodies, cash, and poems were frequently exchanged.

Journeys to hot baths undertaken for purely curative purposes by severely ill individuals can hardly be included under the rubric of leisurely travel. People who relied on the therapeutic powers of warm waters to overcome a physical handicap were seeking to reestablish normalcy rather than escape from it. Not all travelers to hot-spring resorts, however, were plagued by illness, as Yasumi Roan noted in his 1810 *Collection of Travel Precautions (Ryokō yōjinshū)*: "It goes without saying that people go to hot springs for healing purposes, but there are also those who stop over and bathe while on pilgrimage or on a leisurely trip."[42] That bathing at hot-spring resorts did not always coincide with therapy is also confirmed by the genuine surprise of Hishiya Heishichi upon discovering that a certain establishment was reserved for "those who are actually sick" *(jitsubyō no hito)* and did not offer much in terms of amenities.[43] With almost three hundred major resorts scattered throughout the various provinces (this is, at least, Yasumi Roan's estimate in 1810), the maps of hot-spring travelers were just as filled, complex, and varied as those of poets, pilgrims, and philanderers.[44]

For healthy and sick alike, re-creation by immersion in steaming waters was first and foremost of the physical kind. As he entered a bath, Hishiya Heishichi commented, "Suddenly, I forgot all about the hardships I encountered today on the road."[45] But, as Scott Clark has argued, bathing was (and still is) a "metaphor for renewal" in a larger sense, and to many an Edo traveler renewal included the subtle art of reshaping identities.[46] The baths were sites endowed with a plurality of meanings and functions, and as such they generated the temporary illusion of re-creation in more ways than one.

The communal tubs, first of all, served the same equalizing purpose as the open road, for everybody shared the same space and the same experience regardless of status—to use the words of Shikitei Sanba, "a master and his servant are equally naked when they rinse themselves."[47] In his famous novel, Sanba glorified the bathhouses of the floating world as places where one could mingle with a diverse crowd. In the women's bath he portrayed characters as dissimilar as the courtesan and the merchant's wife, the young schoolgirl and the old nun, all converging to the same pool from a myriad different places in life. The benefits of therapeutic baths, moreover, knew no class distinction and could be reaped by individuals across the social board, as Yasumi Roan aptly noted: "From time immemorial—the days when doctors and medicines did not exist—the hot springs of our country have been relieving the sorrows people suffered because of illness or the death of a child. [. . .] Ever since, baths have been popular among everyone, regardless of rank."[48]

At most hot-spring resorts the chances to mix with people of sophistication and culture were considerably high. While soaking in the pools of Hakone in 1842, a doctor's wife by the name of Inamura Kiseko encountered a "man of refinement" *(miyabi otoko)* by the name of Naokatsu, who shared with her a poem as well as excerpts from his diary. Through common literary interests Kiseko created an instant bond with Naokatsu and was able to partake of the somewhat Heianesque refinement *(miyabi)* he exuded.[49] In Hakone in 1845, Fuji Mihoko (?–1865), Kiseko's poetry tutor, came across and struck up a conversation with a young man and his mother, both passionate composers of Chinese poetry and people who, in her eyes, "seemed to enjoy refinement."[50] Whereas travelers like Lady Nakagawa in the seventeenth century and Yuya Shizuko in the eighteenth had largely ignored the existence of bathing facilities in Ikaho and had focused solely on poetic opportunities, nineteenth-century hot-spring visitors like Kiseko and Mihoko acknowledged their immersion into the pools of Hakone while still framing their experience within the context of literary sophistication. Physicality and lyricism did not exclude each other, for travel as re-creation, by then, had become entirely possible even in sites that thrived as commercial enterprises.

Their success as businesses, moreover, did not mean that hot-spring resorts lacked a historical, religious, or poetic dimension altogether. In fact, in many cases the opposite was true. Dōgo in Shikoku could (and did) claim seventh-century ruler Prince Shōtoku (572–621) among its visitors and was mentioned in such illustrious works of literature as *Chronicle of Japan (Nihongi)* and *The Tale of Genji*.[51] The facilities in Arima had hosted sixteenth-century general Toyotomi Hideyoshi (1536–1598); in the late Edo period the pavilion where tea master Sen no Rikkyū (1520–1591) had performed for Hideyoshi, as well as numerous other sites associated with the heyday of the tea ceremony, still enchanted visitors as material testimonies to such glorious precedent.[52] Immersion in the pools where Prince Shōtoku or Hideyoshi had bathed in the past could generate the same sense of communion with history experienced by the literati who stood on the very spots where Kose no Kanaoka had dropped the brush or whence Narihira had gazed at the snows of Mount Fuji. In both cases, travelers were transported to a different time and could reimagine themselves against the background of cultural and historical tradition.

Some of the gendered boundaries that commonly applied in the space of the ordinary tended to dissolve in the steam of the hot springs, also facilitating a sense of novelty, liberation, and re-creation. While men and women were usually kept separate in the public baths in the cities, resorts generally allowed mixed bathing. In Arima, for instance, the basic facility was the communal pool *(aimaku)*, which a document describes as "packed with men and women." For more privacy and more clearly defined gender and status lines a visitor would have had to upgrade to the private, curtained-off bath *(sadame maku yu)*.[53] The water there was no different from that of the communal pool; what some customers paid extra for was the ability to maintain familiar rules of gender and/or status compartmentalization at a site where such rules were normally not enforced. During his 1781 visit to Arima, Motoori Ōhira (1758–1833), the adopted son of nativist scholar Motoori Norinaga, also noticed with much surprise that half of the spectators at a sumo competition organized in conjunction with the Yu no Daijin festival were women.[54] In the space apart of the hot-spring resort (and of the local shrine), the principle according to which women were banned from attending sumo tournaments did not apply.[55]

WHAT ENABLED hot-spring resorts to manage their spaces independently was the argument of healing, which they employed in much the same way as religious establishments exploited the notion of compassion. It is no coincidence, in fact, that many hot-spring resorts served simultaneously as centers of faith and that, like pilgrimages, therapeutic journeys enabled one to effortlessly (and legally) bypass the restrictions of officialdom and obtain a travel permit. To cite one example among many, in the course of the eighteenth and nineteenth centuries, farmers from Narita—men and women—appealed to the authorities by specifying that they were "seriously ill and unable to work in the fields" and received permission to travel to Shiohara hot springs in Shimozuke Province.[56]

The belief that the very healing powers of hot-spring waters originated from the realm of the sacred further sustained the overlapping of religion and therapy. Onsenji (Hot Spring Temple) on Mount Matsudai, near Yunoshima, combined a bathing area inside a cave and a hall dedicated to the Healing Buddha Yakushi Nyorai.[57] In the eastern part of Izu peninsula, Atami blossomed simultaneously as site of healing and as a site of faith. There, baths and shrines stood side by side, the very names of the sacred halls ("Sanctuary Facing the Hot Waters," Yunomae Gongen, and "Running Hot Waters Sanctuary," or Hashiriyu Gongen) evoking such interconnectedness. Hashiriyu Gongen, also known as Izusan Gongen, was in fact known as a center for mountain asceticism *(shugendō),* its fame dating back to the thirteenth century, when the shogun Minamoto no Sanetomo (1192–1219) visited it eight times in eleven years.[58] Other visitors attributed the efficacy of Atami's waters to a perfect combination of (super)natural forces. In 1750 Master Hōkei explained that the local hot springs "combine the yin and the yang, therefore they have therapeutic [powers]. Some have hot waters, some lukewarm, for the union of yin and yang allows for the coexistence of [opposites:] thick and thin, light and heavy."[59] Equally infused with elements of the sacred was the lore surrounding the (second) origins of Arima hot springs: "Once upon a time there came a great flood, the mountains crumbled, and the hot springs disappeared. After many years a holy man by the name of Gyōgi was traveling on a pilgrimage when he came to a sanctuary called Yuya Gongen. He received precious words of admonition and came here on a quest in order to heal the ailments of all people. The hot springs came back a second time."[60] A celebrated monk and religious wanderer, Gyōgi (670–749) conferred a religious aura upon Arima, making it appealing not only as a place of leisure but also as a place of healing, holiness, and compassion.

Those who journeyed to the baths to cure an ailment thus spontaneously turned to the local sites of cult to further increase their chances of recovery. Morimoto Tsuzuko, the wife of a headman from a village in Shinano Province, took her twelve-year-old son to Suwa in 1836 after he injured his leg. While staying at the resort, they also visited many of the local shrines.[61] At the same time, those who headed for religious spaces in hope of regaining their health did not disdain to visit whatever hot-spring resorts they found along the way. When her health failed her, Iwanoshita Isonoko, who ran an inn in Shinagawa, took off on a tour of the Chichibu circuit in 1860; while completing the trip, she also stopped for baths at Ikaho.[62] At hot-spring resorts, in short, some visitors acted upon spirituality as much as they did upon physicality in order to regenerate themselves.

APPEALING AS the prospect of relaxing in tubs while steaming in sultry vapors was, for some travelers physical regeneration was not complete without the diversion (often nuanced with erotic undertones) provided by female attendants known as *yuna.*[63] Officially employed to assist bathers and scrub their backs, certain *yuna* were just as flexible in fulfilling their duties as some of the "waitresses" *(meshimori)* who operated in the inns along the major highways.

While legitimate *yuna* and *meshimori* did exist, many added the arts of flirting and entertaining to their qualifications. In 1781 Motoori Ōhira described the *yuna* at his Arima establishment as "women who explain [to customers] how to use the baths, fetch [their] robes and undergarments, and welcome [new] guests. [. . .] Here at the Nuriya they also bring out cups and bottles, mingle, and sing all sorts of tunes with their peculiar voices."[64] Those who doubled as prostitutes did so against the law and were therefore the targets of a great many legislative efforts on the part of the authorities.[65] At the same time, however, the *yuna* boosted the appeal of some resorts in much the same way as highway prostitutes brought many a post town to fame. It was by virtue of their opportunities for sexual interludes (with *yuna* or other entertainers) that hot springs acquired the status of landmarks on the maps of the erotically inclined. The ever-unabashed *A Diary of Rubbing Thighs,* for example, said of Hakone that "one finds many performers *(geisha)* from Edo, so there are more caves to dig into than one would expect."[66]

In other works of the nineteenth century hot-spring resorts are marketed prominently as sites of sexual recreation and general debauchery. In his *Humorous Record of a Trip to Arima (Kokkei Arima kikō,* 1827), Ōne (Daikon) Tsuchinari presented Arima, not as a complex of therapeutic baths, but rather as a dream destination for courtesan lovers and sake drinkers. "Let's go to Arima and do the fun stuff" is indeed the motto of the two heroes of the novel, Eraiya Tarōsuke from Kyoto and his friend, the Edoite Isōrō Sairoku. One of the two, specifies the author, "did not have any particular health problem. His only addiction was to sake, so he figured he would go to the hot springs"—it is unclear whether to cure the addiction or to fuel it. One suspects the intention was the latter, as the two seem eager to "go to Arima and raise our cups."[67] *Humorous Record of a Trip to Arima* doubled as a courtesans' evaluation booklet, for it presented and ranked Arima's entertainers in much detail. The work claims that the local *yuna,* as a rule, "do not sleep with the customers" because "Arima is a place of healing" where "the *yuna* assist at the baths," but does not deny that they also "keep [the customers] company when they drink." It also adds: "Even the twelve- or thirteen-year-old *yuna* pluck their eyebrows, blacken their teeth, and tie their sash in the front. When summoned to the drinking room, they sing the Arima songs, play drums, and dance. Their appearance spells out old elegance, which adds to the pleasure." Between the lines, *Humorous Record of a Trip to Arima* bespeaks a general expectation on the part of male customers to obtain sexual favors from the *yuna,* at least judging by the disappointed reaction of Sairoku when confronted with the news that "there is not a single one of *those* women in Arima."[68] Overall, distractions of the erotic kind were not exceptional around hot-spring resorts, if we are to judge by Yasumi Roan's advice to travelers, sick and healthy alike, to refrain from overeating, excessive drinking, and sexual activities while spending time at the baths.[69]

AS WELL AS being sites of physical and spiritual transformation, nineteenth-century hot springs distinguished themselves as thriving economic microcosms. By the late Edo period Atami offered not only "countless sacred areas and splendid views," but also "plenty of local specialties, animals and fish, that all the travelers seek."[70] The proliferation of commercial facilities in Atami even prompted author Santō Kyōsan to remind his readers about the miraculous healing powers associated with the local baths because, "although Atami is the most famous therapeutic resort in the Kantō region, I hear that it is also a place of leisure *(yusan no chi)* and many people ignore all its benefits."[71]

As businesses in touch with the expectations of the market, hot-spring resorts offered not only health, history, sex, and the sacred, but also the dream of reinventing oneself through flights of the imagination. At Yunoshima, customers could soak in the company of others or do so privately in the Curtained Bath *(makuyu)* and in the Split-Curtain Bath *(kirimaku)*; they could enjoy the comfort of a predictable experience in the Regular Bath *(tsuneyu)* or a splash of novelty in the Fresh Water Bath *(arayu)*; they could aim for luxury and possibly see themselves as courtiers in the Palace Bath *(goshoyu)*; and maybe even bathe to catch a glimpse of enlightenment in the Mandala Bath *(mandarayu)*. Each of these facilities had its own distinctive atmosphere, varying degrees of water temperature, and unique healing powers, which ranged from improving circulation to "curing" syphilis or healing wounds and boils.[72] The distinction in names was in this sense necessary, but at the same time the bestowal of such grand titles as Mandala Bath and Palace Bath is also indicative of the extent to which entrepreneurs strove to appeal to the re-creational ambitions of many a traveler.

Located at a distance of less than fifty miles from Edo and, most important, on the eastern side of the checkpoint, the hot springs of Hakone attracted throngs of Edoites with many of the same promises: relaxation, regeneration, re-creation. "Men and women from the capital [*miyako*, in this case meaning Edo], young and old, come to bathe here all the time. The view of nearby Enoshima, Kamakura, and Kanazawa is particularly splendid and the atmosphere is cheerful. This is a good place for therapeutic baths," wrote Yasumi Roan in 1810.[73] Hakone's cluster of seven hot springs enticed customers of all types with an array of facilities and services. Miyanoshita, Sokokura, Kiga, Tōnosawa, and Yumoto catered mostly to the healthy with their amenities, while Dōgashima and Ashinoyu targeted the sick by emphasizing first and foremost the therapeutic powers of their waters. The recreationally oriented baths at Tōnosawa, for example, were all set at different temperatures, with some even featuring hot waterfalls *(takiyu)*.[74] By contrast, the nauseating smell and the turbid color of its waters coupled with its remote location at the top of the pass had probably precluded Ashinoyu's development as a recreational area but had boosted its image as a true healing center.[75] Flexibility toward the demands of the market, combined with a keen understanding of the need to provide re-creation in many forms, were the prerequisites for the commercial success of hot-spring resorts in the late Edo period.

When all else failed, to acquire physical regeneration visitors could always turn to the good old souvenir and local specialties stands, where healing took the form of commodities. The shops at Yunoshima, for example, transformed the idea of therapeutic bathing into a tangible souvenir by selling mineral incrustations, the poetically labeled Hot Water Flowers *(yu no hana)*.[76] Even today, travelers buy the incrustations and, upon return, dissolve them in hot water to concoct a homemade version of the hot-spring experience.[77] In an age when commoners did not have private baths at home, however, the Hot Water Flowers probably just served as reminders of the journey and as a way to reconnect with the extraordinary, not unlike the other trinkets travelers collected along the road. Elsewhere, the beneficial virtues of hot springs were marketed in connection with local gastronomies. At the resorts of Yūfuku in Iwami Province, for example, visitors enjoyed the benefits of the local waters not only by bathing in them but also by eating rice and drinking tea prepared with them, presumably thus achieving a sense of regeneration from the inside out that further enhanced the illusion of being completely transformed.[78]

Hot-spring resorts embodied all the complexity of early modern landscapes, existing as they did at the intersection of faith, medicine, history, eroticism, lyricism, and commercialism. They catered to the religiously oriented and to the money squanderers, to the healthy and to the sick, to the fun-seeking and to the elegant. A poem included in the journal of Inamura Kiseko, who visited Hakone in 1842, reveals how hot-spring spaces challenged, questioned, and complicated the neat compartments with which officialdom tried to organize landscapes and, by extension, lives.

Omohikiya I thought
Azuma no miyako I'd look for accommodation
nadokoro o on Hakone Mountain,
Hakone no yama ni one of the famous sites
yadori min to wa of the eastern capital.[79]

In the space of thirty-one syllables Kiseko managed to demolish much of the geopolitical architecture erected by the Tokugawa, while laying down the foundations for her own spatial hierarchies. She identified Edo as one center among many, "the eastern capital," with a touch of yearning for the culturally superior Kamigata in her choice of the word "Azuma" to indicate the East. At the same time, by referring to Hakone (in Sagami Province) as one of Edo's famous sites, she insinuated that her understanding of the city's boundaries did not coincide with the official topography of government maps, but was a much more fluid entity that paid no heed to the confines of Musashi Province proper. And finally, while officialdom heralded the mountain as the site of one of its pillars—the inflexible barrier—to Kiseko Hakone it was simply a *nadokoro,* a "famous site" where she could find shelter, step out of the ordinary, and enjoy her journey.

AS SITES where renewal could be experienced at the immediate physical level and where re-creation could take the form of instant gratification, brothels and baths loomed large on the maps of Edo period travelers. Though frivolous on the surface, bodily engagements with the sites of travel in fact sustained new and complex ways of relating to, taming, and internalizing the unfamiliar. Travelers who chose to establish a physical connection with a site also joined the growing chorus of voices that questioned the monopoly of any single entity over the landscape. Even in roadside teahouses and at hot-spring resorts travelers were able to dig deeply through multiple layers of significance, construct personal hierarchies, and select and combine modes of interaction—monetary and physical, certainly, but also religious, lyrical, and historical if they so wished. The cartographies of physical re-creation pointed travelers who arrived at the busy intersection of travel and life in yet another possible direction, making a significant contribution to the pervasive discourse on space, mobility, and individual agency along the roads of the floating world.

Conclusion
Dreaming of Walking near Fuji

> The world is a bundle of roads. Follow them and you will find everything: life and death, misery and happiness, tears and consolation, adventures and love.
> —Sebastiano Vassalli, *La Chimera*

> The proverb says that shame is thrown aside when one travels.
> —Jippensha Ikku, *Shank's Mare*

IN THE COURSE of the Edo period spaces were continuously appropriated, contested, redefined, and consumed through maps and interpretive frames, through cultural exploits and the sanctity of the written word, through cash transactions and physical intercourse. The tug-of-war between sites of power to lay claim to specific areas of competence and to control and interpret spaces created flexible terrains on which individual interpretations collided and hierarchies were continuously rearranged. Consequently, the power relationships established with and within space also evolved and multiplied, as the landscape became a projection of the travelers' ambitions. Movements through malleable spaces thus became instruments of debate and platforms of contestation. Since the seventeenth century, the domination from above of the political sphere, which looked down on the landscape as its own domain (*tenka,* the realm "under heaven"), and the sacralization from below of the religious authorities, which looked up toward the peaks as projections of paradise, became complemented by increasingly varied forms of engagement: erudite citation, iconization by way of replicas and simulacra, acquisition by monetary exchange, incorporation/ingestion, physical immersion, and even sexual intercourse. The opportunity to choose between such an array of interactions enabled individual travelers to claim agency while bypassing or disregarding rules and modes pertaining to other discourses. As an ever-morphing act, travel helps to unmask a clear disjunction between theory and practice or, as Jilly Traganou put it, between "regulations upon space" and "practices within space."[1] On a road laden with multiple layers of significance, it rested with the individual traveler to determine which aspects of that vast portfolio would come to the fore, which would find room in the memoirs, and which would never be considered. Travel was infinitely more than a journey between departure and destination. It was, for some, an act of total self-assertion—selective, conscious, meditated, and carefully executed.

Travel writing provided the white canvas on which stories and lives could be rearranged, re-created, and commemorated. The narratives that travelers produced while on the road followed the trajectory of their aspirations. Writing in itself is the act of organizing information, making selections, and categorizing according to one's likes and dislikes; it entails the production of an individual set of standards and the creation of a personalized order. Already by the seventeenth century, travel and its own monument to itself, travel writing, had asserted their role in Edo culture and society as, first and foremost, (pre)texts—pretexts to leave the space of the ordinary, to question superimposed productions of spaces, to construct individual geographies, and to reconceptualize one's persona. They maintained this role throughout the course of the Edo period. Not all travelers chose to articulate their aspirations through writing, however. Examined here is but a fragment of the population of wayfarers who moved along the roads of Edo Japan. Though most likely a minority, they raised voices that deserve to be heard, for they help us to assign meaning to the multifaceted and pervasive culture of movement of the period.

What this study has tried to provide through an examination of travel texts and "maps" is an insight into the social and individual imagination of the Edo period. In a sense, it is an attempt to catch a glimpse of a much more intricate aspect of Edo culture and society—the history of knowledge and memory, and of their trajectories from status-bound and exclusive to public and collective, trajectories unquestionably directed by the expansion of education and commercialism. But dreams and aspirations (collective and individual alike) are slippery subjects that more often than not hide between lines or amid icons already dense with meaning. Difficult to verbalize, difficult to grasp, they are impossibly tricky for the historian to recover with any sense of certainty. Leave it, then, to Isoda Koryūsai (1735–1790) to come to the rescue of the text-bound historian with a mesmerizing image that, in the limited space of one woodblock print (19.1 x 25.4 cm), concisely summarizes what countless travelers (as well as the historian in question) have spilled rivers of ink attempting to articulate (Figure 14). *Dreaming of Walking near Fuji* (1770–1773) captures and freezes in time the hopes and desires of two characters from the floating world, a (very feminine) young man and a woman. At home, the two have dozed off midday, leaning against each other. Various objects are scattered on the floor around them—a pipe, a tobacco kit, a game box. Though these items are suggestive of leisurely times, the two are not in the least concerned with material things at the moment: they are dreaming, and in their dream—depicted in the upper portion of the illustration—they are traveling. Sedge hats on their heads, sandals on their feet, they are leisurely strolling at the foot of Mount Fuji. He holds a staff and leads the way with confidence; his back turned toward the mountain, he is intently staring at his travel companion, perhaps wondering why she is not keeping up with his pace. She has slowed down for a reason: looking up toward the sky, she is enraptured by the apparition of Fuji's snow-covered peak rising above the clouds. In the dream the household items and the enclosing walls have disappeared, making room for open skies, floating clouds, a majestic falcon, and an awe-inspiring peak—the man and the woman are now surrounded not by the quotidian but by the extraordinary. What the dream of movement meant to these two is clear: liberation from the everyday. Out of the house, away from all that is predictable and commonplace, they have finally achieved that state of complete disengagement that is the prerequisite for re-creation.

As the juxtaposition of movement and immobility in this image suggests, motion is, in a sense, the antithesis of order: it displaces what ought to stay put; it reconfigures what ought to be stable; it frees what ought to be contained. This was the great promise and at the same time the great threat of travel as re-creation on the roads of Edo Japan. In that nineteenth-century celebration of roaming and freedom that is *Shank's Mare,* Jippensha Ikku proclaims that those who travel enjoy the opportunity to remove themselves from the conventions that apply "when they live in the same row of houses." Freed from expectations and routines, he adds, they naturally tend to reimagine themselves without constrictions, so much so that even "the flower-like Kyōto woman can scratch her head with the skewer from the dumpling."[2] Ikku (and before him Koryūsai) simply put on paper what throngs of travelers had known for centuries: that mobility equals power—the power to experience novelty, the power to question, the power to envision and effect change. Only two days after her departure, the anonymous townswoman who traveled to Sagami in 1767 "understood that, along the road, there are plenty of sights one does not normally see" and realized "this is one of the novelties of travel."[3] At the end of this journey across the early modern culture of movement and along some of its intersections it has become clear that the modes of re-creational travel were manifold and open to everyone—to lump them together under the generic label of *tourism,* redolent as it is of superficiality

Fig. 14. Idealizing travel as re-creation. Isoda Koryūsai, *Dreaming of Walking near Fuji*, 1770–1773, woodblock print, ink and color on paper, 19.1 x 25.4 cm. Courtesy Arthur M. Sackler Gallery, Smithsonian Institution, Washington, DC (The Anne van Biema Collection, S2004.3.24).

and conformism, of shallow Kodak moments and oblivious crowds corralled between one attraction and the next, would do Edo travelers a great disservice, depriving their creations of any nuance, their interactions with the landscape of any meaning, and their experiences of any individuality.

Given the complexity of early modern movements, it also becomes evident that the road represented much more than a functional connective from point A to point B. It was an ever-mutating stage, ready to accommodate all sorts of new performances while still resonating with echoes of the old ones. This was, perhaps, the single defining feature of re-creational travel in Edo Japan, a characteristic destined to change in the years following the Meiji Restoration of 1868. With the advent of the modern age and of new modes of transportation—most notably the train—reaching the destination, rather than experiencing the road, became the goal of many travelers.[4] In this respect, the act of journeying and of being in between (the points of departure and arrival) lost its edge as a complete and long-term immersion into novelty. In the days of the *floating* world, however, the road was still a palimpsest onto which discourses converged and shaped landscapes, allowing for the same site to renew itself continually while becoming enriched with further layers of meanings for the next traveler to unravel.

It may seem somewhat ironic that a study of travel, defined as the removal of the self from a defined social space and time, may in the end provide some insight into the dynamics at play in the everyday lives of people—that the extraordinary, in other words, may illuminate and explain the ordinary. And yet this was the case with movement and the floating world: discussing one helps us better understand the complex and ever-changing character of the other. The many mutations of the spaces of travel tell the story of a fluid system of hierarchies developing against a political and ideological background that theoretically allowed little room for contestation. The production of memoirs as texts of identity illuminates on one side the dynamic character of gender relations inside and outside the household, and on the other the process through which identities were configured and reconfigured within and without society. Understanding the pervasiveness of and importance vested in souvenirs and amenities contributes to a fuller assessment, not only of Edo's creative commercial economy, but also of the way in which locations and entrepreneurs appropriated the historical, lyrical, or religious heritage of a site and transformed the recreational and re-creational desires of travelers into marketable commodities. While this is first and foremost a study of individual ideas, identities, and imaginations, it is also undeniable that the travel culture of the Edo period reveals—sometimes directly, sometimes obliquely—a more general social history. What we see through the lens of travel is the picture of a society in flux. Following the routes of early modern wayfarers allows us to catch glimpses of the changes that gradually brought the era of status-based knowledge to an end and the age of collective, up-for-sale knowledge to a glorious beginning. And if there is indeed an element of irony in making arguments about a society based on the stories of those who stepped out of it for a while, so be it. The travelers of the floating world would crack a smile and move on.

Notes

Introduction: Everything Flows

Epigraph: Richard Lane, *Images from the Floating World* (New York: G. P. Putnam's Sons, 1978), 11.

1. See Thomas Keirstead, "Gardens and Estates: Medievality and Space," *Positions* 1.2 (1993): 289–320, esp. 312.
2. Matsuo Bashō, *The Narrow Road to the Deep North and Other Travel Sketches,* trans. Nobuyuki Yuasa (London: Penguin Books, 1966), 97.
3. Some of these exceptions are discussed in Chapter 3.
4. David Moerman, "The Ideology of Landscape and the Theater of State: *Insei* Pilgrimage to Kumano (1090–1220)," *Japanese Journal of Religious Studies* 24.3–4 (Fall 1997): 347–374.
5. Judith Adler, "Travel as Performed Art," *American Journal of Sociology* 94.6 (May 1989): 1368.
6. Jippensha Ikku, *Hizakurige or Shank's Mare,* trans. Thomas Satchell (Rutland [VT] and Tokyo: Tuttle, 1960), 237.
7. Ibid.
8. Nelson H. H. Graburn, "Tourism: The Sacred Journey," in Valene L. Smith, ed., *Hosts and Guests: The Anthropology of Tourism* (Philadelphia: University of Pennsylvania Press, 1977), 22.
9. The pivotal reference work in this respect is Henri Lefebvre, *The Production of Space,* trans. Donald Nicholson-Smith (Oxford and Cambridge [MA]: Blackwell, 1991). On the fluid character of early modern space, see Marcia Yonemoto, *Mapping Early Modern Japan: Space, Place, and Culture in the Tokugawa Period (1603–1868)* (Berkeley: University of California Press, 2003), and Jilly Traganou, *The Tōkaidō Road: Traveling and Representation in Edo and Meiji Japan* (New York and London: Routledge Curzon, 2004).
10. Travel, of course, was but one of the many areas in which clashing discourses

met, and the disjunction between officialdom and popular practice became evident. Herman Ooms' *Tokugawa Village Practice: Class, Status, Power, Law* (Berkeley: University of California Press, 1996) discusses the gap between law (theory) and custom (practice) against the backdrop of rural communities. On the dichotomy between law and practice, see also Takeuchi Makoto, "Festivals and Fights: The Law and the People of Edo," in James L. McClain, John M. Merriman, and Ugawa Kaoru, eds., *Edo and Paris: Urban Life and the State in the Early Modern Era* (Ithaca, NY: Cornell University Press, 1994), 384–406. Gregory M. Pflugfelder analyzes three discordant discourses (popular, political, and medical) on male-male sexuality in his *Cartographies of Desire: Male-Male Sexuality in Japanese Discourse, 1600–1950* (Berkeley: University of California Press, 1999). Constantine N. Vaporis' pivotal work on travel in the Edo period, *Breaking Barriers: Travel and the State in Early Modern Japan* (Cambridge, MA: Harvard University Press, 1994) also explores the tension between law and practice in the context of travel, but, unlike this study, does so mostly from the viewpoint of the authority.

11. Eric J. Leed, *The Mind of the Traveler: From Gilgamesh to Global Tourism* (New York: Basic Books, 1991), 220–221.

12. Martha C. Tocco, "Norms and Texts for Women's Education in Tokugawa Japan," in Dorothy Ko, Jahyun Kim Haboush, and Joan Piggott, eds., *Women and Confucian Cultures in Premodern China, Korea, and Japan* (Berkeley: University of California Press, 2003), 194.

13. Dean MacCannell, *The Tourist: A New Theory of the Leisure Class* (New York: Schocken Books, 1976); James Buzard, *The Beaten Track: European Tourism, Literature, and the Ways to Culture, 1800–1918* (Oxford: Clarendon Press, 1993); Chris Rojek and John Urry, eds., *Touring Cultures: Transformations of Travel and Theory* (London and New York: Routledge, 1997); John Urry, *The Tourist Gaze: Leisure and Travel in Contemporary Societies* (London and Newbury Park: Sage Publications, 1990); Judith Adler, "The Origins of Sightseeing," *Annals of Tourism Research* 16.1 (1989): 7–29; Adler, "Travel as Performed Art"; Hasan Zafer Doğan, "Forms of Adjustment: Sociocultural Impacts of Tourism," *Annals of Tourism Research* 16.2 (1989): 216–236; James Duncan and Derek Gregory, eds., *Writes of Passage: Reading Travel Writing* (London and New York: Routledge, 1999).

14. Maruyama Yasunari, *Kinsei shukueki no kisoteki kenkyū*, 2 vols. (Tokyo: Yoshikawa Kōbunkan, 1975); Igarashi Tomio, *Kinsei sekisho no kisoteki kenkyū: Nakasendō Usui sekisho o chūshin to shite* (Tokyo: Taga Shuppan, 1986); Kodama Kōta, *Kinsei shukueki seido no kenkyū* (Tokyo: Yoshikawa Kōbunkan, 1957).

15. Vaporis, *Breaking Barriers,* 238, 239.

16. Hiruma Hisashi, "Samazamana kōdō bunka," in Takeuchi Makoto, ed., *Nihon no kinsei 14, Bunka no taishūka* (Tokyo: Chūō Kōronsha, 1993), 319–350.

17. For example, Nelson H. H. Graburn, *To Pray, Pay and Play: The Cultural Structure of Japanese Tourism* (Aix-en-Provence: Centre des Hautes Études Touristiques, 1983). Other studies tackling the issue—some more directly than others—include the various works by Constantine N. Vaporis, particularly *Breaking Barriers* and "*Caveat Viator:* Advice to Travelers in the Edo Period," *Monumenta Nipponica* 44.4 (Winter 1989): 461–483; and Susanne Formanek, "Pilgrimage in the Edo Period, Forerunner of Modern Domestic

Tourism? The Example of the Pilgrimage to Mount Tateyama," in Sabine Frühstück and Sepp Linhart, eds., *The Culture of Japan as Seen through Its Leisure* (Albany: State University of New York Press, 1998), 165–193.

18. Konno Nobuo, *Edo no tabi* (Tokyo: Iwanami Shoten, 1986), 99. Shinjō quoted in Vaporis, *Breaking Barriers,* 236–238.

19. Nishiyama Matsunosuke, "Edo bunka to chihō bunka," in *Iwanami kōza Nihon rekishi 13, Kinsei 5* (Tokyo: Iwanami Shoten, 1963), 161–207; Nishiyama Matsunosuke, *Edo Culture: Daily Life and Diversions in Urban Japan, 1600–1868,* ed. and trans. Gerald Groemer (Honolulu: University of Hawai'i Press, 1997); Vaporis, *Breaking Barriers.*

20. Victor Turner and Edith Turner, *Image and Pilgrimage in Christian Culture: Anthropological Perspectives* (New York: Columbia University Press, 1978), 20.

21. Nam-lin Hur, *Prayer and Play in Late Tokugawa Japan: Asakusa Sensōji and Edo Society* (Cambridge, MA: Harvard University Press, 2000), 76 and 80. Hur draws primarily on the works of Orikuchi Shinobu and William R. La Fleur. In Japanese see Higuchi Kiyoyuki, *Tabi to Nihonjin* (Tokyo: Kōdansha, 1980), and, by the same author, *Asobi to Nihonjin* (Tokyo: Kōdansha, 1980). Shinno Toshikazu, "Tabi, junrei, yusan—Kinsei sankei jijō," in Takeuchi Makoto, ed., *Nihon no kinsei 14, Bunka no taishūka* (Tokyo: Chūō Kōronsha, 1993), 131–168, also translated into English as "Journeys, Pilgrimages, Excursions: Religious Travels in the Early Modern Period," trans. Laura Nenzi, *Monumenta Nipponica* 57.4 (Winter 2002): 447–471. As Turner and Turner's quote cited above indicates, scholars outside the field of Japanese studies have also argued against a compartmentalization of secular and sacred travel. A recent example is that of Ellen Badone and Sharon R. Roseman, according to whom "dichotomous distinctions between the sacred and the secular obscure more than they illuminate." Ellen Badone and Sharon R. Roseman, "Approaches to the Anthropology of Pilgrimage and Tourism," in Ellen Badone and Sharon R. Roseman, eds., *Intersecting Journeys: The Anthropology of Pilgrimage and Tourism* (Urbana and Chicago: University of Illinois Press, 2004), 2.

22. Examples of rural rituals include *dengaku* (lit. "field music") and *sarugaku* (lit. "monkey music"), religious/theatrical events featuring music and dance, originally associated with the agricultural cycle. Temporary exhibits of sacred statues were called *kaichō*. In the case of *kagura* dances, the complementarity of faith and recreation is evident in the name itself, written using the characters for "gods" *(kami)* and "recreation" *(asobi)*. For a discussion of sumo wrestling as a religious act *(kami asobi),* see Herbert E. Plutschow, *Chaos and Cosmos: Ritual in Early and Medieval Japanese Literature* (Leiden and New York: E. J. Brill, 1990), 58–59.

23. Hur, *Prayer and Play,* 89.

24. Shinno Toshikazu, "Journeys, Pilgrimages, Excursions," 469. Convergences of sacred and profane, of religious and burlesque, are in fact common to other cultures: Carnival (leading to Lent and eventually Easter) in the Catholic tradition, or "the gastronomic masquerades of the Saturnalia, Lupercalia, and other winter feasts of pagan Rome" are fitting examples. Emmanuel Le Roy Ladurie, *Carnival in Romans,* trans. Mary Feeney (New York: George Braziller, 1979), 26.

25. Evidence suggests that it was not in the interest of religious institutions to draw

such lines either: temples and shrines were actually the sites where travel as recreation and commercialization originated (see Chapter 6).

26. Arakida Reijo, "Hatsuuma no nikki," in Furuya Chishin, *Edo jidai joryū bungaku zenshū*, vol. 3 (Tokyo: Nihon Tosho Sentaa, 1979), 73.

27. Yonemoto, *Mapping Early Modern Japan;* Marcia Yonemoto, "The 'Spatial Vernacular' in Tokugawa Maps," *Journal of Asian Studies* 59.3 (August 2000): 647–666; Traganou, *The Tōkaidō Road*. On the "quiet revolution in knowledge" brought about by the wide availability of printed matter, see also Mary Elizabeth Berry, *Japan in Print: Information and the Nation in the Early Modern Period* (Berkeley: University of California Press, 2006). The quotation is from page 18.

28. "Diary" is also a term that I use in a general sense to refer to travel memoirs, jottings, and recollections, many (but not all) of which are organized in daily entries. In most cases the titles (generally assigned by the authors themselves) contain the word *kikō* (lit. "travelogue"), *nikki* (lit. "daily record," "diary"), or simply the suffix -*ki* ("record").

29. Yonemoto, *Mapping Early Modern Japan;* Herbert Plutschow, *A Reader in Edo Period Travel* (Kent, UK: Global Oriental, 2006). A 1990 article by Harold Bolitho also anticipated some of the arguments developed in these studies: Harold Bolitho, "Travelers' Tales: Three Eighteenth-Century Travel Journals," *Harvard Journal of Asiatic Studies* 50.2 (December 1990): 485–504.

30. Marguerite Yourcenar, "Reflections on the Composition of *Memoirs of Hadrian*," in *Memoirs of Hadrian,* trans. Grace Frick (New York: Farrar, Straus and Company, 1963), 341.

Chapter 1: Maps, Movements, and the Malleable Spaces of Edo Japan

Epigraphs: Jorge Luis Borges, *Selected Non-Fictions,* ed. Eliot Weinberger (New York: Viking, 1999), 137; Stephen Bann, "The Map as Index of the Real: Land Art and the Authentication of Travel," *Imago Mundi* 46 (1994): 9.

1. Marcia Yonemoto makes a similar claim in *Mapping Early Modern Japan*.

2. By political discourse, or discourse of officialdom, I refer almost exclusively to the standards set by the Tokugawa. The body of laws issued at a regional level by individual domain lords—while pertaining to political discourse in general—is too large and diverse to be considered in this study.

3. For a study of the techniques employed in surveying lands for taxation purposes, see Philip C. Brown, "The Mismeasure of Land: Land Surveying in the Tokugawa Period," *Monumenta Nipponica* 42.2 (Summer 1987): 115–155. Also of interest on the topic of land surveys is Maruyama Yasunari, *Kinsei shukueki no kisoteki kenkyū*, 1:74–86.

4. See Constantine N. Vaporis, "Post Stations and Assisting Villages: Corvée Labor and Peasant Contention," *Monumenta Nipponica* 41.1 (Winter 1986): 377–414.

5. In this respect consider the spiral development around Edo castle as discussed in James L. McClain and John Merriman, "Edo and Paris: Cities and Power," in James L. McClain, John Merriman, and Ugawa Kaoru, eds., *Edo and Paris: Urban Life and the*

State in the Early Modern Era (Ithaca, NY: Cornell University Press, 1994) 3–38 (and particularly 14–29).

6. Kodama Kōta, *Kinsei kōtsū shiryōshū 8, Bakufu hōrei 1* (Tokyo: Yoshikawa Kōbunkan, 1978), 53, no. 94.

7. Kodama Kōta, *Kinsei kōtsū shiryōshū 9, Bakufu hōrei 2* (Tokyo: Yoshikawa Kōbunkan, 1979), 115–116, no. 655; document dated 1803/2. Yamamoto Mitsumasa, "*Bunken nobe ezu* o yomu," in Kanagawa Kinseishi Kenkyūkai, ed., *Edo jidai no Kanagawa: Furuezu de miru fūkei* (Yokohama: Yūrindō, 1994), 94. For a discussion of how the work of the surveyors was carried out in the segments of the Tōkaidō running through the provinces of Tōtōmi and Suruga, see Honda Takahide, "*Tōkaidō bunken nobe ezu* sakusei no kiso chōsa," in Shizuokaken Chiikishi Kenkyūkai, ed., *Tōkaidō kōtsūshi no kenkyū* (Osaka: Seibundō, 1996), 269–299.

8. Before the Tenpō era (survey of 1835, completed in 1838) provincial cartographic surveys had been launched in ca. 1633, 1644 (completed in ca. 1656), and 1697 (completed in 1702). See Oda Takeo, *Chizu no rekishi, Nihon-hen* (Tokyo: Kōdansha Gendai Shinsho, 1974), 61–84; Unno Kazutaka, "Cartography in Japan," in D. Woodward and J. B. Harley, eds., *The History of Cartography: Cartography in the Traditional East and Southeast Asian Societies*, vol. 2, bk. 2 (Chicago: University of Chicago Press, 1994), Appendix 11.8, 472. For the production of provincial maps and their evolution over time, see also Hirotada Kawamura, "*Kuni-ezu* (provincial maps) Compiled by the Tokugawa Shogunate in Japan," *Imago Mundi* 41 (1989): 70–75. According to Marcia Yonemoto, the Tokugawa government produced a total of five complete sets of provincial maps and four maps of Japan in the course of its history. Yonemoto, *Mapping Early Modern Japan*, 9.

9. Kodama Kōta, *Kinsei kōtsū shiryōshū 9, Bakufu hōrei 2*, 110–111, no. 644.

10. Ibid., 48, no. 582. Ordinance of 1775/intercalary 12. In the following year (1776/5) obtaining permission to travel along remote mountain roads became a requirement for such lords: ibid., 50, no. 585.

11. Ujinaga and Dōin produced an itinerary map comprised of five folding books, drawn to scale of 3 *bu* = 1 *chō* (1:12,000). Unno Kazutaka, "Cartography in Japan," 423–424.

12. A complaint signed by the Road Magistrate on 1805/7 reveals how numerous travelers chose to ignore the official designation of stages and frequently availed themselves of the services provided by the "midway villages." Kodama Kōta, *Kinsei kōtsū shiryōshū 9, Bakufu hōrei 2*, 123–124, no. 664.

13. Ooms, *Tokugawa Village Practice*, 287.

14. Yamamoto Mitsumasa, "*Bunken nobe ezu* o yomu." On the use of cartography as part of a political strategy, see also J. B. Harley, "Maps, Knowledge, and Power," in Denis Cosgrave and Stephen Daniels, eds., *The Iconography of Landscape* (Cambridge: Cambridge University Press, 1988), 277–312. In many cases, the government did not authorize the construction of bridges for strategic reasons.

15. Jilly Traganou, "Geographic Representations of the Tōkaidō from Edo to Meiji Japan," *Portolan* 47 (Spring 2000): 16. Also in Traganou, *The Tōkaidō Road*, 41. Traganou notices also that equally enlarged (when compared to their representations in nonofficial maps) are other nuclei of shogunal power such as Fuchū Castle. See also Jilly Traganou,

"Representing Mobility in Tokugawa and Meiji Japan," in Nicolas Fiévé and Paul Waley, eds., *Japanese Capitals in Historical Perspective: Place, Power and Memory in Kyoto, Edo and Tokyo* (London and New York: Routledge Curzon, 2003), 183. Another example of the Tokugawa's penchant for "hierarchical sizing" is discussed in Karen M. Gerhart, *The Eyes of Power: Art and Early Tokugawa Authority* (Honolulu: University of Hawai'i Press, 1999), 130.

16. Such is the claim in Ōto Yoshifuru and Yamaguchi Osamu, eds., *Tōkaidō 1* (Tokyo: Chikuma Shobō, 1976), 18–19.

17. Vaporis, *Breaking Barriers;* Vaporis, *"Caveat Viator";* Nishiyama Matsunosuke, "Edo bunka to chihō bunka."

18. Similarly devoid of human figures was the original map produced by Ujinaga and Dōin.

19. See, for example, the list of authorities in charge of releasing travel permits for women, in Ishii Ryōsuke, *Kinsei hōsei shiryō sōsho* (Tokyo: Kōbundō Shobō, 1941), 3:167. See also Kodama Kōta, *Kinsei kōtsū shiryōshū 8, Bakufu hōrei 1,* 145–146, no. 216.

20. Kodama Kōta, *Kinsei kōtsū shiryōshū 8, Bakufu hōrei 1,* 204, no. 293. Document dated 1668.

21. Ibid., 146, no. 217.

22. Ibid., 316, no. 428.

23. For the specific edict that established the alternate attendance policy, see ibid., 106, no. 169.

24. Ibid.

25. Ibid., 315–316, no. 427.

26. Yuasa Gentei, "Bunkai zakki," in Nihon Zuihitsu Taisei Henshūbu, ed., *Nihon zuihitsu taisei 7* (Tokyo: Yoshikawa Kōbunkan, 1927), 587.

27. Kodama Kōta, *Kinsei kōtsū shiryōshū 8, Bakufu hōrei 1,* 214–216, no. 305.

28. Kodama Kōta, *Kinsei kōtsū shiryōshū 9, Bakufu hōrei 2,* 34, no. 567.

29. Ibid., 132, no. 673.

30. Kodama Kōta, *Kinsei kōtsū shiryōshū 8, Bakufu hōrei 1,* 369, no. 469.

31. Mark Ravina, *Land and Lordship in Early Modern Japan* (Stanford, CA: Stanford University Press, 1999), 16.

32. The efforts of the Tokugawa to make Edo the material symbol of their power were not limited to the management of roads and traffic. Architecture also played a key role in buttressing government authority. See William H. Coaldrake, "Metaphors of the Metropolis: Architectural and Artistic Representations of the Identity of Edo," in Nicolas Fiévé and Paul Waley, eds., *Japanese Capitals in Historical Perspective,* 129–149. And, by the same author, *Architecture and Authority in Japan* (London: Routledge, 1996), and "Building a New Establishment: Tokugawa Iemitsu's Consolidation of Power and the Taitokuin Mausoleum," in McClain, Merriman, and Ugawa, eds., *Edo and Paris,* 153–172.

33. *Musashi wa oyoso Nihon tōzai no chūgoku ni atareri.* Miura Jōshin, *Keichō kenmonshū,* ed. Nakamaru Kazunori (Tokyo: Shin Jinbutsu Ōraisha, 1969), 63.

34. Ōto Yoshifuru, "Kinsei no Sagami," in Ōto Yoshifuru and Yamaguchi Osamu, eds., *Tōkaidō 1* (Tokyo: Chikuma Shobō, 1976), 159–160.

35. For the original text of the edict, see Kodama Kōta, *Kinsei kōtsū shiryōshū 8, Bakufu hōrei 1*, 42–43.

36. The capital of the Western Zhou dynasty (1027?–771 BC) was located near modern-day Xi'an. In the eighth century BC, the dynasty suffered a series of attacks and was forced to relocate east, near present-day Luoyang. This stage is usually referred to as the Eastern Zhou (771–256 BC).

37. Translation adapted from Herman Ooms, *Tokugawa Ideology: Early Constructs, 1570–1680* (Princeton, NJ: Princeton University Press, 1985), 184.

38. See, for example, the ordinance sent to the post station of Numazu: the horses are allowed to transport goods "all the way up to Hara and all the way down to Mishima" (respectively, the next post stations west and east of Numazu). The same linguistic choices are made for edicts directed to all post stations. Kodama Kōta, *Kinsei kōtsū shiryōshū 8, Bakufu hōrei 1*, 15–20.

39. Edict in ibid., 43, no. 81.

40. Ibid., 200–201, no. 289.

41. Kodama Kōta, *Kinsei kōtsū shiryōshū 9, Bakufu hōrei 2*, 11–12, no. 548.

42. See, for instance, the 1711 ordinance signed by the Magistrate, according to which, at the checkpoints of Hakone, Nebugawa, and Yagurazawa, outgoing women *(seki yori soto ni deru onna)* must present papers. Kodama Kōta, *Kinsei kōtsū shiryōshū 8, Bakufu hōrei 1*, 319–320, no. 433.

43. Ibid., 386–388, no. 489. For ships coming toward Edo from regions such as Awa, Shimōsa, or Kazusa, however, the official prudently (or inadvertently) used the safer expression "come and go" *(ōrai suru)*.

44. Ibid., 389–390, no. 491; document dated 1721/1/26.

45. Mark Ravina explores the multiple languages of power in *Land and Lordship in Early Modern Japan*, 28–45.

46. Alternatively, the prudent "travel" *(ryokō)* or "go and return" *(yukigaeri)* were also used. Simply descriptive, they did not imply any power relation, and did not characterize Edo as subordinate. See, for example, Kodama Kōta, *Kinsei kōtsū shiryōshū 8, Bakufu hōrei 1*, 179, no. 260; 110–111, no. 644; Kodama Kōta, *Kinsei kōtsū shiryōshū 9, Bakufu hōrei 2*, 48, no. 582.

47. Kodama Kōta, *Kinsei kōtsū shiryōshū 8, Bakufu hōrei 1*, 315–316, no. 427.

48. See Ronald P. Toby, *State and Diplomacy in Early Modern Japan: Asia in the Development of the Tokugawa Bakufu* (Stanford, CA: Stanford University Press, 1984), 38, 42, 179; Ronald P. Toby, "Carnival of the Aliens: Korean Embassies in Edo-Period Art and Popular Culture," *Monumenta Nipponica* 41.4 (Winter 1986): 415–456. There were twelve such visits in the course of the Edo period.

49. Kodama Kōta, *Kinsei kōtsū shiryōshū 8, Bakufu hōrei 1*, 232, no. 327.

50. Ibid., 321–323, no. 438; 323, no. 439; Kodama Kōta, *Kinsei kōtsū shiryōshū 9, Bakufu hōrei 2*, 8, no. 544.

51. Miura Jōshin, *Keichō kenmonshū*, 74.

52. Morioka Sadakata, "Morioka Sadakata nikki," *Tosa shidan* 54 (March 1936): 118.

53. Ibid., 124.

54. Nishikiori Gobei Yoshikura, "Nakasendō jūshi kakine tōkai kikō," in Harada Tomohiko, Yamori Kazuhiko, Nishikawa Kōji, and Moriya Katsuhisa, eds., *Nihon toshi seikatsu shiryō shūsei 8, Shukuba machi hen* (Tokyo: Gakushū Kenkyūsha, 1977), 580–581, 590, 592, 597, 607–608, and 613–614.

55. See James Foard, "Ippen and Pure Land Buddhist Wayfarers in Medieval Japan," in James Foard, Richard Payne, and Michael Solomon, eds., *The Pure Land Tradition: History and Development* (Berkeley: Regents of the University of California, 1996), 357–397.

56. See, for instance, Paul L. Swanson, "*Shugendō* and the Yoshino-Kumano Pilgrimage: An Example of Mountain Pilgrimage," *Monumenta Nipponica* 36.1 (Spring 1981): 55–79. Allan Grapard, "Flying Mountains and Walkers of Emptiness: Toward a Definition of Sacred Space in Japanese Religions," *History of Religions* 21. 3 (1982): 195–221. Also by the same author see "Geosophia, Geognosis, and Geopiety: Orders of Significance in Japanese Representations of Space," in D. Boden and R. Friedland, eds., *NowHere: Time, Space, and Modernity* (Berkeley: University of California Press, 1994), 372–401.

57. Representations of space in religious terms were not limited to mandalas. Since antiquity, maps of the country served as ritual implements in ceremonial rites, as fortune-telling tools, and as talismans against earthquakes. See Unno Kazutaka, "Maps of Japan Used in Prayer Rites or as Charms," *Imago Mundi* 46 (1993): 65–83.

58. Elizabeth ten Grotenhuis, *Japanese Mandalas: Representations of Sacred Geography* (Honolulu: University of Hawai'i Press, 1999), 167, 173.

59. Ibid., 6.

60. See also Nishiyama Masaru's study of *Ise sankei mandara* and *Nachi sankei mandara*. Nishiyama Masaru, *Seichi no sōzōryoku, Sankei mandara o yomu* (Kyoto: Hōzōkan, 1978), 147–207. Elizabeth ten Grotenhuis looks at Kasuga and Kumano (Nachi) mandalas in her *Japanese Mandalas*.

61. In her study of mandalas, Elizabeth ten Grotenhuis refers to gates and torii as "liminal markers." Ten Grotenhuis, *Japanese Mandalas*, 4.

62. Unno Kazutaka, "Cartography in Japan," 366.

63. Small exceptions were allowed for the sake of security. Jilly Traganou argues that at times clouds were purposely inserted to conceal strategic sites. Traganou, "Geographic Representations of the Tōkaidō from Edo to Meiji Japan," 16; and Traganou, "Representing Mobility in Tokugawa and Meiji Japan," 183.

64. Their identity has been an issue of contention among scholars, who alternatively identify the three deities as (from right to left) a praying bodhisattva, Amida, and Yakushi; or as the bodhisattva Seishi, Shaka, and Amida; or again as a praying bodhisattva, Yakushi, and Amida. Miyake Toshiyuki, "Fuji mandara to kyōten mainō," in Gorai Shigeru, ed., *Shugendō no bijutsu, geinō, bungaku* 1 (Tokyo: Meicho Shuppan, 1980), 425. Other Fuji mandalas include Dainichi, the Buddhist manifestation of the mountain's Shinto deity, Konohana Sakuya Hime.

65. Ten Grotenhuis, *Japanese Mandalas*, 150, 152.

66. Miyake Toshiyuki, "Fuji mandara to kyōten mainō," 434–435. Motonobu's mandala measures 180 x 117.5 cm. By comparison, some of the Edo period mandalas were as small as 35 x 20 cm.

67. On the origins of sacred mountains, see Grapard, "Flying Mountains and Walkers of Emptiness," 199–201. Among the most illustrious examples of mandalized mountains are the Yoshino and Kumano complexes, associated respectively with the Diamond and Womb mandalas. Swanson, "*Shugendō* and the Yoshino-Kumano Pilgrimage," 59.

68. Noda Senkōin, "Nihon kyūhō shugyō nikki," in Miyamoto Tsuneichi, Tanigawa Ken'ichi, and Haraguchi Torao, eds., *Nihon shomin seikatsu shiryō shūsei* (Tokyo: San'ichi Shobō, 1969), 2:10.

69. Kiyokawa Hachirō, *Saiyūsō,* ed. Oyamatsu Katsuichirō (Tokyo: Iwanami Shoten, 1993), 221 and 256.

70. This holds true across cultures and time, as exemplified, among others, by mountain cults related to Mount Olympus, to the Himalayas, or to the Potala in Lhasa. Luigi Tomasi, "*Homo Viator:* From Pilgrimage to Religious Tourism via the Journey," in William H. Swatos Jr. and Luigi Tomasi, eds., *From Medieval Pilgrimage to Religious Tourism: The Social and Cultural Economics of Piety* (Westport [CT] and London: Praeger, 2002), 10–13.

71. Allan Grapard, "The Textualized Mountain-Enmountained Text: The Lotus Sutra in Kunisaki," in George J. Tanabe and Willa Jane Tanabe, eds., *The Lotus Sutra in Japanese Culture* (Honolulu: University of Hawai'i Press, 1989), 159–190.

72. Ōyama in Sagami, for instance, was officially open only from 6/27 to 7/17.

73. Allan Grapard, "The State Remains, but Mountains and Rivers Are Destroyed," in Karen K. Gaul and Jackie Hiltz, eds., *Landscapes and Communities on the Pacific Rim: Cultural Perspectives from Asia to the Pacific Northwest* (Armonk, NY: M. E. Sharpe, 2000), 108–129.

74. For an overview of the origins and place of the Western Provinces tour, see James Foard, "The Boundaries of Compassion: Buddhism and National Tradition in Japanese Pilgrimage," *Journal of Asian Studies* 41.2 (February 1982): 231–251; as well as Mark MacWilliams, "Living Icons: *Reizō* Myths of the Saikoku Kannon Pilgrimage," *Monumenta Nipponica* 59.1 (Spring 2004): 35–82. For the Shikoku *henro,* see Nathalie Kouamé, *Pèlerinage et société dans le Japon des Tokugawa: Le pèlerinage de Shikoku entre 1598 et 1868* (Paris: École française d'Extrême-Orient, 2001), and Ian Reader, *Making Pilgrimages: Meaning and Practice in Shikoku* (Honolulu: University of Hawai'i Press, 2005).

75. The completion of the so-called *rokujūrokubu,* a tour of all the sacred places in the country, was also referred to as *kaikoku junrei,* or a *circuit around* the sixty-six provinces, a term that reinforced the notion of circumambulatory movement within the space of the sacred.

76. Foard, "The Boundaries of Compassion," 237.

77. Byron Earhart, "Mount Fuji and Shugendo," *Japanese Journal of Religious Studies* 16.2–3 (1989): 213. For a visual rendition of the circular route around Fuji's crater, see Miyazaki Fumiko, "Female Pilgrims and Mt. Fuji: Changing Perspectives on the Exclusion of Women," *Monumenta Nipponica* 60.3 (Autumn 2005): 376 (fig. 9).

78. Ishikawa Eisuke, ed., *Ōedo Senkōin tabi nikki* (Tokyo: Kōdansha Bunko, 1997), 330.

79. Hara Jun'ichirō, "Ōyama, Fuji, Enoshima," *Chihōshi kenkyū* 48.4 (August 1998): 25.

80. Suzuki Shōzō, "Fuji zenjō dōchū nikki," in Miwa Chōshi Hensan Iinkai, ed., *Miwa chōshi, Shiryōhen, Kinsei* (Miwa, 1992), 1314.

81. Iwahana Michiaki, "Dōchūki ni miru Dewa sanzan sankei no tabi," *Rekishi chirigaku*, no. 139 (December 1987): 10.

82. Kanamori Atsuko, *Sekishonuke Edo no onnatachi no bōken* (Tokyo: Shōbunsha, 2001), 38–39.

83. Maeda Yoshi, *Edo jidai joryū bungeishi, Chihō o chūshin ni, Tabi nikki hen* (Tokyo: Kasama Shoin, 1998), 379–394. A map of Hisako's route appears in Maeda Yoshi, "Tabi nikki no josei," in Enchi Fumiko, ed., *Jinbutsu Nihon no josei shi 6, Nikki ni tsuzuru aikan* (Tokyo: Shūeisha, 1977), 236.

84. Timon Screech, "The Strangest Place in Edo: The Temple of the Five Hundred Arhats," *Monumenta Nipponica* 48.4 (Winter 1993): 423.

85. Cited in Foard, "The Boundaries of Compassion," 236; italics mine.

86. Ooms notices that the character *shō* in Tōshō daigongen is the same as *terasu* in Amaterasu. Ooms, *Tokugawa Ideology*, 162, 183, 176.

87. Gerhart, *The Eyes of Power*, 80.

88. Ooms, *Tokugawa Ideology*, 175.

89. See Earhart, "Mount Fuji and Shugendo"; Royall Tyler, "The Tokugawa Peace and Popular Religion: Suzuki Shōsan, Kakugyō Tōbutsu, and Jikigyō Miroku," in Peter Nosco, ed., *Confucianism and Tokugawa Culture* (Princeton, NJ: Princeton University Press, 1984), 92–119.

90. Martin Colcutt, "Mt. Fuji as the Realm of Miroku. The Transformation of Maitreya in the Cult of Mt. Fuji in Early Modern Japan," in Alan Sponberg and Helen Hardacre, eds., *Maitreya: The Future Buddha* (Cambridge: Cambridge University Press, 1998), 248–269. The proliferation of Fuji replicas is discussed in more detail in Chapter 6.

91. Nakao Takashi, ed., *Koji junrei jiten* (Tokyo: Tōkyōdō Shuppan, 1973), 7–9, 47–48, 87.

92. Yourcenar, "Reflections on the Composition of *Memoirs of Hadrian*," 341.

93. Quoted in Haruo Shirane, *Traces of Dreams: Landscape, Cultural Memory, and the Poetry of Bashō* (Stanford, CA: Stanford University Press, 1998), 190; italics mine.

94. Matsuo Bashō, *The Narrow Road to the Deep North*, 106–107.

95. Kikusha-ni, "Taorigiku," in Katsumine Shinpū, *Keishū haika zenshū* (Tokyo: Shūeikaku, 1922), 328. Also known as Michinoku, the Rikuoku region comprised the early modern provinces of Iwashiro, Iwaki, Rikuzen, Rikuchū, and Mutsu. See Figure 1.

96. Senbai, "Enoshima kikō," in Fujisawa Shishi Hensan Iinkai, ed., *Fujisawa shishi 2, Shiryōhen* (Fujisawa, 1973), 1215.

97. Tsuchiya Ayako, "Tabi no inochige," in Furuya Chishin, ed., *Edo jidai joryū bungaku zenshū*, vol. 3 (Tokyo: Nihon Tosho Sentaa, 1979), 383.

98. "As obstacles to freedom of movement and as points beyond which home disappears—or recedes a significant distance—such places broke the journeys' spatial unity and therefore the travelers gave them significance." Herbert E. Plutschow, *Four Japanese Travel Diaries of the Middle Ages* (Ithaca, NY: Cornell University Press, 1981), 4.

99. See Katagiri Yōichi, *Utamakura utakotoba jiten* (Tokyo: Kasama Shoin, 1999), 1, 226–227.

100. Matsuo Bashō, *The Narrow Road to the Deep North,* 113.

101. See examples in Traganou, *The Tōkaidō Road,* 157.

102. For example, the version reproduced in Kodama Kōta, ed., *Tōkaidō 2* (Tokyo: Chikuma Shobō, 1977), 34. Originally in the collection of the Setsu Gatōdō gallery in Tokyo, it now belongs to a private collector.

103. *Tales of Ise,* episode 9, in Helen Craig McCullough, ed. and trans., *Tales of Ise: Lyrical Episodes from Tenth-Century Japan* (Stanford, CA: Stanford University Press, 1968), 75–76.

104. My use of the term "lyrical" in reference to this type of space representation emphasizes the artwork's homage to an immediately recognizable literary model of the past. As such, it coincides—but not completely—with the definition of lyrical landscape given by art historian James Cahill, who has produced a fascinating comparative study of poetic paintings in Song and Ming China and late Edo Japan. His understanding of poetic travelscapes acknowledges the artists' efforts to recover a "lost poetic world" and to "give pictorial form to poetic ideas," but Cahill's emphasis on the subtlety of the evocation does not seem to apply to the case studies I present here. Theirs is not an oblique hint, but rather an encyclopedia-like reference. The viewer does not strive to recover the association to literary precedent, for it is served to him on a silver platter. In the same study, Cahill indeed acknowledges that, while it does not fit his definition, Sōtatsu's rendition of *Tales of Ise* can be taken as an example of poetic landscape. James Cahill, *The Lyric Journey: Poetic Painting in China and Japan* (Cambridge, MA: Harvard University Press, 1996), especially 55, 14, and 135.

105. Minamoto (Koga) Michichika, "Takakura-in Itsukushima gokō ki," in Plutschow, *Four Japanese Travel Diaries of the Middle Ages,* 37.

106. *Makotoni nisenri no hoka made tazunekinikeri to oboyuruni.* Nijō uses the expression "two thousand *ri*," which effectively translates to almost five thousand miles (1 *ri* = 2.44 miles). Nijō, *Towazugatari,* ed. Fukuda Hideichi (Tokyo: Shinkōsha, 1978), 233. For an English translation of the diary, see Karen Brazell, trans., *The Confessions of Lady Nijō* (Stanford, CA: Stanford University Press, 1973).

107. Arakida Reijo, "Hatsuuma no nikki," in Furuya Chishin, ed., *Edo jidai joryū bungaku zenshū,* 3:25.

108. Ibid., 46.

109. Steven D. Carter, "Travel as Poetic Practice in Medieval and Early Modern Japan," *Journeys: The International Journal of Travel and Travel Writing* 5.1 (May 2004): 38–42.

110. Nakagawa Hisamori's wife, "Ikahoki," in Furuya Chishin, ed., *Edo jidai joryū bungaku zenshū* 3:5.

111. Ibid., 21.

112. Plutschow, *Four Japanese Travel Diaries of the Middle Ages,* 42.

113. Nakagawa Hisamori's wife, "Ikahoki," 21.

114. Jurgis Elisonas, "Notorious Places: A Brief Excursion into the Narrative

Topography of Early Edo," in McClain, Merriman, and Ugawa, eds., *Edo and Paris,* 253–291.

115. Ibid., 285.

116. Nishikiori Gobei Yoshikura, "Nakasendō jūshi kakine tōkai kikō," 602.

Chapter 2: At the Intersection of Travel and Gender

Epigraphs: "Jiin bōsha nyonin kakaeoku kinshi no oboe," in Umeda Yoshihiko, *Nihon shūkyō seidoshi 3, Kinsei hen* (Tokyo: Tōsen Shuppan, 1972), 289; Lefebvre, *The Production of Space,* 86.

1. Such diaries include *Record of the Azuma Road* (*Azuma michi no ki,* 1602) kept by Maeda Matsuko, the wife of the Kanazawa lord, as she traveled to Edo to serve as hostage; *Roadbook of the Takahara Lord* (*Takahara-in dono omichi no ki,* 1633) by Tokugawa Haru, also traveling between Nagoya and Edo for the same purpose; *Record of [a Trip to] Ikaho* (*Ikahoki*), the 1639 diary of Nakagawa Hisamori's wife's journey from Edo to Ikaho hot springs; *The Tsukushi Region* (*Tsukushitai*), the memoir seventeen-year-old Yoshimi Renko, a samurai's daughter, wrote in the 1660s as she traveled from Ogura to Nagoya on her bridal procession; Inoue Tsūjo's famous record of her journey from Marugame to Edo to serve under her domain lord's mother (*Tōkai Journal,* or *Tōkai kikō,* 1681) as well as the diary she wrote on her way home in 1689 *(Homecoming Diary,* or *Kika nikki)*; Confucian scholar's daughter Mukai Chine's diary of a trip to Ise in 1686 *(Ise Journal,* or *Ise kikō)*; and *Record of the Road to Yamashiro Hot Springs* (*Yamashiro onsen michi no ki*), also known as *Record [of a Trip to] Yumoto* (*Yumoto no ki*), the 1687 journal composed by Nagaye Toyohashi, the mistress of a chief retainer *(karō).*

2. Fukai Jinzō, *Kinsei josei tabi to kaidō kōtsū* (Toyama: Hashira Shobō, 1995), 140. The maps include *Tōkaidō ezu* (1681–1683, ten scrolls) and *Tōkaidō bunken ezu* (1690, illustrated by Hishikawa Moronobu).

3. Of these, twenty-nine were categorized as (married) women, eleven as unmarried girls, four as widows, and five as nuns *(ama).*

4. The remaining four had been issued for a dead man, an insane male traveler with shaved head (possibly a monk, or someone pretending to be a monk), and two insane males. Kodama Kōta, *Kinsei kōtsū shiryōshū 8, Bakufu hōrei 1,* 365–366, no. 465. It was common procedure for barrier officials to collect the permits issued by the superintendent *(rusui)* and send them back to the issuing authority, which would match the number of issued documents with the number of documents collected at checkpoints.

5. Ibid., 390, no. 492.

6. Nagaoka-shi, *Nagaoka shishi, Shiryōhen 3, Kinsei 2* (Nagaoka, 1994), 306. Some seventeenth-century cases are discussed in Chapter 3.

7. Quoted in Shiba Keiko, "Tabi nikki kara mita kinsei josei no ikkōsatsu," in Kinsei Joseishi Kenkyūkai, ed., *Edo jidai no joseitachi* (Tokyo: Yoshikawa Kōbunkan, 1990), 151.

8. Kaibara Ekiken (with an intro. by Shingoro Takaishi), *Women and Wisdom of Japan* (London: J. Murray, 1905), 40, 42, 43.

9. Yamakawa Kikue, *Women of the Mito Domain: Recollections of Samurai Family Life,* trans. Kate Wildman Nakai (Tokyo: University of Tokyo Press, 1992), 16–17.

10. Original document in Kodama Kōta, *Kinsei kōtsū shiryōshū 9, Bakufu hōrei 2,* 233, no. 753. Dated 1835/2/28.

11. Maeda Yoshi, *Edo jidai joryū bungeishi,* 57–89. See also Maeda Yoshi, "*Kōshin kikō* to sono chosha Jugen-in," *Fukuoka Jogakuin Tanki Daigaku Kiyō,* no. 3 (March 1967): 19–37.

12. Although the girl did not leave an account of her journey, one of her attendants wrote a travelogue recording the trip back to Edo, and then to Kyoto, that she took with two other women in 1777 after the young bride had passed away. See Okada Koiso, "Oku no araumi," in Furuya Chishin, ed., *Edo jidai joryū bungaku zenshū,* vol. 3 (Tokyo: Nihon Tosho Sentaa, 1979), 245–274.

13. For the details on the institutional framework of barriers, see Vaporis, *Breaking Barriers,* chapters 3 ("A Curious Institution") and 4 ("Permits and Passages").

14. Kodama Kōta, *Kinsei kōtsū shiryōshū 8, Bakufu hōrei 1,* 21–22, no. 37 and 62, no. 109.

15. Document in ibid., 72–73, no. 122; italics mine.

16. Ibid., 86, no. 144.

17. Ibid., 90, no. 150.

18. Ishii Ryōsuke, ed., *Kinsei hōsei shiryō sōsho 3,* 168–169.

19. For instance, a 1796 communication between the Council of Elders and the Finance Magistrate on how to fill out travel permits for women specifies that even in the cases of prominent women belonging to families whose retinue exceeded 10,000 bushels, the documents must specify whose mother or wife the traveler in question was. Kodama Kōta, *Kinsei kōtsū shiryōshū 9, Bakufu hōrei 2,* 102, no. 633.

20. A last, if obvious, marker of strategic irrelevance mentioned in the document and common to both sexes was death.

21. Kodama Kōta, *Kinsei kōtsū shiryōshū 9, Bakufu hōrei 2,* 188–189, no. 713.

22. Ishii Ryōsuke, ed., *Kinsei hōsei shiryō sōsho 3,* 168–169.

23. At Arai, Tsūjo was denied transit because her passport categorized her as a married woman when in fact she wore the long-sleeved kimono typical of unmarried girls. See Vaporis, *Breaking Barriers,* 157. The verses are taken from Inoue Tsūjo, "Tōkai kikō," in Inoue Tsūjo Zenshū Shūtei Iinkai, ed., *Inoue Tsūjo zenshū* (Marugame, 1973), 47. For a discussion of Tsūjo's writings, see Donald Keene, *Travelers of a Hundred Ages* (New York: Columbia University Press, 1999), 329–335.

24. In Ishii Ryōsuke, ed., *Kinsei hōsei shiryō sōsho 3,* 80.

25. Imamura Yoshitaka and Takahashi Hideo, eds., *Akitahan machibureshū* (Tokyo: Miraisha, 1972), 2:362.

26. Pflugfelder, *Cartographies of Desire,* 138.

27. The print by Hiroshige and Toyokuni is reproduced in many works, among which are Vaporis, *Breaking Barriers,* 169, and Fujiwara Chieko, ed., *Ukiyoe ni miru Edo no tabi* (Tokyo: Kawade Shobō Shinsha, 2000), 29 (partial reproduction).

28. The traditional style of adult males, known as *hanbatsu,* called for the forehead

and top of the head to be shaven and for the remaining hair to be tied in a topknot folded on the top of the head. The appropriate hairstyle for youngsters was called *sōhatsu*.

29. Ishii Ryōsuke and Harafuji Hiroshi, eds., *Mondōshū 3, Shōrei sen'yō, shōke hitsubunshū* (Tokyo: Sōbunsha, 1999), 79.

30. Ihara Saikaku, "Kōshoku ichidai otoko," in Teruoka Yasutaka and Higashi Akimasa, eds., *Ihara Saikakushū 1* (Tokyo: Shogakkan, 1996), 244. For a discussion of the age limits for boyhood, see also Pflugfelder, *Cartographies of Desire,* 30–34. Erotic prints depicting sexual encounters between young boys and adult males are reproduced in abundance in Gary P. Leupp, *Male Colors: The Construction of Homosexuality in Tokugawa Japan* (Berkeley: University of California Press, 1995).

31. Kiyokawa Hachirō, *Saiyūsō,* 41–44. Masa's ordeal is also recounted in Vaporis, *Breaking Barriers,* 214. I explore popular resistance to *nukemairi* in greater detail in "To Ise at All Costs: Religious and Economic Implications of Early Modern *Nukemairi,*" *Japanese Journal of Religious Studies* 33.1 (2006): 75–114.

32. Anne Walthall, "The Family Ideology of the Rural Entrepreneurs in Nineteenth Century Japan," *Journal of Social History* 23.3 (Spring 1990): 475.

33. Ibid.

34. Vaporis, *Breaking Barriers,* 198.

35. Kodama Kōta, *Kinsei kōtsū shiryōshū 8, Bakufu hōrei 1,* 22, no. 38, and 33–34, no. 60.

36. Ryusaku Tsunoda, Wm. Theodore De Bary, and Donald Keene, eds., *Sources of Japanese Tradition* (New York: Columbia University Press, 1958), 1:306; italics mine.

37. "Various Stipulations for Temples and Shrines" (Shojiin jōmoku, 1667). Quoted in Hur, *Prayer and Play,* 25.

38. One of the earliest ordinances in this respect was "Tokugawa Ieyasu kinsei," issued in 1600.

39. For a complete list in chronological order of the various ordinances, see Umeda Yoshihiko, *Nihon shūkyō seidoshi 3,* 52–57.

40. "Tōeisan hatto," in ibid., 359–361.

41. "Nikkōsan jōmoku," in ibid., 362–367.

42. See edict in ibid., 374–376.

43. Ibid.

44. "Notification on the Supervision of Discipline for Buddhist Monks" (Sōryo fūki torishimari ni tsuki tasshi), in Umeda Yoshihiko, *Nihon shūkyō seidoshi 3,* 294–295; italics mine. Secondary temples were minor halls within the main temple's grounds, whereas branch temples were affiliated with the headquarters but located outside the precincts.

45. "Orders to Temples and Shrines of All Denominations" (Shoshū jiin gechijō), in ibid., 274–275.

46. "Osadamegaki hyakkajō," in ibid., 315–323.

47. "On the Supervision of Temples and Shrines" (Jiin torishimari kata no koto, 1829), in ibid., 424–425.

48. "Ordinance on Mourning" (Fukuki rei), in ibid., 283–289.

49. Takeuchi Makoto, "Festivals and Fights," 384–406.

50. Shizuoka-ken, *Shizuoka kenshi, Shiryōhen 13, Kinsei 5* (Shizuoka, 1990), 507–509.

51. The five pungent plants *(goshin)* included leeks, chives, garlic, onions, and scallions. They were all taboo according to Buddhist dietary rules. *Kemari* indicates a type of soccer game. "Stipulations of Ishiyama Temple of the Shingon School" (Shingonshū Ishiyamadera jōmoku), in Umeda Yoshihiko, *Nihon shūkyō seidoshi 3,* 173–174.

52. "Laws of Kongō Temple on Mount Amano" (Amanosan Kongōji shiki), in ibid., 234–237.

53. Suzuki Masataka, *Nyonin kinsei* (Tokyo: Yoshikawa Kōbunkan, 2002).

54. As Karen Smyers has noted, however, Shinto doctrine held an ambiguous position vis-à-vis the correlation between blood (a source of pollution) and fertility (seen in a positive light). Karen A. Smyers, "Women and Shinto: The Relation between Purity and Pollution," *Japanese Religions* 12.4 (July 1983): 7–18.

55. Momoko Takemi, " 'Menstruation Sutra' Belief in Japan," *Japanese Journal of Religious Studies* 10.2–3 (June/September 1983): 230. See also Sugano Noriko, "Nyonin jōbutsu Ketsubonkyō engi," *Teikyō Shigaku* 20 (February 2005): 191–201.

56. Among the numerous studies on the legends related to Kōya, see Susan Matisoff, "Barred from Paradise? Mount Kōya and the Karukaya Legend," in Barbara Ruch, ed., *Engendering Faith: Women and Buddhism in Premodern Japan* (Ann Arbor: Center for Japanese Studies, University of Michigan, 2002), 463–500.

57. "Kōyasan tsūnenshū," in *Kinsei bungei sōsho 2, Meishoki 2* (Tokyo: Kokusho Kankōkai, 1910), 62. According to Buddhist tradition, the Five Hindrances *(goshō)* refer to the impossibility of women becoming Brahma (creators), heavenly lords, devils, saints, and Buddhas because of their heavy karmic burdens. Such impediments are also known as the Five Clouds *(itsutsu no kumo).*

58. Ibid., 212–213.

59. In Narabayashi Tadao, ed., "Okagemairi," in Miyamoto Tsuneichi, Harada Tomohiko, and Haraguchi Torao, eds., *Nihon shomin seikatsu shiryō shūsei,* vol. 12 (Tokyo: San'ichi Shobō, 1971), 88.

60. Arakida Reijo, "Hatsuuma no nikki," in Furuya Chishin, ed., *Edo jidai joryū bungaku zenshū,* 3:79. Mount Shosha is also known as Mount Sosa, or Engyō Temple.

61. Shinkō-in Myōjitsu, "Mokuzu," in ibid., 3:282.

62. Yamanashi Shigako, "Harumichigusa," in Toyoda Chōshi Hensan Iinkai, ed., *Toyoda chōshi, Betsuhen 1, Tōkaidō to Tenryūgawa Ikeda wataribune, Furoku 2, Kikōbun* (Toyoda-chō, 1999), 375.

63. Kurosawa Tokiko, "Jōkyō nikki," quoted in Fukai Jinzō, *Kinsei josei tabi to kaidō kōtsū,* 68. For Taseko, see Anne Walthall, *The Weak Body of a Useless Woman: Matsuo Taseko and the Meiji Restoration* (Chicago: University of Chicago Press, 1998), 158.

64. Kiyokawa Hachirō, *Saiyūsō,* 271.

65. By contrast, the logic of compassion could also carve out areas that excluded men and safeguarded women, as in the case of divorce temples. See Anne Dutton, "Temple Divorce in Tokugawa Japan: A Survey of Documentation on Tōkeiji and Mantokuji," in Ruch, ed., *Engendering Faith,* 209–245; in the same volume see also Wright, "Mantokuji: More Than a 'Divorce Temple,' " 247–276. Sachiko Kaneko and Robert E. Morrell specify

that divorce temples provided "a way out, sanctuary, asylum, for those whom the world would break in its grip." Sachiko Kaneko and Robert E. Morrell, "Sanctuary: Kamakura's Tōkeiji Convent," *Japanese Journal of Religious Studies* 10.2–3 (June/September 1983): 196.

66. Hur, *Prayer and Play*, 91.

67. Makoto Ueda, *Far Beyond the Field: Haiku by Japanese Women, an Anthology* (New York: Columbia University Press, 2003), 70.

68. Kikusha-ni, "Taorigiku," 355.

69. "Memorandum on the New Prohibitions Regarding Temples" (Shinji kinshi no oboe, 1658), in Umeda Yoshihiko, *Nihon shūkyō seidoshi* 3: 270–271. See also "Unofficial Notice Regarding the Scrutiny of Prostitutes and Theatrical Troupes within the Precincts of Temples and Shrines" (Jisha keidai shibai narabini yūjo gimmi ni tsuki naitatsu, 1714), in ibid., 293.

70. See Hur, *Prayer and Play*, 104–107.

71. Ihara Saikaku, *The Japanese Family Storehouse or the Millionaires' Gospel Modernised*, trans. G. W. Sargent (Cambridge: Cambridge University Press, 1959), 46.

72. Katsu Kokichi, *Musui's Story: The Autobiography of a Tokugawa Samurai*, trans. Teruko Craig (Tucson: University of Arizona Press, 1988), 25–33.

73. The temple was a True Pure Land institution at the dependence of the Higashi Honganji. See Koyama Chōshi Hensan Senmon Iinkai, *Koyama chōshi 2, Kinsei shiryōhen 1* (Koyama, 1991), 617.

74. Konno Oito, "Sangū dōchū shōyōki," in Honjō-shi, ed., *Honjō shishi shiryōhen IV* (Honjō, 1988), 611.

75. Emontarō, "Ise sangū shukuhaku oboechō," in Gifu-ken, ed., *Gifu kenshi, Shiryōhen, Kinsei 7* (Gifu, 1971), 547.

76. Suzuki Masataka, *Nyonin kinsei*, 104.

77. Kiyokawa Hachirō, *Saiyūsō*, 263. Another source, *Ise sangū meisho zue* (1797), indicates the fifteenth day of the seventh month as the time apart of Mii Temple. Ashida Koreto, ed., *Ise sangū meisho zue* (Tokyo: Tōyōdō, 1944), 317.

78. Kanamori Atsuko, *Sekishonuke Edo no onnatachi no bōken*, 168.

79. Konno Oito, "Sangū dōchū shōyōki," 626.

80. Kanamori Atsuko, *Sekishonuke Edo no onnatachi no bōken*, 168–170.

81. Suzuki Mihoko, "Kawagoe no kikō," in Saitama Kenshi Hensan Jimusho, ed., *Saitama sōsho 2* (Tokyo: Sanmeisha, 1968), 531–532.

82. A detailed study of Mount Fuji's complex relationship with women can be found in Miyazaki Fumiko, "Female Pilgrims and Mt. Fuji." The Meiji government abolished *nyonin kinsei* in 1872, but as Miyazaki shows, Mount Fuji had already fully opened the summit to women twelve years prior.

83. Miyata Noboru, *Onna no reiryoku to ie no kami* (Kyoto: Jinbun Shoin, 1983), 92–99.

84. Miyazaki Fumiko, "Female Pilgrims and Mt. Fuji," 355–356.

85. Suzuki Shōzō, "Fuji zenjō dōchū nikki," 1314.

86. Miyazaki Fumiko, "Female Pilgrims and Mt. Fuji," 354–355.

87. Shibuya-ku, *Shibuyaku shiryōshū 2* (Tokyo: Shibuya-ku, 1980), 33.

88. *Tsuki no sawari mo naku.* Kouamé, *Pèlerinage et société dans le Japon des Tokugawa,* 70–71.

89. Examples include Hantaji (stage no. 50, the Eastern Temple) and Kongōchōji (stage no. 26, the Western Temple). Onzanji (stage no. 18) and Muroto-san Hatsumisaki Temple (also known as Tōji, stage no. 24, in Tosa Province) also enforced restrictions, while at Zenjinji in Iyo Province (stage no. 64) the front hall was exclusively for women, but the inner hall denied them access. Takeda Akira, *Junrei to minzoku* (Tokyo: Iwasaki Bijutsusha, 1969), 173, 176, and 188.

90. Such temples included Tatsue Temple, Tanema Temple, Enkō Temple, and Ishide Temple—stages 19, 34, 39, and 51 respectively.

91. Takeda Akira, *Junrei to minzoku,* 191, 165.

92. Maeda Takashi, *Junrei no shakaigaku* (Tokyo: Minerva Shobō, 1971), 189.

93. Kouamé, *Pèlerinage et société dans le Japon des Tokugawa,* 126. In 1714 an ordinance asked local villagers along well-known side roads to function as makeshift guides and take pilgrims back to the official route.

94. Reader, *Making Pilgrimages,* 73.

Chapter 3: Women on the Road

Epigraphs: Leed, *The Mind of the Traveler,* 221; Yourcenar, "Reflections on the Composition of *Memoirs of Hadrian,*" 327; Inoue Tsūjo, "Tōkai kikō," 48.

1. The association between travel and an extra-normative, "liminal" experience derives from the works of Victor Turner, particularly *Dramas, Fields, and Metaphors* (Ithaca, NY: Cornell University Press, 1974), and *Process, Performance, and Pilgrimage: A Study in Comparative Symbology* (New Delhi: Concept Publishing, 1979).

2. I am borrowing the words of Caroline Walker Bynum, who has produced an inspiring collection of essays on the ways in which women in medieval Europe carved out autonomous spaces within the religious sphere, exploiting certain elements to their advantage in a process comparable to the one discussed in this work. Caroline Walker Bynum, *Fragmentation and Redemption: Essays on Gender and the Human Body in Medieval Religion* (New York: Zone Books, 1991), 17.

3. In Ishii Ryōsuke, ed., *Kinsei hōsei shiryō sōsho 3,* 122–123.

4. *Source of Prosperity and Longevity for Women (Onna kotobuki hōraidai,* 1819), in Emori Ichirō, *Edo jidai josei seikatsu ezu daijiten,* vol. 3: *Katei, Shakai* (Tokyo: Ōzorasha, 1993), 58–59. As Yokota Fuyuhiko has compellingly argued, many moralistic texts of the Edo period, including *The Greater Learning for Women (Onna daigaku),* emphasized modesty in an attempt to counterbalance the ideal of sexually promiscuous females envisioned in popular erotic fiction. "The relationship between these two types of books," claims Yokota, "was fundamentally Janus faced." On one side erotic manuals winked at indulgence, on the other educational textbooks sternly advocated respectability. For every whore and dancer idolized in popular fiction, moralistic manuals celebrated a mother and a virtuous daughter. Yokota Fuyuhiko, "Imagining Working Women in Early Modern Japan" (trans.

Mariko Asano Tamanoi), in Hitomi Tonomura, Anne Walthall, and Haruko Wakita, eds., *Women and Class in Japanese History* (Ann Arbor: Center for Japanese Studies, University of Michigan, 1999), 153–167. The quotation is from p. 165.

5. For expedients such as cross-dressing and alternate roads, see Vaporis, *Breaking Barriers,* 182–193.

6. Ivan Morris, *The World of the Shining Prince: Court Life in Ancient Japan* (New York, Tokyo, and London: Kodansha International, 1994), 210–212.

7. Murasaki Shikibu, *The Tale of Genji,* trans. Royall Tyler (New York: Penguin Books, 2001), 23.

8. Barbara Ambros, "Liminal Journeys: Pilgrimages of Noblewomen in Mid-Heian Japan," *Japanese Journal of Religious Studies* 24.3–4 (Fall 1997): 301. For the ways in which noblewomen manipulated relationships with men, see 331–334.

9. Morris, *The World of the Shining Prince,* 201.

10. Janet R. Goodwin discusses itinerant female entertainers of the Heian and Kamakura periods—*asobime* and *kugutsu* in particular—in "Shadows of Transgression: Heian and Kamakura Constructions of Prostitution," *Monumenta Nipponica* 55.3 (Autumn 2000): 327–368. Their degree of agency, she emphasizes, is an issue of contention among scholars (see 343–346).

11. *A Tale of Flowering Fortunes* (*Eiga monogatari,* 1027–1092) portrays them as elegant entertainers who traveled on boats; in *The Tale of Genji* they cross the path of the Shining Prince at Sumiyoshi Shrine. See Terry Kawashima, *Writing Margins: The Textual Construction of Gender in Heian and Kamakura Japan* (Cambridge, MA: Harvard University Press, 2001), 69–71.

12. Sugawara no Takasue no musume, *Sarashina nikki;* quoted in Kawashima, *Writing Margins,* 68. Donald Keene discusses *The Sarashina Diary* in *Travelers of a Hundred Ages,* 48–56.

13. Amino Yoshihiko argues that numerous aristocrats and political figures between the late Heian and Kamakura periods had *yūjo, shirabyōshi,* and dancers for mothers. Amino Yoshihiko, "Chūsei no tabibitotachi," in *Hyōhaku to teichaku, teijū shakai e no michi* (Tokyo: Shogakkan, 1984), 182–183.

14. Hitomi Tonomura, "Re-envisioning Women in the Post-Kamakura Age," in Jeffrey P. Mass, ed., *The Origins of Japan's Medieval World: Courtiers, Clerics, Warriors, and Peasants in the Fourteenth Century* (Stanford, CA: Stanford University Press, 1997), 159.

15. Kawashima, *Writing Margins,* 15. The trend toward "wife taking" became evident in the fourteenth century but, in certain cases, existed since the late Heian period. Tonomura, "Re-envisioning Women in the Post-Kamakura Age," 152.

16. For the argument that the narratives of female aristocrats became, in the medieval period, "more public log than personal statement," see Tonomura, "Re-envisioning Women in the Post-Kamakura Age," 140–144.

17. Ibid., 164.

18. See Amino Yoshihiko, "Chūsei no tabibitotachi," 153–266. On the topic of female travelers in the medieval period, see also Hosokawa Ryōichi, "Chūsei no tabi o

suru josei—Shūkyō, geinō, kōeki," in Okano Haruko, ed., *Onna to otoko no jikū, Nihon joseishi saikō 3, Onna to otoko no ran, Chūsei* (Tokyo: Fujiwara Shoten, 1996), 341–378. For itinerant nuns in the medieval and early modern periods, see Barbara Ruch, "Woman to Woman: *Kumano bikuni* Proselytizers in Medieval and Early Modern Japan," in Barbara Ruch, ed., *Engendering Faith: Women and Buddhism in Premodern Japan* (Ann Arbor: Center for Japanese Studies, University of Michigan, 2002), 537–580.

19. Tonomura, "Re-envisioning Women in the Post-Kamakura Age," 157. In his treatise *Shōbōgenzō*, Dōgen claims that "Learning the Law of Buddha and achieving release from illusion have nothing to do with whether one happens to be a man or a woman"; Stanley Weinstein, "The Concept of Reformation in Japanese Buddhism," in Saburo Ota, ed., *Studies in Japanese Culture*, vol. 2 (Tokyo: P.E.N. Club, 1973), 82. Quoted in Barbara Ruch, "The Other Side of Culture in Medieval Japan," in Kozo Yamamura, ed., *The Cambridge History of Japan*, vol. 3: *Medieval Japan* (Cambridge: Cambridge University Press, 1990), 506.

20. "Bennonaishi nikki," in Nagasaki Ken, Tonomura Natsuko, Iwasa Miyoko, Inada Toshinori, and Itō Kei, eds., *Chūsei nikki kikōshū* (Tokyo: Shogakkan, 1994), 239. See also Keene, *Travelers of a Hundred Ages*, 145–148.

21. See a visual representation in Amino Yoshihiko, "Chūsei no tabibitotachi," 192.

22. Ibid., 190–194. For *asobime* and *kugutsu*, see also Kawashima, *Writing Margins*, 27–72.

23. Amino Yoshihiko, "Chūsei no tabibitotachi," 175–176.

24. In Kawashima, *Writing Margins*, 298–300.

25. Amino Yoshihiko, "Chūsei no tabibitotachi," 178.

26. Terry Kawashima cites the case of a group of *kugutsu* who in 1114 filed a suit against an official accused of hurting one of them and looting some of their goods. The official was found guilty and was incarcerated. Kawashima, *Writing Margins*, 47.

27. On the liberating power and creative outlet provided by the act of taking the tonsure in the medieval period, see Ruch, "The Other Side of Culture in Medieval Japan," 507–511.

28. Tonomura, "Re-envisioning Women in the Post-Kamakura Age," 166.

29. See Katsuura Noriko, "Tonsure Forms for Nuns: Classification of Nuns according to Hairstyle" (trans. Virginia Skord Waters), in Ruch, ed., *Engendering Faith*, 109–129.

30. James C. Dobbins, *Letters of the Nun Eshinni: Images of Pure Land Buddhism in Medieval Japan* (Honolulu: University of Hawai'i Press, 2004), 86. According to Hitomi Tonomura, however, even within the clergy differences persisted between men and women, as the notion of a gender-based division of labor (men outside, women inside) percolated into the religious sphere as well. Monks from certain denominations, for instance, toiled outside, building roads and bridges, while the nuns remained inside, washing the monks' soiled clothes. Tonomura, "Re-envisioning Women in the Post-Kamakura Age," 166. For a discussion of the notion of "men outside, women inside," see Yasuko Tabata, "Women's Work and Status in the Changing Medieval Economy," in Tonomura, Walthall, and Wakita, eds., *Women and Class in Japanese History*, 113–116.

31. Dobbins, *Letters of the Nun Eshinni*, 83.

32. Ruch, "The Other Side of Culture in Medieval Japan," 510.

33. Abutsu, "Fitful Slumbers" (trans. John R. Wallace), *Monumenta Nipponica* 43.4 (Winter 1988): 402. The dating of the work is a matter of disagreement among scholars, who date it to either the 1240s or the 1250s. See John R. Wallace, "Fitful Slumbers: Nun Abutsu's *Utatane*," *Monumenta Nipponica*, 43:4 (Winter 1988): 396–397.

34. Abutsu, "Fitful Slumbers," 415–416.

35. Ibid., 411, and Abutsu, "Izayoi nikki," in Nagasaki Ken, Tonomura Natsuko, Iwasa Miyoko, Inada Toshinori, and Itō Kei, eds., *Chūsei nikki kikōshū* (Tokyo: Shogakkan, 1994), 280 and 282. For an English translation, see Edwin O. Reischauer and Joseph K. Yamagiwa, *Translations from Early Japanese Literature* (Cambridge, MA: Harvard University Press, 1972), 52–119. See also "The Diary of the Waning Moon," in Keene, *Travelers of a Hundred Ages*, 136–140.

36. Nijō, *Towazugatari*, 253. *The Confessions of Lady Nijō (Towazugatari)* is also discussed in Keene, *Travelers of a Hundred Ages*, 155–162.

37. Nijō, *Towazugatari*, 277.

38. Ibid., 254.

39. Ibid., 251.

40. Abutsu, "Fitful Slumbers," 415.

41. Fujiwara Keishi, "Nakatsukasa no naishi nikki," in Fukuda Hideichi, Iwasa Miyoko, Kawazoe Shōji, Ōsone Shōsuke, Kubota Jun, and Tsurusaki Hiroo, eds., *Chūsei nikki kikōshū* (Tokyo: Iwanami Shoten, 1995), 214–270. See also Keene, *Travelers of a Hundred Ages*, 149–154.

42. Tonomura, "Re-envisioning Women in the Post-Kamakura Age," 155–156.

43. Quoted in Hotate Michihisa, "Himen no onna to romen no onna, Chūsei josei no soto aruki," in Sōgō Joseishi Kenkyūkai, ed., *Bunka to josei* (Tokyo: Yoshikawa Kōbunkan, 1998), 252.

44. Tonomura, Walthall, and Wakita, eds., *Women and Class in Japanese History*, 8.

45. See, for instance, Ichijō Kaneyoshi, *Fujikawa's Diary* (*Fujikawa no ki*, 1473), and Shōkō's *Shōkō's Diary* (*Shōkō nikki*, 1473). Both are mentioned by Inada Toshinori in an appendix to Nagasaki Ken et al., eds., *Chūsei nikki kikōshū*, 605.

46. Iwasa argues that the "long vacuum" lasted until the resurfacing of female travel diaries with Inoue Tsūjo (1681). Examples of travelogues by women of the Edo period antedating Tsūjo's, however, do exist and are discussed in this study. Nagasaki Ken et al., eds., *Chūsei nikki kikōshū*, 597. It should also be noticed that Lee Butler mentions the journeys of sixteenth-century court women to hot-spring resorts in " 'Washing Off the Dust': Baths and Bathing in Late Medieval Japan," *Monumenta Nipponica* 60.1 (Spring 2005): 28. He bases his evidence on a collective court women's diary titled *Oyudononoue no nikki*.

47. Tsuchiya Ayako, "Tabi no inochige," 367–368.

48. On the evolution of these modes of transportation between the late medieval and the early Edo period, see Miyajima Shin'ichi, "Hideyoshi wa kago ni nottaka," *Nihon Rekishi*, no. 669 (February 2004): 32–34.

49. Michel de Certeau, *The Practice of Everyday Life,* trans. Steven F. Rendall (Berkeley: University of California Press, 1984), 111. De Certeau makes this point regarding the train.

50. Tsuchiya Ayako, "Tabi no inochige," 367.

51. Ibid., 396.

52. Ibid., 368.

53. Inoue Tsūjo, "Tōkai kikō," 44. Tsūjo's diaries are discussed also in Keene, *Travelers of a Hundred Ages,* 328–335.

54. Inoue Tsūjo, "Kika nikki," in Inoue Tsūjo Zenshū Shūtei Iinkai, ed., *Inoue Tsūjo zenshū* (Marugame, 1973), 71.

55. Tsuchiya Ayako, "Tabi no inochige," 368.

56. Kikusha-ni, "Taorigiku," 317. The title of her memoir puns on the word *kiku,* chrysanthemum, which is also the first character in the name Kikusha-ni.

57. Ibid., 319, 415, 344, and 328.

58. Ibid., 322.

59. Ibid., 409. Bashō makes a similar statement in the opening lines of his *The Narrow Road to the Deep North (Oku no hosomichi).* Matsuo Bashō, *The Narrow Road to the Deep North,* 97.

60. Kikusha-ni, "Taorigiku," 322.

61. Ibid., 410.

62. For a chronology of Noriko's life, see Maeda Yoshi, *Edo jidai joryū bungeishi,* 247–248.

63. Seigen-in Noriko, "Kaihen shūjiki" (ed. Itasaka Yōko), *Kumamoto Tandai Ronshū* 55, *Shiryō* (July 1977): 1–26.

64. Seigen-in Noriko, "Aoba no yamaji" (ed. Itasaka Yōko), *Aichi Kenritsu Daigaku Setsurin, Shiryō honkoku* 27 (February 1979): 72.

65. Maeda Yoshi, *Edo jidai joryū bungeishi,* 249–273. See also Maeda Yoshi, "Shinryū-in Takako to tabi nikki *Koshi no yamafumi,*" *Fukuoka Jogakuin Tanki Daigaku Kiyō,* no. 14 (February 1978): 1–17.

66. Takejo, "Kanoene michi no ki," in Furuya Chishin, *Edo jidai joryū bungaku zenshū,* vol. 3 (Tokyo: Nihon Tosho Sentaa, 1979), 214. See also Keene, *Travelers of a Hundred Ages,* 335–340.

67. Takejo, "Kanoene michi no ki," 205. The quotation from "the writings of old" is a reference to *The Book of Rites* of Confucian tradition.

68. *Shinkokinshū,* no. 1701. My translation.

69. Ono no Komachi, *Kokinshū,* no. 938. Translation in Laurel Rasplica Rodd and Mary Catherine Henkenius, *Kokinshū: A Collection of Poems Ancient and Modern* (Princeton, NJ: Princeton University Press, 1984), 319.

70. Takejo, "Kanoene michi no ki," 214.

71. Nagashima Atsuko, "Bakumatsu nōson josei no kōdō no jiyū to kaji rōdō, Bushū Tachibanagun Namamugi mura *Sekiguchi nikki* o sozai toshite," in Kinsei Joseishi Kenkyūkai, ed., *Ronshū kinsei joseishi* (Tokyo: Yoshikawa Kōbunkan, 1986), 139–173. Nagashima's definition of "outing" includes long journeys as well as short visits to acquaintances in the same village.

72. See Maeda Yoshi, "Tabi nikki no josei," 238; and Maeda Yoshi, "Itō Tsunetari monjin Kuwahara Hisako to *Shikinami no shū*," *Fukuoka Jogakuin Tanki Daigaku Kiyō*, no. 13 (January 1977): 1–18.

73. Shiba Keiko, *Kinsei onna tabi nikki* (Tokyo: Yoshikawa Kōbunkan, 1997), 178, fig. 2.

74. Ihara Saikaku, "Kōshoku ichidai otoko," 122.

75. *Hiru mo hito o shinobazu*. Ihara Saikaku, "Kōshoku ichidai onna," in Teruoka Yasutaka and Higashi Akimasa, eds., *Ihara Saikakushū* 1 (Tokyo: Shogakkan, 1996): 443.

76. See Kanamori Atsuko, *Sekishonuke Edo no onnatachi no bōken*, 91–92. Unfortunately, Kanamori does not provide any further reference for the case and never mentions the year in which the incident happened. Other cases are presented in Vaporis, *Breaking Barriers*, 182–184.

77. Miyazaki Fumiko, "Female Pilgrims and Mt. Fuji," 353.

78. Quoted in Fukai Jinzō, "Kinsei ni okeru nukemairi no tenkai to sono shutai," *Rekishi* 50 (1977): 134.

79. Ishii Ryōsuke ed., *Kinsei hōsei shiryō sōsho 1*, 322–323. In other cases male travelers of commoner stock even presented themselves, cunningly, as members of the samurai class. Hisashichi, a commoner from Nihonbashi Shinagawachō, was arrested in 1827 as he traveled along the Tōkaidō posing as a retainer of the Protector of Bitchū. Hisashichi was on his way to Osaka in the company of the kabuki actor Onoe Kikugorō. Accused of "lying about his status" *(mibun o magirashi)*, he was sent into exile. The case is included in Ishii Ryōsuke, ed., *Oshioki reiruishū 12, Tenpō ruishū 2* (Tokyo: Meicho Shuppan, 1973), 438–439.

80. Large-scale *okagemairi* occurred in 1650, 1705, 1771, and 1830–1831.

81. Quoted in Fujitani Toshio, *Okagemairi to eejanaika* (Tokyo: Iwanami Shoten, 1972), 91–92.

82. Emori Ichirō, *Edo jidai josei seikatsu ezu daijiten*, 3:58–59.

83. Senkaku Tōshi, "Kamakura nikki," in Fujisawa Shishi Hensan Iinkai, ed., *Fujisawa shishi 2, Shiryōhen* (Fujisawa, 1973): 1221.

84. Fukai Jinzō, *Kinsei josei tabi to kaidō kōtsū*, 155.

85. In Makoto Ueda, ed. and trans., *Light Verse from the Floating World: An Anthology of Japanese Senryu* (New York: Columbia University Press, 1999), 261.

86. Ishii Ryōsuke, ed., *Kinsei hōsei shiryō sōsho 1*, 323–324.

87. Ibid., 324–326.

88. Vaporis, *Breaking Barriers*, 175–182.

89. Quoted in Fukai Jinzō, *Kinsei josei tabi to kaidō kōtsū*, 38.

90. Miyake Yoshiemon, "Zenkōji Tateyama sankei tabi nikki," in Gifu-ken, ed., *Gifu kenshi, Shiryōhen, Kinsei 7* (Gifu, 1971), 544–545.

91. Tatsu, the woman who climbed Mount Fuji disguised as a man, was a member of the Fujidō association, a group operating under the principle that men and women should reverse their power relation ("The woman is up. The man is down"). Therefore, Tatsu's obedience to the *nyonin kinsei* rule that regulated access to the top of Mount Fuji was arguably subordinated to her belief in the principles of Fujidō.

92. Timon Screech discusses the Edo period obsession with voyeurism, peeping, and stolen gazes in *Sex and the Floating World: Erotic Images in Japan, 1700–1820* (Honolulu: University of Hawai'i Press, 1999), 197–236.

Chapter 4: Palimpsests

Epigraphs: Sei Shōnagon, *The Pillow Book of Sei Shōnagon,* trans. Ivan Morris (New York: Columbia University Press, 1991), 25; Hayashi Razan, *Tsurezuregusa nozuchi* (1621; printed 1667), quoted in Linda H. Chance, "Constructing the Classic: *Tsurezuregusa* in Tokugawa Readings," *Journal of the American Oriental Society* 117.1 (January–March 1997): 43.

1. For a discussion of the intersections between travel, travel writing, and constructions of power, see Duncan and Gregory, eds., *Writes of Passage.* Gregory writes that travel diaries are "literally 'passages' that mark and are marked by words in motion. They are always more (and always less) than a direct record of experience" (Derek Gregory, "Scripting Egypt, Orientalism and the Cultures of Travel," in ibid., 116–117). For a comparative case study of a late nineteenth- to early twentieth-century Western woman manipulating her identity by means of travel narratives, see Loredana Polezzi, "Between Gender and Genre: The Travels of Estella Canziani," in Glenn Hooper and Tim Youngs, eds., *Perspectives on Travel Writing* (Aldershot [UK] and Burlington [VT]: Ashgate, 2004), 121–137.

2. Dorinne Kondo, *Crafting Selves: Power, Gender, and Discourse of Identity in a Japanese Workplace* (Chicago: University of Chicago Press, 1990), 74.

3. See ibid., 260. On the different ways in which men and women in medieval Europe lived and talked about their lives, see Bynum, *Fragmentation and Redemption,* 34–43 and 175–179. Catherine Barnes Stevenson reaches a conclusion similar to Kondo's in regard to Victorian female travelers in Africa who, compared to their male counterparts, tended to produce "more private, fragmented, episodic" works; Catherine Barnes Stevenson, "Women Travellers and the Art of Travel Writing," in Catherine Barnes Stevenson, ed., *Victorian Women Travel Writers in Africa* (Boston: Twayne Publishers, 1982), 10. Others have ascribed the lack of structure in women's narratives to the difficulties female authors encountered when they stepped into a male domain. When a female narrator speaks from the fringes of a male-developed and male-controlled field, "her voice may come out distorted, her narrative fragmented and ruptured," argues Ronald P. Loftus in "Female Self-Writing: Takamure Itsue's *Hi no kuni no onna no nikki,*" *Monumenta Nipponica* 51.2 (Summer 1996): 155–156. By the same author see also *Telling Lives: Women's Self-Writing in Modern Japan* (Honolulu: University of Hawai'i Press, 2004).

4. Kondo, *Crafting Selves,* 78.

5. Ikegawa Shunsui, "Fuji nikki," in Miyamoto Tsuneichi, Takeuchi Toshimi, and Mori Kahei, eds., *Nihon shomin seikatsu shiryō shūsei,* vol. 3 (Tokyo: San'ichi Shobō, 1969), 377.

6. Quoted in Takeuchi Makoto, "Shomin bunka no naka no Edo," in Takeuchi Makoto, ed., *Nihon no kinsei 14, Bunka no taishūka* (Tokyo: Chūō Kōronsha, 1993), 35.

7. Kiyokawa Hachirō, *Saiyūsō*, 220.

8. Nishikawa Yūko, "Diaries as Gendered Text" (trans. Anne Walthall), in Tonomura, Walthall, and Wakita, eds., *Women and Class in Japanese History*, 241–255.

9. Quoted in Shirane, *Traces of Dreams*, 189. See also Edward Kamens, *Utamakura, Allusion, and Intertextuality in Traditional Japanese Poetry* (New Haven, CT: Yale University Press, 1997).

10. Suzuki Mihoko, "Kawagoe no kikō," 533–534. Mihoko was the wife of a merchant. Her diary was written in 1770.

11. Anne Walthall, "Matsuo Taseko and the Meiji Restoration: Texts of Self and Gender," in Tonomura, Walthall, and Wakita, eds., *Women and Class in Japanese History*, 221.

12. For Nakako, see Maeda Yoshi, *Edo jidai joryū bungeishi*, 15–16 and 159–192. By the same author see also "Kutsukake Nakako to *Azumaji no nikki*," *Fukuoka Jogakuin Tanki Daigaku Kiyō*, no. 20 (February 1984): 11–33.

13. Bettina Gramlich-Oka, "Tadano Makuzu and Her *Hitori Kangae*," *Monumenta Nipponica* 56.1 (Spring 2001): 1–38.

14. Ueda, *Far Beyond the Field*, xix–xx.

15. Plutschow, *Four Japanese Travel Diaries of the Middle Ages*, 7.

16. Maeda Yoshi, "Kinsei keishū shijin Hara Saihin to Bōsō no tabi, Hara Saihin kenkyū sono ichi," *Fukuoka Jogakuin Tanki Daigaku Kiyō*, no. 12 (March 1976): 13–29. The original titles of the two diaries are *Tōyū nikki* and *Tōyū mansō*, respectively.

17. *Jibun wa onna to iu yori wa, hitori no ningen toshite kokorozasu michi o ayumitai.* Maeda Yoshi, "Tabi nikki no josei," 229–230, 224, 226.

18. McCullough, ed. and trans., *Tales of Ise*, 75.

19. Tokugawa Haru, "Takahara-in dono omichi no ki," ed. Ōi Tasuko, *Edoki onnakō*, no. 10 (1999): 98; Seigen-in Noriko, "Kaihen shūjiki," 6; Tsuchiya Ayako, "Tabi no inochige," 380.

20. Takejo, "Kanoene michi no ki," 210–211.

21. Hōkei-shi, "Atami kikō," in Yanase Kazuo, ed., *Hekichūdō sōsho 14* (Kyoto: Nozomigawa Shoten, 1996), 215. For Nagakubo Sekisui, see Plutschow, *A Reader in Edo Period Travel*, 47.

22. Kiyokawa Hachirō, *Saiyūsō*, 398.

23. Ibid., 141, 136. Later in life Hachirō became openly involved with the loyalist movement, so it is likely that his recollection of fourteenth-century loyalist Masashige was, in part, politically inspired.

24. Arakida Reijo, "Hatsuuma no nikki," 76–77. Genji's exile to Suma is narrated in chapters 12 and (partially) 13 of *The Tale of Genji*.

25. Plutschow, *A Reader in Edo Period Travel*, 70.

26. Ibid., 91.

27. Kiyokawa Hachirō, *Saiyūsō*, 216.

28. Kawai Tsugunosuke, "Chiritsubo," in Miyamoto Tsuneichi, Tanigawa Ken'ichi, and Haraguchi Torao, eds., *Nihon shomin seikatsu shiryō shūsei*, 2:404.

29. Kiyokawa Hachirō, *Saiyūsō*, 91.

30. Ibid., 87.

31. Tsuchiya Ayako, "Tabi no inochige," 387.

32. Peter F. Kornicki, "Unsuitable Books for Women? *Genji Monogatari* and *Ise Monogatari* in Late Seventeenth-Century Japan," *Monumenta Nipponica* 60.2 (Summer 2005): 147–193.

33. For a detailed study on the importance of the literary past in Bashō's journeys, see Shirane, *Traces of Dreams,* and Steven D. Carter, "On a Bare Branch: Bashō and the *Haikai* Profession," *Journal of the American Oriental Society* 117.1 (January–March 1997): 57–69.

34. Tomita Koreyuki, "Ōshū kikō," in Haraguchi Torao, Takeuchi Toshimi, and Miyamoto Tsuneichi, eds., *Nihon shomin seikatsu shiryō shūsei,* vol. 20 (Tokyo: San'ichi Shobō, 1972), 363–377.

35. See Hishiya Heishichi, "Tsukushi kikō," in ibid., 197, 223, 229, and 230.

36. Mukai Kyorai and Chine, "Ise kikō," in Ōuchi Hatsuo et al., eds., *Kyorai sensei zenshū* (Kyoto: Rakushisha Hōzonkai, 1982), 164–167.

37. Since the Heian period, fog *(kiri)* was traditionally associated with the autumn, while mist *(kasumi)* designated the springtime. The deer's sad cry evoked the gloominess of the fall. Clover was also associated with the season because its flowers bloom at the beginning of autumn. See Katagiri Yōichi, *Utamakura utakotoba jiten,* 135, 189, 336.

38. Nakagawa Hisamori's wife, "Ikahoki," 1.

39. See, for example, *Kokinshū,* poems nos. 437, 438, 439, 440, 442, 443, and *Man'yōshū,* scroll 2, poem no. 110, and scroll 12, poem no. 3065.

40. Nakagawa Hisamori's wife, "Ikahoki," 6. Narihira composed the following poem at Mount Asama:

Shinano naru	Surely no one
Asama no take ni	far or near
tatsu keburi	but marvels to see
ochikochibito no	the smoke rising from the peak
mi ya wa togamenu	of Asama in Shinano.

In McCullough, ed. and trans., *Tales of Ise,* 74.

41. Nakagawa Hisamori's wife, "Ikahoki," 5 and 9–10.

42. McCullough, ed. and trans., *Tales of Ise,* 80.

43. Nakagawa Hisamori's wife, "Ikahoki," 5, 10, 20.

44. McCullough, ed. and trans., *Tales of Ise,* 80.

45. Nakagawa Hisamori's wife, "Ikahoki," 5, 11.

46. In reference to Matsuo Bashō, Carter argues that the interaction with tradition represented "a professional resolve that [was] meant to connect him with the élite of the past and to show his worthiness to be counted in their number in the present." Carter, "On a Bare Branch," 67. See also Shirane, *Traces of Dreams.*

47. The verses, originally included in *Kaidōki,* the thirteenth-century record of a journey between Kyoto and Kamakura, are variously attributed to Kamo no Chōmei, to Minamoto no Mitsuyuki, and to Fujiwara no Hideyoshi. See "Kaidōki," in Nagasaki Ken, Tonomura Natsuko, and Iwasa Miyoko, eds., *Chūsei nikki kikōshū* (Tokyo: Shogakkan, 1994), 67.

Enoshima ya	Ah, Enoshima.
Sashite shioji ni	Profound must be
ato taruru	the oath of the gods
kami wa chikai no	who manifest themselves
fukaki naru beshi	along your tidal path.

Tokugawa Mitsukuni, "Kamakura nikki," in Fujisawa Shishi Hensan Iinkai, *Fujisawa shishi 2, Shiryōhen* (Fujisawa, 1973), 1206, and Hakuei, "Miura kikō," in ibid., 1213.

48. Arakida Reijo, "Hatsuuma no nikki," 60.

49. A disciple of Kamo no Mabuchi and a priest for the Inner Shrine, Arakida Hisaoyu excelled as a scholar of ancient writings. He is the author of a commentary on the *Man'yōshū*. See Mark Teeuwen, "Poetry, Sake, and Acrimony: Arakida Hisaoyu and the Kokugaku Movement," *Monumenta Nipponica* 52.3 (Autumn 1997): 295–325.

50. Atsuko Sakaki, *Obsessions with the Sino-Japanese Polarity in Japanese Literature* (Honolulu: University of Hawai'i Press, 2006), 119.

51. Arakida Reijo, "Hatsuuma no nikki," 28.

52. Plutschow, *Chaos and Cosmos*, 90.

53. See, for example, *Man'yōshū*, no. 3253.

54. Arakida Reijo, "Nochi no uma no nikki," in Furuya Chishin, ed., *Edo jidai joryū bungaku zenshū,* vol. 3 (Tokyo: Nihon Tosho Sentaa, 1979), 126–127.

55. Ibid., 107–108.

56. *Kokinshū*, no. 303, in Rodd and Henkenius, *Kokinshū*, 134.

57. Episode 23, in McCullough, ed. and trans., *Tales of Ise,* 89.

Kimi ga atari	Though rain may fall,
mitsutsu o oran	I forbid you, clouds,
Ikomayama	to veil Mount Ikoma,
kumo na kakushi so	for I live only
ame wa furu to mo	to gaze toward my beloved.

Saigyō in *Shinkokinshū*, no. 585: "Ikoma's peak / is veiled in clouds. / Is it raining on Toyama then / in Akishino?" Heiachirō H. Honda, trans., *The Shin Kokinshu: The 13th Century Anthology Edited by Imperial Edict* (Tokyo: Hokuseido Press, 1970), 158. On the same subject, see also *Tales of Ise,* episode 67, *Shinkokinshū*, no. 1368, and *Man'yōshū*, no. 3032.

58. Arakida Reijo, "Nochi no uma no nikki," 116. For Nunobiki Falls, see *Kokinshū*, nos. 922 (Ariwara no Yukihira), 923 (Ariwara no Narihira, also included in *Tales of Ise,* episode 87), and 927 (Tachibana no Nagamori).

59. Arakida Reijo, "Nochi no uma no nikki," 128.

60. Arakida Reijo, "Hatsuuma no nikki," 40, 64, 57; Arakida Reijo, "Nochi no uma no nikki," 121. During the Genpei Wars, a warrior named Kajiwara Genta Kagesue filled up his quiver with plum branches and used them during battle in lieu of arrows. The story is told in the Noh play *Quiver (Ebira)* and was also performed in puppet plays *(jōruri)*.

61. Arakida Reijo, "Hatsuuma no nikki," 55.

62. Matsuo Bashō, *The Narrow Road to the Deep North*, 118.

63. Arakida Reijo, "Nochi no uma no nikki," 119.

64. Arakida Reijo, "Hatsuuma no nikki," 40, 46; italics mine.

65. Ibid., 101.

66. On the cultural and social pursuits of wealthy farmers, see Roger K. Thomas, "Plebeian Travelers on the Way of Shikishima: Waka Theory and Practice during the Late Tokugawa Period" (Ph.D. diss., Indiana University, 1991); Thomas C. Smith, *The Agrarian Origins of Modern Japan* (Stanford, CA: Stanford University Press, 1959), 177–179; and Anne Walthall, "The Cult of Sensibility in Rural Tokugawa Japan: Love Poetry by Matsuo Taseko," *Journal of the American Oriental Society* 117.1 (January–March 1997): 70–86.

67. Anne Walthall has argued that, by appropriating the poetic tradition, rural entrepreneurs distinguished themselves from uneducated country peasants, bridged the gap between them and the samurai class, created a (cultural) community within the (social) community, and crafted an "emotionally and intellectually satisfying identity." Walthall, "The Cult of Sensibility," 70.

68. Ibid., 85.

69. Miura Jōshin, *Keichō kenmonshū*; quoted in Cecilia Segawa Seigle, *Yoshiwara: The Glittering World of the Japanese Courtesan* (Honolulu: University of Hawai'i Press, 1993), 18.

70. "Peasant men who had been marginalized in the political world of their time found that the extraordinary circumstances surrounding the coming of the barbarians gave them a chance to express themselves to their rulers. In the cracks that opened if only briefly and only slightly in the bastion of male privilege, a handful of women who had been silenced as women found an opportunity to speak as well." Walthall, *The Weak Body of a Useless Woman*, 109. See also Thomas, "Plebeian Travelers on the Way of Shikishima."

71. De Certeau, *The Practice of Everyday Life*, 79.

72. See Iwatsuki Akie, "Yuya Shizuko kashū *Chirinokori*," *Edoki onnakō*, no. 10 (1999): 60–70, and Fukai Jinzō, *Kinsei josei tabi to kaidō kōtsū*, 177.

73. The mist *(kasumi)* indicates the beginning of spring. Wild geese *(karigane)* were traditionally associated with two seasons, fall (when they fly south), and spring (when they fly back north). The bush warbler *(uguisu)* also serves as a seasonal reference, as it sings in the spring and was traditionally associated with plum blossoms. See Katagiri Yōichi, *Utamakura utakotoba jiten*, 104–105, 123–124, and 69–70. The image of "grass pillows" appears, for example, in *Man'yōshū* (Prince Arima, scroll no. 2), *Kokinshū* (Utsuku, no. 376), *Shinkokinshū* (Tsurayuki, Travel), and *Tales of Ise* (sec. 83).

74. Yuya Shizuko, "Ikaho no michi yukiburi," in Furuya Chishin, ed., *Edo jidai joryū bungaku zenshū*, 3:322. Note that the third line has six instead of five syllables.

75. Sei Shōnagon, *The Pillow Book*, 254.

76. Yuya Shizuko, "Ikaho no michi yukiburi," 320.

77. Shizuko incorrectly locates Sano no Funabashi in Shimozuke.

78. Yuya Shizuko, "Ikaho no michi yukiburi," 324.

79. *Man'yōshū*, book 14, poem no. 3420 (my translation):

>   *Kaminotsuke*   As the pontoon bridge at Sano
>   *Sano no funabashi*   in Kōzuke
>   *torihanashi*   comes apart
>   *oya wa sakuredo*   my parents try to separate us,
>   *wa wa sakaru gae*   but I will not let that happen.

Minamoto no Toshiyori Ason (1055–1129) also composed a poem on Sano no Funabashi included in the tenth scroll of *Gosen wakashū*. See also Katagiri Yōichi, *Utamakura utakotoba jiten*, 178.

80. In 1681, for example, Inoue Tsūjo had traveled through Yatsuhashi and had been told that the moor of old had been reclaimed and was now a cultivated field, that of the famous bridge only a few posts remained, and that the irises were gone: in short, that there was "nothing left worth seeing" *(goranzubeku mo nashi)*; Inoue Tsūjo, "Tōkai kikō," 46. The encounter of Narihira with the irises of Yatsuhashi is narrated in *Tales of Ise*, episode 9. See McCullough, ed. and trans., *Tales of Ise*, 74–75.

81. "Azumaji no nikki," in Kamakurashi Shishi Hensan Iinkai and Kodama Kōta, eds., *Kamakura shishi, Kinsei kindai kikō chishi hen* (Tokyo: Yoshikawa Kōbunkan, 1985), 164–182.

82. Kikuchi Tamiko, "Enoshima no ki," in ibid., 349 and 350–354.

83. Ibid., 352.

84. See, for example, Laura Moretti, *Chikusai il ciarlatano* (Venice: Cafoscarina, 2003), 32–42.

85. Le Roy Ladurie, *Carnival in Romans*, 316.

86. *Mi no shugyō ni narubeki waza narikeri*; Hishiya Heishichi, "Tsukushi kikō," 179.

87. Vaporis, *"Caveat Viator,"* 470.

88. Shinno Toshikazu, "Journeys, Pilgrimages, Excursions," 459. In the same article Shinno also discusses the general implications of travel as a rite of passage, especially pp. 455–460.

89. "The gods seemed to have possessed my soul and turned it inside out, and roadside images seemed to invite me from every corner," wrote Matsuo Bashō in the opening lines of *The Narrow Road to the Deep North*, 97. Among the female travelers considered here, Arakida Reijo completed at least three journeys, composing a different travelogue each time. Hara Saihin (1798–1859) also traveled extensively: to Edo in 1828, to the Bōsō peninsula in 1847, and to her home province of Chikuzen in the fall of 1848. In 1856 she began a tour of Hizen and Satsuma that lasted until 1858.

90. Shinno Toshikazu discusses the pilgrimage monuments of the northeastern regions of Japan in his "Journeys, Pilgrimages, Excursions."

91. Shinkō-in Myōjitsu, "Mokuzu," 307.

92. Yasumi Roan, *Gendaiyaku Ryokō yōjinshū*, ed. Sakurai Masanobu (Tokyo: Yasaka Shobō, 1993), 74.

93. Takejo, "Kanoene michi no ki," 214.

94. Both Kuwahara Hisako (1791–1853) and Oda Ieko (1788–1870) were educated

merchant wives from Chikuzen. They knew each other, were both disciples of scholar Itō Tsunetari, and traveled together to Ise, Zenkōji, and Nikkō in 1841. Ieko authored *Diary of the Azuma Road (Azumaji nikki)*, while Hisako wrote *Diary of a Pilgrimage to Futara (Futara mōde nikki)*. Kutsukake Nakako (1749–1829) was born into a mercantile family near Shiojiri and married a Shinano merchant. She titled her memoir of a tour of the Chichibu circuit *Diary of the Azuma Road*. See Maeda Yoshi, "Itō Tsunetari monjin Kuwahara Hisako to *Shikinami no shū*"; Maeda Yoshi, *Edo jidai joryū bungeishi*, 379–394; Maeda Yoshi, "Kutsukake Nakako to *Azumaji no nikki*."

95. Keene, *Travelers of a Hundred Ages*, 329.

96. Ibid., 335.

97. Kikuchi Tamiko, "Enoshima no ki," 349.

98. Ibid., 351.

99. Sei Shōnagon claimed that *The Pillow Book* was "written entirely for my own amusement," adding, "I was careful to keep my book hidden. But now it has become public, which is the last thing I expected. [...] Whatever people may think of my book, I still regret that it ever came to light." Sei Shōnagon, *The Pillow Book*, 263–264.

100. Kikuchi Tamiko, "Enoshima no ki," 348–349.

101. *Tamakushige*, literally "jewel comb box," is a pillow word *(makura kotoba)* that modifies *hako* (lit. "box") of Hakone.

102. Reference to *Kokinshū*, no. 764:

Yama no i no	Though the mountain spring
asaki kokoro mo	is shallow-hearted I am
omowanu o	not why does my love
kage bakari nomi	never visit only his
hito no miyu ran	reflection appears to me.

In Rodd and Henkenius, *Kokinshū*, 268–269.

103. Inamura Kiseko, "Hakone no ki," *Edoki onnakō*, no. 9 (1998): 195.

Chapter 5: Print Matters

Epigraph: Jippensha Ikku, "Jōdan shitsukonashi," in Tanahashi Masahiro, ed., *Jippensha Ikkushū* (Tokyo: Kokusho Kankōkai, 1997), 53.

1. Tsuchiya Ayako, "Tabi no inochige," 393.

2. Kiyokawa Hachirō, *Saiyūsō*, 242, 253.

3. In the seventeenth century some 701 publishing houses were operating in Kyoto, 185 in Osaka, and 242 in Edo. Katsuhisa Moriya, "Urban Networks and Information Networks," trans. Ronald P. Toby, in Chie Nakane and Shinzaburō Ōishi, eds., *Tokugawa Japan: The Social and Economic Antecedents of Modern Japan* (Tokyo: University of Tokyo Press, 1990), 115.

4. Engelbert Kaempfer, *Kaempfer's Japan: Tokugawa Culture Observed*, ed. and trans. Beatrice M. Bodart-Bailey (Honolulu: University of Hawai'i Press, 1999), 269.

5. Ibid., 342–343.

6. Coaldrake, "Metaphors of the Metropolis: Architectural and Artistic Representations of the Identity of Edo," 144.

7. Marcia Yonemoto, "Nihonbashi: Edo's Contested Center," *East Asian History* 17/18 (1999): 49–70.

8. "Nihon dōchū meisho zukushi," in Imai Kingo, ed., *Dōchūki shūsei 1* (Tokyo: Ōzorasha, 1998), 3–76.

9. "Dōchūki," in ibid., 1:79–134.

10. "Shokoku annai tabi suzume," in ibid., 5:5–6. *Menqiu* is an eighth-century Chinese text by Li Han. It was used as a textbook for children to memorize the names and deeds of famous men of the past. Known in Japan as *Mōgyū*, it enjoyed such popularity that a proverb of the Heian period, alluded to in this introduction, said, "[Even] the sparrows of the Kangaku-in chirp the *Mōgyū*." Records show that it was used to educate the son of Emperor Seiwa in 878. In *The Pillow Book,* section 166, Sei Shōnagon also makes an allusion to the text. The first printed edition appeared in Japan in 1596. In the Edo period *Mōgyū* was still a popular primer for Confucian studies. Playwright Chikamatsu Monzaemon (1653–1724), novelist Ihara Saikaku, and poet/painter Yosa Buson (1716–1783) all drew on its anecdotes. See Li Han, *Meng Ch'iu: Famous Episodes from Chinese History and Legend,* trans. Burton Watson (Tokyo: Kodansha International, 1979).

11. "Shokoku annai tabi suzume," 350. Sasaki Takatsuna and Kajiwara Kagesue are famous for participating in the 1180 battle at the Uji River.

12. "Shokoku yasumi kaibun no ezu," in Imai Kingo, ed., *Dōchūki shūsei,* 2:70.

13. Moronobu later cooperated with cartographer Ochikochi Dōin to transform the first official road map of the Tōkaidō into a commercially marketable piece. In the resulting work—*Detailed Illustrated Map of the Tōkaidō (Tōkaidō bunken ezu)*—Moronobu added what the cartographies of officialdom so prominently lacked: people. Unno Kazutaka, "Cartography in Japan," 424.

14. Imai Kingo, ed., *Dōchūki shūsei,* 2:317.

15. Peter Kornicki, *The Book in Japan: A Cultural History from the Beginnings to the Nineteenth Century* (Leiden: Brill, 1998), 258.

16. Conrad Totman, *Early Modern Japan* (Berkeley: University of California Press, 1993), 354.

17. Ibid., 433.

18. Tocco, "Norms and Texts for Women's Education in Tokugawa Japan," 202.

19. Peter Kornicki, "Literacy Revisited: Some Reflections on Richard Rubinger's Findings," *Monumenta Nipponica* 56.3 (Autumn 2001): 383. Kornicki's article is a reaction to Richard Rubinger, "Who Can't Read and Write? Illiteracy in Meiji Japan," *Monumenta Nipponica* 55.2 (Summer 2000): 163–198. Kornicki warns that "literacy is an uncommonly slippery issue" and that the very definition of literacy presents problems. In the case of early modern Japan, for example, the notion of literacy encompassed various degrees of reading and writing proficiency, ranging from the simple ability to read basic *kana* books to the skill of reading an imported, unpunctuated Chinese text.

20. Herbert Passin, *Society and Education in Japan,* cited in Henry D. Smith II, "The

History of the Book in Edo and Paris," in James L. McClain, John M. Merriman, and Ugawa Kaoru, eds., *Edo and Paris: Urban Life and the State in the Early Modern Era* (Ithaca, NY: Cornell University Press, 1994), 336.

21. Emori Ichirō, *Edo jidai josei seikatsu ezu daijiten*, vol. 5: *Shiki, Dōshokubutsu, Meisho* (Tokyo: Ōzorasha, 1993), 286, 244–253.

22. Ibid., 134–137, 143.

23. *Kokinshū*, no. 409, anonymous, usually attributed to Kakinomoto no Hitomaro. In Rodd and Henkenius, *Kokinshū*, 165. For the primers in question, see Emori, *Edo jidai josei seikatsu ezu daijiten*, 5:240–241 and 246.

24. Saitō Gesshin (Yukinari), "Edo meisho zue," in Ikeda Yasaburō, ed., *Nihon meisho fūzoku zue 4, Edo no maki 2* (Tokyo: Kadokawa Shoten, 1980), 160–161 and 168.

25. Franziska Ehmcke, "The Tōkaidō Woodblock Print Series as an Example of Intertextuality in the Fine Arts," in Susanne Formaneck and Sepp Linhart, eds., *Written Texts—Visual Texts, Woodblock-Printed Media in Early Modern Japan* (Amsterdam: Hotei Publishing, 2005), 120–121.

26. The print is reproduced in Fujiwara Chieko, ed., *Ukiyoe ni miru Edo no tabi*, 61.

27. "Ise sangū kondate dōchūki," in Haraguchi Torao, Takeuchi Toshimi, and Miyamoto Tsuneichi, eds., *Nihon shomin seikatsu shiryō shūsei*, vol. 20 (Tokyo: San'ichi Shobō, 1972), 619. "Persimmon" *(kaki)* alludes to the family name of the poet.

28. Masukawa Kōichi, *Sugoroku* (Tokyo: Hōsei Daigaku Shuppankyoku, 1995), 2:92–93. Masukawa mentions a Pure Land *sugoroku (Jōdo sugoroku)* from 1666, the final stage of which was heaven.

29. Reproduced in Takahashi Junji, ed., *Nihon esugoroku shūsei* (Tokyo: Kashiwa Bijutsu Shuppan, 1994), 87.

30. Reproduced in ibid., 46.

31. See also Gerald Groemer, "Singing the News: *Yomiuri* in Japan during the Edo and Meiji Periods," *Harvard Journal of Asiatic Studies* 54.1 (1994): 233–261.

32. The print is reproduced in Chris Uhlenbeck and Merel Molenaar, *Mount Fuji: Sacred Mountain of Japan* (Leiden: Hotei Publishing, 2000), 27 (plate 21).

33. A detailed analysis of this image appears in Nakamachi Keiko, "Ukiyo-e Memories of *Ise Monogatari*," trans. Henry Smith and Miriam Wattles, *Impressions* 22 (2000): 61–67.

34. *Musashi ni mo / miyako no teburi / nisashi tsutsu / ima wa hitogara / yasashi kari keri.* Asai Ryōi, "Edo meishoki," in Asakura Haruhiko, ed., *Nihon meisho fūzoku zue 3, Edo no maki 1* (Tokyo: Kadokawa Shoten, 1979), 8.

35. Ibid., 51.

36. As Jurgis Elisonas has shown, *Guide to Edo's Famous Sites* was in fact a poorly adapted rendition of a manual on the red-light district of Kyoto (the incongruously titled *Tale of Naniwa,* or *Naniwa monogatari,* 1655) and may have been compiled without Ryōi ever having set foot in the East. Elisonas, "Notorious Places," 259–262.

37. Itō Yoshio, "Ishu Hyakunin isshu," in Suzuki Tsutomu, ed., *Hyakunin isshu* (Tokyo: Sekai Bunkasha, 1975), 152. On *Hyakunin isshu*, see also Joshua S. Mostow, *Pictures of the Heart: The Hyakunin Isshu in Word and Image* (Honolulu: University of Hawai'i Press, 1996).

38. Smith, "The History of the Book in Edo and Paris," 334.
39. Kiyokawa Hachirō, *Saiyūsō*, 231.
40. Ibid., 281–282.
41. "Edo meisho hanagoyomi," in Asakura Haruhiko, ed., *Nihon meisho fūzoku zue 3, Edo no maki 1,* 72–105 (example of Tōto on p. 77). In the same collection are also "Ehon Edo miyage," 210–335 (Tōto on pp. 211, 212, 213, 214), and Saitō Gesshin's "Tōto saijiki," 108–207.
42. Saitō Gesshin, "Edo meisho zue," 433.
43. Ibid., 150. The episode of Nitta Shirō Tadatsune entering the cave is narrated in *Mirror of the East (Azuma kagami)*, Kennin 3 (1203)/6/3. Nitta had entered with five other men by order of Yoriie (not, as *Edo meisho zue* would have it, Yoritomo). In the cave the men encountered the deity of the mountain; overcome by surprise, Nitta's companions dropped dead on the spot. The following day, he was the only one to come out.
44. Saitō Gesshin, "Edo meisho zue," 433.
45. Ibid., 205.
46. Chigata Nakamichi, "Shokoku meibutsu ōrai," unpublished ms., University of California Berkeley, East Asia Collection. Examples of Hiroshige's prints from the *Famous Products* series are included in Elvehjem Museum of Art, *The Edward Burr Van Vleck Collection of Japanese Prints* (Madison: Elvehjem Museum of Art, University of Wisconsin-Madison, 1990), 91–92.
47. Howard Hibbett, *The Chrysanthemum and the Fish: Japanese Humor since the Age of the Shoguns* (Tokyo, New York, and London: Kodansha International, 2002), 142.
48. Jippensha Ikku, *Shank's Mare,* 88–89.
49. Ibid., 47–48.
50. Ibid., 48–51.
51. Jippensha Ikku, "Jōdan shitsukonashi," 53.

Chapter 6: Icons of Escapism

Epigraphs: *Monzen ni / amazake uri no / kireisa yo.* Miyake Yoshiemon, "Zenkōji Tateyama sankei tabi nikki," 543; Borges, *Selected Non-Fictions,* 409.
1. Jippensha Ikku, *Shank's Mare,* 237.
2. Grapard, "The State Remains, but Mountains and Rivers Are Destroyed," 120–121.
3. Kaibara Ekiken, "Jinshin kikō," in Takada Mamoru and Hara Michio, eds., *Kinsei kikō shūsei,* series Sōsho Edo bunko 17 (Tokyo: Kokusho Kankōkai, 1991), 43.
4. Ikegawa Shunsui, "Fuji nikki," 375.
5. Kanzaki Noritake compares the activities of early modern *oshi* to modern travel agencies in "A Comparative Analysis of the Tourist Industry," in Umesao Tadao, Harumi Befu, and Ishimori Shuzo, eds., *Japanese Civilization in the Modern World, 9: Tourism* (Osaka: National Museum of Ethnology, 1995), 48.
6. Kanagawa-ken Kikaku Chōsabu Kenshi Henshūshitsu, *Kanagawa kenshi, Tsūshi-*

hen 2, Kinsei 1 (Kanagawa, 1974), 772–773. Nishiyama Masaru, *Seichi no sōzōryoku, Sankei mandara o yomu,* 147–207. Susanne Formanek discusses the specific case of Tateyama's *oshi* and their advertising activities in "Pilgrimage in the Edo Period, Forerunner of Modern Domestic Tourism? The Example of the Pilgrimage to Mount Tateyama."

7. Teeuwen, "Poetry, Sake, and Acrimony," 315–316.

8. Kaempfer, *Kaempfer's Japan,* 108.

9. Ihara Saikaku, *The Japanese Family Storehouse,* 89, 90; Ihara Saikaku, *This Scheming World,* trans. Masanori Takatsuka and David C. Stubbs (Rutland [VT] and Tokyo: Tuttle, 1965), 36.

10. In one story, a mother from Noda village (Settsu Province) runs away with her infant son. "She came all the way to the residence of a certain *onshi* from Yamada, but did not tell him she had fled on an unauthorized pilgrimage. The *onshi* thought she was commendable and showed her around the two shrines, paying for all travel expenses"; in Narabayashi Tadao, ed., "Okagemairi," 90.

11. Ihara Saikaku, *The Japanese Family Storehouse,* 89.

12. "Shokoku annai tabi suzume," 186–187, 201.

13. "Shokoku irozato annai," in Geinōshi Kenkyūkai, ed., *Nihon shomin bunka shiryō shūsei 9, Asobi* (Tokyo: San'ichi Shobō, 1974), 12.

14. Fujisawa Shishi Hensan Iinkai, *Fujisawa shishi 2, Shiryōhen* (Fujisawa, 1973), 1118–1120.

15. Hirano Eiji, "Fujikō Ōyamakō no junpai to yusan," *Chihōshi kenkyū* 48.4 (August 1998): 31. See also Fujisawa Shishi Hensan Iinkai, *Fujisawa shishi 2, Shiryōhen,* 1130–1133.

16. Senkaku Tōshi, "Kamakura nikki," 1221–1222.

17. Maeda Takashi, *Junrei no shakaigaku,* 114–115.

18. Hirano Eiji, "Fujikō Ōyamakō no junpai to yusan," 30.

19. Ibid., 31. *Tomeonna* were prostitutes/waitresses usually sent by teahouses and inns to street corners or the gates of villages and towns with the specific purpose of stopping wayfarers, advertising the services of their establishments, and at times quite literally dragging people in.

20. See Kanagawa-ken Kikaku Chōsabu Kenshi Henshūshitsu, *Kanagawa kenshi, Tsūshi-hen 2, Kinsei 1,* 762.

21. Jijūken Ikkishi, "Kamakura ki," in Kamakurashi Shishi Hensan Iinkai and Kodama Kōta, eds., *Kamakura shishi, Kinsei kindai kikō chishi hen* (Tokyo: Yoshikawa Kōbunkan, 1985), 122.

22. "Azumaji no nikki," 173–174.

23. Hishiya Heishichi, "Tsukushi kikō," 169.

24. Ibid.

25. In his diary Heishichi also includes an illustration of the site; ibid., 170.

26. *Man'yōshū,* III, no. 306.

Ise no umi no	Would that they were flowers,
okitsu shiranami	the white surges far upon

> *hana nimoga*   the sea of Ise—
> *tsutsumite imo ga*   I would wrap and bring them home
> *iezuto ni semu*   as a souvenir for my beloved wife.

English translation from *The Manyōshū: One Thousand Poems Selected and Translated from the Japanese, with Text in Romaji and an Introduction, Notes, Maps, Biographical Notes, Chronological Table, Etc.* (Tokyo: Iwanami Shoten, 1940), 88.

27. *Man'yōshū*, XX, no. 4409. English translation in ibid., 178.

28. Sōkyū, "Miyako no tsuto," trans. Herbert Plutschow, in Herbert Plutschow, *Four Japanese Travel Diaries of the Middle Ages,* (Ithaca, NY: Cornell University Press, 1981), 73–74.

29. Kaempfer, *Kaempfer's Japan,* 322.

30. Ikegawa Shunsui, "Fuji nikki," 375.

31. Jippensha Ikku, *Shank's Mare,* 47.

32. Hishiya Heishichi, "Tsukushi kikō," 204.

33. Inoue Shunji, trans., *Kojiki* (Fukuoka: Nihon Shuji Kyoiku Renmei, 1966), 26. I discuss this episode and other implications of gastronomic travel in Laura Nenzi, "*Ise sangū kondate dōchūki,* un'odissea religioso-gastronomica del periodo Edo," in *Atti del XXVI Convegno di Studi sul Giappone, Torino, 26–28 Settembre 2002* (Venice: Cartotecnica Veneziana Editrice, 2002), 357–369.

34. Asahi Monzaemon, "Ōmurōchūki," in Nagoya-shi Kyōiku Iinkai, ed., *Nagoya sōsho, Zokuhen,* vol. 11 (Nagoya, 1968): 54.

35. See Chapter 4, note 47, and discussion in Chapter 4.

36. Iwamura Yasuhisa, "Kamakura sanshō nikki," in Fujisawa Shishi Hensan Iinkai, ed., *Fujisawa shishi 2, Shiryōhen,* 1226, 1228.

37. "Ah, Odawara. / The scent of *uirō* / on a misty night" *(Odawara ya / uirō niou / yoi oboro).* Kikusha-ni, "Taorigiku," 344.

38. In this case, our hero mistakenly takes the medicine for a rice cake and gulps it down, to everyone's amusement. Jippensha Ikku, *Shank's Mare,* 41.

39. Furukawa Koshōken, "Saiyū zakki," in Miyamoto Tsuneichi, Tanigawa Ken'ichi, and Haraguchi Torao, eds., *Nihon shomin seikatsu shiryō shūsei,* vol. 2 (Tokyo: San'ichi Shobō, 1969), 381.

40. Nakamura Ito, "Ise mōde no nikki," in Toyoda Chōshi Hensan Iinkai, ed., *Toyoda chōshi, Betsuhen 1, Tōkaidō to Tenryūgawa Ikeda wataribune, Furoku 2, Kikōbun* (Toyoda-chō, 1999), 515.

41. Ōkiyo Keijun (Jippōan), "Jippōan yūreki zakki," in Fujisawa Shishi Hensan Iinkai, ed., *Fujisawa shishi 2, Shiryōhen* (Fujisawa, 1973), 1231.

42. Kiyokawa Hachirō, *Saiyūsō,* 71.

43. Konno Oito, "Sangū dōchū shōyōki," 611.

44. "Fuji Ōyama dōchū zakki" (1836), in Fujisawa Shishi Hensan Iinkai, ed., *Fujisawa shishi 2, Shiryōhen,* 1253.

45. Kusunoki Masashige, also known as Chūshin Nanko, was a loyal supporter of Emperor Go-Daigo in the Nanbokuchō period. He committed ritual suicide after

suffering a defeat at the hands of Ashikaga Takauji in 1336. A biographical sketch of Masashige appears in Ivan Morris, *The Nobility of Failure: Tragic Heroes in the History of Japan* (New York: Holt, Rinehart and Winston, 1975), 106–142.

46. "Ise sangū kondate dōchūki," 618. Shu Shunsui (1600–1682) was a Chinese man of letters who fled to Nagasaki after the decline of the Ming dynasty. He was later hired by the lord of Mito, Tokugawa Mitsukuni, and participated in the compilation of *Great History of Japan (Dai Nihon shi)*.

47. See Kiyokawa Hachirō, *Saiyūsō*, 87–88, 311–312.

48. Ibid., 162. Tekkai is the mountain at the foot of which the battle took place.

49. Ri-in, "Enoshima kikō," in Kamakurashi Shishi Hensan Iinkai and Kodama Kōta, eds., *Kamakura shishi, Kinsei kindai kikō chishi hen* (Tokyo: Yoshikawa Kōbunkan, 1985), 395–396; *italics mine*. Not much is known about Ri-in's identity. The style and content of her diary, *Account of a Trip to Enoshima* (*Enoshima kikō*, 1855), suggest that she might have belonged to a mercantile family based in Edo.

50. A reference to the Nanbokuchō period, when Emperor Go-Daigo, expelled from Kyoto, established a court on the mountain (1336).

51. Kiyokawa Hachirō, *Saiyūsō*, 344.

52. Katagiri Yōichi, *Utamakura utakotoba jiten*, 184.

53. Saigyō in *Shinkokinshū*, no. 987. The translation is from Honda, *The Shin Kokinshu*, 274.

54. Shigako plays on the homophony between "rice jelly" and "rain" *(ame)*. Yamanashi Shigako, "Harumichigusa," 374.

55. According to local lore, a pregnant woman had been assassinated in the proximity of the rock. A wandering monk had found the body and delivered the child. When the boy grew up he avenged his mother by tracking down and killing her assassin. Hachirō mentions the anecdote: "In the past, a pregnant woman was cut down. Later she was avenged. Everyone knows this story." Kiyokawa Hachirō, *Saiyūsō*, 395.

56. Ibid., 395–396. For more on Sayo no Nakayama's many identities, see Ehmcke, "The Tōkaidō Woodblock Print Series," 114–117.

57. Ōkiyo Keijun (Jippōan), "Jippōan yūreki zakki," 1231–1233, 1239.

58. "Azumaji no nikki," 168–169.

59. Shinkō-in Myōjitsu, "Mokuzu," 294–295. Matsuo Bashō was actually buried at Yoshinaka Temple in Zeze, Ōmi Province. See Shirane, *Traces of Dreams*, 281. A late Edo traveler, the Tosa official Morioka Sadakata, mentions this "real" grave in his travel diary: Morioka Sadakata, "Morioka Sadakata nikki," 125.

60. Urry, *The Tourist Gaze*, 7.

61. Helen Hardacre discusses the case of one Shikoku replica created in Kōza county (Sagami Province) between 1817 and 1820 in *Religion and Society in Nineteenth-Century Japan: A Study of the Southern Kantō Region, Using Late Edo and Early Meiji Gazetteers* (Ann Arbor: Center for Japanese Studies, University of Michigan, 2002), 145–147. Also touching on the role of replicas are Ian Reader and Paul L. Swanson in "Editors' Introduction: Pilgrimage in the Japanese Religious Tradition," *Japanese Journal of Religious Studies* 24.3–4 (1997): 236.

62. Kiyokawa Hachirō, *Saiyūsō,* 273.
63. Takeda Akira, *Junrei to minzoku,* 189.
64. Saitō Gesshin, "Edo meisho zue," 370.
65. Screech, "The Strangest Place in Edo," 423.
66. Quoted in ibid., 410.
67. Igarashi Tomio, "Edo jidai no dōchūki ni arawareta shomin no tabi, Dōchūki to kikōbun no hikakuteki kōsatsu," *Gunma Joshi Tanki Daigaku Kiyō* 11 (January 1984): 2–3.
68. See Saitō Gesshin, "Edo meisho zue," 145, 148, 69, 310, 223, 365, 487 (for Kumano), 510–511 (Sanjūsangendō), 47 (Ise), 72 and 104 (Kashima), 538 (Katori), 350–351 (Western Provinces), 124, 322, and 433 for Kamakura Hachimangū. For Benzaiten, see 318 (Inokashira), 519 (Honjo), 124–125 (Haneda), 386 (Biwajima), 518–519 (Fukagawa), 550 (Ushigome), 125 (Kurishima), 458–459, 444–445 (Matsuhashi), 511–513 (Susaki), 150 (Sukan), 174–175 (Seto), 59 (Zōjōji), 412–413 (Shinobazu). In Kyoto, Kiyokawa Hachirō notices a replica *(utsushi)* of the eighty-eight-stage Shikoku circuit in the hills behind Ninnaji. See Kiyokawa Hachirō, *Saiyūsō,* 291.
69. Saitō Gesshin, "Tōto saijiki," 198, 203–204, 196–197.
70. Saitō Gesshin, "Edo meisho zue," 426.
71. Saitō Gesshin, "Tōto saijiki," 198–199.
72. Martin Colcutt, "Mt. Fuji as the Realm of Miroku," 248–269. *Souvenir of Edo: A Picture Book (Ehon Edo miyage),* a guide to the city published between 1850 and 1868, includes representations of miniaturized surrogates of Mount Fuji in Tomigaoka (Fukagawa), Ōkubo Nishimuki Tenjin, Takada, and Teppōzu Minato Inari. "Ehon Edo miyage," 320, 318, 310, and 229.
73. Saitō Gesshin, "Tōto saijiki," 148.
74. Asai Ryōi, "Edo meishoki," 18.
75. Saitō Gesshin, "Tōto saijiki," 148.
76. See MacCannell, *The Tourist,* 91–107.
77. As many travel guides explained, the straw snakes had become a popular souvenir since the Kan'ei era (1624–1644), when a local farmer named Kihachi first made and sold such snakes to curious bystanders during the festival. When a plague epidemic hit on the seventh month of that year, the houses that displayed the snakes were spared and the fame of the souvenirs skyrocketed thereafter. See Saitō Gesshin, "Tōto saijiki," 148.
78. Ibid., 148.
79. Suzuki Shōzō, "Fuji zenjō dōchū nikki," 1315.
80. Traganou, "Geographic Representations of the Tōkaidō from Edo to Meiji Japan," 22. Elsewhere Traganou argues that, with the advent of the railroad in the Meiji period, "space [was] measured as distance, distance [was] measured as time, time [was] measured as money." Traganou, "Representing Mobility in Tokugawa and Meiji Japan," 198.

Chapter 7: Bodies, Brothels, and Baths

Epigraphs: Bynum, *Fragmentation and Redemption,* 20; Lefebvre, *The Production of Space,* 162.

1. Suzanne E. Cahill, "Discipline and Transformation: Body and Practice in the Lives of Daoist Holy Women of Tang China," in Dorothy Ko, Jahyun Kim Haboush, and Joan Piggott, eds., *Women and Confucian Cultures in Premodern China, Korea, and Japan* (Berkeley: University of California Press, 2003), 251. On the body as a platform for debate in medieval Japan, see Hitomi Tonomura, "Black Hair and Red Trousers: Gendering the Flesh in Medieval Japan," *American Historical Review* 99.1 (February 1994): 129–154.

2. For a discussion of womb projections onto vast geographical areas, see Helen Hardacre, "The Cave and the Womb World," *Japanese Journal of Religious Studies* 10.2–3 (June/September 1983): 149–176. For the Fuji caves, see Miyata Noboru, *Onna no reiryoku to ie no kami,* 92–99.

3. Winston Davis, *Japanese Religion and Society: Paradigms of Structure and Change* (Albany: State University of New York Press, 1992), 73. More examples on the physicality of religion and culture can be found in Thomas P. Kasulis, "The Body—Japanese Style," in Thomas P. Kasulis, Roger T. Ames, and Wimal Dissanayake, eds., *Self as Body in Asian Theory and Practice* (Albany: State University of New York Press, 1993), 299–319.

4. Walthall, *The Weak Body of a Useless Woman,* 231.

5. "Azumaji no nikki," 166–167.

6. Marta V. Vicente and Luis R. Corteguera, "Women in Texts: From Language to Representation," in Marta V. Vicente and Luis R. Corteguera, eds., *Women, Texts and Authority in the Early Modern Spanish World* (Aldershot [UK] and Burlington [VT]: Ashgate, 2003), 10.

7. Inoue Tsūjo, "Tōkai kikō," 48.

8. Minamori Reiko, "Chiyojo no kage ni kakureta Sakajiriya Karyō *Wataridori,*" *Edoki onnakō,* no. 9 (1998): 174.

9. Both examples are cited in Chapter 6.

10. I am borrowing the expression Gregory M. Pflugfelder uses as the title of his 1999 monograph on male-male sexuality.

11. "The only thing separating the new-born baby's first bath from the cleansing of the corpse is life." Robert W. Leutner, *Shikitei Sanba and the Comic Tradition in Edo Fiction* (Cambridge, MA: Harvard University Press, 1985), 137.

12. Yonemoto, *Mapping Early Modern Japan,* 129–172.

13. On the creation of licensed spaces of transgression, see Nicolas Fiévé, "Social Discrimination and Architectural Freedom in the Pleasure District of Kyoto in Early Modern Japan," in Nicolas Fiévé and Paul Waley, eds., *Japanese Capitals in Historical Perspective: Place, Power and Memory in Kyoto, Edo and Tokyo* (London and New York: Routledge Curzon, 2003), 67–99. See also Seigle, *Yoshiwara.*

14. Many such edicts are collected in Kodama Kōta, *Kinsei kōtsū shiryōshū 8–9, Bakufu hōrei 1–2.* The continuous reissuance of these warnings is in itself testimony that none succeeded in eliminating the practice.

15. "Shokoku irozato annai," 23, 12.
16. Hishiya Heishichi, "Tsukushi kikō," 206, 226.
17. Kiyokawa Hachirō, *Saiyūsō*, 240.
18. Ihara Saikaku, *The Japanese Family Storehouse*, 106.
19. Kaempfer, *Kaempfer's Japan*, 142.
20. "Shokoku irozato annai," 22.
21. Furukawa Koshōken, "Saiyū zakki," 382–383. For more on Koshōken, see Plutschow, *A Reader in Edo Period Travel*, 89–123; Bolitho, "Travelers' Tales: Three Eighteenth-Century Travel Journals." See also Screech, *Sex and the Floating World*, 274.
22. Hishiya Heishichi, "Tsukushi kikō," 206–209, 213.
23. Timon Screech, for example, mentions the aptly titled *Sexual Travel Diary* (*Kōshoku tabi nikki*, 1687) by an anonymous author. See Screech, *Sex and the Floating World*, 18. Howard Hibbett discusses the erotic literature of the Edo period in *The Chrysanthemum and the Fish*, 89–129.
24. Hiraga Gennai, "Nanshoku saiken mitsu no asa," in Geinōshi Kenkyūkai, ed., *Nihon shomin bunka shiryō shūsei 9, Asobi* (Tokyo: San'ichi Shobō, 1974), 103.
25. *Shunga* on the theme of travel made their debut on the market in the late eighteenth century. Screech, *Sex and the Floating World*, 269.
26. Yonemoto, *Mapping Early Modern Japan*, 129–172. Particularly intriguing is her discussion of the "Land of the Rising Moon" (143–149) and of the "Map of Nape-of-the-Neck Mountain" (163–166).
27. Screech, *Sex and the Floating World*, 248. The same author also mentions Koikawa Shōzan's *A Travel Pillow for the Fifty-three Stations (Tabimakura gojūsantsugi)* as an example of sexual iconization of the Tōkaidō.
28. Higashiōji Taku, ed., *Tōkaidō gojūsantsugi hizasuri nikki*, Ukiyoe bijutsu meihinkan 1 (Tokyo: Gabundō, 1984), 8.
29. Ibid.
30. *Hara no tatsu hodo henoko ga tateba tōni jinkyo o suru darō*. The pun is based on the homophony between the name of the local town, Hara, and the expression for "getting angry" *(hara ga tatsu)*. Higashiōji Taku, ed., *Tōkaidō gojūsantsugi hizasuri nikki*, 28.
31. Ibid., 12, 14, 4, 18.
32. Ibid., 42.
33. Jippensha Ikku, *Tōkaidōchū hizakurige*, vol. 1, ed. Asō Isoji (Tokyo: Iwanami Shoten, 1992), 130.
34. Konno Nobuo, *Edo no tabi*, 42–43.
35. Enomoto Myōshin, "Issenkoji michi no ki," in Warabi-shi, ed., *Enomoto ke kiroku, Warabi shishi chōsa hōkokusho 4* (Warabi, 1987), 68.
36. Maeda Isamu, *Edogo no jiten* (Tokyo: Kōdansha, 1979), 543.
37. Kikusha-ni, "Taorigiku," 348.
38. Anne Walthall, ed., *The Human Tradition in Modern Japan* (Wilmington, DE: SR Books, 2002), 51; italics mine. Yet another example provided by Anne Walthall is that of Matsuo Taseko, who on the occasion of her 1862–1863 journey to Kyoto spent one evening strolling around the pleasure quarter of Osaka and visiting the local teahouses

in the company of a nativist fellow. See Walthall, *The Weak Body of a Useless Woman*, 172–173.

39. Butler, " 'Washing Off the Dust,' " 8, 16.

40. Jippensha Ikku, *Shank's Mare*, 42–44. As the story goes, Kita and Yaji reach Odawara and check into an inn owned by a man from the Kansai region. He has installed a tub typical of western Japan, the proper use of which the two heroes ignore. Instead of asking, they attempt to figure it out by themselves, with disastrous consequences: they scorch their feet and end up destroying the tub in the process. See also Leutner, *Shikitei Sanba,* 164. Here, a man from the Kansai region, new to Edo, comes into the public bath, mistakes a dirty loincloth soaking in a bucket for a clean towel, and starts scrubbing his face with it.

41. Recounted in Yamakawa Kikue, *Women of the Mito Domain,* 52–53.

42. Yasumi Roan, *Gendaiyaku Ryokō yōjinshū,* 92–93. For an English-language selection of items from Roan's guide, see Vaporis, *"Caveat Viator."*

43. Hishiya Heishichi, "Tsukushi kikō," 245.

44. Roan gives a specific figure, a total of 292 resorts across forty provinces. He does, however, add: "There are countless resorts scattered in the mountains all over the country. These resorts have been described in the works of others who have advertised them, so I am not including them here." Yasumi Roan, *Gendaiyaku Ryokō yōjinshū,* 95, 121, 114.

45. Hishiya Heishichi, "Tsukushi kikō," 217.

46. Scott Clark, *Japan: A View from the Bath* (Honolulu: University of Hawai'i Press, 1994), 147.

47. Leutner, *Shikitei Sanba,* 137.

48. Yasumi Roan, *Gendaiyaku Ryokō yōjinshū,* 92.

49. Inamura Kiseko, "Hakone no ki," 192.

50. Fuji Mihoko, "Hakone nikki," ed. Hasegawa Ikuko, *Edoki onnakō,* no. 10 (1999): 85.

51. See Kouamé, *Pèlerinage et société dans le Japon des Tokugawa,* 221.

52. "Arima meisho kagami," in *Kinsei bungei sōsho 2, Meishoki 2* (Tokyo: Kokusho Kankōkai, 1910), 434. Kiyokawa Hachirō, *Saiyūsō,* 318.

53. Ōne Tsuchinari, "Kokkei Arima kikō," in Itasaka Yōko, ed., *Edo onsen kikō* (Tokyo: Heibonsha, 1987), 33, 25.

54. Motoori Ōhira, "Arima nikki," in ibid., 86.

55. On the exclusion of women from sumo spaces, see Suzuki Masataka, *Nyonin kinsei,* 22–25.

56. Narita Shishi Hensan Iinkai, ed., *Narita shishi, Kinsei hen, Shiryōshū 5, jō, Monzenchō 1* (Narita, 1976), 179, 412–413 (appeals from 1780 and 1840, respectively).

57. Hishiya Heishichi, "Tsukushi kikō," 245.

58. Yunoue Takashi, *Mitsu no Tōkaidō* (Shizuoka: Shizuoka Shinbunsha, 2000), 108–115.

59. Hōkei-shi, "Atami kikō," 221.

60. Motoori Ōhira, "Arima nikki," 75. Yuya is written with characters that are normally read "Kumano."

61. Morimoto Tsuzuko, "Suwa nikki," *Edoki onnakō,* no. 11 (2000): 79–82.

62. Shiba Keiko, *Kinsei onna tabi nikki,* 8–9.

63. For the etymology of the word *yuna,* see Butler, "'Washing Off the Dust,'" 24–25.

64. Motoori Ōhira, "Arima nikki," 80.

65. On the Tokugawa's vain attempts to stifle the erotic activities of the *yuna,* see Clark, *Japan,* 32–33.

66. Higashiōji Taku, ed., *Tōkaidō gojūsantsugi hizasuri nikki,* 22.

67. Ōne Tsuchinari, "Kokkei Arima kikō," 19, 8, 17, 19.

68. Ibid., 50, 4, 51. Though informed by one of the *yuna* that there are no prostitutes, Sairoku remains insistent. The woman threatens to call the innkeeper, adding "and he'll scold you good."

69. Yasumi Roan, *Gendaiyaku Ryokō yōjinshū,* 94.

70. Ibid., 101, 103.

71. Santō Kyōsan, "Atami onsen zui," in Shizuoka-ken, ed., *Shizuoka kenshi, Shiryō 15, Kinsei 7* (Shizuoka, 1991), 1017.

72. Hishiya Heishichi, "Tsukushi kikō," 244.

73. Yasumi Roan, *Gendaiyaku Ryokō yōjinshū,* 106.

74. Iwasaki Masasumi, "Hakone nanayu," in Ōto Yoshifuru and Yamaguchi Osamu, eds., *Tōkaidō 1* (Tokyo: Chikuma Shobō, 1976), 172.

75. A. J. C. Geerts, "The Mineral Springs of Ashi-no-Yu in the Hakone Mountains," *Transactions of the Asiatic Society of Japan* 9 (1881): 50, 52.

76. Hishiya Heishichi, "Tsukushi kikō," 245.

77. Scott Clark talks about the modern-day version of this practice in *Japan,* 136.

78. Yasumi Roan, *Gendaiyaku Ryokō yōjinshū,* 118.

79. Inamura Kiseko, "Hakone no ki," 192.

Conclusion: Dreaming of Walking near Fuji

Epigraphs: "Il mondo è un gomitolo di strade e seguendole trovi tutto: vita e morte, miseria e felicità, lacrime e consolazione, avventure e amore" (Sebastiano Vassalli, *La Chimera* [Turin: Einaudi, 1990], 213); Jippensha Ikku, *Shank's Mare,* 237.

1. Traganou, "Geographic Representations of the Tōkaidō from Edo to Meiji Japan," 13.

2. Jippensha Ikku, *Shank's Mare,* 237.

3. *Tabi to iu mono no mezurashiki.* "Azumaji no nikki," 167.

4. Traganou, "Geographic Representations of the Tōkaidō from Edo to Meiji Japan," 22. By the same author see also "Representing Mobility in Tokugawa and Meiji Japan," 197.

Bibliography

Abutsu. "Fitful Slumbers." Trans. John R. Wallace. *Monumenta Nipponica* 43.4 (Winter 1988): 399–416.

———. "Izayoi nikki." In *Chūsei nikki kikōshū*. Shinpen Nihon koten bungaku zenshū 48, ed. Nagasaki Ken, Tonomura Natsuko, Iwasa Miyoko, Inada Toshinori, and Itō Kei, 265–304. Tokyo: Shogakkan, 1994.

Adler, Judith. "The Origins of Sightseeing." *Annals of Tourism Research* 16.1 (1989): 7–29.

———. "Travel as Performed Art." *American Journal of Sociology* 94.6 (May 1989): 1366–1391.

Ambros, Barbara. "Liminal Journeys: Pilgrimages of Noblewomen in Mid-Heian Japan." *Japanese Journal of Religious Studies* 24.3–4 (Fall 1997): 301–345.

Amino Yoshihiko. "Chūsei no tabibitotachi." In *Hyōhaku to teichaku, teijū shakai e no michi*, 153–266. Nihon minzoku bunka taikei 6. Tokyo: Shogakkan, 1984.

Arakida Reijo. "Hatsuuma no nikki." In *Edo jidai joryū bungaku zenshū*, vol. 3, ed. Furuya Chishin, 25–101. Tokyo: Nihon Tosho Sentaa, 1979.

———. "Nochi no uma no nikki." In *Edo jidai joryū bungaku zenshū*, vol. 3, ed. Furuya Chishin, 103–134. Tokyo: Nihon Tosho Sentaa, 1979.

"Arima meisho kagami." In *Kinsei bungei sōsho 2, Meishoki 2*, 412–436. Tokyo: Kokusho Kankōkai, 1910.

Asahi Monzaemon. "Ōmurōchūki." *Nagoya sōsho, Zokuhen*, vol. 11, ed. Nagoya-shi Kyōiku Iinkai. Nagoya, 1968.

Asai Ryōi. "Edo meishoki." In *Nihon meisho fūzoku zue 3, Edo no maki 1*, ed. Asakura Haruhiko, 5–70. Tokyo: Kadokawa Shoten, 1979.

Asakura Haruhiko, ed. *Nihon meisho fūzoku zue 3, Edo no maki 1*. Tokyo: Kadokawa Shoten, 1979.

Ashida Koreto, ed. *Ise sangū meisho zue*. Tokyo: Tōyōdō, 1944.

"Azumaji no nikki." In *Kamakura shishi, Kinsei kindai kikō chishi hen*, ed. Kamakurashi Shishi Hensan Iinkai and Kodama Kōta, 164–182. Tokyo: Yoshikawa Kōbunkan, 1985.

Badone, Ellen, and Sharon R. Roseman. "Approaches to the Anthropology of Pilgrimage and Tourism." In *Intersecting Journeys: The Anthropology of Pilgrimage and Tourism,* ed. Ellen Badone and Sharon R. Roseman, 1–23. Urbana and Chicago: University of Illinois Press, 2004.

Bann, Stephen. "The Map as Index of the Real: Land Art and the Authentication of Travel." *Imago Mundi* 46 (1994): 9–18.

"Bennonaishi nikki." In *Chūsei nikki kikōshū*. Shinpen Nihon koten bungaku zenshū 48, ed. Nagasaki Ken, Tonomura Natsuko, Iwasa Miyoko, Inada Toshinori, and Itō Kei, 143–264. Tokyo: Shogakkan, 1994.

Berry, Mary Elizabeth. *Japan in Print: Information and the Nation in the Early Modern Period.* Berkeley: University of California Press, 2006.

Bolitho, Harold. "Travelers' Tales: Three Eighteenth-Century Travel Journals." *Harvard Journal of Asiatic Studies* 50.2 (December 1990): 485–504.

Borges, Jorge Luis. *Selected Non-Fictions.* Ed. Eliot Weinberger. New York: Viking, 1999.

Brown, Philip C. "The Mismeasure of Land: Land Surveying in the Tokugawa Period." *Monumenta Nipponica* 42.2 (Summer 1987): 115–155.

Butler, Lee. " 'Washing Off the Dust': Baths and Bathing in Late Medieval Japan." *Monumenta Nipponica* 60.1 (Spring 2005): 1–41.

Buzard, James. *The Beaten Track: European Tourism, Literature, and the Ways to Culture, 1800–1918.* Oxford: Clarendon Press, 1993.

Bynum, Caroline Walker. *Fragmentation and Redemption: Essays on Gender and the Human Body in Medieval Religion.* New York: Zone Books, 1991.

Cahill, James. *The Lyric Journey: Poetic Painting in China and Japan.* Cambridge, MA: Harvard University Press, 1996.

Cahill, Suzanne E. "Discipline and Transformation: Body and Practice in the Lives of Daoist Holy Women of Tang China." In *Women and Confucian Cultures in Premodern China, Korea, and Japan,* ed. Dorothy Ko, Jahyun Kim Haboush, and Joan Piggott, 251–278. Berkeley: University of California Press, 2003.

Carter, Steven D. "On a Bare Branch: Bashō and the *Haikai* Profession." *Journal of the American Oriental Society* 117.1 (January–March 1997): 57–69.

———. "Travel as Poetic Practice in Medieval and Early Modern Japan." *Journeys: The International Journal of Travel and Travel Writing* 5.1 (May 2004): 23–46.

Chance, Linda H. "Constructing the Classic: *Tsurezuregusa* in Tokugawa Readings." *Journal of the American Oriental Society* 117.1 (January–March 1997): 39–56.

Chigata Nakamichi. "Shokoku meibutsu ōrai." Unpublished ms. University of California Berkeley, East Asia Collection.

Clark, Scott. *Japan: A View from the Bath.* Honolulu: University of Hawai'i Press, 1994.

Coaldrake, William H. "Building a New Establishment: Tokugawa Iemitsu's Consolidation of Power and the Taitokuin Mausoleum." In *Edo and Paris: Urban Life and the State in the Early Modern Era,* ed. James L. McClain, John M. Merriman, and Ugawa Kaoru, 153–172. Ithaca, NY: Cornell University Press, 1994.

———. *Architecture and Authority in Japan.* London: Routledge, 1996.

———. "Metaphors of the Metropolis: Architectural and Artistic Representations of the Identity of Edo." In *Japanese Capitals in Historical Perspective: Place, Power and Memory in Kyoto, Edo and Tokyo*, ed. Nicolas Fiévé and Paul Waley, 129–149. London and New York: Routledge Curzon, 2003.

Colcutt, Martin. "Mt. Fuji as the Realm of Miroku: The Transformation of Maitreya in the Cult of Mt. Fuji in Early Modern Japan." In *Maitreya: the Future Buddha*, ed. Alan Sponberg and Helen Hardacre, 248–269. Cambridge: Cambridge University Press, 1998.

Davis, Winston. *Japanese Religion and Society: Paradigms of Structure and Change*. Albany: State University of New York Press, 1992.

de Certeau, Michel. *The Practice of Everyday Life*. Trans. Steven F. Rendall. Berkeley: University of California Press, 1984.

Dobbins, James C. *Letters of the Nun Eshinni: Images of Pure Land Buddhism in Medieval Japan*. Honolulu: University of Hawai'i Press, 2004.

"Dōchūki." In *Dōchūki shūsei 1*, ed. Imai Kingo, 79–134. Tokyo: Ōzorasha, 1998.

Doğan, Hasan Zafer. "Forms of Adjustment: Sociocultural Impacts of Tourism." *Annals of Tourism Research* 16.2 (1989): 216–236.

Duncan, James, and Derek Gregory, eds. *Writes of Passage: Reading Travel Writing*. London and New York: Routledge, 1999.

Dutton, Anne. "Temple Divorce in Tokugawa Japan: A Survey of Documentation on Tōkeiji and Mantokuji." In *Engendering Faith: Women and Buddhism in Premodern Japan*, ed. Barbara Ruch, 209–245. Ann Arbor: Center for Japanese Studies, University of Michigan, 2002.

Earhart, Byron. "Mount Fuji and Shugendo." *Japanese Journal of Religious Studies* 16.2–3 (1989): 205–226.

"Edo meisho hanagoyomi." In *Nihon meisho fūzoku zue 3, Edo no maki 1*, ed. Asakura Haruhiko, 72–105. Tokyo: Kadokawa Shoten, 1979.

Ehmcke, Franziska. "The Tōkaidō Woodblock Print Series as an Example of Intertextuality in the Fine Arts." In *Written Texts—Visual Texts: Woodblock-Printed Media in Early Modern Japan*, ed. Susanne Formaneck and Sepp Linhart, 109–139. European Studies on Japan 3. Amsterdam: Hotei Publishing, 2005.

"Ehon Edo miyage." In *Nihon meisho fūzoku zue 3, Edo no maki 1*, ed. Asakura Haruhiko, 210–335. Tokyo: Kadokawa Shoten, 1979.

Elisonas, Jurgis. "Notorious Places: A Brief Excursion into the Narrative Topography of Early Edo." In *Edo and Paris: Urban Life and the State in the Early Modern Era*, ed. James L. McClain, John M. Merriman, and Ugawa Kaoru, 253–291. Ithaca, NY: Cornell University Press, 1994.

Elvehjem Museum of Art. *The Edward Burr Van Vleck Collection of Japanese Prints*. Madison: Elvehjem Museum of Art, University of Wisconsin-Madison, 1990.

Emontarō. "Ise sangū shukuhaku oboechō." In *Gifu kenshi, Shiryōhen, Kinsei 7*, ed. Gifuken, 546–549. Gifu, 1971.

Emori Ichirō. *Edo jidai josei seikatsu ezu daijiten*, vol. 3: *Katei, Shakai*. Tokyo: Ōzorasha, 1993.

———. *Edo jidai josei seikatsu ezu daijiten*, vol. 5: *Shiki, Dōshokubutsu, Meisho*. Tokyo: Ōzorasha, 1993.

Enomoto Myōshin. "Issenkoji michi no ki." In *Enomoto ke kiroku, Warabi shishi chōsa hōkokusho 4,* ed. Warabi-shi, 57–76. Warabi, 1987.

Fiévé, Nicolas. "Social Discrimination and Architectural Freedom in the Pleasure District of Kyoto in Early Modern Japan." In *Japanese Capitals in Historical Perspective: Place, Power and Memory in Kyoto, Edo and Tokyo,* ed. Nicolas Fiévé and Paul Waley, 67–99. London and New York: Routledge Curzon, 2003.

Fiévé, Nicolas, and Paul Waley, eds. *Japanese Capitals in Historical Perspective: Place, Power and Memory in Kyoto, Edo and Tokyo.* London and New York: Routledge Curzon, 2003.

Foard, James. "The Boundaries of Compassion: Buddhism and National Tradition in Japanese Pilgrimage." *Journal of Asian Studies* 41.2 (February 1982): 231–251.

———. "Ippen and Pure Land Buddhist Wayfarers in Medieval Japan." In *The Pure Land Tradition: History and Development,* 357–397. Berkeley Buddhist Studies 3, ed. James Foard, Richard Payne, and Michael Solomon. Berkeley: Regents of the University of California, 1996.

Formanek, Susanne. "Pilgrimage in the Edo Period, Forerunner of Modern Domestic Tourism? The Example of the Pilgrimage to Mount Tateyama." In *The Culture of Japan as Seen through Its Leisure,* ed. Sabine Frühstück and Sepp Linhart, 165–193. Albany: State University of New York Press, 1998.

Fuji Mihoko. "Hakone nikki." Ed. Hasegawa Ikuko. *Edoki onnakō,* no. 10 (1999): 80–91.

"Fuji Ōyama dōchū zakki." In *Fujisawa shishi 2, Shiryōhen,* ed. Fujisawa Shishi Hensan Iinkai, 1252–1254. Fujisawa, 1973.

Fujisawa Shishi Hensan Iinkai. *Fujisawa shishi 2, Shiryōhen.* Fujisawa, 1973.

Fujitani Toshio. *Okagemairi to eejanaika.* Tokyo: Iwanami Shoten, 1972.

Fujiwara Chieko, ed. *Ukiyoe ni miru Edo no tabi.* Tokyo: Kawade Shobō Shinsha, 2000.

Fujiwara Keishi. "Nakatsukasa no naishi nikki." In *Chūsei nikki kikōshū.* Shin Nihon koten bungaku taikei 51, ed. Fukuda Hideichi, Iwasa Miyoko, Kawazoe Shōji, Ōsone Shōsuke, Kubota Jun, and Tsurusaki Hiroo, 214–270. Tokyo: Iwanami Shoten, 1995 (1st ed. 1990).

Fukai Jinzō. "Kinsei ni okeru nukemairi no tenkai to sono shutai." *Rekishi* 50 (1977): 132–156.

———. *Kinsei josei tabi to kaidō kōtsū.* Toyama: Hashira Shobō, 1995.

Fukuda Hideichi, Iwasa Miyoko, Kawazoe Shōji, Ōsone Shōsuke, Kubota Jun, and Tsurusaki Hiroo, eds. *Chūsei nikki kikōshū.* Shin Nihon koten bungaku taikei 51. Tokyo: Iwanami Shoten, 1995 (1st ed. 1990).

Furukawa Koshōken. "Saiyū zakki." In *Nihon shomin seikatsu shiryō shūsei,* vol. 2, ed. Miyamoto Tsuneichi, Tanigawa Ken'ichi, and Haraguchi Torao, 329–395. Tokyo: San'ichi Shobō, 1969.

Furuya Chishin. *Edo jidai joryū bungaku zenshū.* 4 vols. Tokyo: Nihon Tosho Sentaa, 1979 (1st ed. 1919).

Geerts, A. J. C. "The Mineral Springs of Ashi-no-Yu in the Hakone Mountains." *Transactions of the Asiatic Society of Japan* 9 (1881): 48–52.

Gerhart, Karen M. *The Eyes of Power: Art and Early Tokugawa Authority.* Honolulu: University of Hawai'i Press, 1999.

Goodwin, Janet R. "Shadows of Transgression: Heian and Kamakura Constructions of Prostitution." *Monumenta Nipponica* 55.3 (Autumn 2000): 327–368.
Graburn, Nelson H. H. "Tourism: The Sacred Journey." In *Hosts and Guests: The Anthropology of Tourism,* ed. Valene L. Smith, 17–31. Philadelphia: University of Pennsylvania Press, 1977.
———. *To Pray, Pay and Play: The Cultural Structure of Japanese Tourism.* Aix-en-Provence: Centre des Hautes Études Touristiques, 1983.
Gramlich-Oka, Bettina. "Tadano Makuzu and Her *Hitori Kangae.*" *Monumenta Nipponica* 56.1 (Spring 2001): 1–20.
Grapard, Allan. "Flying Mountains and Walkers of Emptiness: Toward a Definition of Sacred Space in Japanese Religions." *History of Religions* 21.3 (1982): 195–221.
———. "The Textualized Mountain-Enmountained Text: The Lotus Sutra in Kunisaki." In *The Lotus Sutra in Japanese Culture,* ed. George J. Tanabe and Willa Jane Tanabe, 159–190. Honolulu: University of Hawai'i Press, 1989.
———. "Geosophia, Geognosis, and Geopiety: Orders of Significance in Japanese Representations of Space." In *NowHere: Time, Space, and Modernity,* ed. D. Boden and R. Friedland, 372–401. Berkeley: University of California Press, 1994.
———. "The State Remains, but Mountains and Rivers Are Destroyed." In *Landscapes and Communities on the Pacific Rim: Cultural Perspectives from Asia to the Pacific Northwest,* ed. Karen K. Gaul and Jackie Hiltz, 108–129. Armonk, NY: M. E. Sharpe, 2000.
Gregory, Derek. "Scripting Egypt, Orientalism and the Cultures of Travel." In *Writes of Passage: Reading Travel Writing,* ed. James Duncan and Derek Gregory, 114–150. London and New York: Routledge, 1999.
Groemer, Gerald. "Singing the News: *Yomiuri* in Japan during the Edo and Meiji Periods." *Harvard Journal of Asiatic Studies* 54.1 (1994): 233–261.
Hakuei. "Miura kikō." In *Fujisawa shishi 2, Shiryōhen,* ed. Fujisawa Shishi Hensan Iinkai, 1212–1215. Fujisawa, 1973.
Hara Jun'ichirō. "Ōyama, Fuji, Enoshima." *Chihōshi kenkyū* 48.4 (August 1998): 24–28.
Hardacre, Helen. "The Cave and the Womb World." *Japanese Journal of Religious Studies* 10.2–3 (June/September 1983): 149–176.
———. *Religion and Society in Nineteenth-Century Japan: A Study of the Southern Kantō Region, Using Late Edo and Early Meiji Gazetteers.* Michigan Monograph Series in Japanese Studies no. 41. Ann Arbor: Center for Japanese Studies, University of Michigan, 2002.
Harley, J. B. "Maps, Knowledge, and Power." In *The Iconography of Landscape,* ed. Denis Cosgrave and Stephen Daniels, 277–312. Cambridge: Cambridge University Press, 1988.
Hibbett, Howard. *The Chrysanthemum and the Fish: Japanese Humor since the Age of the Shoguns.* Tokyo, New York, and London: Kodansha International, 2002.
Higashiōji Taku, ed. *Tōkaidō gojūsantsugi hizasuri nikki.* Ukiyoe bijutsu meihinkan 1. Tokyo: Gabundō, 1984.
Higuchi Kiyoyuki. *Asobi to Nihonjin.* Nihonjin no rekishi 8. Tokyo: Kōdansha, 1980.

———. *Tabi to Nihonjin.* Nihonjin no rekishi 7. Tokyo: Kōdansha, 1980.
Hiraga Gennai. "Nanshoku saiken mitsu no asa." In *Nihon shomin bunka shiryō shūsei 9, Asobi,* ed. Geinōshi Kenkyūkai, 101–111. Tokyo: San'ichi Shobō, 1974.
Hirano Eiji. "Fujikō Ōyamakō no junpai to yusan." *Chihōshi kenkyū* 48.4 (August 1998): 29–32.
Hiruma Hisashi. "Samazamana kōdō bunka." In *Nihon no kinsei 14, Bunka no taishūka,* ed. Takeuchi Makoto, 319–350. Tokyo: Chūō Kōronsha, 1993.
Hishiya Heishichi. "Tsukushi kikō." In *Nihon shomin seikatsu shiryō shūsei,* vol. 20, ed. Haraguchi Torao, Takeuchi Toshimi, and Miyamoto Tsuneichi, 155–262. Tokyo: San'ichi Shobō, 1972.
Hōkei-shi. "Atami kikō." In *Hekichūdō sōsho 14,* ed. Yanase Kazuo. Kyoto: Nozomigawa Shoten, 1996 (1st ed. 1969): 215–231.
Honda, Heiachirō H., trans. *The Shin Kokinshu: The 13th Century Anthology Edited by Imperial Edict.* Tokyo: Hokuseido Press, 1970.
Honda Takahide. "*Tōkaidō bunken nobe ezu* sakusei no kiso chōsa." In *Tōkaidō kōtsūshi no kenkyū,* ed. Shizuokaken Chiikishi Kenkyūkai, 269–299. Osaka: Seibundō, 1996.
Hosokawa Ryōichi. "Chūsei no tabi o suru josei—Shūkyō, geinō, kōeki." In *Onna to otoko no jikū, Nihon joseishi saikō 3, Onna to otoko no ran, Chūsei,* ed. Okano Haruko, 341–378. Tokyo: Fujiwara Shoten, 1996.
Hotate Michihisa. "Himen no onna to romen no onna, Chūsei josei no soto aruki." In *Bunka to josei.* Nihon joseishi ronshū 7, ed. Sōgō Joseishi Kenkyūkai, 251–269. Tokyo: Yoshikawa Kōbunkan, 1998.
Hur, Nam-lin. *Prayer and Play in Late Tokugawa Japan: Asakusa Sensōji and Edo Society.* Cambridge, MA: Harvard University Press, 2000.
Igarashi Tomio. "Edo jidai no dōchūki ni arawareta shomin no tabi, Dōchūki to kikōbun no hikakuteki kōsatsu." *Gunma Joshi Tanki Daigaku Kiyō* 11 (January 1984): 1–10.
———. *Kinsei sekisho no kisoteki kenkyū: Nakasendō Usui sekisho o chūshin to shite.* Tokyo: Taga Shuppan, 1986.
Ihara Saikaku. *The Japanese Family Storehouse or the Millionaires' Gospel Modernised.* Trans. G. W. Sargent. Cambridge: Cambridge University Press, 1959.
———. *This Scheming World.* Trans. Masanori Takatsuka and David C. Stubbs. Rutland (VT) and Tokyo: Tuttle, 1965.
———. "Kōshoku ichidai onna." In *Ihara Saikakushū 1.* Shinpen Nihon koten bungaku zenshū 66, ed. Teruoka Yasutaka and Higashi Akimasa, 391–568. Tokyo: Shogakkan, 1996.
———. "Kōshoku ichidai otoko." In *Ihara Saikakushū 1.* Shinpen Nihon koten bungaku zenshū 66, ed. Teruoka Yasutaka and Higashi Akimasa, 17–250. Tokyo: Shogakkan, 1996.
Ikegawa Shunsui. "Fuji nikki." In *Nihon shomin seikatsu shiryō shūsei,* vol. 3, ed. Miyamoto Tsuneichi, Takeuchi Toshimi, and Mori Kahei, 373–382. Tokyo: San'ichi Shobō, 1969.
Imai Kingo, ed. *Dōchūki shūsei.* 47 vols. Tokyo: Ōzorasha, 1996–1998.

Inamura Kiseko. "Hakone no ki." *Edoki onnakō,* no. 9 (1998): 185–195.
Imamura Yoshitaka and Takahashi Hideo, eds. *Akitahan machibureshū.* 3 vols. Tokyo: Miraisha, 1971–1973.
Inoue, Shunji, trans. *Kojiki.* Fukuoka: Nihon Shuji Kyoiku Renmei, 1966.
Inoue Tsūjo. "Kika nikki." In *Inoue Tsūjo zenshū,* ed. Inoue Tsūjo Zenshū Shūtei Iinkai, 55–105. Marugame, 1973.
———. "Tōkai kikō." In *Inoue Tsūjo zenshū,* ed. Inoue Tsūjo Zenshū Shutei Iinkai, 37–54. Marugame, 1973.
"Ise sangū kondate dōchūki." In *Nihon shomin seikatsu shiryō shūsei,* vol. 20, ed. Haraguchi Torao, Takeuchi Toshimi, and Miyamoto Tsuneichi, 601–620. Tokyo: San'ichi Shobō, 1972.
Ishii Ryōsuke, ed. *Kinsei hōsei shiryō sōsho.* 3 vols. Tokyo: Kōbundō Shobō, 1938–1941.
———, ed. *Oshioki reiruishū 12, Tenpō ruishū 2.* Tokyo: Meicho Shuppan, 1973.
Ishii Ryōsuke and Harafuji Hiroshi, eds. *Mondōshū 3, Shōrei sen'yō, shōke hitsubunshū.* Tokyo: Sōbunsha, 1999.
Ishikawa Eisuke, ed. *Ōedo Senkōin tabi nikki.* Tokyo: Kōdansha Bunko, 1997.
Itō Yoshio. "Ishu Hyakunin isshu." In *Hyakunin isshu.* Nihon no koten, Bekkan 1, ed. Suzuki Tsutomu, 150–153. Tokyo: Sekai Bunkasha, 1975.
Iwahana Michiaki. "Dōchūki ni miru Dewa sanzan sankei no tabi." *Rekishi chirigaku,* no. 139 (December 1987): 1–14.
Iwamura Yasuhisa. "Kamakura sanshō nikki." In *Fujisawa shishi 2, Shiryōhen,* ed. Fujisawa Shishi Hensan Iinkai, 1226–1229. Fujisawa, 1973.
Iwasaki Masasumi. "Hakone nanayu." In *Tōkaidō* 1. Edo jidai zushi 14, ed. Ōto Yoshifuru and Yamaguchi Osamu, 171–175. Tokyo: Chikuma Shobō, 1976.
Iwatsuki Akie. "Yuya Shizuko kashū *Chirinokori.*" *Edoki onnakō,* no. 10 (1999): 60–70.
Jijūken Ikkishi. "Kamakura ki." In *Kamakura shishi, Kinsei kindai kikō chishi hen,* ed. Kamakurashi Shishi Hensan Iinkai and Kodama Kōta, 106–137. Tokyo: Yoshikawa Kōbunkan, 1985.
Jippensha Ikku. *Hizakurige or Shank's Mare.* Trans. Thomas Satchell. Rutland (VT) and Tokyo: Tuttle, 1960.
———. *Tōkaidōchū hizakurige.* Ed. Asō Isoji. 2 vols. Tokyo: Iwanami Shoten, 1992.
———. "Jōdan shitsukonashi." In *Jippensha Ikkushū.* Sōsho Edo bunko 43, ed. Tanahashi Masahiro, 37–68. Tokyo: Kokusho Kankōkai, 1997.
Kaempfer, Engelbert. *Kaempfer's Japan: Tokugawa Culture Observed.* Ed. and trans. Beatrice M. Bodart-Bailey. Honolulu: University of Hawai'i Press, 1999.
Kaibara Ekiken. *Women and Wisdom of Japan.* Intro. by Shingoro Takaishi. Wisdom of the East. London: J. Murray, 1905.
———. "Jinshin kikō." In *Kinsei kikō shūsei.* Sōsho Edo bunkō 17, ed. Takada Mamoru and Hara Michio, 5–48. Tokyo: Kokusho Kankōkai, 1991.
"Kaidōki." In *Chūsei nikki kikōshū.* Shinpen Nihon koten bungaku zenshū 48, ed. Nagasaki Ken, Tonomura Natsuko, and Iwasa Miyoko, 11–84. Tokyo: Shogakkan, 1994.
Kamakurashi Shishi Hensan Iinkai and Kodama Kōta, eds. *Kamakura shishi, Kinsei kindai kikō chishi hen.* Tokyo: Yoshikawa Kōbunkan, 1985.

Kamens, Edward. *Utamakura, Allusion, and Intertextuality in Traditional Japanese Poetry.* New Haven, CT: Yale University Press, 1997.

Kanagawa-ken Kikaku Chōsabu Kenshi Henshūshitsu. *Kanagawa kenshi, Tsūshi-hen 2, Kinsei 1.* Kanagawa, 1974.

Kanagawa Kinseishi Kenkyūkai, ed. *Edo jidai no Kanagawa: Furuezu de miru fūkei.* Yokohama:Yūrindō, 1994.

Kanamori Atsuko. *Sekishonuke Edo no onnatachi no bōken.* Tokyo: Shōbunsha, 2001.

Kaneko, Sachiko, and Robert E. Morrell. "Sanctuary: Kamakura's Tōkeiji Convent." *Japanese Journal of Religious Studies* 10.2–3 (June/September 1983): 195–228.

Kanzaki, Noritake. "A Comparative Analysis of the Tourist Industry." In *Japanese Civilization in the Modern World, 9: Tourism,* 39–49. Senri Ethnological Studies no. 38, ed. Umesao Tadao, Harumi Befu, and Ishimori Shuzo. Osaka: National Museum of Ethnology, 1995.

Kasulis, Thomas P. "The Body—Japanese Style." In *Self as Body in Asian Theory and Practice,* ed. Thomas P. Kasulis, Roger T. Ames, and Wimal Dissanayake, 299–319. Albany: State University of New York Press, 1993.

Katagiri Yōichi. *Utamakura utakotoba jiten.* Tokyo: Kasama Shoin, 1999.

Katsu Kokichi. *Musui's Story: The Autobiography of a Tokugawa Samurai.* Trans. Teruko Craig. Tucson: University of Arizona Press, 1988.

Katsuura Noriko. "Tonsure Forms for Nuns: Classification of Nuns according to Hairstyle." Trans. Virginia Skord Waters. In *Engendering Faith: Women and Buddhism in Premodern Japan,* ed. Barbara Ruch, 109–129. Ann Arbor: Center for Japanese Studies, University of Michigan, 2002.

Kawai Tsugunosuke. "Chiritsubo." In *Nihon shomin seikatsu shiryō shūsei,* vol. 2, ed. Miyamoto Tsuneichi, Tanigawa Ken'ichi, and Haraguchi Torao, 397–439. Tokyo: San'ichi Shobō, 1969.

Kawamura, Hirotada. "*Kuni-ezu* (provincial maps) Compiled by the Tokugawa Shogunate in Japan." *Imago Mundi* 41 (1989): 70–75.

Kawashima, Terry. *Writing Margins: The Textual Construction of Gender in Heian and Kamakura Japan.* Cambridge, MA: Harvard University Press, 2001.

Keene, Donald. *Travelers of a Hundred Ages.* New York: Columbia University Press, 1999.

Keirstead, Thomas. "Gardens and Estates: Medievality and Space." *Positions* 1.2 (1993): 289–320.

Kikuchi Tamiko. "Enoshima no ki." In *Kamakura shishi, Kinsei kindai kikō chishi hen,* ed. Kamakurashi Shishi Hensan Iinkai and Kodama Kōta, 348–358. Tokyo: Yoshikawa Kōbunkan, 1985.

Kikusha-ni. "Taorigiku." In *Keishū haika zenshū,* ed. Katsumine Shinpū, 315–433. Tokyo: Shūeikaku, 1922.

Kiyokawa Hachirō. *Saiyūsō.* Ed. Oyamatsu Katsuichirō. Tokyo: Iwanami Shoten, 1993.

Kodama Kōta. *Kinsei shukueki seido no kenkyū.* Tokyo: Yoshikawa Kōbunkan, 1957.

———, ed. *Tōkaidō* 2. Edo jidai zushi 15. Tokyo: Chikuma Shobō, 1977.

———. *Kinsei kōtsū shiryōshū 8–9, Bakufu hōrei 1–2.* Tokyo: Yoshikawa Kōbunkan, 1978–1979.

Kondo, Dorinne. *Crafting Selves: Power, Gender, and Discourse of Identity in a Japanese Workplace.* Chicago: University of Chicago Press, 1990.

Konno Nobuo. *Edo no tabi.* Tokyo: Iwanami Shoten, 1986.

Konno Oito. "Sangū dōchū shōyōki." In *Honjō shishi shiryōhen IV,* ed. Honjō-shi, 610–641. Honjō, 1988.

Kornicki, Peter F. *The Book in Japan: A Cultural History from the Beginnings to the Nineteenth Century.* Leiden: Brill, 1998.

———. "Literacy Revisited: Some Reflections on Richard Rubinger's Findings." *Monumenta Nipponica* 56.3 (Autumn 2001): 381–394.

———. "Unsuitable Books for Women? *Genji Monogatari* and *Ise Monogatari* in Late Seventeenth-Century Japan." *Monumenta Nipponica* 60.2 (Summer 2005): 147–193.

Kouamé, Nathalie. *Pèlerinage et société dans le Japon des Tokugawa: Le pèlerinage de Shikoku entre 1598 et 1868.* Paris: École française d'Extrême-Orient, 2001.

Koyama Chōshi Hensan Senmon Iinkai. *Koyama chōshi 2, Kinsei shiryōhen 1.* Koyama, 1991.

"Kōyasan tsūnenshū." In *Kinsei bungei sōsho 2, Meishoki 2.* Tokyo: Kokusho Kankōkai, 1910.

Lane, Richard. *Images from the Floating World.* New York: G. P. Putnam's Sons, 1978.

Leed, Eric J. *The Mind of the Traveler: From Gilgamesh to Global Tourism.* New York: Basic Books, 1991.

Lefebvre, Henri. *The Production of Space.* Trans. Donald Nicholson-Smith. Oxford (UK) and Cambridge (MA): Blackwell, 1991.

Le Roy Ladurie, Emmanuel. *Carnival in Romans.* Trans. Mary Feeney. New York: George Braziller, 1979.

Leupp, Gary P. *Male Colors: The Construction of Homosexuality in Tokugawa Japan.* Berkeley: University of California Press, 1995.

Leutner, Robert W. *Shikitei Sanba and the Comic Tradition in Edo Fiction.* Cambridge, MA: Harvard University Press, 1985.

Li Han. *Meng Ch'iu: Famous Episodes from Chinese History and Legend.* Trans. Burton Watson. Tokyo: Kodansha International, 1979.

Loftus, Ronald P. "Female Self-Writing: Takamure Itsue's *Hi no kuni no onna no nikki.*" *Monumenta Nipponica* 51.2 (Summer 1996): 153–179.

———. *Telling Lives: Women's Self-Writing in Modern Japan.* Honolulu: University of Hawai'i Press, 2004.

MacCannell, Dean. *The Tourist: A New Theory of the Leisure Class.* New York: Schocken Books, 1976.

MacWilliams, Mark. "Living Icons: *Reizō* Myths of the Saikoku Kannon Pilgrimage." *Monumenta Nipponica* 59.1 (Spring 2004): 35–82.

Maeda Isamu. *Edogo no jiten.* Tokyo: Kōdansha, 1979.

Maeda Takashi. *Junrei no shakaigaku.* Tokyo: Minerva Shobō, 1971.

Maeda Yoshi. "*Kōshin kikō* to sono chosha Jugen-in." *Fukuoka Jogakuin Tanki Daigaku Kiyō,* no. 3 (March 1967): 19–37.

———. "Kinsei keishū shijin Hara Saihin to Bōsō no tabi, Hara Saihin kenkyū sono ichi." *Fukuoka Jogakuin Tanki Daigaku Kiyō,* no. 12 (March 1976): 13–29.

———. "Itō Tsunetari monjin Kuwahara Hisako to *Shikinami no shū*." *Fukuoka Jogakuin Tanki Daigaku Kiyō*, no. 13 (January 1977): 1–18.

———. "Tabi nikki no josei." In *Jinbutsu Nihon no josei shi 6, Nikki ni tsuzuru aikan*, ed. Enchi Fumiko, 207–244. Tokyo: Shūeisha, 1977.

———. "Shinryū-in Takako to tabi nikki *Koshi no yamafumi*." *Fukuoka Jogakuin Tanki Daigaku Kiyō*, no. 14 (February 1978): 1–17.

———. "Kutsukake Nakako to *Azumaji no nikki*." *Fukuoka Jogakuin Tanki Daigaku Kiyō*, no. 20 (February 1984): 11–33.

———. *Edo jidai joryū bungeishi, Chihō o chūshin ni, Tabi nikki hen*. Tokyo: Kasama Shoin, 1998.

(The) Manyōshū: One Thousand Poems Selected and Translated from the Japanese, with Text in Romaji and an Introduction, Notes, Maps, Biographical Notes, Chronological Table, Etc. Tokyo: Iwanami Shoten, 1940.

Maruyama Yasunari. *Kinsei shukueki no kisoteki kenkyū*. 2 vols. Tokyo: Yoshikawa Kōbunkan, 1975.

Masukawa Kōichi. *Sugoroku*. Vol. 2. Mono to ningen no bunkashi 79. Tokyo: Hōsei Daigaku Shuppankyoku, 1995.

Matisoff, Susan. "Barred from Paradise? Mount Kōya and the Karukaya Legend." In *Engendering Faith: Women and Buddhism in Premodern Japan*, ed. Barbara Ruch, 463–500. Ann Arbor: Center for Japanese Studies, University of Michigan, 2002.

Matsuo Bashō. *The Narrow Road to the Deep North and Other Travel Sketches*. Trans. Nobuyuki Yuasa. London: Penguin Books, 1966.

McClain, James L., and John M. Merriman. "Edo and Paris: Cities and Power." In *Edo and Paris: Urban Life and the State in the Early Modern Era*, ed. James L. McClain, John M. Merriman, and Ugawa Kaoru, 3–38. Ithaca, NY: Cornell University Press, 1994.

McClain, James L., John M. Merriman, and Ugawa Kaoru, eds. *Edo and Paris: Urban Life and the State in the Early Modern Era*. Ithaca, NY: Cornell University Press, 1994.

McCullough, Helen Craig, ed. and trans. *Tales of Ise: Lyrical Episodes from Tenth-Century Japan*. Stanford, CA: Stanford University Press, 1968.

Minamori Reiko. "Chiyojo no kage ni kakureta Sakajiriya Karyō *Wataridori*." *Edoki onnakō*, no. 9 (1998): 172–180.

Minamoto (Koga) Michichika. "Takakura-in Itsukushima gokō ki." Trans. Herbert Plutschow. In *Four Japanese Travel Diaries of the Middle Ages*. Cornell University East Asia Papers 25, ed. Herbert Plutschow, 25–43. Ithaca, NY: Cornell University Press, 1981.

Miura Jōshin. *Keichō kenmonshū*. Ed. Nakamaru Kazunori. Tokyo: Shin Jinbutsu Ōraisha, 1969.

Miyajima Shin'ichi. "Hideyoshi wa kago ni nottaka." *Nihon Rekishi*, no. 669 (February 2004): 32–34.

Miyake Toshiyuki. "Fuji mandara to kyōten mainō." In *Shugendō no bijutsu, geinō, bungaku 1*. Sangaku shūkyōshi kenkyū sōsho 14, ed. Gorai Shigeru, 420–448. Tokyo: Meicho Shuppan, 1980.

Miyake Yoshiemon. "Zenkōji Tateyama sankei tabi nikki." In *Gifu kenshi, Shiryōhen, Kinsei 7,* ed. Gifu-ken, 541–546. Gifu, 1971.
Miyata Noboru. *Onna no reiryoku to ie no kami.* Kyoto: Jinbun Shoin, 1983.
Miyazaki, Fumiko. "Female Pilgrims and Mt. Fuji: Changing Perspectives on the Exclusion of Women." *Monumenta Nipponica* 60.3 (Autumn 2005): 339–391.
Moerman, David. "The Ideology of Landscape and the Theater of State: *Insei* Pilgrimage to Kumano (1090–1220)." *Japanese Journal of Religious Studies* 24.3–4 (Fall 1997): 347–374.
Moretti, Laura. *Chikusai il ciarlatano.* Venice: Cafoscarina, 2003.
Morimoto Tsuzuko. "Suwa nikki." *Edoki onnakō,* no. 11 (2000): 79–82.
Morioka Sadakata. "Morioka Sadakata nikki." *Tosa shidan* 54 (March 1936): 118–127.
Moriya, Katsuhisa. "Urban Networks and Information Networks." Trans. Ronald P. Toby. In *Tokugawa Japan: The Social and Economic Antecedents of Modern Japan,* ed. Chie Nakane and Shinzaburō Ōishi, 97–123. Tokyo: University of Tokyo Press, 1990.
Morris, Ivan. *The Nobility of Failure: Tragic Heroes in the History of Japan.* New York: Holt, Rinehart and Winston, 1975.
———. *The World of the Shining Prince: Court Life in Ancient Japan.* New York, Tokyo, and London: Kodansha International, 1994 (1st ed. 1964).
Mostow, Joshua S. *Pictures of the Heart: The Hyakunin Isshu in Word and Image.* Honolulu: University of Hawai'i Press, 1996.
Motoori Ōhira. "Arima nikki." In *Edo onsen kikō,* ed. Itasaka Yōko, 57–125. Tokyo: Heibonsha, 1987.
Mukai Kyorai and Chine. "Ise kikō." In *Kyorai sensei zenshū,* ed. Ōuchi Hatsuo et al., 164–167. Kyoto: Rakushisha Hōzonkai, 1982.
Murasaki Shikibu. *The Tale of Genji.* Trans. Royall Tyler. New York: Penguin Books, 2001.
Nagaoka-shi. *Nagaoka shishi, Shiryōhen 3, Kinsei 2.* Nagaoka, 1994.
Nagasaki Ken, Tonomura Natsuko, Iwasa Miyoko, Inada Toshinori, and Itō Kei, eds. *Chūsei nikki kikōshū.* Shinpen Nihon koten bungaku zenshū 48. Tokyo: Shogakkan, 1994.
Nagashima Atsuko. "Bakumatsu nōson josei no kōdō no jiyū to kaji rōdō, Bushū Tachibana-gun Namamugi mura *Sekiguchi nikki* o sozai toshite." In *Ronshū kinsei joseishi,* ed. Kinsei Joseishi Kenkyūkai, 139–173. Tokyo: Yoshikawa Kōbunkan, 1986.
Nakagawa Hisamori's wife. "Ikahoki." In *Edo jidai joryū bungaku zenshū,* vol. 3, ed. Furuya Chishin, 1–21. Tokyo: Nihon Tosho Sentaa, 1979.
Nakamachi Keiko. "Ukiyo-e Memories of *Ise Monogatari.*" Trans. Henry Smith and Miriam Wattles. *Impressions* 22 (2000): 54–85.
Nakamura Ito. "Ise mōde no nikki." In *Toyoda chōshi, Betsuhen 1, Tōkaidō to Tenryūgawa Ikeda wataribune, Furoku 2, Kikōbun,* ed. Toyoda Chōshi Hensan Iinkai, 514–515. Toyoda-chō, 1999.
Nakao Takashi, ed. *Koji junrei jiten.* Tokyo: Tōkyōdō Shuppan, 1973.
Narabayashi Tadao, ed. "Okagemairi." In *Nihon shomin seikatsu shiryō shūsei,* vol. 12, ed. Miyamoto Tsuneichi, Harada Tomohiko, and Haraguchi Torao, 85–149. Tokyo: San'ichi Shobō, 1971.

Narita Shishi Hensan Iinkai, ed. *Narita shishi, Kinsei hen, Shiryōshū 5, jō, Monzenchō 1.* Narita, 1976.

Nenzi, Laura. "*Ise sangū kondate dōchūki*, un'odissea religioso-gastronomica del periodo Edo." *Atti del XXVI Convegno di Studi sul Giappone, Torino, 26–28 Settembre 2002,* 357–369. Venice: Cartotecnica Veneziana Editrice, 2002.

———. "Women's Travel Narratives in Early Modern Japan: Genre Imperatives, Gender Consciousness and Status Questioning." *Journeys: The International Journal of Travel and Travel Writing* 5.1 (May 2004): 47–72.

———. "Cultured Travelers and Consumer Tourists in Edo-Period Sagami." *Monumenta Nipponica* 59.3 (Autumn 2004): 285–319.

———. "To Ise at All Costs: Religious and Economic Implications of Early Modern *Nukemairi*." *Japanese Journal of Religious Studies* 33.1 (2006): 75–114.

"Nihon dōchū meisho zukushi." In *Dōchūki shūsei 1*, ed. Imai Kingo, 3–76. Tokyo: Ōzorasha, 1998.

Nijō. *The Confessions of Lady Nijō.* Trans. Karen Brazell. Stanford, CA: Stanford University Press, 1973.

———. *Towazugatari.* Ed. Fukuda Hideichi. Shinkō Nihon koten shūsei 20. Tokyo: Shinkōsha, 1978.

Nishikawa Yūko. "Diaries as Gendered Text." Trans. Anne Walthall. In *Women and Class in Japanese History*, ed. Hitomi Tonomura, Anne Walthall, and Haruko Wakita, 241–255. Ann Arbor: Center for Japanese Studies, University of Michigan, 1999.

Nishikiori Gobei Yoshikura. "Nakasendō jūshi kakine tōkai kikō." In *Nihon toshi seikatsu shiryō shūsei 8, Shukuba machi hen,* ed. Harada Tomohiko, Yamori Kazuhiko, Nishikawa Kōji, and Moriya Katsuhisa, 579–614. Tokyo: Gakushū Kenkyūsha, 1977.

Nishiyama Masaru. *Seichi no sōzōryoku, Sankei mandara o yomu.* Kyoto: Hōzōkan, 1978.

Nishiyama Matsunosuke. "Edo bunka to chihō bunka." In *Iwanami kōza Nihon rekishi 13, Kinsei 5,* 161–207. Tokyo: Iwanami Shoten, 1963.

———. *Edo Culture: Daily Life and Diversions in Urban Japan, 1600–1868.* Ed. and trans. Gerald Groemer. Honolulu: University of Hawai'i Press, 1997.

Noda Senkōin. "Nihon kyūhō shugyō nikki." In *Nihon shomin seikatsu shiryō shūsei,* vol. 2, ed. Miyamoto Tsuneichi, Tanigawa Ken'ichi, and Haraguchi Torao, 5–262. Tokyo: San'ichi Shobō, 1969.

Oda Takeo. *Chizu no rekishi, Nihon-hen.* Tokyo: Kōdansha Gendai Shinsho, 1974.

Okada Koiso. "Oku no araumi." In *Edo jidai joryū bungaku zenshū*, vol. 3, ed. Furuya Chishin, 245–274. Tokyo: Nihon Tosho Sentaa, 1979.

Ōkiyo Keijun (Jippōan). "Jippōan yūreki zakki." In *Fujisawa shishi 2, Shiryōhen,* ed. Fujisawa Shishi Hensan Iinkai, 1230–1239. Fujisawa, 1973.

Ōne Tsuchinari. "Kokkei Arima kikō." In *Edo onsen kikō*, ed. Itasaka Yōko, 4–56. Tokyo: Heibonsha, 1987.

Ooms, Herman. *Tokugawa Ideology: Early Constructs, 1570–1680.* Princeton, NJ: Princeton University Press, 1985.

———. *Tokugawa Village Practice: Class, Status, Power, Law.* Berkeley: University of California Press, 1996.

Ōto Yoshifuru. "Kinsei no Sagami." In *Tōkaidō 1. Edo jidai zushi 14*, ed. Ōto Yoshifuru and Yamaguchi Osamu, 159–165. Tokyo: Chikuma Shobō, 1976.
Ōto Yoshifuru and Yamaguchi Osamu, eds. *Tōkaidō 1. Edo jidai zushi 14*. Tokyo: Chikuma Shobō, 1976.
Pflugfelder, Gregory M. *Cartographies of Desire: Male-Male Sexuality in Japanese Discourse, 1600–1950*. Berkeley: University of California Press, 1999.
Plutschow, Herbert E. *Four Japanese Travel Diaries of the Middle Ages.* Cornell East Asia Papers 25. Ithaca, NY: Cornell University Press, 1981.
———. *Chaos and Cosmos: Ritual in Early and Medieval Japanese Literature*. Leiden and New York: E. J. Brill, 1990.
———. *A Reader in Edo Period Travel*. Kent, UK: Global Oriental, 2006.
Polezzi, Loredana. "Between Gender and Genre: The Travels of Estella Canziani." In *Perspectives on Travel Writing*. Studies in European Cultural Transition, vol. 19, ed. Glenn Hooper and Tim Youngs, 121–137. Aldershot (UK) and Burlington (VT): Ashgate, 2004.
Ravina, Mark. *Land and Lordship in Early Modern Japan*. Stanford, CA: Stanford University Press, 1999.
Reader, Ian. *Making Pilgrimages: Meaning and Practice in Shikoku*. Honolulu: University of Hawai'i Press, 2005.
Reader, Ian, and Paul L. Swanson. "Editors' Introduction: Pilgrimage in the Japanese Religious Tradition." *Japanese Journal of Religious Studies* 24.3–4 (1997): 225–270.
Reischauer, Edwin O., and Joseph K. Yamagiwa. *Translations from Early Japanese Literature*. Cambridge, MA: Harvard University Press, 1972 (1st ed. 1951).
Ri-in. "Enoshima kikō." In *Kamakura shishi, Kinsei kindai kikō chishi hen*, ed. Kamakurashi Shishi Hensan Iinkai and Kodama Kōta, 395–402. Tokyo: Yoshikawa Kōbunkan, 1985.
Rodd, Laurel Rasplica, and Mary Catherine Henkenius. *Kokinshū: A Collection of Poems Ancient and Modern*. Princeton, NJ: Princeton University Press, 1984.
Rojek, Chris, and John Urry, eds. *Touring Cultures: Transformations of Travel and Theory*. London and New York: Routledge, 1997.
Rubinger, Richard. "Who Can't Read and Write? Illiteracy in Meiji Japan." *Monumenta Nipponica* 55.2 (Summer 2000): 163–198.
Ruch, Barbara. "The Other Side of Culture in Medieval Japan." In *The Cambridge History of Japan*, vol. 3: *Medieval Japan*, ed. Kozo Yamamura, 500–543. Cambridge: Cambridge University Press, 1990.
———, ed. *Engendering Faith: Women and Buddhism in Premodern Japan*. Ann Arbor: Center for Japanese Studies, University of Michigan, 2002.
———. "Woman to Woman: *Kumano bikuni* Proselytizers in Medieval and Early Modern Japan." In *Engendering Faith: Women and Buddhism in Premodern Japan*, ed. Barbara Ruch, 537–580. Ann Arbor: Center for Japanese Studies, University of Michigan, 2002.
Saitō Gesshin (Yukinari). "Tōto saijiki." In *Nihon meisho fūzoku zue 3, Edo no maki 1*, ed. Asakura Haruhiko, 108–207. Tokyo: Kadokawa Shoten, 1979.

———. "Edo meisho zue." In *Nihon meisho fūzoku zue 4, Edo no maki 2*, ed. Ikeda Yasaburō. Tokyo: Kadokawa Shoten, 1980.

Sakaki, Atsuko. *Obsessions with the Sino-Japanese Polarity in Japanese Literature*. Honolulu: University of Hawai'i Press, 2006.

Santō Kyōsan. "Atami onsen zui." In *Shizuoka kenshi, Shiryō 15, Kinsei 7*, ed. Shizuoka-ken, 1015–1021. Shizuoka, 1991.

Screech, Timon. "The Strangest Place in Edo: The Temple of the Five Hundred Arhats." *Monumenta Nipponica* 48.4 (Winter 1993): 407–428.

———. *Sex and the Floating World: Erotic Images in Japan, 1700–1820*. Honolulu: University of Hawai'i Press, 1999.

Sei Shōnagon. *The Pillow Book of Sei Shōnagon*. Trans. Ivan Morris. New York: Columbia University Press, 1991.

Seigen-in Noriko "Kaihen shūjiki." Ed. Itasaka Yōko. *Kumamoto Tandai Ronshū* 55: Shiryō (July 1977): 1–26.

———. "Aoba no yamaji." Ed. Itasaka Yōko. *Aichi Kenritsu Daigaku Setsurin, Shiryō honkoku* 27 (February 1979): 46–75.

Seigle, Cecilia Segawa. *Yoshiwara: The Glittering World of the Japanese Courtesan*. Honolulu: University of Hawai'i Press, 1993.

Senbai. "Enoshima kikō." In *Fujisawa shishi 2, Shiryōhen*, ed. Fujisawa Shishi Hensan Iinkai, 1215–1218. Fujisawa, 1973.

Senkaku Tōshi. "Kamakura nikki." In *Fujisawa shishi 2, Shiryōhen*, ed. Fujisawa Shishi Hensan Iinkai, 1218–1223. Fujisawa, 1973.

Shiba Keiko. "Tabi nikki kara mita kinsei josei no ikkōsatsu." In *Edo jidai no joseitachi*, ed. Kinsei Joseishi Kenkyūkai, 147–184. Tokyo: Yoshikawa Kōbunkan, 1990.

———. *Kinsei onna tabi nikki*. Rekishi Bunka Library 13. Tokyo: Yoshikawa Kōbunkan, 1997.

Shibuya-ku. *Shibuyaku shiryōshū* 2. Tokyo: Shibuya-ku, 1980.

Shinkō-in Myōjitsu. "Mokuzu." In *Edo jidai joryū bungaku zenshū*, vol. 3, ed. Furuya Chishin, 275–310. Tokyo: Nihon Tosho Sentaa, 1979.

Shinno Toshikazu. "Tabi, junrei, yusan—Kinsei sankei jijō." In *Nihon no kinsei 14, Bunka no taishūka*, ed. Takeuchi Makoto, 131–168. Tokyo: Chūō Kōronsha, 1993.

———. "Journeys, Pilgrimages, Excursions: Religious Travels in the Early Modern Period." Trans. Laura Nenzi. *Monumenta Nipponica* 57.4 (Winter 2002): 447–471.

Shirane, Haruo. *Traces of Dreams: Landscape, Cultural Memory, and the Poetry of Bashō*. Stanford, CA: Stanford University Press, 1998.

Shizuoka-ken. *Shizuoka kenshi, Shiryōhen 13, Kinsei 5*. Shizuoka, 1990.

"Shokoku annai tabi suzume." In *Dōchūki shūsei 5*, ed. Imai Kingo, 3–505. Tokyo: Ōzorasha, 1998.

"Shokoku irozato annai." In *Nihon shomin bunka shiryō shūsei 9, Asobi*, ed. Geinōshi Kenkyūkai, 5–24. Tokyo: San'ichi Shobō, 1974.

"Shokoku yasumi kaibun no ezu." In *Dōchūki shūsei 2*, ed. Imai Kingo, 65–250. Tokyo: Ōzorasha, 1998.

Smith, Henry D., II. "The History of the Book in Edo and Paris." In *Edo and Paris: Urban*

Life and the State in the Early Modern Era, ed. James L. McClain, John M. Merriman, and Ugawa Kaoru, 332–352. Ithaca, NY: Cornell University Press, 1994.

Smith, Thomas C. *The Agrarian Origins of Modern Japan.* Stanford, CA: Stanford University Press, 1959.

Smyers, Karen A. "Women and Shinto: The Relation between Purity and Pollution." *Japanese Religions* 12.4 (July 1983): 7–18.

Sōkyū. "Miyako no tsuto." Trans. Herbert Plutschow. In *Four Japanese Travel Diaries of the Middle Ages.* Cornell University East Asia Papers 25, ed. Herbert Plutschow, 61–75. Ithaca, NY: Cornell University Press, 1981.

Stevenson, Catherine Barnes. "Women Travellers and the Art of Travel Writing." In *Victorian Women Travel Writers in Africa,* ed. Catherine Barnes Stevenson, 1–12. Boston: Twayne Publishers, 1982.

Sugano Noriko. "Nyonin jōbutsu Ketsubonkyō engi." *Teikyō Shigaku* 20 (February 2005): 191–201.

Suzuki Masataka. *Nyonin kinsei.* Rekishi Bunka Library 138. Tokyo: Yoshikawa Kōbunkan, 2002.

Suzuki Mihoko. "Kawagoe no kikō." In *Saitama sōsho 2,* ed. Saitama Kenshi Hensan Jimusho, 529–534. Tokyo: Sanmeisha, 1968.

Suzuki Shōzō. "Fuji zenjō dōchū nikki." In *Miwa chōshi, Shiryōhen, Kinsei,* ed. Miwa Chōshi Hensan Iinkai, 1313–1315. Miwa, 1992.

Swanson, Paul L. "*Shugendō* and the Yoshino-Kumano Pilgrimage: An Example of Mountain Pilgrimage." *Monumenta Nipponica* 36.1 (Spring 1981): 55–79.

Tabata, Yasuko. "Women's Work and Status in the Changing Medieval Economy." In *Women and Class in Japanese History,* ed. Hitomi Tonomura, Anne Walthall, and Haruko Wakita, 99–118. Ann Arbor: Center for Japanese Studies, University of Michigan, 1999.

Takada Mamoru and Hara Michio, eds. *Kinsei kikō shūsei.* Sōsho Edo bunkō 17. Tokyo: Kokusho Kankōkai, 1991.

Takahashi Junji, ed. *Nihon esugoroku shūsei.* Tokyo: Kashiwa Bijutsu Shuppan, 1994.

Takeda Akira. *Junrei to minzoku.* Minzoku mingei sōsho 43. Tokyo: Iwasaki Bijutsusha, 1969.

Takejo. "Kanoene michi no ki." In *Edo jidai joryū bungaku zenshū,* vol. 3, ed. Furuya Chishin, 205–216. Tokyo: Nihon Tosho Sentaa, 1979.

Takemi, Momoko. " 'Menstruation Sutra' Belief in Japan." *Japanese Journal of Religious Studies* 10.2–3 (June/September 1983): 229–246.

Takeuchi Makoto. "Shomin bunka no naka no Edo." In *Nihon no kinsei 14, Bunka no taishūka,* ed. Takeuchi Makoto, 7–54. Tokyo: Chūō Kōronsha, 1993.

———. "Festivals and Fights: The Law and the People of Edo." In *Edo and Paris: Urban Life and the State in the Early Modern Era,* ed. James L. McClain, John M. Merriman, and Ugawa Kaoru, 384–406. Ithaca, NY: Cornell University Press, 1994.

Teeuwen, Mark. "Poetry, Sake, and Acrimony: Arakida Hisaoyu and the Kokugaku Movement." *Monumenta Nipponica* 52.3 (Autumn 1997): 295–325.

ten Grotenhuis, Elizabeth. *Japanese Mandalas: Representations of Sacred Geography.* Honolulu: University of Hawai'i Press, 1999.

Teruoka Yasutaka and Higashi Akimasa, eds. *Ihara Saikakushū*. Shinpen Nihon koten bungaku zenshū 66–69. Tokyo: Shogakkan, 1996.

Thomas, Roger K. "Plebeian Travelers on the Way of Shikishima: Waka Theory and Practice during the Late Tokugawa Period." Ph.D. diss., Indiana University, 1991.

Toby, Ronald P. *State and Diplomacy in Early Modern Japan: Asia in the Development of the Tokugawa Bakufu*. Stanford, CA: Stanford University Press, 1984.

———. "Carnival of the Aliens: Korean Embassies in Edo-Period Art and Popular Culture." *Monumenta Nipponica* 41.4 (Winter 1986): 415–456.

Tocco, Martha C. "Norms and Texts for Women's Education in Tokugawa Japan." In *Women and Confucian Cultures in Premodern China, Korea, and Japan,* ed. Dorothy Ko, Jahyun Kim Haboush, and Joan Piggott, 193–218. Berkeley: University of California Press, 2003.

Tokugawa Haru. "Takahara-in dono omichi no ki." Ed. Ōi Tasuko. *Edoki onnakō*, no. 10 (1999): 97–99.

Tokugawa Mitsukuni. "Kamakura nikki." In *Fujisawa shishi 2, Shiryōhen,* ed. Fujisawa Shishi Hensan Iinkai, 1204–1209. Fujisawa, 1973.

Tomasi, Luigi. "*Homo Viator:* From Pilgrimage to Religious Tourism via the Journey." In *From Medieval Pilgrimage to Religious Tourism: The Social and Cultural Economics of Piety,* ed. William H. Swatos Jr. and Luigi Tomasi, 1–24. Westport [CT] and London: Praeger, 2002.

Tomita Koreyuki. "Ōshū kikō." In *Nihon shomin seikatsu shiryō shūsei,* vol. 20, ed. Haraguchi Torao, Takeuchi Toshimi, and Miyamoto Tsuneichi, 363–377. Tokyo: San'ichi Shobō, 1972.

Tonomura, Hitomi. "Black Hair and Red Trousers: Gendering the Flesh in Medieval Japan." *American Historical Review* 99.1 (February 1994): 129–154.

———. "Re-envisioning Women in the Post-Kamakura Age." In *The Origins of Japan's Medieval World: Courtiers, Clerics, Warriors, and Peasants in the Fourteenth Century,* ed. Jeffrey P. Mass, 138–169. Stanford, CA: Stanford University Press, 1997.

Tonomura, Hitomi, Anne Walthall, and Haruko Wakita, eds. *Women and Class in Japanese History*. Ann Arbor: Center for Japanese Studies, University of Michigan, 1999.

Totman, Conrad. *Early Modern Japan*. Berkeley: University of California Press, 1993.

Toyoda Chōshi Hensan Iinkai. *Toyoda chōshi, Betsuhen 1, Tōkaidō to Tenryūgawa Ikeda wataribune, Furoku 2, Kikōbun*. Toyoda-chō, 1999.

Traganou, Jilly. "Geographic Representations of the Tōkaidō from Edo to Meiji Japan." *Portolan* 47 (Spring 2000): 12–31.

———. "Representing Mobility in Tokugawa and Meiji Japan." In *Japanese Capitals in Historical Perspective: Place, Power and Memory in Kyoto, Edo and Tokyo,* ed. Nicolas Fiévé and Paul Waley, 172–207. London and New York: Routledge Curzon, 2003.

———. *The Tōkaidō Road: Traveling and Representation in Edo and Meiji Japan*. London and New York: Routledge Curzon, 2004.

Tsuchiya Ayako. "Tabi no inochige." In *Edo jidai joryū bungaku zenshū,* vol. 3, ed. Furuya Chishin, 365–408. Tokyo: Nihon Tosho Sentaa, 1979.

Tsunoda, Ryusaku, Wm. Theodore De Bary, and Donald Keene, eds. *Sources of Japanese Tradition.* New York: Columbia University Press, 1958.

Turner, Victor. *Dramas, Fields, and Metaphors.* Ithaca, NY: Cornell University Press, 1974.

———. *Process, Performance, and Pilgrimage: A Study in Comparative Symbology.* New Delhi: Concept Publishing, 1979.

Turner, Victor, and Edith Turner. *Image and Pilgrimage in Christian Culture: Anthropological Perspectives.* New York: Columbia University Press, 1978.

Tyler, Royall. "The Tokugawa Peace and Popular Religion: Suzuki Shōsan, Kakugyō Tōbutsu, and Jikigyō Miroku." In *Confucianism and Tokugawa Culture,* ed. Peter Nosco, 92–119. Princeton, NJ: Princeton University Press, 1984.

Ueda, Makoto, ed. and trans. *Light Verse from the Floating World: An Anthology of Japanese Senryu.* New York: Columbia University Press, 1999.

———. *Far Beyond the Field: Haiku by Japanese Women: An Anthology.* New York: Columbia University Press, 2003.

Uhlenbeck, Chris, and Merel Molenaar. *Mount Fuji: Sacred Mountain of Japan.* Leiden: Hotei Publishing, 2000.

Umeda Yoshihiko. *Nihon shūkyō seidoshi 3, Kinsei hen.* Tokyo: Tōsen Shuppan, 1972.

Unno, Kazutaka. "Maps of Japan Used in Prayer Rites or as Charms." *Imago Mundi* 46 (1993): 65–83.

———. "Cartography in Japan." In *The History of Cartography: Cartography in the Traditional East and Southeast Asian Societies,* vol. 2, bk. 2, ed. D. Woodward and J. B. Harley, 346–477. Chicago: University of Chicago Press, 1994.

Urry, John. *The Tourist Gaze: Leisure and Travel in Contemporary Societies.* London and Newbury Park: Sage Publications, 1990.

Vaporis, Constantine N. "Post Stations and Assisting Villages: Corvée Labor and Peasant Contention." *Monumenta Nipponica* 41.1 (Winter 1986): 377–414.

———. "*Caveat Viator:* Advice to Travelers in the Edo Period." *Monumenta Nipponica* 44.4 (Winter 1989): 461–483.

———. *Breaking Barriers: Travel and the State in Early Modern Japan.* Cambridge, MA: Harvard University Press, 1994.

Vassalli, Sebastiano. *La Chimera.* Turin: Einaudi, 1990.

Vicente, Marta V., and Luis R. Corteguera. "Women in Texts: From Language to Representation." In *Women, Texts and Authority in the Early Modern Spanish World,* ed. Marta V. Vicente and Luis R. Corteguera, 1–15. Aldershot (UK) and Burlington (VT): Ashgate, 2003.

Wallace, John R. "Fitful Slumbers: Nun Abutsu's *Utatane.*" *Monumenta Nipponica* 43.4 (Winter 1988): 391–398.

Walthall, Anne. "The Family Ideology of the Rural Entrepreneurs in Nineteenth Century Japan." *Journal of Social History* 23.3 (Spring 1990): 463–483.

———. "The Cult of Sensibility in Rural Tokugawa Japan: Love Poetry by Matsuo Taseko." *Journal of the American Oriental Society* 117.1 (January–March 1997): 70–86.

———. *The Weak Body of a Useless Woman: Matsuo Taseko and the Meiji Restoration.* Chicago: University of Chicago Press, 1998.

———. "Matsuo Taseko and the Meiji Restoration: Texts of Self and Gender." In *Women and Class in Japanese History,* ed. Hitomi Tonomura, Anne Walthall, and Haruko Wakita, 217–240. Ann Arbor: Center for Japanese Studies, University of Michigan, 1999.

———, ed. *The Human Tradition in Modern Japan.* The Human Tradition around the World 3. Wilmington, DE: SR Books, 2002.

Wright, Diana E. "Mantokuji: More Than a "Divorce Temple." In *Engendering Faith: Women and Buddhism in Premodern Japan,* ed. Barbara Ruch, 247–276. Ann Arbor: Center for Japanese Studies, University of Michigan, 2002.

Yamakawa Kikue. *Women of the Mito Domain: Recollections of Samurai Family Life.* Trans. Kate Wildman Nakai. Tokyo: University of Tokyo Press, 1992.

Yamamoto Mitsumasa. "*Bunken nobe ezu* o yomu." In *Edo jidai no Kanagawa: Furuezu de miru fūkei,* ed. Kanagawa Kinseishi Kenkyūkai, 94–97. Yokohama: Yūrindō, 1994.

Yamanashi Shigako. "Harumichigusa." In *Toyoda chōshi, Betsuhen 1, Tōkaidō to Tenryūgawa Ikeda wataribune, Furoku 2, Kikōbun,* ed. Toyoda Chōshi Hensan Iinkai, 373–376. Toyoda-chō, 1999.

Yasumi Roan. *Gendaiyaku Ryokō yōjinshū.* Ed. Sakurai Masanobu. Tokyo: Yasaka Shobō, 1993.

Yokota Fuyuhiko. "Imagining Working Women in Early Modern Japan." Trans. Mariko Asano Tamanoi. In *Women and Class in Japanese History,* ed. Hitomi Tonomura, Anne Walthall, and Haruko Wakita, 153–167. Ann Arbor: Center for Japanese Studies, University of Michigan, 1999.

Yonemoto, Marcia. "Nihonbashi: Edo's Contested Center." *East Asian History* 17/18 (1999): 49–70.

———. "The Spatial Vernacular in Tokugawa Maps." *Journal of Asian Studies* 59.3 (August 2000): 647–666.

———. *Mapping Early Modern Japan: Space, Place, and Culture in the Tokugawa Period (1603–1868).* Berkeley: University of California Press, 2003.

Yourcenar, Marguerite. "Reflections on the Composition of *Memoirs of Hadrian.*" In *Memoirs of Hadrian,* trans. Grace Frick. New York: Farrar, Straus and Company, 1963.

Yuasa Gentei. "Bunkai zakki." In *Nihon zuihitsu taisei 7,* ed. Nihon Zuihitsu Taisei Henshūbu, 551–711. Tokyo: Yoshikawa Kōbunkan, 1927.

Yunoue Takashi. *Mitsu no Tōkaidō.* Shizuoka: Shizuoka Shinbunsha, 2000.

Yuya Shizuko. "Ikaho no michi yukiburi." In *Edo jidai joryū bungaku zenshū,* vol. 3, ed. Furuya Chishin, 317–334. Tokyo: Nihon Tosho Sentaa, 1979.

Index

Abe no Seimei, 125
Abutsu, 77–79; *The Diary of the Waning Moon (Izayoi nikki)*, 77–78, 117; in Edo period travel diaries, 36; *Fitful Slumbers (Utatane)*, 77
Adler, Judith, 5
adult men. See *otona*
adult, married women. See *onna*
Akasaka, 174–175
Akashi: as famous place and lyrical trope, 37, 94–95, 127, 128; in women's educational manuals and textbooks, 128; woodblock prints of, 129–130
Akiba, Mount, 61
Akisato Ritō, 129
alternate attendance system. See *sankinkōtai*
ama. See nunhood: in travel permits
Amano, Mount, 59
Amaterasu (Sun Goddess), 7, 34, 65, 200n86
Ambros, Barbara, 73
Andō Hiroshige: *Famous Products of All Provinces (Shokoku meisan)*, 139; *The Fifty-three Stages of the Tōkaidō Highway (Tōkaidō gojūsantsugi;* Hoeidō series), 175; *Illustration of the Crowds of Pilgrims Going to Enoshima, in Sagami Province, for the Benzaiten Exhibit (Sōshū Enoshima Benten kaichō sankei gunshū no zu)*, 88–89 fig. 8; *One Hundred Famous Views of Edo (Meisho Edo hyakkei)*, 161, 162 fig. 13; *Viewing Mount Fuji from a Tea House at Zōshigaya (Zōshigaya Fujimi chaya)*, 135, 135 fig. 11, 138
Anjin, 157
Anthology of Ten Thousand Leaves. See *Man'yōshū*

Aoyama, 107
Arai checkpoint (Imagire), 17 fig. 2; creation of, 49; inspections at, 23, 53, 72; regulations of, 19; transit through, 86; women and, 51, 167, 203n23
Arakida Hisaoyu, 105, 216n49
Arakida Reijo, 8, 41–42, 60, 104–108, 218n89
aratameonna, 50, 53, 72
Arima hot springs: facilities at, 180; in *Humorous Record of a Trip to Arima*, 182; origins and history of, 179; prostitutes (*yuna*) at, 182
Ariwara no Narihira, 43, 97, 172, 179; in art, 38–40, 38 fig. 6, 40 fig. 7; in board games, 130–131; in Edo period travel diaries, 97–98, 102–104, 164; in guidebooks, 129; as literary icon for cultured travelers, 114, 140; parodies and "actualizations" of, 130–131, 132 fig. 10, 133, 174; in women's educational manuals and textbooks, 126–128. See also descent to the East; *Tales of Ise;* Yatsuhashi
Asahi Monzaemon, 150–151
Asai Ryōi: *Guide to Edo's Famous Sites (Edo meishoki)*, 133, 161, 221n36; *Tales of the Floating World (Ukiyo monogatari)*, 1
Asakusa Temple (Sensōji), 55, 62
Asama, Mount, 102, 143, 215n40
Ashikaga Takauji, 225n45
Ashinoyu. See Hakone hot springs
asobime. See entertainers: before the Edo period
Atami, 98; commercial facilities at, 183; hot springs, 180–181, 183
Azuma, 112, 133, 184–185

250   INDEX

Azuma kagami (Mirror of the East), 173, 222n43
Azuma kudari. See descent to the East

Bandō circuit, 30–32, 31 fig. 5; surrogates and replicas of, 158, 159
Bann, Stephen, 13
barriers. *See* checkpoints
Bathhouse of the Floating World, The (Ukiyoburo). See Shikitei Sanba
baths: gender and, 180; and physical regeneration, 178; re-creational meaning of, 167–168, 177–178; and regional differences, 177, 229n40; social function of, 178; as spaces apart, 177–178. *See also* hot-spring resorts
Bennonaishi nikki (The Diary of Lady Ben), 75
Benten. *See* Benzaiten
Benzaiten: cave of, 88, 112; commercial activities related to, 142, 143–145, 153; cult of, 159; exhibits, 89 fig. 8; and forged historical artifacts, 156. *See also* Enoshima
bikuni. See nunhood: in travel permits
Blood Bowl Sutra (Ketsubonkyō), 59–60
board games *(sugoroku)*, 129, 130–131, 136–137, 136 fig. 12
bodies: healing of, 152, 165, 178; as mediators between travelers and spaces, 166–167, 171–172, 176–177, 178, 185; as *meibutsu*, 167, 174–177; and pollution, 59–60, 63–64, 65–66, 165, 205n54 *(see also* childbirth: as source of pollution; *nyonin kinsei)*; as sites of contestation and/or empowerment, 72–76, 91, 165, 166. *See also* cross-dressing and impersonation; tonsure
Borges, Jorge Luis, 13, 141
Buke shohatto (Laws for the Military Households), 20, 24
bunjin (literati): female, 96, 104, 105; identity as, 96, 105–106; and the recovery of literary precedent, 92–93, 104–108, 117; townswomen acting as, 108–114
Butler, Lee, 177, 210n46
Buzard, James, 5
Bynum, Caroline Walker, 165

Cahill, James, 201n104
Carter, Steven D., 42, 104
cartography. *See* maps

centers: lyrical, 41–43; political, 21–26, 32, 34; religious, 34–35; vs. peripheries, 25–26, 41–42, 45, 102–104, 107, 133–135, 168
checkpoints *(sekisho)*, 6, 17 fig. 2, 19–20, 23, 43, 79; in board games, 137; gendered policies of, 49–51, 158, 197n42; illegal bypassing of, 86–87, 89–91 *(see also* women's roads); transit permits for (see *tegata). See also* Arai checkpoint; *aratameonna;* Hakone checkpoint
Chichibu circuit, 31 fig. 5, 32, 181; surrogates and replicas of, 158
Chigata Nakamichi, 139
childbirth: protection during, 66, 75, 131–132, 153; as source of pollution, 57–58, 60, 74
Chronicle of Great Peace (Taiheiki), 154
Chronicle of Japan (Nihongi), 179
Chronicle of the Year's Events in the Eastern Capital (*Toto saijiki;* Saito Gesshin Yukinari), 134, 159, 160 table 1, 161
Clark, Scott, 178
cloistering and confinement of women, 4; before the Edo period, 73, 77, 79–80; in the Edo period, 48–49, 50–51, 52, 54, 80–82 (see also *sankinkōtai:* women as hostages of)
Coaldrake, William, 122
Collection of Ancient and Recent Poems (Kokinshū), 84, 128, 130, 215n39, 217n73, 219n102
Collection of Travel Precautions (Ryokō yōjinshū; Yasumi Roan), 115, 116, 178, 179, 183
commercialism, 4, 122, 133–140, 141, 156, 175, 187; and historical sites, 147, 154; and hot-spring resorts, 179, 183–184; and Mount Fuji, 135–138; and sacred spaces, 35, 141–148, 153
commodification: of bodies, 174–175; of history, 5, 147, 153, 154, 190; of lyricism, 5, 129, 153–154, 190; of Nagasaki's foreignness, 152; of religion, 147, 153, 190. *See also meibutsu* and souvenirs
Confucianism, 85, 99, 211n67, 220n10
Corteguera, Luis, 166
cross-dressing and impersonation, 72, 86–88, 212n79

Davis, Winston, 165
de Certeau, Michel, 110

descent to the East *(Azuma kudari):* in art, 38 fig. 6, 39; Edo period emulations of, 102–104, 111–112; parodies of, 130–131, 132 fig. 10, 133, 174. *See also* Ariwara no Narihira; *Tales of Ise*
Detailed Illustrated Map of the Tōkaidō (Tōkaidō bunken ezu), 202n1, 220n13
Dewa, 31 fig. 5, 32
diaries. *See* travel diaries
Diary of Lady Ben, The (Bennonaishi nikki), 75
Diary of Rubbing Thighs, A (Tōkaidō gojūsantsugi hizasuri nikki), 173–175, 182
Diary of the Waning Moon, The (Izayoi nikki; Abutsu), 77–78, 117
divorce temples, 205n65
Dobbins, James C., 77
dōchū bugyō (Road Magistrate), 14, 16, 21, 27, 41, 50, 72
Dōgashima. *See* Hakone hot springs
Dōgen, 74, 209n19
Dōgo hot springs, 179
Dreaming of Walking near Fuji (Isoda Koryūsai), 187–189, 189 fig. 14

Edo: as cultural center, 102, 134; famous places in, 33, 43; guidebooks about, 43, 134 (see also *Edo meishoki; Edo meisho zue; Ehon Edo miyage; Tōto saijiki*); lack of historical and literary pedigree in, 42, 133–134; as political center, 21–26, 32, 185, 196n32; wealth of, 43
Edo meishoki (Guide to Edo's Famous Sites; Asai Ryōi), 133, 161, 221n36
Edo meisho zue (Illustrated Guide to Edo's Famous Places; Saitō Gesshin Yukinari), 128–129, 131–132, 137–138, 159
Ehmcke, Franziska, 129
Ehon Edo miyage (Souvenir of Edo: A Picture Book), 134, 163, 226n72
Elisonas, Jurgis, 43, 133
Emontarō, 63
Enomoto Myōshin, 176
Enoshima: Iwamotoin, 143–145; lyrical and literary heritage of, 104, 151, 216n47; *oshi* and impersonators, 145; souvenirs and specialty products of, 139, 149–154 passim, 156, 164. *See also* Benzaiten
entertainers: before the Edo period, 73–76, 208nn10–11, 208n13; in the Edo period, 89, 182 (see also Takejo)
eroticism: and food, 174; and historical precedent, 174; and lyrical or literary precedent, 174; maps of, 167–177 passim, 182, 228n26; and the Tōkaidō, 173–175, 228n27; and travel guides, 169–176 passim, 228n23

famous places. *See meisho*
Fifty-three Stages of the Tōkaidō Highway, The (Tōkaidō gojūsantsugi; Andō Hiroshige), 175
Fifty-three Stages on the Tōkaidō: A Diary of Rubbing Thighs (Tōkaidō gojūsantsugi hizasuri nikki), 173–175, 182
Finance Magistrate. *See kanjō bugyō*
floating world *(ukiyo):* culture, 1, 47, 125, 140; definition of, 1. *See also ukiyoe*
food: erotic lore behind, 174; forbidden and taboo, 56, 59; and religion, 153, 205n51; as way to evaluate or bond with a location, 134, 150–156 passim, 167. *See also meibutsu* and souvenirs: gastronomic
forgeries, 156, 161
freedom of movement. *See* travel, as liberation
Fuji Mihoko, 179
Fuji, Mount, 31 fig. 5; Baggage Express, 146; in board games, 130–131, 136–137, 136 fig. 12; caves of, 64, 138, 165, 173, 222n43; and commercialism, 135–138; confraternities, 29, 161; cult of, 34, 161 (*see also* Konohana Sakuya Hime); in erotic maps, 173–174; in guidebooks, 137–138; in lyrical maps, 38–41, 38 fig. 6, 40 fig. 7; in official maps, 18 fig. 3, 27; pilgrimage to, 32, 94, 161; in religious maps (mandalas), 27, 28 fig. 4, 29, 37, 198n64; surrogates and replicas of, 35, 137–138, 161, 162 fig. 13, 163, 226n72; and *Tales of Ise,* 38–40, 38 fig. 6, 40 fig. 7, 127–128, 127 fig. 9, 130, 132 fig. 10, 133; in travel diaries, 44, 78; and women, 64–65, 86, 206n82, 212n91; in women's educational manuals and textbooks, 127–128, 127 fig. 9; in woodblock prints, 132 fig. 10, 133, 135–136, 135 fig. 11, 162 fig. 13, 188–189, 189 fig. 14
Fujiki Ichi (Jugen-in), 49
Fuji sankei mandara (Mandala of a Pilgrimage to Mount Fuji; Kanō Motonobu). *See under* mandalas
Fujisawa, 174–175

Fujiwara Keishi (Lady Nakatsukasa), 79
Fujiwara: Shigeaki, 76; Tameaki, 94; Teika, 96, 134
Fukai Jinzō, 46
Furukawa Koshōken, 98–99, 152–153, 170–171
Fuwa checkpoint, 78

gastronomies. *See* food
gender: boundaries, 51, 77, 175, 180, 209n430; consciousness and relations, 99, 112, 113–114, 166, 190; and mobility, 2, 4, 45–55; 71–91, 166; and official discourse, 14, 45–46, 48–49, 55–58; and the recovery of the past, 4, 97–101, 104, 107 (*see also* women's educational manuals and textbooks); re-creation of, 93, 96–97, 112–114 (*see also* cross-dressing and impersonation); and sacred space, 55–67, 131–132 (see also *nyonin kinsei*); and writing, 72, 74, 93–97, 101, 109, 213n3
Genji monogatari (Murasaki Shikibu). See *Tale of Genji, The*
Genpei Wars, 74, 98, 216n60
Genroku era, 46, 125
Go-Daigo, 98, 224n45, 225n50
Go-Fukakusa, 78
Gohyaku Rakandō (Temple of the Five Hundred Arhats), 33, 158
Gokaidō, 16, 17 fig. 2, 20–21
Gokaidō bunken nobe ezu (Illustrated Map and Survey of the Five Main Roads), 16, 27, 30
Goyu, 21, 174–176
Gramlich-Oka, Bettina, 96
Greater Learning for Women, The (Onna daigaku), 48, 207n4
Guide to the Brothels of All Provinces (Shokoku irozato annai), 169–170
Guide to Edo's Famous Sites (Edo meishoki, Asai Ryōi), 133, 161, 221n36
Guide to the Local Specialties of All Provinces (Shokoku meibutsu ōrai; Chigata Nakamichi), 139
guidebooks. *See* travel guides
Gyōgi, 181

Haguro, Mount, 31 fig. 5, 32, 63, 153
Hakone, Mount, 118, 184–185
Hakone checkpoint, 17 fig. 2, 140, 185; regulations of, 19, 197n42; transit through, 53, 86, 137; women and, 47, 82, 85

Hakone hot springs, 179, 182, 183–184
Hakone sanctuary, 140
Hakone, souvenirs and specialty products of, 139, 140, 149
Hakuei, 104
Hamana, Lake, 21
Hamana Bridge, 153
Hara, 173–174, 175
Hara Saihin, 96–97, 218n89
Harumichi no Tsuraki, 106
Hayashi Razan, 92
Heian: courtiers, 42, 72–73, 80; Edo period recovery, emulation, and "actualization" of, 95, 97–102 passim, 130–131, 133 (*see also* descent to the East: Edo period emulations of); period, 37, 72–73, 99. *See also* Kyoto; *miyabi*
Hibbett, Howard, 139
Hiei, Mount, 31 fig. 5, 34, 55; of the East (Tōeisan Kan'eiji), 34, 56; other surrogates and replicas of, 158; and women, 56, 61, 158
Hiko, Mount, 31 fig. 5, 142
Hiraga Gennai, 173, 174
Hiruma Hisashi, 6
Hishikawa Moronobu, 124, 202n1, 220n13
Hishiya Heishichi: on the hardships of travel, 115, 178; and literary precedent, 100; on Mount Yuka, 147–148; and Nagasaki, 150, 169, 170, 171–172
historical precedent: commodification of, 154; erotic renditions of, 174; in guidebooks, 123–124; recollections of, 113, 153, 179
Hōjō: Nagauji (Sōun), 152; Ujimasa, 123; Ujinaga, 16, 196n18
Hōkei-shi (Master Hōkei), 98, 181
Honzakadōri, 17 fig. 2, 20
Hōshō Hakuō (Senbai), 36
Hosorogi checkpoint, 82
hot-spring resorts: commercialism at, 179, 183–184; estimated number of, 178, 229n44; and gender boundaries, 180; historical pedigree of, 179–180; and literary travelers, 179; prostitutes at (see *yuna*); re-creation at, 183, 184; religious origins of, 180–181; souvenirs and specialty products of, 184; as spaces apart, 168, 177–178, 180, 184–185; therapeutic travel to, 46, 83, 101, 178–185 passim, 210n46. *See also* baths

Humorous Record of a Trip to Arima (Kokkei Arima kikō; Ōne Tsuchinari), 182
Hur, Nam-lin, 61, 62
Hyakunin isshu (One Hundred Poets, One Poem Each), 134

Ichifuri checkpoint, 17 fig. 2, 91
Ichikawa checkpoint, 90
Ichinotani, 99, 154
ichirizuka (mile markers), 22, 23, 43
identity: affirmation of, 3, 92–96, 101–108, 187; re-creation of, before the Edo period, 75–76; re-creation of, in the Edo period, 2, 3–4, 71–72, 96, 100, 187, 190, 213n1 (*see also* bodies: as sites of contestation and/or empowerment; cross-dressing and impersonation; gender: re-creation of; nunhood: as liberation; tonsure; travel, as liberation; travel diaries: as instruments of re-creation; widowhood: as liberation)
Igarashi Tomio, 5, 158–159
Ihara Saikaku, 53–54, 91, 170, 220n10; *The Life of an Amorous Man (Kōshoku ichidai otoko),* 86, 172; *The Life of an Amorous Woman (Kōshoku ichidai onna),* 86
Ikaho, 42, 101–102, 110, 179, 181
Ikegawa Shunsui, 94, 95, 142, 149
Ikoma, Mount, 107
Ikuta no Mori, 107, 126
Illustrated Guide to Edo's Famous Places (Edo meisho zue; Saitō Gesshin Yukinari), 128–129, 131–132, 137–138, 159
Illustrated Guide to the Famous Places in the Capital (Miyako meisho zue), 122
Illustrated Guide of the Famous Sites along the Tōkaidō (Tōkaidō meisho zue; Akisato Ritō), 129
Illustrated Map and Survey of the Five Main Roads (Gokaidō bunken nobe ezu), 16, 27, 30
Illustrated Map and Survey of the Tōkaidō (Tōkaidō bunken nobe ezu), 16, 18–19, 18 fig. 3, 39
Illustrated Maps of All Provinces Easy to View in Any Order (Shokoku yasumi kaibun no ezu), 124–125
Imagire. *See* Arai checkpoint
Inamura Kiseko, 118, 179, 184–185
Inoue Tsūjo: at Arai checkpoint, 51, 203n23; gender consciousness of, 71; status consciousness of, 51; travel diaries of, 117, 167, 202n1, 210n46; traveling in palanquin, 81; in Yatsuhashi, 218n80
Ise, 31 fig. 5, 34, 62, 105; clergy and *onshi* of, 8, 105, 142, 143, 223n10; commercialism in, 143; in guidebooks, 123, 143, 173; mandalas of, 198n60; pilgrimage to, 33, 58, 63, 115 (see also *okagemairi*); Shrine, 55, 60; souvenirs and specialty products of, 143; surrogates and replicas of, 159
Ise monogatari. See Tales of Ise
Ishiyama Temple, 58–59
Isoda Koryūsai, 187–189, 189 fig. 14
Iwahana Michiaki, 32
Iwamotoin. *See* Enoshima: Iwamotoin
Iwamura Yasuhisa, 151–152
Iwanoshita Isonoko, 181
Iwasa Miyoko, 80
Izayoi nikki (The Diary of the Waning Moon; Abutsu), 77–78, 117

Jijūken Ikkishi, 147
Jikigyō Miroku, 34
Jippensha Ikku: celebrating recreational travel, 2, 121, 140, 141, 186, 188; as commercial author, 139; on regional diversity, 177, 229n40; *Shank's Mare (Tōkaidōchū hizakurige)* as catalogue of commodities and *meibutsu,* 139–140, 150, 152, 174
Jippōan, 153, 156
jisha bugyō (Magistrate of Temples and Shrines), 55, 64–65, 143–144
Jugen-in (Fujiki Ichi), 49

Kaempfer, Engelbert, 122–123, 143, 149, 170
Kaibara Ekiken, 48, 117, 142
Kajiwara Kagesue, 124, 216n60, 220n10
Kakinomoto no Hitomaro, 130, 221n23
Kakugyō, 34
Kamakura: commercialism in, 146–147; famous sites of, 113, 146–147; Great Buddha, 112, 146; Hachimangū and replicas thereof, 146, 147, 159, 163, 167; period, 22, 79; souvenirs and specialty products of, 139, 149
kamikiri. See widowhood: in travel permits
Kamo, River, 127
Kamo no Chōmei, 36, 104, 151, 215n47
Kamo no Mabuchi, 96, 110, 216n49
Kanagawa, 112, 113, 175

Kanazawa (Musashi Province), 113, 129, 154. *See also* Kose no Kanaoka
Kan'eiji. *See* Hiei, Mount: of the East
kanjō bugyō (Finance Magistrate), 20, 21, 48
Kannon, 29, 32, 58, 123, 159
Kanō Motonobu, 27–29, 28 fig. 4
Karyō-ni, 167
Katsu Kokichi, 62
katsurame, 75
Kawai Tsugunosuke, 99
Kawanakajima, 99
Kenkō Hōshi, 129
Ketsubonkyō (Blood Bowl Sutra), 59–60
Kiga: checkpoint, 19, 58; hot springs (*see* Hakone hot springs)
Kikuchi Tamiko, 113–114, 116–117, 121
Kikusha-ni: on flexible spaces, 61–62; and lyricism, 36; as a nun, 81–83, 166; on prostitutes, 176; on souvenirs and *meibutsu*, 152, 167, 224n37
Ki no Tsurayuki, 36, 96; *Tosa Diary (Tosa nikki)*, 96, 117
Kiso Fukushima checkpoint, 17 fig. 2, 87
Kiso Road, 21, 83, 99, 139
Kiyokawa Hachirō: on commercialism, 134, 154–156 passim; and gendered writing, 94–95; on prostitutes, 169; and the recollection of historical precedent, 98–99, 121–122, 154–156 passim, 214n23; on sacred spaces, 29, 61
kō. *See* pilgrimage: confraternities
Kōbō Daishi, 35, 66, 156, 158
Kobotoke checkpoint, 137
Kodama Kōta, 5
Kojiki (Record of Ancient Matters), 7, 124, 150
Kokinshū (Collection of Ancient and Recent Poems), 84, 128, 130, 215n39, 217n73, 219n102
Kokkei Arima kikō (Humorous Record of a Trip to Arima; Ōne Tsuchinari), 182
Kondo, Dorinne, 93
Kondō Kiyoharu, 134
Konno Nobuo, 7, 175
Konno Oito, 63
Konohana Sakuya Hime, 65, 137, 198n64
Konpira, 31 fig. 5
koonna (young unmarried girls), 51–52, 202n3
Kose no Kanaoka, 113, 128, 154, 157, 179
Kōshoku ichidai onna (The Life of an Amorous Woman; Ihara Saikaku), 86

Kōshoku ichidai otoko (The Life of an Amorous Man; Ihara Saikaku), 86, 172
Kōshūdōchū, 16, 17 fig. 2, 21
Kōya, Mount, 31 fig. 5; surrogates and replicas of, 35, 158; and women, 60, 63–64
kudaru (to move down from), 22–26
kugutsu. *See* entertainers: before the Edo period
Kumano: and Nachi, 32, 198n60; pilgrimages to, 2; as projection of Womb mandala, 165, 199n67; surrogates and replicas of, 159
Kurosawa Tokiko, 61
Kusunoki Masashige, 98, 154, 214n23, 224n45
Kutsukake Nakako, 95–96, 116, 219n94
Kuwahara Hisako, 33, 85–86, 116, 218n94
Kyoto: as cultural center, 34, 41, 102; famous sites of, 29, 41, 108; guides to, 122; in the Ōnin era, 79; as political center, 22–23, 32, 34, 41; surrogates and replicas of its famous sites, 159

Lady Nakagawa. *See* Nakagawa Hisamori's wife
Lady Nakatsukasa (Fujiwara Keishi), 79
Lady Nijō. *See* Nijō
Laws for the Military Households (Buke shohatto), 20, 24
Leed, Eric J., 4, 71
Lefebvre, Henri, 45, 165
Le Roy Ladurie, Emmanuel, 115
Life of an Amorous Man, The (Kōshoku ichidai otoko; Ihara Saikaku), 86, 172
Life of an Amorous Woman, The (Kōshoku ichidai onna; Ihara Saikaku), 86
literacy: definition of, 220n19; expansion of, 93, 108–109, 121, 126, 131; and status (*see* status: and access to education and knowledge)
literati. *See bunjin*
lyrical and literary precedent: commodification of, 129, 153–154; commoners and the recollection of, 121, 126; elite women and the recollection of, 92, 101–104; erotic renditions of, 174; in guidebooks, 123, 129; literati's recollection of, 36, 92–93, 104–108; rules on the recollection of, 36, 94–95; townspeople and the recollection of, 93, 108–114; in women's educational

INDEX 255

manuals and textbooks, 126–128; in woodblock prints, 129–130. *See also* gender: and the recovery of the past; *utamakura* and codified poetic tropes

MacCannell, Dean, 5, 162
Magistrate of Temples and Shrines. See *jisha bugyō*
Makura no sōshi (Sei Shōnagon). See *Pillow Book, The*
mandalas: Diamond and Womb, 199n67; of Ise, 198n60; *Mandala of a Pilgrimage to Mount Fuji (Fuji sankei mandara;* Kanō Motonobu), 14, 27, 28 fig. 4, 29, 30, 39; manipulation of geography in, 29; of Mount Fuji in the Edo period, 29; of Nachi, 198n60
Manpukuji, 61
Man'yōshū (Anthology of Ten Thousand Leaves): cited in Edo period travel diaries, 100, 102, 215n39; commentaries on, 216n49; and established poetic tropes, 217n73, 217n79, 223n26; farewell poems in, 106; Prince Aki's poem in, 215n39; songs of the frontier guards, 2, 149
maps: definition of, 8; erotic, 167–177 passim, 182, 228n26; land surveys for, 14, 194n3; lyrical, 14, 36–43, 30 fig. 6, 40 fig. 7, 201n104; official, 13–26 passim, 18 fig. 3, 27, 30, 37–41 passim, 52 (see also *Illustrated Map and Survey of the Five Main Roads*; *Illustrated Map and Survey of the Tōkaidō*); religious, 14, 26–35, 198n57 (*see also* mandalas); as sources, 8–9
Mariko, 139, 150, 174, 175
marriage: practices, 74, 208n15; and travel, 46, 49–51, 202n1
Maruyama Yasunari, 5
Master Hōkei (Hōkei-shi), 98, 181
Matsuo Bashō: cited in late Edo period travel diaries and literature, 36, 96, 100, 129; disciples of, 96; *The Narrow Road to the Deep North (Oku no hosomichi)*, 1, 211n59, 218n89; as prototypical literary traveler, 36; *The Records of a Travel-worn Satchel (Oi no kobumi)*, 36; and the recovery of historical precedent, 37, 99–100, 107–108, 215n46; tomb of, 157, 225n59
Matsuo Taseko, 61, 228n38
meibutsu and souvenirs: before the Edo period, 148–149, 223n26; as counterparts to educated recollections, 4–5, 152, 157, 163–164; definition and categories of, 149; forged, 156, 161; gastronomic, 137, 139, 150, 153–156 passim, 174, 184; historical, 154; at hot-spring resorts, 184; as landmarks, 150; lyrical, 153–154; medicinal, 152–153, 184, 224n38 (*see also* Odawara: *uirō*); religious, 63, 149, 153. *See also* bodies: as *meibutsu*; commercialism; prostitutes: as ways to evaluate a location and as *meibutsu*
Meiji, 189, 226n80
meisho (famous places), 43, 123–124, 141. See also *utamakura* and codified poetic tropes
Menqiu (Mōgyū), 124, 220n10   michiyuki?
Mii Temple, 61, 63, 206n77
mile markers *(ichirizuka)*, 22, 23, 43
Minamoto: (Koga) Michichika, 41, 43; Sanetomo, 146, 181; Yoriie, 222n43; Yorimitsu, 154; Yorinobu, 107; Yoritomo, 131, 138, 155; Yoriyoshi, 107; Yoshiie, 107; Yoshinaka, 123; Yoshitsune, 113, 154, 174
Mino Road, 19
Minobu, Mount, 31 fig. 5, 55, 176
Mirror of the East (Azuma kagami), 173, 222n43
Mishima, 174, 197n38
Mitate Narihira Azuma kudari (A Parody of Narihira's Journey to the East; Suzuki Harunobu), 132 fig. 10, 133
Miura Jōshin, 22, 25, 109
Miya, River, 60, 108, 143
miyabi, 41, 80, 179
Miyake Yae and Yoshiemon, 91, 141
Miyako meisho zue (Illustrated Guide to the Famous Places in the Capital), 122
Miyanoshita. See Hakone hot springs
Miyata Noboru, 64
Miyazaki Fumiko, 64
Mogami, River, 127
Mōgyū (Menqiu), 124, 220n10
money: coining of, 142; eclipsing erudition, 155, 163; eclipsing status, 109, 141; as offering, 143; time as, 226n80
Monmu, Emperor, 123
monzenchō. See *monzenmachi*
monzenmachi, 142–143, 148
Morimoto Tsuzuko, 181

256   INDEX

Morioka: Sadakata, 25–26, 225n59; Sadayoshi, 25–26
Morris, Ivan, 73
Motoori: Norinaga, 105, 180; Ōhira, 180, 182
mountains: and asceticism *(yamabushi and shugendō)*, 2, 26, 29, 32, 55, 64, 181; as sacred spaces, 27, 28 fig. 4, 29–30. *See also names of individual mountains*
Mukai Chine and Kyorai, 100–101, 202n1
Murasaki Shikibu. See *Tale of Genji, The*
Muromachi period, 79
Musashi: battle, 123; as center, 22; as poetic trope, 102

Nachi. *See* Kumano: and Nachi
Nagakubo Sekisui, 98
Nagasaki: as exotic Other, 150, 152–153, 169–172; pleasure district of, 170–171; souvenirs and specialty products of, 152
Nagashima Atsuko, 85
Nakagawa Hisamori's wife (Lady Nakagawa): on Edo as a center, 42–43, 102–104, 107, 108; replicating Narihira's descent to the East, 102–104; travel diary and narrative choices of, 101–102
Nakamura Ito, 153
Nakasendō, 16, 17 fig. 2, 21, 23, 33, 123
Nakatsukasa, Lady. *See* Fujiwara Keishi
Nanbokuchō, 98, 224n45, 225n50
Narihira. *See* Ariwara no Narihira
Narrow Road to the Deep North, The (*Oku no hosomichi;* Matsuo Bashō), 1, 211n59, 218n89
Nebugawa checkpoint, 47, 197n42
New Collection of Ancient and Recent Poems (*Shinkokinshū*), 84, 100, 107, 216n57, 217n73
Nihonbashi, 22, 26, 32, 123
Nihongi (Chronicle of Japan), 179
Nijō, 41, 78–79
Nikkō: 31 fig. 5; Road (Nikkōdōchū), 16, 17 fig. 2, 21; Tōshōgū (Ieyasu's mausoleum), 21, 34, 200n86; and women pilgrims, 56
Nishikiori Gobei Yoshikura, 26, 44
Nishimiya Hide, 176–177
Nitta Shirō Tadatsune, 138, 173, 222n43
noboru (to move up to), 22–26
Noda Senkōin, 29, 32
Nozawa Ukō, 96

nukemairi, 54, 87, 89, 91, 223n10
nunhood: as liberation, 72, 76–79, 81–84; in travel permits, 51, 202n3
Nunobiki Falls, 107
nyonin kinsei (women-free zones): disregard for and exceptions to, 63–66, 86; mountains as, 29, 60–61, 91; Mount Fuji and, 64, 86, 206n82; Mount Kōya and, 60; origins of, 59; respect for, 91; Shikoku and, 66, 206n82; surrogates and replicas as alternatives to, 158

Ochikochi Dōin, 16, 196n18, 220n13
Oda Ieko, 86, 116, 218n94
Oda Nobunaga, 55, 123
Odawara: historical precedent of, 152; souvenirs and specialty products of, 156; *uirō,* 152, 167, 224n37, 224n38
Ōe, Mount, 154
Ogasawara, Aunt, 177
Oguri Hankan, 174
ōharame, 75
Oi no kobumi (*The Records of a Travel-Worn Satchel;* Matsuo Bashō), 36
okagemairi, 60, 87, 212n80
Okuhara Sadayū, 48–49
Oku no hosomichi (*The Narrow Road to the Deep North;* Matsuo Bashō), 1, 211n59, 218n89
One Hundred Poets, One Poem Each (*Hyakunin isshu*), 134
One Hundred Provisions (*Osadamegaki hyakkajō*), 57
Ōne Tsuchinari, 182
Ōnin era, 79
onna (adult, married women), 50–52, 165, 202n3
Onna daigaku (*The Greater Learning for Women*), 48, 207n4
onna no michi (women's roads), 90–91
onshi. See oshi: from Ise
Ooms, Herman, 18, 34
ōraimono. See women's educational manuals and textbooks
Osadamegaki hyakkajō (*One Hundred Provisions*), 57
oshi: holiness of, 165; impersonators, 145, 146; from Ise, 142, 143, 223n10; as travel agents, 142
Ōshūdōchū, 16, 17 fig. 2
Ōta Nanpo, 153–154

otona (adult men), 52–54
outcastes, 18, 62
Ōyama, 31 fig. 5; commercialism in, 142, 146; *oshi,* 146; pilgrimage season for, 199n72

palanquins: as forms of cloistering, 80–81, 166; inspection of, 50, 72; travel in, 83
parody, 114, 132 fig. 10, 133, 139
Parody of Narihira's Journey to the East, A (*Mitate Narihira Azuma kudari;* Suzuki Harunobu), 132 fig. 10, 133
Pflugfelder, Gregory, 52, 227n10
pilgrimage: circuits, 27, 30–32, 31 fig. 5, 158, 199n75; confraternities *(kō),* 29, 33, 63, 88; economic implications of, 62–64, 142–146; as excuse, 54–55, 87; monuments, 115, 218n90; official regulation of, 52, 54–55, 56, 58; and recreation, 7–8, 193n21; as rites of passage and learning opportunities, 54, 115; unauthorized (see *nukemairi; okagemairi*)
Pillow Book, The (*Makura no sōshi;* Sei Shōnagon), 92, 95, 219n99, 220n10; parodies of, 114
pleasure quarters: courtesans of, 7, 109, 172; Edo Yoshiwara, 62, 168, 169; guides to, 168–169, 170, 172–173, 221n36; Kyoto Shimabara, 169; Nagasaki Maruyama, 169–172; as spaces of re-creation, 109–110, 168
Plutschow, Herbert, 9, 96
poetic tropes. See *utamakura* and codified poetic tropes
pregnancy, 65, 66, 131
Prince Aki, 148
Prince Shōtoku (Shōtoku Taishi), 107, 179
print industry: and commercialism, 140; and eroticism, 172; in Kansai and Kantō, 133–134, 219n3; rise of, 3, 121–122, 126. *See also* travel fiction; travel guides; *ukiyoe*
prostitutes, 7; along highways, 168, 181–182; at hot-spring resorts (see *yuna*); as people apart, 85; in religious spaces, 62; as ways to evaluate a location and as *meibutsu,* 167–177, 182. *See also* entertainers; pleasure quarters; *tomeonna*

Ravina, Mark, 21
Reader, Ian, 66
Record of Ancient Matters (*Kojiki*), 7, 124, 150

Records of a Travel-worn Satchel, The (*Oi no kobumi;* Matsuo Bashō), 36
Reiheishidō, 17 fig. 2, 21
Ri-in, 154, 225n49
Road Magistrate. See *dōchū bugyō*
rōnin. See samurai: masterless
Ryokō yōjinshū (*Collection of Travel Precautions;* Yasumi Roan), 115, 116, 178, 179, 183

Saigyō: cited in Edo period travel diaries and literature, 96, 100, 107; poetry by, 155, 216n57
Saikoku *henro. See* Western Provinces circuit
Saitō Gesshin Yukinari: *Edo meisho zue,* 128–129, 131–132, 137–138, 159; on surrogates and replicas, 163; *Tōto saijiki,* 134, 159, 160 table 1, 161
Sakai Hanjirō, 94–95
samurai: before the Edo period, 22, 74; masterless *(rōnin),* 56, 62, 86; women and mobility, 48–49, 79–86 passim
sankinkōtai (alternate attendance system), 14; regulations of, 20, 24; women as hostages of, 46, 50, 83, 101, 202n1
Sano no Funabashi, 111–112, 114, 217n77, 218n79
Santō Kyōsan, 183
Sarashina Diary (*Sarashina nikki*), 73, 117
Sasaki Takatsuna, 124, 220n10
Sayo no Nakayama, 155–156
Screech, Timon, 158
Seigen-in Noriko, 83
Sei Shōnagon: in Edo period travel diaries, 95, 111, 117; *The Pillow Book* (*Makura no sōshi*), 92, 95, 114, 219n99, 220n10
Sekigawa checkpoint, 91
Sekiguchi family, 85–86
sekisho. See checkpoints
Senbai (Hōshō Hakuō), 36
Senkaku Tōshi, 88–89, 145
Sen no Rikkyū, 179
Sensōji (Asakusa Temple), 55, 62
sex: hot-spring resorts and, 181–183; religious compounds and, 56–57, 62; travel and, 167–177, 228n25. *See also* maps: erotic; travel guides: for the erotic traveler
Shank's Mare (*Tōkaidōchū hizakurige;* Jippensha Ikku): as catalogue of commodities and *meibutsu,* 139–140, 150, 152, 174; as celebration of travel and

freedom, 188; Kita and Yaji from, 121; on regional diversity, 177, 229n40
Shiba Keiko, 86
Shiba Sonome, 96
Shiga Pass, 106
Shikitei Sanba, 168, 178; *The Bathhouse of the Floating World (Ukiyoburo)*, 177
Shikoku circuit (Shikoku *henro*), 30–32, 31 fig. 5; and commercialism, 145; surrogates and replicas of, 35, 158–159, 225n61, 226n68; and women, 65–66
Shinagawa, 21, 174–175
Shinano, 151, 154
Shining Prince. See *Tale of Genji, The*
Shinjō Tsunezō, 7
Shinkō-in Myōjitsu, 60, 116, 157
Shinkokinshū (New Collection of Ancient and Recent Poems), 84, 100, 107, 216n57, 217n73
Shinryū-in Takako, 84
Shirakawa barrier, 36
Shokoku annai tabi suzume (Travel Sparrow, A Guide to All Provinces), 123–124, 134, 143
Shokoku irozato annai (Guide to the Brothels of All Provinces), 169–170
Shokoku meibutsu ōrai (Guide to the Local Specialties of All Provinces; Chigata Nakamichi), 139
Shokoku yasumi kaibun no ezu (Illustrated Maps of All Provinces Easy to View in Any Order), 124–125
Shosha, Mount, 60–61
Shōtetsu, 36
Shōtoku Taishi (Prince Shōtoku), 107, 179
shugendō. See mountains: and asceticism
Shu Shunsui, 154, 225n46
Sokokura. See Hakone hot springs
Souvenir of Edo: A Picture Book (Ehon Edo miyage), 134, 163, 226n72
souvenirs. See *meibutsu* and souvenirs
spaces: gendered (*see* gender: and sacred space); lyrical (*see* maps: lyrical; *meisho; utamakura* and codified poetic tropes); political (*see* checkpoints; maps: official); religious, 55–66, 148 (*see also* maps: religious; mountains: as sacred spaces); surrogates and replicas of, 35, 157–164 passim, 160 table 1
spaces, flexible meanings of: along the roads and at travel sites, 2, 3, 13–14, 43, 66, 184, 186–190 passim (*see also* Sayo no Nakayama); commercial publishing and, 140; Mount Fuji and, 43–44; in relation to gender, 45–46, 67; travelers' understanding of, 91, 122, 184–185; urban sites and, 123
specialty products. See *meibutsu* and souvenirs
status: and access to education and knowledge, 93, 109, 121, 126, 187, 190; affirmation or re-creation of (*see under* identity); consciousness, 111, 112, 180; disregard for, 178–179; markers of, 50, 51, 76–77, 80–83 passim; system, 14, 45–46, 49–50; and travel, 2, 19, 46, 72–73, 80–91 passim
Sue no Matsuyama, 36, 149
sugoroku. See board games
sukegō (assisting village-system), 14
Suma, 37, 98–99
sumo, 7, 180, 229n55
Suwa: checkpoint, 137; hot springs, 181
Suzuka, 101, 106
Suzuki Bokushi, 54
Suzuki Harunobu, 132 fig. 10, 133
Suzuki Masataka, 59, 63
Suzuki Mihoko, 64
Suzuki Shōzō, 32, 64, 163

Tachibanaya Buhei, 153
Tadano Makuzu, 96
Taiheiki (Chronicle of Great Peace), 154
Taira: Atsumori, 99, 154; Kiyomori, 99; Tadanori, 99; Yasuyori, 107
Takeda Shingen, 99, 152, 154
Takejo, 84–85, 98, 116, 117
Takeuchi Makoto, 58
Takizawa Bakin, 96
Takuan, 129
Tale of Genji, The (Genji monogatari; Murasaki Shikibu), 73, 121, 172; criticism of, 99; in Edo period travel diaries, 98, 104, 110; famous sites associated with, 37, 98–99, 179; parodies of, 114; in women's educational manuals and textbooks, 126
Tales of the Floating World (Ukiyo monogatari; Asai Ryōi), 1
Tales of Ise (Ise monogatari), 97–98, 112, 217n73; in art, 39–40; in board games, 130–131; criticism of, 99; in Edo period travel diaries, 97–98, 102–104, 107,

216n57; famous sites associated with (*see* Asama, Mount; Fuji, Mount: and *Tales of Ise;* Utsunoyama; Yatsuhashi); parodies of, 114, 132 fig. 10, 133; in women's educational manuals and textbooks, 127–128. *See also* Ariwara no Narihira; descent to the East
Tateyama, 91
Tawaraya Sōtatsu, 38 fig. 6, 39, 201n104
Teeuwen, Mark, 142
tegata (checkpoint transit permits): requests for, 47, 52, 180; for women, 50, 65, 203n19, 203n23
Tekkai, Mount, 154, 225n48
Temple of the Five Hundred Arhats (Gohyaku Rakandō), 33, 158
temple schools *(terakoya)*, 126. *See also* women's educational manuals and textbooks
ten Grotenhuis, Elizabeth, 29
terakoya. *See* temple schools
Tocco, Martha, 4
Toda Mosui, 43
Tōeisan. *See* Hiei, Mount: of the East
Togakushi, Mount, 61
Tōkaidō, 17 fig. 2; as eroticized space, 173–176, 228n27; famous sites of, 42, 121, 123, 173, 175; guidebooks to, 123, 129; as political space, 16–23 passim, 18 fig. 3
Tōkaidō bunken ezu (Detailed Illustrated Map of the Tōkaidō), 202n1, 220n13
Tōkaidō bunken nobe ezu (Illustrated Map and Survey of the Tōkaidō), 16, 18–19, 18 fig. 3, 39
Tōkaidōchū hizakurige (Shank's Mare; Jippensha Ikku): as catalogue of commodities and *meibutsu*, 139–140, 150, 152, 174; as celebration of travel and freedom, 121, 188; on regional diversity, 177, 229n40
Tōkaidō gojūsantsugi (Fifty-three Stages of the Tōkaidō Highway; Andō Hiroshige), 175
Tōkaidō gojūsantsugi hizasuri nikki (Fifty-three Stages on the Tōkaidō: A Diary of Rubbing Thighs), 173–175, 182
Tōkaidō meisho zue (Illustrated Guide of the Famous Sites along the Tōkaidō; Akisato Ritō), 129
Tokugawa: Hidetada, 14, 23, 34, 49; Ieharu, 23; Iemitsu, 34, 50; Ienari, 14; Ienobu, 20; Ieyasu, 21, 23, 34, 46, 49, 75, 97,

204n38; Ieyoshi, 25; Mitsukuni, 104, 225n46; Nariaki, 176; Yoshimune, 23; Yoshinao, 97
tomeonna, 146, 223n19
Tomita Koreyuki, 100
Tonomura, Hitomi, 74, 76, 209n30
Tōnosawa. *See* Hakone hot springs
tonsure, 51, 76–77, 81–83, 87, 165
tororojiru (yam gruel). *See* Mariko
Tosa (school), 39, 40 fig. 7
Tosa nikki (Tosa Diary; Ki no Tsurayuki), 96, 117
Totman, Conrad, 126
Tōto saijiki (Chronicle of the Year's Events in the Eastern Capital, Saitō Gesshin Yukinari), 134, 159, 160 table 1, 161
Toyotomi Hideyoshi, 25, 75, 152, 179
Traganou, Jilly, 8, 19, 186
travel, before the Edo period, 1–2, 41, 72–80, 148–149
travel, as liberation, 2–5, 9, 92, 177, 186–190; art depicting, 187–188, 189 fig. 14; by way of physical engagements, 167; by way of replicas and surrogates, 158–159; by way of writing and erudition, 108–114, 187; for women 4, 71–72, 177
travel diaries: as genre, 93–95, 194n28; as instruments of re-creation, 92–93, 95, 108–118, 187; as sources, 9, 95; as souvenirs, 149; writing, editing, and publishing of, 116–117. *See also* gender: and writing
travel fiction, 9, 139–140, 163. See also *Humorous Record of a Trip to Arima;* Jippensha Ikku
travel guides: seventeenth century, 122–125, 133–134; eighteenth century, 128–129; nineteenth century, 128–129, 131–132, 134, 137–139, 159; for the erotic traveler, 169–176 passim, 228n23; used by Edo period travelers, 121–122
Travel Sparrow, A Guide to All Provinces, The (Shokoku annai tabi suzume), 123–124, 134, 143
Tsuchiya Ayako, 37, 80–81, 99, 101, 121
Tsurumi Bridge, 112

Ueda Akinari, 98
Ueda, Makoto, 96
Uesugi Kenshin, 99, 152
uirō. *See* Odawara: *uirō*

Uji Bridge, 124
Uge River, 220n10
ukiyo. *See* floating world
Ukiyoburo (The Bathhouse of the Floating World). See Shikitei Sanba
ukiyoe, 122, 129–130, 135–136, 135 fig. 11
Ukiyo monogatari (Tales of the Floating World; Asai Ryōi), 1
Urashima Tarō, 113
Urry, John, 5, 157
Usui checkpoint, 17 fig. 2
Utagawa: Hiroshige (*see* Andō Hiroshige); Kunisada, 130, 173, 175; Sadafusa, 131; Toyokuni, 133, 203n27
utamakura and codified poetic tropes, 117, 141, 157; animals as, 101, 217n73; cherry blossoms as, 37, 111; in the diaries of educated travelers, 41, 100–102, 106, 110–112; flowers and plants as, 102; in guidebooks, 124; lack of, 43, 150; for loneliness and melancholy, 37; origins of, 37; places as, 36, 94–95, 101, 106, 112, 126–127; seasonal, 100–101, 215n37, 217n73
Utsunoyama, 97–98

Vaporis, Constantine, 5, 6
Vassalli, Sebastiano, 186
Vicente, Marta, 166
Viewing Mount Fuji from a Tea House at Zōshigaya (Zōshigaya Fujimi chaya; Andō Hiroshige), 135, 135 fig. 11, 138

wakashu (young boys), 52–54, 165
Walthall, Anne, 54, 95, 109, 166, 217n67
Warring States period, 75, 79
Western Lake (China), 129, 154
Western Provinces circuit (Saikoku *henro*), 30–32, 31 fig. 5, 33–34, 58; surrogates and replicas of, 159, 160 table 1
widowhood: as liberation, 72, 76, 81–85; in travel permits, 51, 202n3
women-free zones. *See nyonin kinsei*
women's educational manuals and textbooks, 72, 88, 126–128, 127 fig. 9, 207n4

women's roads *(onna no michi),* 90–91
woodblock prints, 8, 29, 124, 129–130, 152–153. *See also ukiyoe*

Yagurazawa: checkpoint, 197n42; Road, 146
Yakushi Nyorai, 66, 150, 180, 198n64
Yamabe no Akahito, 128
yamabushi. See mountains: and asceticism
Yamanashi Shigako, 61, 155
Yanagase checkpoint, 82, 91
Yasumi Roan *(Collection of Travel Precautions; Ryokō yōjinshū),* 115, 116, 178, 179, 183
Yatsuhashi: Ariwara no Narihira and, 112, 129, 130; Edo period board games and, 130; Edo period guidebooks and, 129; Edo period travelers and, 112, 114, 152, 218n80
Yokota Fuyuhiko, 207n4
Yōmei, Emperor, 123
Yonemoto, Marcia, 8, 9, 122, 168
Yoneyama, 153
Yoshida, 21, 174–176
Yoshino: and cherry blossoms, 36–37, 95, 155; as famous site, 83, 105, 127, 155; as sacred space, 199n67; souvenirs and specialty products of, 155
Yoshiwara. *See* pleasure quarters: Edo Yoshiwara
young boys. *See wakashu*
young unmarried girls. *See koonna*
Yourcenar, Marguerite, 35, 71
Yuasa Gentei, 20
Yui Shōsetsu, 98
yūjo. See entertainers: before the Edo period
Yuka, Mount, 147–148
Yumoto, 139
yuna, 181–183, 230n63, 230n65, 230n68
Yunoshima, 183, 184
Yuya Shizuko, 110–112, 114, 116, 126, 179

Zenkōji, 31 fig. 5, 33, 47, 83, 150
zenni. See nunhood: in travel permits
Zōshigaya Fujimi chaya (Viewing Mount Fuji from a Tea House at Zōshigaya; Andō Hiroshige), 135, 135 fig. 11, 138